CW00920037

Wiltshire Record Society

(formerly the Records Branch of the Wiltshire
Archaeological and Natural History Society)

VOLUME 77

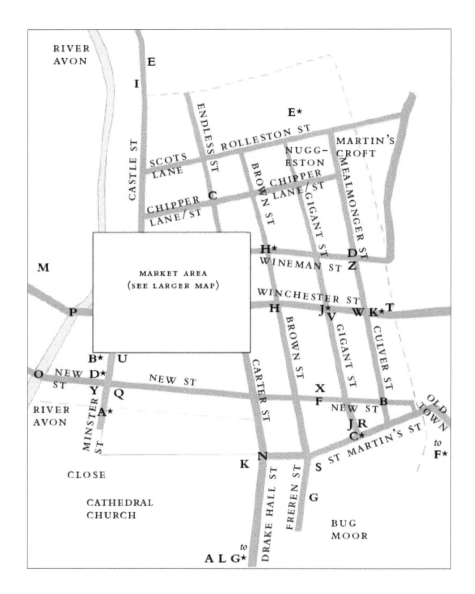

KEY TO SALISBURY MAP

Note that two long stretches of street were sometimes given alternative or double names, used interchangeably, as follows: Castle Street/Minster Street; Culver Street/Mealmonger Street. The name or description 'high street' might be applied to Carter Street, Endless Street, Drake Hall Street or Minster Street. The northern section of Gigant Street was sometimes distinguished as 'on the way to St Edmund's church'.

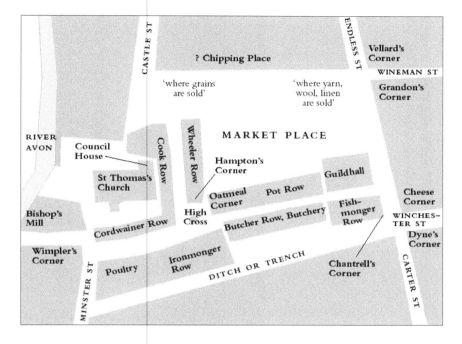

Not all corners, rows and named buildings encountered in the Domesday Books have been entered or are currently locatable. Certain or probable locations are abbreviated on the map opposite as follows:

A	Ayleswade Bridge	S	Franciscan Friary
B	Barnwell Cross	T	Gatehouse
C	Bedred Row	U	George's Inn
D	Bert's Corner	V	Glastonbury's Corner
E	Beyond the Bar	W	Holy Ghost Corner
F	Black Bridge	X	Holy Trinity Hospital
G	Buckland's Place	Y	Hott Corner
H	Bull Hall	Z	Ive's Corner
I	Bunt's Place	A★	North Gate
J	Clark's Place	B★	Pinnock's Inn
K	Common Hall	C★	Ro Corner
L	De Vaux College	D★	Rose
M	Dominican Friary	E★	St Edmund's Church
N	East Gate	F★	St Martin's Church
O	Fisherton Lower Bridge	G★	St Nicholas's Hospital
P	Fisherton Upper Bridge	H★	Stint's Corner
Q	Florentine's Corner	J★	Stratford's Corner
R	Focket Place	K★	Warr's Corner

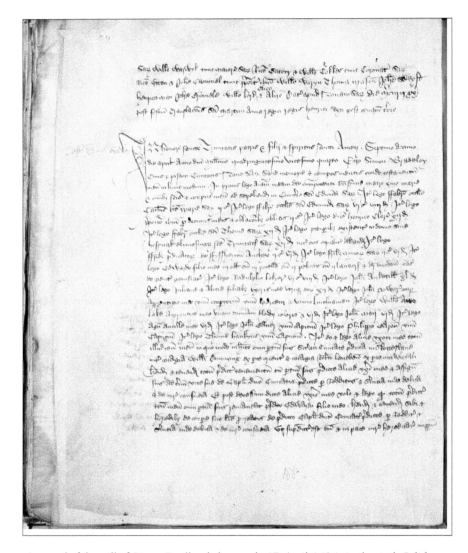

*Approval of the will of Simon Bradley, baker, made 17 April 1424, in the sixth Salisbury Domesday Book, WSA G23/1/214, f. 95v (see pp. 149–50, entry **2549**).*

SALISBURY DOMESDAY BOOKS
1413–1478

edited by

JOHN CHANDLER

and

DOUGLAS CROWLEY

CHIPPENHAM

2024

Published on behalf of the Wiltshire Record Society
by The Hobnob Press,
8 Lock Warehouse, Severn Road,
Gloucester GL1 2GA
www.hobnobpress.co.uk

© Wiltshire Record Society, 2024
c/o Wiltshire and Swindon History Centre,
Cocklebury Road, Chippenham SN15 3QN

www.wiltshirerecordsociety.org.uk

ISBN 978–0–901333–54–4

Typeset by John Chandler

CONTENTS

PREFACE

Salisbury's good fortune in having preserved in the Domesday Books a record of its 14th- and 15th-century property transactions became apparent when the first part of this trilogy, detailing the years 1317–1413, was published as volume 75 in the Society's series in 2022. With the publication of the present volume, covering 1413–78, the editors' task in presenting the rich contents of the books is complete. A third volume will draw on the evidence from the Domesday Books and other contemporary sources to attempt a topographical analysis of the tenurial history of the city, over a period when it prospered and grew to become one of the largest trading communities in the kingdom.

As was acknowledged in the preface to volume 75, Dr Crowley and Dr Chandler record with gratitude the help that they have been given by the staff of the Wiltshire and Swindon History Centre throughout, and in particular the service that Jane Silcocks gave in photographing each folio of the books, enabling Dr Crowley to prepare the work remotely. They also wish formally to thank Wiltshire Council for permission to edit them. Once again Dr Chandler is grateful to Emily Naish, Salisbury Cathedral Archivist, for access to material in her care, and he has been encouraged by the interest that Salisbury historians and archaeologists have shown in this ongoing project.

Tom Plant
General Editor

INTRODUCTION

There were seven Domesday books of Salisbury, into each of which were written transcripts, all recording the transfer of real property in the city, of wills, charters, deeds, and other documents. The charters and deeds were witnessed, and the wills approved, in the court of the bishop of Salisbury. What brought the books into existence has been described in the introduction to volume 75 of the Wiltshire Record Society's series of publications. Four of the books survive, the third, fifth, sixth, and seventh, and their physical appearance and archival history have also been described in that volume. Although books one, two, and four do not survive, a list of their contents appears in book six. Volume 75 contains an edition of books three and five and of the list of contents of books one, two, and four. This volume contains an edition of the documents transcribed in the remainder of book six and in the whole of book seven. Those two books are to be found in the Wiltshire and Swindon Archives and have the call numbers WSA G 23/1/214–15.

Domesday book six contains, apart from the list of contents, transcripts of 433 charters, deeds, and other writings and of 77 wills. The documents recorded by the transcripts are of the period 1413–34 except for nine, the earliest of which is dated 1311 and the latest 1411. Book seven contains transcripts of 89 charters, deeds, and other writings and of 3 wills. The documents recorded range in date from 1408 to 1478. The purpose of book six, which followed the pattern of books three and five, has been explained in volume 75 of the society's series. In the period 1413–34 there was an average of 23 charters, deeds, wills, and other documents passing through the bishop's court each year. The purpose of book seven was clearly different. For the period 1435–78 there was an average of only two documents a year passing through that court, and in 17 of the years none at all. The systematic witnessing of charters and deeds, and the approving of wills, evidently ceased there about 1434. Documents continued to be witnessed by the court but the record does not show that the wills were approved there. Book seven was kept open for transfers of real property to be recorded and published in it even though there was apparently no longer a gain to the bishop or to the mayor and commonalty of the city in that being done. Presumably it was kept open because the parties to a document sometimes thought that to enter the document in a public register was worth the expense of having it done, and because there was a gain to the clerk who charged to make the transcription. The usefulness of the register to the parties seems to have had a resurgence in the period 1458–73 when 69 of the 92 documents were transcribed.

Salisbury was not the only urban area in which, in the Middle Ages, conveyances were witnessed before a court, and in towns and other cities instruments by which real property was transferred were written into the court records or, as they were in Salisbury, into separate registers. Such towns and cities are referred to in volume 75 of the society's series. Nor are the Domesday books the only source of information about real property in Salisbury in the 14th and 15th centuries, and other sources are also referred to in volume 75. The archives of the cathedral, of the city, and of other city institutions all contain medieval deeds, and there are smaller accumulations and single deeds elsewhere. Copies of the wills of citizens and other inhabitants of Salisbury survive among diocesan and archdiocesan records and in the records of the Prerogative Court of Canterbury, although not all of them record the transfer of real property. Taken together all those sources contain for the 14th and 15th centuries far fewer charters, deeds, and wills recording the transfer of real property than the 185 wills and 1,233 other documents transcribed in Domesday books three, five, six, and seven. Those Domesday books, supplemented by the 290 wills and 1,063 other documents listed as the contents of books one, two, and four, are the prime source of information about such transfers in that period.

Although for the 14th and 15th centuries the Domesday books are indeed the prime source for the transfer of real property in the city, and for the street-by-street location of the property transferred and of abutting premises, other sources list inhabitants of the city and in some cases indicate which of the four wards of the city they may have lived in. A rental of 1455, although later than most of the information contained in the Domesday books, contains much information about real property, including the location of tenements by ward, descriptions of tenements, reference to abutting tenements, and the names of tenants. All those sources are referred to in volume 75.

To those studying Salisbury, especially as it was in the Middle Ages, the value of the documents transcribed in the Domesday books is as great as it is obvious, and it has been discussed in volume 75. The names of streets and rows and of locations around the market place are given, and many of the tenements standing in those places, especially at the street corners, can be located precisely. Owners of tenements, and occasionally their tenants, are named, the descent of tenements can sometimes be traced, and familial relationships are often rehearsed.

This volume completes the edition of the documents transcribed in Salisbury's Domesday books. Those using it are reminded that, before the title page and as in the first volume, maps and a key depict and list the streets and principal landmarks of the city using their medieval names. It is intended to produce a third volume which will aim for a tenement-by-tenement account of the city's tenurial history.

In general the method of editing Domesday books six and seven in this volume is the same as that used for books three and five in volume 75, where it is explained in more detail. As in that volume all the entries presented below are translated from Latin and given in an abbreviated form. In the case of charters and deeds common form has been omitted, and in the case of wills the order in which the testator recorded dispositions has not been respected. An attempt has been made to give each forename, surname, and place name a standard and modern form and to use it throughout the edition. Dates have been modernized, and regnal and all other years have been converted to the year of grace as it is now reckoned.

Marginal drawing of a face and hat, WSA G 23/1/214, f. 96.

SALISBURY DOMESDAY BOOKS

BOOK 6

(in WSA G 23/1/214)

1 December 1311, at Salisbury
2170 By their charter Robert of Worcester, the rector of Collingbourne Kingston (*Collingbourne Abbatis*), and William of Ludgershall, the rector of Chiseldon, granted to Philip Aubin and his wife Alice Theobald the following rent which they held in Salisbury: a rent of 40s. a year issuing from Robert of Knoyle's chief tenement in Winchester Street; 40s. from John Needler's chief tenement in that street; 40s. from Henry of Figheldean's chief tenement in that street; 6s. from Richard Garlickmonger's tenement in that street; 20s. from a tenement of Thomas Batter in the same street; 10s. from Robert Inways's shop on the west side of the Guildhall (*Gialde*); 4s. from John Tucker's chief tenement in Chipper Street; 5s. 4d. from two shops near the graveyard of St. Thomas's church on the north side of a tenement of the provost of St. Edmund's church; 5s. from Henry Fox's tenement opposite the butchers' stalls; 6s. from Robert of Alton's three shops in Rolleston Street; 16s. from a tenement of Peter of Ringwood, called Carter, in the high street; 40s. from a tenement formerly that of Gillian, a daughter of Michael Spicer, in New Street; 4s. from Nicholas of Hinton's tenement in that street; 10s. from William Pitt's tenement in Brown Street; 10s. from John Gilmin's tenement in the same street; 4s. from Alexander Cook's tenement in Culver Street. Robert and William also granted to Philip and Alice the following tenements which they held in Salisbury: a tenement in Winchester Street called the Bull Hall, with a sollar and a cellar next to it in the same street beside the gate of Robert of Knoyle's chief tenement; a tenement in the high street formerly that of Catherine the poulterer; a tenement in that street which was formerly that of the sister of the master Walter of Blandford; a tenement in New Street which was formerly that of Agnes, Philip's mother; a tenement in St. Martin's Street which was formerly Thomas Farrow's. The rent and the tenements are to be held for ever by Philip and Alice and Philip's heirs. Clause of warranty for £1,000 cash paid to the grantors in advance. Seals: those of Robert and William and, for greater security, the common seal of the city. Named witnesses: the bailiff, the mayor, a coroner, the reeves, Robert of Knoyle, Henry Baldry, Henry Spicer, Richard of Tidworth, Nicholas Plubel, Robert Cheese, Adam Ironmonger, Simon of Oxford, Thomas Ironmonger, and John Bishop

28 April 1361, at Salisbury
2171 By her deed Alice, the relict of Philip Longenough, of late a citizen of Salisbury, granted to Philip Aubin, of Winchester, a citizen of that city [?Salisbury;

cf. 2172], a rent of 20*s*. a year to be received for ever by him and his heirs and assigns from her two shops, with sollars, and a lower shop which stand conjoined in Carter Street in front of a tenement of hers. *This entry repeats one made in book 2 [496] and again in book 5 [1656], q.v.*

1 September 1361, at Salisbury

2172 By his charter Philip Aubin, a citizen of Salisbury, granted to Stephen Haim, a citizen of Winchester, a rent of 40*s*. a year issuing from a tenement, formerly William Stringer's, in Winchester Street, a rent of 20*s*. a year issuing from a tenement, formerly Walter Boreham's, in Winchester Street, and a rent of 20*s*. a year issuing from two shops, with sollars, and a lower shop which stand conjoined in Carter Street in front of a tenement of late that of Alice, the relict of Philip Longenough. *This entry repeats one made in book 3 [552], q.v.*

3 February 1393, at Salisbury

2173 A deed of John Brewer and his wife Alice. John and Alice held for their life [Ive's Corner], a messuage, with shops, cottages, yards, and gardens, in Wineman Street [and Mealmonger Street: *cf. 1746, 1959–60*], opposite Gilbert Oword's tenement, between Robert Sexhampcote's tenement on the west side and William Warmwell's cottages on the north side. The reversion of the messuage pertains for ever to Robert Play and Richard Jewell and their heirs and assigns by a grant which by his deed James Ive, a kinsman and heir of Ralph Ive, perfected for Robert and Richard. John and Alice, on the grant to Robert and Richard, attorned to them by means of their fealty and the payment of 4*d*., undertaking that they would be submissive to them and their heirs and assigns as is fitting according to the terms of the grant to them. Seals: those of John and Alice and the mayoral seal of the city

19 March 1393, at Salisbury

2174 Approval of the will of Nicholas Whichbury, called Baker, a citizen of Salisbury, made on 24 April 1391. <u>Interment</u>: in St. Martin's church, opposite the high cross, beside the tomb of his wife Sarah. <u>Bequests</u>: 20*s*. to the fabric of that church, 12*d*. each to the fraternity of the light of St. John, the fraternity of the light of the high cross, and the fraternity of the light of the Holy Trinity, 10*s*. to the high altar for his forgotten tithes and benefactions, 2*s*. 6*d*. to the parochial chaplain to pray for his soul and the soul of his wife Sarah, and 6*d*. each to the deacon and the sacristan; 6*s*. 8*d*. to the fabric of the cathedral church, and ½ mark to the fraternity of the light of the high cross; 2*s*. each to the fabric of St. Edmund's church and the fabric of St. Thomas's church; 12*d*. each to the fabric of Christ's church, Twinham, and the fabric of the church of Wimborne Minster; 6*d*. to each resident annual chaplain celebrating mass in the city on the day of his burial to pray for his soul; 6*d*. to each friar wearing a habit, in the church of the Dominicans of Fisherton and in the church of the Franciscans of Salisbury, to pray for his soul; 30 lb. of wax should be bought for candles to be made from it for burning around his corpse and his grave on the day of his burial, without a limit being set in any way; 20s. for the improvement and repair of the ways of Winchester Street ... [*MS. illegible*] there was need for the easement of water and carts according to the stipulation of his executors; ... to paupers, as much for feeding paupers on the day of his burial as ...; ... to Joan, his servant, on condition that she remained with him ...; ... to William, a son of William Prince, of late staying with him, ... his executors should pay to William 13s. 4d. a year for 10 years if he were to keep a wife; 40s. to Christine Hunt, of late his servant; 40d. to John Pope, a chaplain, to pray ... of Whichbury; ½ ... to John, a son of Nicholas Borley; 20d. to John Borley, a son of Agnes, Nicholas's sister; 2s. to John Loader, dyer; 40s. to Nicholas Brown, his chaplain, to celebrate mass on behalf of his soul; 12d. for each of his indigent kinsmen, and for each of the indigent kinsmen of his wife Sarah, to whom otherwise nothing was bequeathed; 13s. 4d. to Nicholas, a son of William Lord; 40d. to each of his other godchildren; 40d. to the fabric of St. Leonard's church, Whitsbury; £4 and a piece of silver, with a cover, having a long foot, to his daughter Margaret; the rest of his goods to his son John Baker, who should pay for them £20 cash which Nicholas appointed to be laid out, at the stipulation of John and his own other executors, on the salvation of his own soul and of the souls mentioned below. <u>Devises</u>: to his son John Baker, grocer, two conjoined tenements, with gardens, in Winchester Street between a tenement formerly William Tenterer's on the east side and a tenement formerly Robert Still's on the west side. Nicholas dwelt in one of the tenements and William Lord dwells in the other. The two, with the gardens, are to be held for ever by John and his issue, and if John were to die without issue they should be sold by Nicholas's executors, their executors, or subsequent executors. The money received from the sale should be laid out by the executors, on celebrating masses, giving alms, repairing ways, visiting paupers, and doing other charitable deeds, on behalf of Nicholas's soul, the souls of his wife Sarah and his son John, and other souls. Nicholas devised to John two conjoined cottages, with a yard (*or* yards), in Gigant Street, on the way to St. Edmund's church, between shops of late William Stanley's on the south side and cottages now John Butterley's on the north side; also a yard in Freren Street between William Godmanstone's yard on the north side and William Ashley's cottage property on the south side. The cottages, with the yard(s), and the yard in Freren Street are to be held for ever by John and his heirs and assigns. Nicholas devised to his son Nicholas Salisbury, a chaplain, a rent of 30s. a year, which he held by a devise of Gilbert of Whichbury, issuing from a tenement, of late John Burgess's, now that of Nicholas's son John Baker, in New Street between a tenement of late Thomas Britford's on the west side and a tenement of late Richard Monk's on the east side. The rent is to be held by Nicholas for life, and after his death it should be held for ever by John Baker and his heirs and assigns so that he and they might find a chaplain to celebrate mass in St. Martin's church, for the year following the elder Nicholas's death, on behalf of that Nicholas's soul, the souls mentioned above, the soul of the younger Nicholas, and other souls. Nicholas devised to his son Nicholas two conjoined shops in New Street between William Warmwell's corner tenement on the west side and Robert Play's tenement on the east side. The shops are to be held for life by Nicholas, and after his death they should be sold by the elder Nicholas's executors, their executors, or subsequent executors. The money received from the sale should be laid out by the executors in the way mentioned above on behalf of the elder Nicholas's soul and the souls mentioned above. Nicholas devised to Joan Ringwood, his servant, a tenement in Brown Street, between a tenement of late John Luckham's on the north side and William Warmwell's tenement on the south side. The tenement should be held by Joan for life on condition that she serves Nicholas, and remains with him, until his death, and after her death it should be sold by Nicholas's executors, their executors, or subsequent executors. The money received from the sale should be laid out by the executors in the way mentioned above on behalf of Nicholas's soul and the souls mentioned above. Executors: his sons John Baker and Nicholas Salisbury. Proved on 14 February 1393 in front of William Glinton, the subdean; the administration was entrusted to John and Nicholas. Approved at a court held in front of the bailiff, the mayor, and other citizens; the seisin of the tenements, shops, and rent was released to the legatees.

5 October 1393, at Winchester
2175 By his charter Stephen Haim, a citizen of Winchester, granted to Thomas Warrener, Thomas Bonham, of Wiltshire, Adam Murray, a clerk, of Eastbourne, Sussex, and William Bailey, draper, of Salisbury, the manor of Forton, near Gravelacre, with the houses, gardens, rent, services, courts, woods, mills, meadows, pastures, feeding rights, ponds, fisheries, vintries, ways, paths, hedges, and ditches, and all his land, tenements, rent, services, and rights in Empshott in Selborne hundred, in Salisbury, and elsewhere in Hampshire and Wiltshire, to be held by them and their heirs and assigns. Clause of warranty. Seal: Stephen's. Named witnesses: John Dovedale, Henry Popham, William Overton, John Butterley, of Salisbury, and William Warmwell

27 June 1399, at London
2176 Proof of the will of John Camel, a citizen of Salisbury, made on 30 December 1398 [*the date of the will as given in the copy is 30 December 1399, evidently in error for 30 December 1398: John Camel is known to have died between 31 July 1398 and 26 February 1399*]. Interment: in St. Thomas's church, on the north side of his wife Edith buried there. Bequests: 100s. to George [Lowthorpe], the rector of that church, for his forgotten tithes; 40 marks to his wife Alice; £50 to the Franciscans of Salisbury to pray for his soul and to hold his obit for ever; £20 to the monastery of Shaftesbury on condition that, on the advice of Robert Hindon, a friar, John's younger daughter Edith might be a nun there; 10 marks to that Edith for her necessities to be placed about her room; his executors, at their discretion, should reward all his servants according to their merits; the rest of his goods to his executors to be laid out on pious uses on behalf of his soul and the souls of others. Devises: to his wife Alice for her life as dower a tenement called Bull Hall, with all its appurtenances as far as the tenement in which William Buckland dwells. John appointed that Edmund Enfield and Richard Spencer, feoffees in a tenement of

late Richard Hart's, should enfeoff Alice in that tenement for her life. He devised to Laurence Gowan and Agnes, his daughter, Laurence's wife, a corner tenement called Dyne's Corner [in Carter Street and Winchester Street], a tenement called Hott Corner [?in Minster Street and New Street], a corner tenement [in Endless Street: *cf. 1639*], of late Robert Play's, between John Mower's tenement on the north side and Walter Bower's cottage property on the east side, and two shops in Brown Street, in which Henry Chubb, baker, dwells. The tenements and the shops are to be held for ever by Laurence and Agnes and their joint issue, as it appears fully in indentures perfected between John Camel and John Gowan, of Norrington, on the marriage of Laurence and Agnes. If Laurence and Agnes were to die without such issue the tenements and the shops would remain for ever to John's son John and Edmund Enfield's son Richard, to be divided equally between them, and to their issue. If John and Richard were to die without issue the tenements and the shops would remain for ever to John Camel's direct heirs and their issue, and if those heirs were to die without issue they should be sold by John Camel's executors, their executors, or subsequent executors. The money received from them should be laid out on pious uses. John devised to Maud, his mother, for her life two conjoined tenements, of late Nicholas Taylor's, opposite the east end of the Guildhall. He devised to his son John a tenement in Castle Street, beyond the bar, in which William Dayhay dwells, and two tenements in Culver Street, between Margery Justice's cottage property on the south side and John Prentice's cottages on the north side, to be held for ever by him and his issue. If John were to die without issue those tenements would remain, and descend step by step, as it is written above concerning that John and Richard Enfield. John devised to that Richard a tenement above a small pit in Winchester Street, which he acquired from Edmund Enfield, to be held for ever by Richard and his issue. If Richard were to die without issue his sister Edith and her issue should hold the tenement for ever, and if Edith were to die without issue the tenement should be sold by John's executors or subsequent executors. The money received from the sale should be laid out on pious uses. John devised to Walter Shirley a tenement in Brown Street, in which William Buckland dwells, between Bull Hall on the south side and a corner tenement of late Nicholas Taylor's on the north side. The tenement is to be held by Walter for the life of John's younger daughter Edith, maintaining it in all things necessary at his own expense and paying a rent of 40s. a year to Edith. After Edith's death the tenement, with the rent, should be sold by John's executors. The money received should be laid out on behalf of John's soul and the souls of others. John devised to Edmund Enfield and his wife Edith a corner tenement [in Wineman Street and Brown Street: *cf. 2202, 2223, 2225*], opposite [Ball's Place], Agnes Ball's tenement, between John Needler's tenement on the east side and the tenement devised to Walter Shirley on the south side. The tenement is to be held by Edmund and Edith for their life and the life of the one of them living longer, and after their death it should be sold by John's executors. The money received from the sale should be laid out on behalf of John's soul and the souls of others. John devised to his son John two conjoined tenements [in Brown Street: *cf. 2229*], behind a tenement in which

Thomas Bleacher dwells, opposite a wide gate of it, formerly John Butterley's, to be held for ever by him and heirs and assigns. He devised to his wife Alice for life, to hold his obit in St. Thomas's church, cottages in Nuggeston and Mealmonger Street which he bought from John Stallington, and after Alice's death the cottages should be sold by his executors. The money received from the sale should be laid out on pious uses on behalf of his soul. John appointed that on Alice's death Bull Hall should remain for ever to his son John and his issue, and if that John were to die without issue it should be sold by the elder John's executors. The money received should be laid out on behalf of the elder John's soul and the souls of others. John appointed the reversion of the tenement, formerly Hart's, devised to Alice for life, to be sold by his executors. The money received from the sale should be released by them to the hospital of the Holy Trinity on condition that the chaplains celebrating mass in it should hold a special commemoration service on behalf of his soul, and that the keepers or masters of the hospital should hold his obit in the hospital every year for ever. John devised to his elder daughter Edith a tenement [opposite the fishermen's stalls: *cf. 1689*], in which Maud Till dwells, after the death of his mother, to be held for ever by her and her issue, and if Edith were to die without issue the tenement should be sold by John's executors as quickly as it could be done to advantage. The money received from the sale should be laid out on pious uses. John devised to his son John a tenement opposite the Guildhall, in which John Long dwells, to be held for ever by him and his issue, and if that John were to die without issue the tenement should be sold by the elder John's executors. The money received from the sale should be laid out by the executors on pious uses. Executors: his wife Alice, Edmund Enfield, and Walter Shirley. Proved in front of John Barnet, an officer of the court of Roger [Walden], the archbishop of Canterbury, and deputed a commissary general. In a letter dated 27 June 1399 John informed Thomas Montagu, the dean of Salisbury, and his officers William Bildeston and Thomas Upton, that, because John Camel possessed goods in various dioceses in the province of Canterbury, the proving of his will pertained to the archbishop of Canterbury and the proving by Edmund Cockerell, the subdean of Salisbury, had been annulled. The administration was entrusted to Walter Shirley, who was required to make an inventory of John Camel's goods and return it to the archbishop or his commissary. John Barnet authorized Thomas Montagu or William Bildeston and Thomas Upton to entrust it to John Camel's wife Alice and Edmund Enfield.

Quindene of Martinmas 1410, at Westminster
2177 In a final agreement reached in the king's court in front of William Thirning, William Hankford, John Cockayne, John Culpepper, and Robert Hill, justices, between Richard Falconer, of Salisbury, Robert Blake, William Winslow, a clerk, and Edward Russell, a clerk, plaintiffs, and William Coventry and his wife Margaret, deforciants, concerning 12 messuages in Salisbury, William and Margaret acknowledged the messuages to be the right of William Winslow, as that which the four plaintiffs held by their gift, and quitclaimed them for themselves, and for Margaret's heirs, to the plaintiffs and William Winslow's heirs.

Clause of warranty. For that acknowledgement and quitclaim the plaintiffs gave 200 marks cash to William and Margaret.

23 September 1411, at Salisbury
2178 By his deed Nicholas Melbury, a citizen of Salisbury, quitclaimed to Henry Summer and his wife Catherine and to Henry's heirs and assigns his right or claim to a tenement, containing three shops, with a sollar, in Carter Street between a tenement of late John Newman's, in which John Bell dwells, on the north side and William Tull's tenement on the south side. Clause of warranty. Seals: Nicholas's and the common and mayoral seals of the city. Named witnesses: the bailiff, the mayor, a coroner, the reeves, John Mower, Richard Spencer, Walter Shirley, William Walter, Thomas Mason, draper, and the clerk

14 June 1413, at Salisbury
2179 Approval of the will of William Warmwell, a citizen of Salisbury, made on 8 October 1412. <u>Interment</u>: in St. Thomas's church, in the middle of the nave. <u>Bequests</u>: [*sum not specified*] to the fabric of that church to be laid out at the discretion of his executors, and 6*d.* to each chaplain; 20*s.* to the fabric of St. Martin's church, to be laid out at the discretion of his executors, to pray for his soul, and 6*d.* to each chaplain; 20*s.* to the fabric of St. Edmund's church, to be laid out in the same way, to pray for his soul, and 4*d.* to each chaplain; 40*s.* to the fabric of the cathedral church, a gold ring worth 13*s.* 4*d.* to the image of the Blessed Mary of Salisbury above the west door, a similar ring to the image of the same Blessed Mary *Gysyue*, and 4*d.* to each vicar chaplain to pray for his soul; 13*s.* 4*d.* for the maintenance of paupers of St. Nicholas's hospital; 4*d.* to each ailing person, of both sexes, lying bedridden in the city or in Fisherton Anger; 13 poor men and 13 poor married women should be clothed in white cloth on the day of his burial; five candles, each weighing 6 lb., should be burned around his corpse on the day of his burial; 20*s.* to the community of Dominicans of Fisherton Anger, 4*d.* to each friar chaplain there singly to pray for his soul on the day of his burial, and 3*d.* to each other friar; 20*s.* to the community of Franciscans of Salisbury, 4*d.* to each friar chaplain, and 3*d.* to each other friar; 13*s.* 4*d.* for the maintenance of the paupers of the almshouse called Almshouse; a piece of silver with a cover each to John Warmwell and Robert Warmwell, sons of his brother, and to his kinsman William Bower; 6*s.* 8*d.* to each of his servants, men and women, remaining with him on the day of his death; from his goods his executors should provide for 3,500 masses to be celebrated on the day of his death on behalf of his soul and the souls of others; within the two years following his death, or more quickly if it could be done advantageously, 3,500*d.* should be handed out at 1*d.* each among feeble paupers, both within the city and outside, at the discretion of his executors; 6*s.* 8*d.* to the hospital of St. Giles, near Wilton; 3*s.* 4*d.* to the lepers' hospital of Harnham; to the altar of St. Michael in St. Thomas's church a missal, a silver and gilt chalice, a silver and gilt ewer with a pax-board from York with silver and gilt decoration, and a psalter, to be chained in the cell, near that altar, where he was accustomed to sit, to serve the altar, provided that the missal,

the chalice, the ewer, and the pax-board should remain in the keeping, and at the disposition, of the wardens of that church for the time being, to the end that they would not be alienated nor kept by any chaplain appointed to the altar or by anyone else; all his armour to John Warmwell, Robert Warmwell, and William Bower, his kinsmen, to be divided among them in equal parts; of the rest of his goods, excluding cash, he bequeathed half to his daughter Joan, at her first choice after the division, and half to his executors to be laid out on behalf of his soul and the souls of others; 53s. 4d. to each of his executors. <u>Devises</u>: to his daughter Joan three conjoined cottages beyond the bar of Castle Street, with a garden (*or* gardens) and a dovecot, between John Starr's tenement on the south side and William's own cottages on the north side, which he held by a grant of Nicholas Harding and John Stoke, executors of Isabel Cole. The cottages, with the garden(s) and dovecot, are to be held for ever by Joan and her issue, and if Joan were to die without issue they would remain for ever to Robert Warmwell and his heirs and assigns on condition that, in the first year that he or his heirs receive any profit as a result of the remainder, he or his heirs or assigns would lay out 100s. in good faith for the salvation of William's soul and the souls of others. William devised to Robert Warmwell two cottages in Castle Street, beside the three cottages devised to Joan on the south side and Henry Summer's tenement on the north side, which he held by a grant of John Lewisham, the executor of John Drury. The cottages are to be held for ever by Robert and his heirs and assigns on condition that, within the two years following William's death, Robert would pay £10 for a chaplain to be found for the same two years [?to celebrate mass] on behalf of William's soul and the souls of others, with any necessary addition for accomplishing that from William's goods, that part of the sum of £10 to be paid by Robert in William's lifetime having been subtracted, if anything more should be paid according to the testimony of William's daughter Joan. William devised to William Dowding a tenement, with an adjacent garden, in Gigant Street between William Stout's tenement on the south side and William Sall's tenement on the north side. The tenement is to be held for ever by William Dowding and his heirs and assigns on condition that, in the two years following William Warmwell's death, he would pay to William's other executors £10 in each year, and if he declined to pay the £20 in the two years, or refused to make the payment, the other executors should sell the tenement. The money issuing from the sale should be laid out on behalf of William Warmwell's soul. William devised to William Bower a tenement, with an adjacent garden, in St. Martin's Street, beside Ivy bridge, between a tenement of the provost of St. Edmund's church on the east side and a tenement of the dean and chapter of Salisbury on the west side. The tenement is to be held for ever by William and his heirs and assigns on condition that, in the year following William's death, he would pay to William's other executors £10 to be laid out by the other executors on behalf of William's soul and the souls of others. If William were unwilling, or refused, to pay the £10 the other executors should sell the tenement, with the garden. The money received from the sale should be laid out by those executors for the salvation of William's soul and the souls of others. William appointed three conjoined cottages in Mealmonger Street between cottages of John Hampton, brewer, on the south side and William Slegge's cottages on the north side, together with a rent of 10s. issuing to him from a tenement [in Nuggeston: cf. *2042–3*; in Mealmonger Street: cf. *2596*] of late Thomas Dunball's, now Thomas Ferring's, to be sold by his executors. The cottages, and the tenement from which the rent issued, were acquired by William from Stephen Haim and John Butterley, executors of William Wishford. The money received from the sale should be laid out by the executors on behalf of William's soul and the souls of others, especially that of William Wishford. William devised to his daughter Joan three conjoined tenements, with a garden (*or* gardens), in Gigant Street, between Christine Handley's tenement on the south side and Robert Russell's tenement on the north side, which William held by a grant of John Upton. He also devised to Joan three cottages in Gigant Street, between cottage property of the provost of St. Edmund's church on the south side and Margaret Godmanstone's cottages on the north side, together with a rent of 5s. issuing from a tenement, of late William Lord's, which William Basket now holds. The tenements, cottages, and rent are to be held for ever by Joan and her issue to hold the anniversary obit of William Warmwell and his wives yearly in St. Thomas's church. If Joan or her heirs delayed in holding the obit for two whole years, and did not hold it, William's executors, their executors, or subsequent executors should enter on the tenements and sell them. The money received from the sale should be laid out, with the oversight of the mayor for the time being, for the salvation of William's soul. William devised to the mayor a rent of 10s., issuing from a tenement, of late John Thorburn's, in Winchester Street, which he acquired from Robert Beechfount, an executor of Richard Ryborough, to be held by the mayor and commonalty in aid of all the charge henceforward to be imposed on them according to the terms of a licence granted by the king and confirmed by the bishop of Salisbury and the dean and chapter of Salisbury. William appointed five cottages, with a rack (*or* racks) and a garden (*or* gardens), in Freren Street, opposite the wall of the Franciscans, to be sold by his executors when, immediately after his death, it could be done advantageously. The money issuing from the sale should be handed out by the executors among the older destitute and poor of the city with all haste. <u>Executors</u>: his daughter Joan, Robert Warmwell, William Bower, and William Dowding, who should do or undertake nothing in contravention of the will, nor any one of them act individually unless with the unanimous assent and wish of the others; if they, or any one of them, were to act contrary to the prescribed terms the action of the one in contravention would be invalid and void. <u>Proved</u> on 12 May 1413 in front of the subdean; the administration was entrusted to the executors. <u>Approved</u> at a court held in front of the bailiff, the mayor, and other citizens; the seisin of the tenements, cottages, gardens, and rent was released to the legatees.

16 June 1413
2180 By his deed Adam Murray, a clerk, of Eastbourne, Sussex, granted to Nicholas Carran and his wife Mercy the manor of Forton, near Gravelacre, [*as in 2175*] and land etc. [*as in 2175*] in Empshott in Selborne hundred, in Salisbury,

and elsewhere in Hampshire and Wiltshire. The manor and the land etc. were held jointly by Adam and, now dead, Thomas Warrener and Thomas Bonham, of Wiltshire, and William Bailey, draper, of Salisbury, by a grant of Stephen Haim, of late a citizen of Winchester, and are to be held for ever by Nicholas and Mercy and their heirs and assigns. Seal: Adam's

20 June 1413
2181 By his deed Adam Murray, a clerk, of Eastbourne, Sussex, quitclaimed to Nicholas Carran and his wife Mercy and their heirs and assigns his right or claim to the manor of Forton, near Gravelacre, [*as in 2175*] and to land etc. [*as in 2175*] in Empshott in Selborne hundred, in Salisbury, and elsewhere in Hampshire and Wiltshire. The manor and the land etc. were held jointly by Adam and, now dead, Thomas Warrener and Thomas Bonham, of Wiltshire, and William Bailey, draper, of Salisbury, by a grant of Stephen Haim, sometime ago a citizen of Winchester. Seal: Adam's

12 July 1413
2182 By his deed Thomas Read, merchant, quitclaimed to John Prentice, a clerk, a son of John Prentice, of late a citizen of Salisbury, and his heirs and assigns his right or claim to a cottage, with a garden, which he held by the younger John's grant on conditions in that matter fulfilled. The cottage stands in Culver Street, on the east side of the street, between Thomas Knoyle's cottage property on the north side and the younger John's own cottages on the south side. Seals: Thomas Read's and the common and mayoral seals of the city. Named witnesses: the bailiff, the mayor, the reeves, John Mower, Richard Spencer, Walter Shirley, William Dowding, and the clerk

26 July 1413, at Salisbury
2183 By their indented charter Richard Spencer and John Jakes, a chaplain, granted to Gunnore, the relict of Thomas Bowyer, of late a citizen of Salisbury, a tenement, with a shop (*or* shops), standing where of late poultry were sold, between a tenement which Walter at the burgh of late held on the east side and Shit Lane on the west side. The tenement, with the shop(s), was of late Richard Falconer's and is to be held for ever by Gunnore and her heirs and assigns, paying to Richard Spencer and John Jakes a rent of 53*s.* 4*d.* a year for the life of Richard Falconer and his wife Alice and the life of the one of them living longer, or at all events to Richard and Alice. In the meantime Gunnore and her heirs and assigns are to maintain the tenement in all things necessary at their own expense so that the rent would not be lost. Clause to permit Richard Spencer and John Jakes to enter on the tenement if the rent were to be in arrear for 15 days, distrain, and keep distresses until the unpaid rent was recovered; also, if the rent were to be in arrear for a quarter, or if Gunnore or her heirs or assigns were not to maintain the tenement so that the rent would be lost during the life of Richard Falconer and Alice, to permit Richard Spencer and John Jakes to repossess and retain the tenement, with the shops, for the life of Richard and Alice and the life of the one

of them living longer, the reversion always pertaining to Gunnore and her heirs. Seals: those of the parties to the parts of the charter in turn and the common and mayoral seals of the city. Named witnesses: the bailiff, the mayor, the reeves, John Mower, Richard Spencer, Walter Shirley, William Sall, and the clerk

2184 By his charter Nicholas, a son and heir of Nicholas Baynton, granted to John Swift, ironmonger, a citizen of Salisbury, two conjoined shops which the elder Nicholas acquired from John Polmond, a burgess of Southampton, in Minster Street, near the graveyard of St. Thomas's church, between a shop formerly Andrew Bone's, now built as a cellar with a sollar of John Swift, on the south side and shops formerly William Mount's on the north side. The shops are to be held for ever by John Swift and his heirs and assigns. Seals: Nicholas's and the common and mayoral seals of the city. Named witnesses: the bailiff, the mayor, the reeves, John Mower, Richard Spencer, Walter Shirley, William Warin, William Dowding, and the clerk

6 September 1413, at Salisbury

2185 By his charter John Prentice, a clerk, a son of John Buddle, called Prentice, of late a citizen of Salisbury, and his wife Catherine, granted to John Shad, draper, and his wife Agnes cottages, with a garden (*or* gardens), now built as four cottages, in Culver Street, on the east side of the street, between Thomas Knoyle's cottage property on the north side and cottage property of late John Camel's, which Richard Spencer holds, on the south side. The cottages, with the garden(s), are to be held for ever by John Shad and Agnes and John's heirs and assigns, to whom John Prentice quitclaimed his right or claim to them. Clause of warranty. Seals: John Prentice's and the common and mayoral seals of the city. Named witnesses: the bailiff, the mayor, the reeves, John Mower, Richard Spencer, Walter Shirley, William Walter, Thomas Read, and the clerk

2186 By their deed William Goodall, barber, and his wife Maud, the relict of Gilbert at the brook, skinner, and at all events Maud, examined in court in front of the bailiff and the mayor and having avowed her will in the matter, granted to William Walter and William Harnhill, barber, citizens of Salisbury, their or Maud's right or claim to a tenement, with a garden next to it, a shop (*or* shops), and rooms. The tenement, of late Gilbert's, stands in Gigant Street between a tenement of late Hugh Hoare's, now John Lewisham's, on the north side and a tenement of late Thomas Chaplin's on the south side, and it is to be held for ever by William Walter and William Harnhill and their heirs and assigns according to the terms of Maud's tenure. Seals: those of William Goodall and Maud and the common and mayoral seals of the city. Named witnesses: the bailiff, the mayor, the reeves, John Mower, Richard Spencer, Nicholas Harding, John Lewisham, and the clerk

2187 By their deed John Brock, a chaplain, and Stephen Edington granted to William Tull, a merchant, [Bert's Corner: *cf. 2071–2*], a corner tenement, which they held with others now dead, by a grant of Richard Bristow and his wife Tamsin and of Roger Capon. The tenement stands in Wineman Street and Culver Street, between a tenement of late Gilbert Oword's on the west side and

Thomas Slegge's cottages on the south side, and is to be held for ever by William and his heirs and assigns. Seals: those of John and Stephen and the common and mayoral seals of the city. Named witnesses: the bailiff, the mayor, the reeves, John Mower, Richard Spencer, Walter Shirley, William Sall, William Dowding, and John Lewisham

4 October 1413, at Salisbury
2188 Approval of the will of Thomas Manning of Fisherton Anger made on 14 August 1413. <u>Interment</u>: in the graveyard of St. Clement's church, Fisherton, [?near] the south door of the church. <u>Bequests</u>: 10*s.* to the fabric of that church; 6*s.* 8*d.* to the fabric of the cathedral church; 3*s.* 4*d.* each to the fabric of St. Thomas's church, of St. Edmund's church, and of St. Martin's church; 6*s.* 8*d.* each to the fabric of Sutton Veny church and of Stratford-sub-Castle church; 6*s.* 8*d.* both to the Dominicans of Fisherton and the Franciscans of Salisbury; 6*s.* 8*d.* to be handed out among paupers in the hospital of the Holy Trinity; 2*s.* to the prisoners in the Guildhall; a harnessed dagger to Nicholas Conner, the rector of the church of Chilmark; 20*s.* to the Carthusian house in Selwood; 10*s.* to the rector of Fisherton for his forgotten tithes; 6*s.* 8*d.* to Thomas Hellier, a chaplain, to pray for his soul; 6*s.* 8*d.* to the lord John Daubeney likewise; £4 3*s.* 4*d.* for 1,000 masses to be celebrated on behalf of his soul immediately after his death; £4 3*s.* 4*d.* to be handed out among paupers on the day of his burial or immediately afterwards; 3*s.* 4*d.* to William Windsor, of Sutton; a suitable gown and 6*s.* 8*d.* to Walter Gaud; a gown, with a hood, and 6*s.* 8*d.* to Stephen at the gate, his household servant; 4*d.* to each prisoner in [Old] Sarum castle; 13*s.* 4*d.* to the little Agnes, his servant, if she wished to remain with his wife; 6*s.* 8*d.* to the lord Richard Jacob to pray for his soul; 2*s.* each to the fraternity of the light of the Holy Trinity, the fraternity of the light of St. Christopher, and the fraternity of the light of the Holy Cross, all in the church of Fisherton; 6*s.* 8*d.* each to William Priest and John Rose, chaplains, to pray for his soul; 13*s.* 4*d.* to William Dinton, butcher, and he remits what more William owes to him; 4*d.* to each pauper in St. Nicholas's hospital; a plain furred gown with a hood, a silver bowl with a cover, and 60*s.* both to his brother the lord John Manning and John Draper, a clerk; 20*s.* to John Wishford, a clerk, [and to] John Draper; 40*s.* to John Everard; 6*s.* 8*d.* each to John at the gate, his household servant, and Thomas, his godson, a son of John Manning, butcher; 12*d.* each to his other godsons; 4*d.* to each person ill and bedridden in Fisherton and Stratford; 6*s.* 8*d.* and a gown, with a hood, to Thomas Good, his household servant; 6*s.* 8*d.* to John, the parochial chaplain of Stratford; 13*s.* 4*d.* each to Isabel, his household servant, and Edith Shipster; 13*s.* 4*d.* to the friar Henry Wallis to pray for his soul. He bequeathed to his wife Maud, besides her purparty, from his contingent goods all his utensils in his house at Fisherton, except those bequeathed above, on condition that she would keep herself celibate and unmarried for life; first of all an indented inventory of the utensils should be made, subscribed to by Maud and Thomas's executors, and Maud should find sufficient security to them for the return to them or their executors of all his purparty concerning the utensils. If Maud were to unite with any other man

by way of marriage Thomas appointed his purparty to be disposed of by his executors or their executors on pious uses for the salvation of his soul and the souls of others. Thomas bequeathed the rest of his goods to his executors to be disposed of on behalf of his soul and the souls of others. <u>Devise</u>: he appointed all the lands and tenements in Salisbury which he acquired from Richard Mawardine and his wife Edith to his brother John and John Draper to be sold. The money issuing from them should be laid out by his executors or their executors on pious uses for the salvation of his soul and the souls of others. <u>Executors</u>: his brother John and John Draper. <u>Proved</u> on 14 September 1413 in front of John Perch, a registrar of Thomas [Arundel], the archbishop of Canterbury; the administration was entrusted to John Manning, reserving the power to entrust it to John Draper when he might come to seek it. <u>Approved</u> at a court held in front of the bailiff, the mayor, and other citizens; the seisin of the land and tenements was released to the legatees.

18 October 1413, at Salisbury
2189 A deed of Alice, the relict, and an executor, of Robert Woodborough, of late a citizen of Salisbury. Robert devised a tenement in Rolleston, near Mealmonger Street, between a tenement then Thomas Dunball's on one side and a yard then Richard Haxton's on the other side, to his daughter Cecily and her issue. If Cecily were to die without issue the tenement would remain for ever to Robert's son John and his issue, and if John were to die without issue it should be sold by Robert's executors or their executors. The money issuing from the sale should be laid out on behalf of Robert's soul. Cecily and John have died without living issue, all Robert's executors are dead except Alice, living in widowhood, and it therefore falls to Alice alone to sell the tenement. By her deed Alice, as Robert's executor, on the strength of the will granted the tenement to William Sall, a citizen of Salisbury, to be held for ever by him and his heirs and assigns as that which he bought from Alice in good faith for a sum of money to fulfil Robert's will. Seals: Alice's and the common and mayoral seals of the city. Named witnesses: the bailiff, the mayor, the coroners, the reeves, John Mower, Richard Spencer, Walter Shirley, William Warin, John Lewisham, and the clerk

1 November 1413, at Salisbury
2190 By his charter William Winslow, a clerk, granted to Henry Harborough, a clerk, William Bowyer, John Malby, and John Wilton, a messuage, with two shops, in Minster Street between Richard Harlwin's shops on the north side and John Spencer's tenement on the south side; also two tenements in St. Martin's Street between a tenement of John Dovedon and his wife Joan on the west side and a tenement of the dean and chapter of Salisbury on the east side; also a cottage, with a garden and a rack, in Freren Street between cottage property of late John Duckton's on the south side and a tenement of late Edith Ashley's on the north side; also a cottage, with a garden, in Drake Hall Street between John Hemby's cottage property on the north side and Nicholas Melbury's cottage property on the south side; also two cottages in Mealmonger Street between

William Mead's tenement on the north side and a cottage of late Richard Leach's on the south side; with all the land and tenements in the city which he held by a grant of William Coventry and his wife Margaret by means of a fine levied in the king's court. The premises are to be held for ever by the grantees and their heirs and assigns. Seals: William Winslow's and the common and mayoral seals of the city. Named witnesses: the bailiff, the mayor, the coroners, the reeves, John Mower, Richard Spencer, William Warin, Walter Shirley, Walter Nalder, and the clerk

2191 By their indented charter Richard Spencer, a citizen of Salisbury, and John Jakes, a clerk, granted to the master Richard Leach, otherwise Falconer, a citizen of Salisbury, and his wife Alice a [corner] messuage, with a cottage (*or* cottages) and a garden (*or* gardens), in Wineman Street between a tenement of Richard Spencer and John Jakes, in which John Pinch, tucker, dwells, on the west side and Nicholas Harding's tenement in Gigant Street on the south side. Richard and John held the messuage, with the cottage(s) and garden(s), with other land in the city and in Stratford, by a grant of Richard Leach. They also granted to Richard and Alice 3½ acres and 1 yardland of arable land in the field of Stratford near Salisbury. The messuage, with the cottage(s) and garden(s), and the land are to be held by Richard and Alice for their life and the life of the one of them living longer, and after their death should remain for ever to William Lord and his wife Joan and to William's heirs and assigns. For the life of Richard and Alice, and the life of the one of them living longer, William and Joan and William's heirs shall maintain the messuage, with the cottage(s), for instance in the matter of the roof, and pay the rent due to the chief lord. Seals: those of Richard Spencer, John Jakes, and William Lord, and the common and mayoral seals of the city, to the part of the charter remaining in the possession of Richard and Alice, and those of Richard Spencer and John Jakes, and the common and mayoral seals of the city, to the part remaining in the possession of William Lord and Joan. Named witnesses: the bailiff, the mayor, the coroners, the reeves, John Mower, William Walter, Nicholas Harding, Walter Shirley, Walter Nalder, William Dowding, and the clerk

15 November 1413, at Salisbury
2192 By his indented charter Nicholas, a son and heir of Nicholas Baynton, of Faulston, granted to Richard Coof and Edward Frith a tenement in Endless Street between a tenement of late Walter Holbury's, now Roger Enterbush's, on the south side and a corner tenement formerly John Pannett's, now William Dunning's, on the north side. The tenement was acquired by the elder Nicholas from George Goss, was held by George by a grant of Margery, the relict of John Pannett, was held by Margery by John's devise, and is to be held for ever by Richard and Edward and their heirs and assigns. Richard and Edward and their heirs and assigns may not build anything in the garden next to the tenement by means of which the windows lighting Nicholas's houses there would be obscured. Clause of warranty. Seals: those of the parties to the parts of the charter in turn, and the common and mayoral seals of the city. Named witnesses: the bailiff, the

mayor, the coroners, the reeves, John Mower, Richard Spencer, Walter Shirley, William Sall, Walter Nalder, and the clerk

13 December 1413, at Salisbury
2193 Approval of the will of Henry Winpenny, butcher, of Salisbury, made on 26 July 1413. Interment: in the south part of St. Thomas's church. Bequests: 6s. 8d. to the fabric of that church, and 3s. 4d. to the high altar for his forgotten tithes and lesser benefactions; 12d. each to the fabric of the cathedral church, the fabric of St. Edmund's church, and the fabric of St. Martin's church; 3s. 4d. both to the Franciscans of Salisbury and the Dominicans of Fisherton; 20d. each to Henry, a son of a younger John Wells, to a daughter of Edward Dubber, and to Gunnore, a daughter of an elder John Wells; the rest of his goods to his wife Maud to be disposed of on behalf of his soul; 20s. to Geoffrey Butcher, of Wilton, for his diligence in helping Maud to fulfil his legacies. Devise: to Maud and her heirs and assigns for ever a shop, or tenement, in Butcher Row between Thomas Knoyle's tenement on the west side and Henry Popham's shop on the east side. Maud should find a chaplain, to be chosen with the assent of the lord James Green, to celebrate mass in St. Thomas's church for a year after Henry Winpenny's death as often as he can on behalf of Henry's soul and the souls of others; she should entreat the parochial chaplain to commend Henry's soul in the pulpit of that church every Sunday among his other prayers, in which it is seemly, for Maud's life, she paying meanwhile to the parochial chaplain for the time being 2s. a year for praying thus for Henry's soul. Executor: Maud; overseer, Geoffrey Butcher. Proved on 31 October 1413 in front of John Hulling, the subdean; the administration was entrusted to the executor. Approved at a court held in front of the bailiff, the mayor, and other citizens; the seisin of the tenement or shop was released to Maud, the legatee.

27 December 1413, at Salisbury
2194 Approval of the will of Cecily, the wife of Richard Ferrer, of Salisbury, made on 1 October 1413. Interment: in the graveyard of St. Edmund's church. Bequests: 2s. to the fabric of that church, and 12d. to the parochial chaplain; a gold ring and 6d. to the fabric of the cathedral church; her best tablecloth, with a towel, and 6d. to the fabric of St. Margaret's church, Woodford; a pair of silver knives to the wife of John Noble; a blue gown, with a hood, and two veils to the wife of Hugh Portesham; a red gown to her kinswoman Christine; the rest of her goods to her husband Richard so that he might dispose of them on behalf of her soul and the souls of others. Devises: to Richard and his heirs and assigns for ever a shop, or corner tenement, in which she lives, opposite the market [place where grains are sold: *cf.* ***2196***] on the way towards Castle Street; also a rent of 7s. a year which she was accustomed to receive from a shop which Richard holds of Agnes Lea, between Cecily's own shop or corner tenement on the west side and another shop of Agnes on the east side. For the 20 years immediately following Cecily's death Richard and his heirs and assigns should hold her obit yearly in St. Edmund's church, commending in that obit the souls of John Ferrer and Robert

Ferrer, of late her husbands, and handing out 6s. 8d. on the day of the obit among
the annual chaplains of the college there and among paupers, both wives and
husbands. If Richard, or his executors or assigns, were to cease to hold the obit
or make the distribution the executors of John and Robert should enter on the
corner tenement and the rent, and sell them so as to hold the obit and make the
distribution. Executors: her husband Richard and her brother Robert Ravald,
with John Noble as overseer. Proved on the last day of December [?rectius October
or November] 1413 in front of John Hulling, the subdean; the administration was
entrusted to Richard Ferrer, reserving the power to entrust it to Robert Ravald
when he might come to seek it. Approved at a court held in front of the bailiff,
the mayor, and other citizens; the seisin of the shop or tenement and the rent was
released to the legatee.

10 January 1414, at Salisbury
2195 A deed of Joan, the relict of William River and a daughter of William
Warmwell, of late a citizen of Salisbury, Robert Warmwell, William Bower, and
William Dowding, executors of William Warmwell, who appointed cottages, by
the name of five cottages, in Freren Street, opposite the wall of the Franciscans,
between a corner tenement formerly John Baldry's, now John Becket's, on the
north side and cottage property of late John Sivier's, now Richard Spencer's,
on the south side, to be sold by them immediately after his death. One of the
cottages stands above a trench of running water there. The money to be raised
from the sale should be laid out by the executors among the older destitute and
poor and on other charitable deeds. William Phebis has paid a sum of money to
the executors to have the cottages, on the strength of the will and by their deed
the executors granted them to him, and they are to be held for ever by William
and his heirs and assigns as that which he bought from the executors in good
faith for the sum of money to be laid out according to the will. Seals: those of
the grantors and the common and mayoral seals of the city. Named witnesses: the
bailiff, the mayor, the coroners, a reeve, William Warin, William Walter, William
Bishop, Walter Nalder, and the clerk
2196 A deed of William Sivier, an executor of John Canning, of Salisbury. John
devised to his wife Joan for life a corner tenement, or shop, opposite the market
place where grains are sold, between Agnes Lea's shops on either side; also a
rent of 7s. a year issuing from a tenement or shop, beside that corner tenement,
between the corner tenement on the west side and another shop of Agnes
opposite that market place on the east side. On Joan's death the corner tenement
and the rent should be sold by John's executors or their executors, and the money
received should be laid out on the salvation of John's soul and the souls of others.
Because it is well known to William that Cecily, who was the wife of Richard
Ferrer and the relict of John Ferrer, acquired the corner tenement and the rent
and devised them to Richard, who survives, to be held for ever by him and his
heirs and assigns, William quitclaimed to Richard and his heirs and assigns his
right or claim to them on the strength of John's will. Seals: William's and the
common and mayoral seals of the city. Named witnesses: the bailiff, the mayor,

the coroners, the reeves, John Mower, Richard Spencer, Walter Shirley, William Warin, William Sall, and the clerk

2197 By his deed John Forest, a citizen of Salisbury, quitclaimed to William Sall, a citizen of Salisbury, and his heirs and assigns his right or claim to a tenement in Rolleston near Mealmonger Street between a tenement of late that of Thomas Dunball on one side and a yard of late Richard Haxton's on the other side. William held the tenement by a grant of Alice, the relict, and an executor, of Robert Woodborough, and John of late held it according to the custom of England after the death of Robert's daughter Cecily. Seals: John's and the common and mayoral seals of the city. Named witnesses: the bailiff, the mayor, the coroners, the reeves, John Mower, William Walter, Nicholas Harding, John Lewisham, William Tull, and the clerk

24 January 1414, at Salisbury
2198 Approval of the will of Thomas Child, a citizen of Salisbury, made on 10 October 1413. Interment: in St. John's chapel in St. Edmund's church. Bequests: 40*d.* to the fabric of the cathedral church; 10*s.* to the fabric of St. Thomas's church, and 4*d.* to each chaplain to pray for his soul; 40*d.* to the fabric of Christ's church, Twinham, to pray for his soul there; 5*s.* both to the Franciscans of Salisbury and the Dominicans of Fisherton to pray for his soul in their divine services; 20*s.* to the fabric of Ditchampton church to commend his soul in prayer among the parishioners on Sundays; to William Hatter the remission of 14*s.* 4*d.* of the debt which William owed to him; to John Russell 10*s.* of his debt; 6*s.* 8*d.* to William Bailiff, taverner; to Field 20*s.* of his debt if he were to pay his whole debt to Thomas's executors, otherwise he should receive nothing of the legacy; 100*s.* to be handed out among paupers coming to the distribution on the day of his burial, ½*d.* each; his executors should arrange for five trental masses of St. Gregory to be celebrated by chaplains within a year after his death or sooner if that seemed best, otherwise the whole sum should be handed out to paupers and the destitute and laid out on other charitable deeds; 6*s.* 8*d.* for the maintenance of paupers and the feeble staying in the hospital of the Holy Trinity to pray devoutly for his soul in their prayers; his executors, as soon as they can, should cause 500 masses to be celebrated after his death and, moreover, 5 marks to be handed out among paupers in the city and outside, where the greatest need requires it, and among the feeble, especially the bedridden, if the largess might but hold out, and otherwise nothing; five wax candles, each weighing 5 lb., should be provided to be burned around his corpse in masses and in his funeral rites; 20*s.* to the fabric of the church of Wilsford, near Amesbury, to pray for his soul and the souls of John Mercer and his wife Margaret, commending in prayer among the parishioners there on Sundays; 40*d.* to the fabric of St. Nicholas's church, Wilton, to pray for his soul and the souls of others; 6*s.* 8*d.* to the fraternity of the art of the tailors of Salisbury, in which he was a fellow; 6*s.* 8*d.* to John Crosier; 6*s.* 8*d.* to John Mowse, a Dominican friar; 20*s.* to the wife of John Place, his kinswoman; a fur tunic, with a hood, to the style of Walter Nalder, and 40*d.*, to Thomas Marlborough; 6*s.* 8*d.* to Isabel, a daughter of John Warminster; 5 marks to each of his executors taking

upon themselves the burden of the administration of this will, and fulfilling the will in good faith; 12*d.* to William Collingdon, of Winterslow; 40*d.* to the most needy and the paupers of that vill, to be shared among them equally; the rest of his goods should be disposed of by his executors or their executors on behalf of his soul and the souls of others. Devises: to his wife Isabel for life a tenement, with a cellar, in Pot Row between a tenement of late Nicholas Longstock's on the east side and Thomas Stabber's shops on the west side. The tenement immediately after Isabel's death, or the reversion in her lifetime, should be sold by Thomas's executors. The money received from the sale should be laid out by the executors on pious uses on behalf of Thomas's soul and the souls of others, without fraud or deceit. Thomas also devised to Isabel for life the reversion of a tenement and shops when they fell due on the death of Margaret, the relict of William of Godmanstone, which he acquired from Margaret [?*rectius* John Montagu: *cf.* **1935**]. The tenement and shops stand in Winchester Street, above the ditch, between Laurence Gowan's tenement on the west side and a tenement of late John Ettshall's on the east side. After Isabel's death, or even in her lifetime, the tenements should be sold by Thomas's executors. The money received from the sale should be kept for discharging all the purchases made by Thomas and the debts of those to whom it pertains; that done satisfactorily, if anything were to remain it should be laid out by the executors, or by others whom they wished to assign it to, on behalf of Thomas's soul and the souls of others. If anyone of Thomas's executors were not to conform to the wish and order of his fellows, or were to do anything to the contrary to prejudice the will, he would meanwhile lose the bequests assigned to him, and if anything were done by him to the detriment of the will it would be of no value and should be utterly condemned in law. Executors: William Walter, John Lake, John Smith, a chaplain, and an elder John Pilk, of Beckington. Proved on 24 October 1413 in front of John Perch, a registrar of Thomas [Arundel], the archbishop of Canterbury. The proof is shown to a commissary of the registrar, and James Green and Edward Curle, priest of Salisbury diocese, were commissioned to entrust the administration to the executors. Approved at a court held in front of the bailiff, the mayor, and other citizens; the seisin of the tenements and of the reversion was released to Isabel.

2199 By their deed William Walter and William Harnhill, barber, citizens of Salisbury, granted to Alice, the relict of Thomas Ham, tailor, their right or claim under a grant of William Goodall, barber, and his wife Alice [*rectius* Maud: *cf.* **2186**], the relict of Gilbert at the brook, skinner, to a tenement, with an adjacent garden, a shop (*or* shops), and rooms. The tenement, which was of late Gilbert's, stands in Gigant Street between a tenement of late Hugh Hoare's, now John Lewisham's, on the north side and Thomas Chaplin's tenement on the south side, and is to be held for ever by Alice and her heirs and assigns. Seals: those of William Walter and William Harnhill and the common and mayoral seals of the city. Named witnesses: the bailiff, the mayor, the coroners, the reeves, John Mower, Richard Spencer, Walter Shirley, William Warin, Walter Nalder, and the clerk

21 February 1414, at Salisbury

2200 By her deed Alice Whitmore quitclaimed to her son John Whitmore, a clerk, her right or claim to a corner tenement, of late John's, in St. Martin's Street and Gigant Street, between cottages of late William Warmwell's in Gigant Street on the north side and a tenement which William of late held in St. Martin's Street on the west side. Seals: Alice's, that of the mayor of Shaftesbury, and the common and mayoral seals of the city of Salisbury. Named witnesses: the mayor, the bailiff, the coroners, Walter Nalder, William Dowding, William Bishop, Robert Warmwell, and the clerk

7 March 1414, at Salisbury

2201 By his charter Thomas Farrant granted to William Packing and his wife Alice two conjoined cottages in Chipper Lane between a tenement of late William Boyland's, now William Packing's, on the west side and a tenement of late William Wishford's, now John Parch's, on the east side. The cottages were acquired by Thomas from Richard Spencer, a citizen of Salisbury, and are to be held for ever by William Packing and Alice and William's heirs and assigns. Clause of warranty. Seals: Thomas's and the common and mayoral seals of the city. Named witnesses: the bailiff, the mayor, the coroners, the reeves, John Mower, Richard Spencer, Walter Shirley, William Walter, Nicholas Bell, and the clerk

2202 By his charter John Needler, a citizen of Salisbury, granted to his son Richard and John Ruddock a tenement, in which he dwells, with a shop (*or* shops) and a garden, in Wineman Street between a tenement of late Robert Kirtlingstoke's, now Nicholas Melbury's, on the east side and a tenement of late Nicholas Taylor's, now Richard Spencer's, on the west side. The tenement, with the shop(s) and garden, is to be held for ever by Richard Needler and John Ruddock and their heirs and assigns. Clause of warranty. Seals: John Needler's and the common and mayoral seals of the city. Named witnesses: the bailiff, the mayor, the coroners, the reeves, John Mower, Richard Spencer, Walter Shirley, William Sall, William Dowding, and the clerk

2203 By his letters of attorney John Needler, a citizen of Salisbury, appointed Walter Short and Roger Enterbush to surrender into the hand of Robert, the bishop of Salisbury, the seisin of a tenement, in which he dwelt, with a shop (*or* shops) and a garden, in Wineman Street [*as in* **2202**] to the use of his son Richard and John Ruddock. Seals: John Needler's and the mayoral seal of the city

21 March 1414, at Salisbury

2204 By his charter John Whitmore, a clerk, granted to Henry Man, of Salisbury, a corner tenement in St. Martin's Street and Gigant Street [*as in* **2200**]. The tenement was acquired by John from Roger Davitt, a chaplain, and executor of Walter Hoare, a clerk, and is to be held for ever by Henry and his heirs and assigns. Clause of warranty. Seals: John's and the common and mayoral seals of the city. Named witnesses: the bailiff, the mayor, the coroners, the reeves, Richard Spencer, Walter Shirley, William Walter, John Becket, and the clerk

2205 By their indented deed Richard Needler and John Ruddock granted to

Alice, the relict of John Needler, a citizen of Salisbury, a tenement, with a shop (*or shops*) and a garden, in which John of late dwelt, in Wineman Street [*as in* **2202**], to be held for her life by her and her assigns. The tenement should be maintained and repaired at their own expense by Alice and her assigns during Alice's life, causing no waste or distress, and after Alice's death it should remain for ever to Richard and his issue. If Richard were to die without issue he and John Ruddock wish, and grant, that it should remain to the executors of John Needler to be sold. [The money issuing from the sale] should be laid out on behalf of John's soul and the souls of others. Clause of warranty: Richard and his heirs warrant the tenement, with the shop(s) and the garden, to Alice and her assigns for Alice's life. Seals: those of the parties to the parts of the deed in turn, and the mayoral seal of the city. Named witnesses: the mayor, the bailiff, the coroners, John Mower, Richard Spencer, William Warin, John Becket, and the clerk

18 April 1414, at Salisbury

2206 Approval of the will of Adam White, a citizen of Salisbury, made on 7 March 1414. <u>Interment</u>: in the graveyard of St. Martin's church. <u>Bequests</u>: 40*d.* to the fabric of that church, and 20*d.* to William [?Spicer], the parochial chaplain; 12*d.* to the fabric of the cathedral church; 6*s.* 8*d.* to the fabric of St. Edmund's church; 40*d.* to William Westage, a chaplain; 2*s.* 6*d.* both to the Franciscans of Salisbury and the Dominicans of Fisherton; 6*s.* 8*d.* and a tunic to Thomas Tonner, his brother; 20*s.* to his elder son John; 40*d.* to each of his daughters; 6 marks cash to his younger son John; 6*s.* 8*d.* and a tunic to John White, of Newton Tony; 4*d.* to each of his godchildren; 40*d.* to 40 priests to celebrate mass before his burial; the rest of his goods to his wife Maud to be disposed of on behalf of his soul. <u>Devise</u>: to Maud a yard in Gigant Street, on a corner, opposite shops of late John Baker's, between a yard of late John Still's on the north side and Shit Lane [?Chipper Street, called Shit Lane: *cf.* **2371**] on the south side. The yard was held by Adam of Isabel, the relict of John Cole. It is to be held for life by Maud, after Maud's death should be held for ever by Adam's younger son John and his issue, and if that John were to die without issue should be sold by Adam's executors or their executors. The money received from the sale should be laid out on celebrating masses, giving alms, and doing other charitable deeds. <u>Executors</u>: his wife Maud and John Brasseler. <u>Proved</u> on 18 March 1414 in front of John Hulling, the subdean; the administration was entrusted to the executors. <u>Approved</u> at a court held in front of the bailiff, the mayor, and other citizens; the seisin of the yard was released to the legatee.

16 May 1414, at Salisbury

2207 By his writing Thomas Read, a merchant, of Salisbury, granted to Thomas Randolph, of Salisbury, and his wife Alice a corner tenement, with a gate, which John Pope, weaver, of late held and dwelt in, in Endless Street and Chipper Street between Sarah Pope's shop in Endless Street on the north side and Thomas's shop, which William Waite, weaver, holds, in Chipper Street on the east side, to be held for ever by them and their heirs and assigns. Clause of warranty. Seals:

Thomas Read's and the common and mayoral seals of the city. Named witnesses:
the bailiff, the mayor, the coroners, the reeves, John Mower, Richard Spencer,
William Walter, Walter Nalder, and the clerk

13 June 1414, at Salisbury
2208 By their indented charter Thomas Randolph, of Salisbury, and his wife
Alice granted to Thomas Read, a merchant, of Salisbury, a corner tenement,
which they held by his grant, in Endless Street and Chipper Street [*as in* **2207**],
to be held for ever by him and his heirs and assigns. Thomas Read and his heirs
and assigns are to pay a rent of 20s. cash a year to Thomas and Alice and their
heirs and assigns and to repair and maintain the tenement at their own expense
so that the rent would not be lost. Clause to permit re-entry if the rent were to
be in arrear for a month, distraint, and the keeping of distresses until the unpaid
rent was recovered; also, if the rent were to be in arrear for a year and sufficient
distresses could not be found, to permit repossession until the unpaid rent was
recovered. Seals: those of the parties to the parts of the charter in turn and the
common and mayoral seals of the city. Named witnesses: the bailiff, the mayor,
the coroners, the reeves, John Mower, Richard Spencer, Walter Shirley, William
Warin, Walter Nalder, and the clerk
2209 By their indented charter John Little, mercer, and his wife Joan granted
to John Manning, a clerk, and John Everard a corner tenement, with a shop (*or*
shops) and a cottage (*or* cottages) attached to it, in Endless Street and Chipper
Street between Nicholas Baynton's tenement called the Abbey in Chipper
Street on the west side and a tenement of late of John … [*MS. blank*], now John
Shute's, in Endless Street on the north side. The tenement, with the shop(s) and
cottage(s), was held by John and Joan by a grant of Richard Spencer, a citizen
of Salisbury, and is to be held for ever by John Manning and John Everard and
their heirs and assigns, paying a rent of 53s. 4d. a year to John and Joan for the
life of John and rendering the rent, charges, and services due to Richard and
anyone else. John Manning and John Everard and their heirs and assigns are to
maintain the tenement, with the shop(s) and cottage(s), in all things necessary so
that the rent would not be lost. Clause to permit re-entry if the rent were to be
in arrear for a month, distraint, and the keeping of distresses until the unpaid rent
was recovered; also to permit permanent repossession if the rent were to be in
arrear for a year and sufficient distresses could not be found. Clause of warranty.
Seals: those of the parties to the parts of the charter in turn and the common and
mayoral seals of the city. Named witnesses: the bailiff, the mayor, the coroners,
the reeves, John Mower, Walter Shirley, William Warin, William Dowding, and
the clerk

23 June 1414, at Salisbury
2210 By their indenture Thomas Mason, draper, the mayor, and the commonalty
granted to John Parch a tenement in Winchester Street between a corner tenement
of late William Hull's, which William Cox now holds, on the east side and a
tenement of late John Baker's, now John Becket's, on the west side. The tenement

is to be held by John of the mayor and commonalty and their successors for 98 years from the date of the indenture paying a rent of 20s. a year to the mayor and commonalty and rendering the rent, charges, and services due to anyone else. John Parch and his assigns are to maintain and repair the tenement in all things necessary at their own expense for that term of years so that the rent would not be lost. Clause to permit re-entry if the rent were to be in arrear for a month, distraint, and the keeping of distresses until the unpaid rent was recovered; also, if the rent were to be in arrear and sufficient distresses could not be found, to permit repossession until the unpaid rent and other losses were recovered. Clause of warranty. Seals: that of the office of mayor and the common seal of the city to one part of the indenture and John Parch's to the other part

27 June 1414, at Salisbury
2211 By his charter Adam, a son and heir of Simon Belch and his wife Christine, a daughter and heir of John Shalford, of late a citizen of Salisbury, granted to John Shad, draper, of Salisbury, a tenement, with shops, a cottage (*or* cottages), and gardens, which descended to him on the death of Christine, his mother. The tenement stands in the high street which is called Drake Hall Street between a tenement of late Nicholas Longborough's, now that of the vicars of the cathedral church, on the south side and Nicholas Bell's cottages on the north side, and, with the shops, cottage(s), and gardens, is to be held for ever by John Shad and his heirs and assigns. Clause of warranty. Seals: Adam's and the common and mayoral seals of the city. Named witnesses: the bailiff, the mayor, the coroners, the reeves, John Mower, Walter Shirley, William Warin, Nicholas Bell, and the clerk
2212 By his deed William Warin, of Salisbury, granted to Thomas Chaffin, called Cardmaker, of Warminster, a rent of a rose a year issuing from a tenement, which Isabel, the relict of Simon Tredinnick, holds for her life by William's grant, in Wheeler Row between shops, on a corner opposite the market, of late John Bonham's on the north side and a tenement of late that of John Franklin, wheeler, afterwards Richard Knolle's, on the south side; also the reversion of the tenement on Isabel's death. The rent and the reversion are to be held for ever by Thomas and his heirs and assigns. Seals: William's and the common and mayoral seals of the city. Named witnesses: the bailiff, the mayor, the coroners, the reeves, John Mower, Richard Spencer, Walter Shirley, William Bishop, Walter Nalder, and the clerk

11 July 1414, at Salisbury
2213 By his deed Adam, a son and heir of Simon Belch and his wife Christine, a daughter and heir of John Shalford, of late a citizen of Salisbury, quitclaimed to John Shad, draper, and his heirs and assigns his right or claim to a tenement, with shops, a cottage (*or* cottages), and gardens, which was of late John Shalford's, in Drake Hall Street [*as in* **2211**]. Clause of warranty. Seals: Adam's and the common and mayoral seals of the city. Named witnesses: the bailiff, the mayor, the coroners, the reeves, John Mower, Richard Spencer, William Dowding, John Becket, and the clerk

2214 By their deed William Warin and William Dowding, citizens of Salisbury, executors of Simon Tredinnick, called Draper, a citizen of Salisbury, quitclaimed to Thomas Chaffin, called Cardmaker, of Warminster, and his heirs and assigns their right or claim to a rent of a rose a year issuing from a tenement which Isabel, Simon's relict, holds for her life in Wheeler Row [*as in 2212*]; also to the reversion of the tenement when it fell due on Isabel's death. Thomas previously acquired the rent and the reversion, as witnessed by another deed shown to William and William [*2212*]. Seals: those of William Warin and William Dowding and the common and mayoral seals of the city. Named witnesses: the bailiff, the mayor, the coroners, the reeves, John Mower, Richard Spencer, Walter Shirley, Walter Nalder, John Becket, and the clerk

25 July 1414, at Salisbury
2215 By his deed William Lord, a citizen of Salisbury, quitclaimed to Thomas Chaffin, called Cardmaker, his right or claim to two tenements which were of late those of Nicholas Taylor, a citizen of Salisbury, one in Wheeler Row [*as in 2212*] and one in Pot Row. Seals: William's and the common and mayoral seals of the city. Named witnesses: the bailiff, the mayor, the coroners, the reeves, John Mower, Walter Shirley, William Dowding, John Becket, John Lewisham, and the clerk

8 August 1414, at Salisbury
2216 A deed of Thomas Bleacher, a kinsman, and an executor, of Robert Play, of late a citizen of Salisbury, who devised to Thomas two conjoined tenements in New Street between cottage property of late John Salisbury's, now that of Nicholas Brown, a clerk, on the west side and a tenement of late William Warmwell's, now John Sydenham's, on the east side. Thomas was esteemed an old man, had no living issue, and therefore wished, as he was obliged to, to carry out Robert's will, preferably in his own lifetime. William at the lea, fishmonger, of Salisbury, has paid to him as the executor a sum of money, the true value of the tenements, to have the tenements on his death and he, on the strength of the will and by his deed, granted the reversion of the tenements, and the tenements when they fell due on his death, to William, to be held for ever by him and his heirs and assigns. Seals: Thomas's and the common and mayoral seals of the city. Named witnesses: the bailiff, the mayor, the coroners, the reeves, John Mower, Richard Spencer, Walter Shirley, William Warin, Walter Nalder, and the clerk

22 August 1414, at Salisbury
2217 By his deed Thomas Bleacher, a kinsman, and an executor, of Robert Play, of late a citizen of Salisbury, quitclaimed to William at the lea, fishmonger, of Salisbury, and his heirs and assigns his right or claim to two conjoined tenements, which were of late Robert's and which Thomas held by Robert's devise, in New Street [*as in 2216*]. Clause of warranty. Seals: Thomas's and the common and mayoral seals of the city. Named witnesses: the bailiff, the mayor, the coroners, the reeves, John Mower, Richard Spencer, William Warin, Walter Nalder, John

Becket, and the clerk

2218 Approval [*dated to the Wednesday after the feast of St. Bartholomew the Apostle (29 August) probably in error for the Wednesday before that feast*] of the will of Maud Baron, the wife of Adam Marris, a citizen of Salisbury, made on 18 December 1413. Interment: in the graveyard of St. Edmund's church. Bequests: a large box to the fabric of that church, to serve in the church for vestments and other necessities while it would last; 6*d*. to the cathedral church; 6*d*. to John Jakes, her confessor; a red gown to Edith Jay; the rest of her goods to her husband Adam [and] to her son John Marris, a clerk, and her daughter Joan to be divided equally between them after the death of Adam. Devise: to Adam a tenement, which she held by a grant and devise of Maud Langford, in Scots Lane between a tenement of late Richard Ryborough's, now John Hain's, on the west side and a tenement of late William Bartlet's, now John Wishford's, on the east side. The tenement is to be held by Adam and his assigns for Adam's life, after Adam's death by John Marris and his assigns for John's life, and after John's death for ever by Joan and her issue. If Joan were to die without issue the tenement should be sold by the executors of Adam, John, and Joan. The money received from the sale should be laid out on behalf of her soul, the souls of Adam, John, and Joan, and the souls of others. It is to be understood that Maud's intention is that the greater part of the money should be for the fabric of St. Edmund's church. Executor: Adam. Witnesses: John Jakes and Richard North, chaplains, Simon Bradley, Robert Stonard, and others. Proved on 22 June 1413 in front of John Hulling, the subdean; the administration was entrusted to the executor. Approved at a court held in front of the bailiff, the mayor, and other citizens; the seisin of the tenement was released to the legatee.

3 October 1414, at Salisbury

2219 By her charter Clarice, the relict of John Preston, grocer, of Salisbury, granted to her son John Preston her land, tenements, rent, services, and reversions in Salisbury [*margin*: concerning a tenement in Carter Street] to be held for ever by him and his heirs and assigns. Clause of warranty. Seals: Clarice's and the common and mayoral seals of the city. Named witnesses: the bailiff, the mayor, William Walter, Walter Shirley, William Warin, Walter Nalder, and Thomas Stabber

2220 Approval of the will of William Sall, a citizen of Salisbury, made on 25 April 1414. Interment: in St. Edmund's church, beside the tomb of Joan, of late his wife. Bequests 20*s*. to the fabric of that church, 6*s*. 8*d*. to the high altar for his forgotten tithes and lesser benefactions, 6*d*. to each collegiate chaplain being present at his funeral rites and sepulchral mass, 4*d*. to each other chaplain being present likewise; 3*s*. 4*d*. to the fabric of the cathedral church; 3*s*. to the fabric of St. Thomas's church; 40*d*. to the fabric of St. Martin's church; 6*s*. 8*d*. both to the Dominicans of Fisherton and the Franciscans of Salisbury to be present at his funeral rites and mass and to pray for his soul; 2*s*. to the ailing and to the hospital of the Holy Trinity called Almshouse. After his burial all his movable goods should be valued by his trustworthy neighbours and whatever pertains to him should remain to his wife Emme and should be released to her, security having previously been received from her by his executors for the return of it to them or their executors after her death. It should then be disposed of on behalf of his soul, Emme's soul, and the souls mentioned below. For the rest of her life Emme should hold William's obit in St. Edmund's church, and she should pay his debts. <u>Devise</u>: to Emme for life his land, tenements, shops, cottages, gardens, rent, and reversions in Salisbury. On Emme's death that property should remain to Richard Coof and Walter Short, [two of] his executors, to be sold, or Richard and Walter may sell the reversion of it in Emme's lifetime as soon as that could be done advantageously. From the money received from the sale two chaplains should be appointed. One should celebrate mass in St. Edmund's church for a year on behalf of William's soul, the souls of Ralph Erghum, John Waltham, and Richard Mitford, of late bishops of Salisbury, the soul of [Nicholas Bubwith], the present bishop of Salisbury, the souls of William's wives Emme and Joan, the souls of Richard Baker, John Barrett, and John Gatcombe, and other souls. The other chaplain should celebrate mass in the church of Ripon, where William was born, for a year on behalf of William's soul and the souls of others. Also from the money received from the sale £20 should be handed out among his poor kinsmen of that district, to each one according to the needs of his condition at the discretion of the executors. If the executors were not troubled by the mayor for the time being, his fellow citizens, or the commonalty concerning the receipts or business of his late period of office as mayor, or of his period in any other office, security being held in that matter, the executors should order £20 from the sale, to be raised as soon as possible, to be offered to the mayor and commonalty to give help to them in common for praying for his soul. If any money were to remain from the sale it should be laid out by the executors, on holding the obit yearly in St. Edmund's church, at all events on celebrating masses, giving alms, repairing ways and bridges, and doing other charitable deeds, on behalf of William's soul, the souls of Joan and Emme, the souls of Richard Baker, John Barrett, and John Gatcombe, and the souls of others. If Richard Coof and Walter Short were to die before the sale of all the property had been perfected what then remained to be sold should be sold by the executors of William's executors with the oversight of the mayor and of four upright men of his fellow citizens chosen by him. The money received should be laid out according to their conscience and discretion and spent in the manner described above. <u>Executors</u>: his wife Emme, Richard Coof, and Walter Short. <u>Proved</u> on 12 June 1414 in front of John Hulling, the subdean; the administration was entrusted to the executors. <u>Approved</u> at a court held in front of the bailiff, the mayor, and other citizens; the seisin of the property was released to the legatees.

17 October 1414, at Salisbury
2221 Approval of the will of Margaret Godmanstone, the relict of William Godmanstone, formerly a citizen of Salisbury, made on 23 July 1414. <u>Interment</u>: in St. Thomas's church, beside the grave of her father and mother. <u>Bequests</u>: a round leaden vessel for making malt to that church, 13*s*. 4*d*. to the high altar for

her forgotten tithes and lesser benefactions, 6s. 8d. to the light of the Holy Trinity
and the Holy Cross, 2s. to the light of St. James, 2s. to the light of St. Michael,
6s. 8d. to James Green, the parochial chaplain, to pray for her soul, 10s. to the
lord Nicholas Gifford, 12d. to each other chaplain to celebrate mass on behalf of
her soul on the day of her burial, 12d. to the deacon, and 6d. to the sacristan; 6s.
8d. to the fabric of the cathedral church; 20s. to the Franciscans of Salisbury, to
be divided among them by her executors, so that they might intercede on behalf
of her soul and the souls of others; 20s. to the Dominicans of Fisherton likewise;
3s. 4d. to the paupers of the hospital of the Holy Trinity, called Almshouse, to be
divided among them in the same way; 6s. 8d. to the paupers of St. Giles's hospital,
near Wilton, likewise; 2s. to the paupers of the hospital of St. Mary Magdalene[,
Wilton]; 4d. to each ailing person lying bedridded in Salisbury; 6s. 8d. each to
the fabric of St. Edmund's church and the fabric of St. Martin's church; 3s. 4d.
to the fabric of St. Clement's church, Fisherton; 40s. to the convent of the house
of friars, Easton, to pray for her soul; 10 marks to be handed out among paupers
on the day of her burial; eight paupers, female and widows, should be dressed
in white clothes on the day of her burial to pray for her soul; five candles, each
weighing 3 lb., should be made for her funeral rites and mass and for her burial;
a book called *Potiphar* to Richard Horn, her godson; 40s. to William Bowyer;
3s. 4d. each to Margaret, a daughter of William River, her goddaughter, and
Robert, a son of Richard at the mill, her godson; 12d. to each of her other
godchildren to whom she has left nothing otherwise; a rosary of amber beads,
with a crucifix attached, to Alice Horn; a gown, with a hood, to Agnes Sherfield;
a belt, in a hanging of which [there is] an image of St. Margaret, to Agnes, the
wife of Henry Linden, called Scarlet, of Southampton; a hood of scarlet, lined
with brown, to Maud Till; 12d. to Maud Steward; 3s. 4d. to William, her servant;
6s. 8d. to Henry Blackmoor; 50s., a piece of silver with a flower in the middle,
a deep mazer, and a basin with a laver to William Bailiff, called Weston, a green
belt furnished with silver to his wife Christine, 6s. 8d. to his son William, and 6s.
8d. to his daughter Alice; 20s., a piece of silver with a flower in the middle, and a
mazer, of which the foot is broken, to William at the lea, and a rosary of amber
beads, with a clasp attached, to his wife Christine; a coverlet, two blankets, two
linen cloths, a tablecloth with a towel, a brass pot with a pan, a best box, a mazer,
and a piece of silver at the discretion of Margaret's executors to Edith, her servant,
and a small mazer [and] a tablecloth with a towel, of a simple grade, to Edith's
daughter Alice; the rest of her goods to her executors to be disposed of on behalf
of her soul and the souls mentioned below. Devises: to William Bailiff, called
Weston, a cottage, with a garden, in Gigant Street, between Thomas Chaplin's
tenement on the north side and Margaret's own cottage, which John Horn holds,
on the south side, to be held for ever by him and his heirs and assigns. Margaret
devised to Edith, her servant, and Edith's daughter Alice a cottage, with a portion
of garden to be assigned to them by her executors, in Brown Street, between
Margaret's own cottage, which John Mason holds, on the north side and William
Hoare's yard on the south side, to be held by them for their life and the life of the
one of them living longer. After the death of Edith and Alice the cottage, with

the portion of garden, should be sold by Margaret's executors, their executors, or subsequent executors, and the reversion might be sold in the lifetime of Edith and Alice, and of the one of them living longer, if it could be done advantageously. The money received from the sale should be laid out, on celebrating masses, giving alms, giving alms to paupers, repairing broken ways and bridges, visiting the feeble, the lame, and the sick, and doing other charitable deeds on behalf of Margaret's soul, the souls of her father and mother, the souls of William Buckland and William Godmanstone, her husbands, the souls of Adam Ludwell and his wife Cecily, the soul of Nicholas Chirstoke, and the souls of others. Margaret appointed all her other land and tenements, with the appurtenant cottages, racks, and gardens, in the city to be sold by her executors immediately after her death if that could be done advantageously. The money received from the sale should be laid out by her executors on pious uses, in the way mentioned above, for the salvation of her soul and the souls mentioned above. <u>Executors</u>: William Bailiff, called Weston, and William at the lea. Everything in the will should be put into effect with the assent of both of them; neither of them may do, or undertake to do, by himself, without the consent of the other, anything to the contrary. If either of them undertook to act on his own it would be utterly invalid and void. <u>Proved</u> on 15 October 1414 in front of an officer of the subdean; the administration was entrusted to the executors. <u>Approved</u> at a court held in front of the bailiff, the mayor, and other citizens; the seisin of the land, tenements, shops, cottages, and gardens was released to the legatees.

31 October 1414, at Salisbury
2222 By their indented charter Laurence Groom and John Mitchell, chaplains, executors of William Buck, a chaplain and a vicar of the cathedral church, on the strength of William's will granted to John Shad, draper, and his wife Agnes seven conjoined cottages, with a garden (*or* gardens), in Gigant Street and Nuggeston between a tenement of late William Sall's on the south side and a tenement of late Richard Knolle's on the east side. The cottages, with the garden(s), are to be held for ever by John and Agnes and John's heirs on condition that, if John and Agnes or their heirs, executors, or assigns were to pay to Laurence and John, or their executors or assigns, 40s. a year for each of the 10 years from the date of the charter, the grant would have its full force and effect. Clause to permit permanent repossession if the cottages were not repaired adequately during the 10 years or if a payment were defaulted on for a quarter of a year. Seals: those of the parties to the parts of the charter in turn and the common and mayoral seals of the city. Named witnesses: the bailiff, the mayor, the coroners, the reeves, John Mower, Walter Shirley, William Walter, Walter Nalder, and the clerk
2223 A deed of Walter Warwick, a chaplain, an executor of John Turk, a canon of the cathedral church, an executor of John Ball, of late a citizen of Salisbury. John Ball devised to his wife Agnes for life [Ball's Place], a [corner] tenement, in which John dwelt, with shops, a cottage (*or* cottages), a gate (*or* gates), a yard (*or* yards), a garden, and a dovecot, in Wineman Street and Brown Street between shops of late those of John Webb, of Woodlands, which William Buckland then held, on

the north side and a tenement which Henry Louden, weaver, then held on the east side. On Agnes's death the tenement, with its appurtenances, was to remain for ever to John Ball's sons Nicholas and Thomas and their issue, and if Nicholas and Thomas were to die without issue it should be sold by John's executors, their executors, or subsequent executors. The money received should be laid out on behalf of John's soul and the souls of others. Because Agnes has died, Nicholas and Thomas have died without living issue, and all John Ball's executors have died the sale of the tenement, with its appurtenances, pertains to Walter, as an executor of an executor of John, to be made on the strength of the will. By his deed Walter granted to Walter Shirley and John Lewisham, citizens of Salisbury, and Richard Christchurch, a merchant, the tenement, with its appurtenances, to be held for ever by them and their heirs and assigns as that which Walter, John, and Richard bought from him in good faith for a sum of money to be laid out according to the terms of John Ball's will. Seals: Walter Warwick's and the common and mayoral seals of the city. Named witnesses: the bailiff, the mayor, a coroner, the reeves, John Mower, William Warin, William Walter, William Bishop, Nicholas Bell, and the clerk

2224 By his charter Robert Deverill, a citizen of Salisbury, granted to William Phebis, a citizen of Salisbury, three shops, with a sollar (*or* sollars), which, by the name of a tenement, he held, with other tenements in the city, by a grant of Thomas Bowyer, of late a citizen of Salisbury, and which were formerly those of John Fish, of Salisbury. The shops stand conjoined in the street on the way to the upper bridge of Fisherton, near the church of the Dominicans there, between a shop next to a tenement called Scalding House on the east side and a shop of John Butt, a cordwainer, on the west side, and are to be held for ever by William and his heirs and assigns. Clause of warranty. Seals: Robert's and the common and mayoral seals of the city. Named witnesses: the bailiff, the mayor, the coroners, the reeves, John Mower, William Walter, William Dowding, John Becket, William Bishop, Thomas Mason, and the clerk

2225 Approval of the will of Richard Spencer, a citizen of Salisbury, made on 4 October 1414. <u>Interment</u>: in St. Edmund's church, in the place where the church bells are rung. <u>Bequests</u>: 13s. 4d. each to the fabric of the cathedral church and the fabric of St. Martin's church; 40s. to the fabric of St. Edmund's church, 12d. to each collegiate chaplain and 6d. to each annual chaplain to pray for his soul and the souls of others, and 40s. and the lights burning around his corpse on the day of his burial to the provost for his forgotten tithes and lesser benefactions; 6s. 8d. to the fabric of St. Thomas's church; 13s. 4d. to the Franciscans of Salisbury, 6d. to each friar of the convent to pray for his soul and the souls of others, and all his marble stones, being in their keeping, to the friars to pray for his soul and the souls of others; 13s. 4d. to the Dominicans of Fisherton to pray for his soul and the souls of others, and 6d. to each friar of the convent being present at his funeral rights and mass on the day of his burial to pray for his soul and the souls of others; 4d. to each ailing bedridden person in the city to pray for his soul and the souls of others; 6s. 8d. to the fabric of the hospital of the Holy Trinity called Almshouse, and 2d. to each needy person lying bedridden in it to pray for his soul and the souls of others; 13 paupers should be clothed in black cloth on the day of his burial; 40s. and a pair of vestments to the fabric of Kington St. Michael church, 6s. 8d. to the vicar to pray for his soul and the souls of others, 40d. to the vicar to commend his soul and the souls of others for a year in that church in front of the parishioners on every Sunday and on solemn festivals, and 9 marks, to be received from Richard's executors, to a chaplain, chosen by the executors and the parishioners of that church, to celebrate mass there for the year following Richard's death on behalf of Richard's soul and the souls of others; 40s. to the convent of nuns at Kington, to be divided equally among them, to pray for Richard's soul and the souls of others; 12d. to each of his godchildren to pray for his soul; £10 should be handed out by his executors to the needy, the lame, and the feeble on the day of his burial; £20 for his funeral expenses on the day of his burial; as many wax candles should be burned around his corpse as might cost at most 5 marks; John Harries should pay to his executors £20 of the £40 which he owes to him, and the other £20 Richard bequeaths to John's offspring; 20s. each to Henry Blackmoor, Agnes Crase, Alice Popes; 20s. and a bowl with a cover to his brother John, to whom he remits £8 which he owes to him; Richard remits to William Penton, dyer, 10 marks of the debt which he owes to him; 10 marks to John Marshall likewise; he remits 100s. of the debt which William Deller, dyer, owes to him; 40s. to John Porquin likewise; he remits 100s. of the debt which John Corscombe owes to him; 6s. 8d. to Richard, his chaplain; 40d. each to Alice, his servant, and Robert, his apprentice; 20d. to Agnes, his servant; 100s. to John Hampton, his servant, on condition that in good faith John informed Richard's executors about the debts which Richard owes and about all the debtors who owe any sums of money to him, and that he offered help to the executors to levy Richard's debts and to do other things about the necessary matters mentioned above; 100s. each to William Algar, a chaplain, and William Lord; the rest of his goods to his wife Edith. <u>Devises</u>: to Edith for life as dower a chief tenement, in which he dwelt, in Winchester Street between Nicholas Harding's tenement on the west side and Robert Ashley's tenement on the east side; also to Edith for life his share of the land and tenements which were of late those of John Thorburn, otherwise called John Taylor, in Winchester Street on a corner [of Brown Street: cf. *2316, 2376*]; Richard Oword and William Lord, the feoffees, should make an estate to Edith for life in a messuage, with a shop (*or* shops), a rack (*or* racks), a cottage (*or* cottages), and a garden, in which Richard Mill dwells, in Carter Street; also to Edith for life two tenements in Gigant Street, on the way to St. Edmund's church, between Richard Weston's tenement on the south side and Margaret Godmanstone's cottage property on the north side; also to Edith for life a yard, with a rack (*or* racks), of late Robert Goyland's, in Gigant Street; also to Edith two tenements in Rolleston and Brown Street of which John Shute holds one and John Brewer holds the other. Richard also devised to Edith rent of £7 3s. 4d. a year: *viz.* 4 marks issuing from John Deansbury's tenement in Southampton, 40s. from a corner tenement of late John Little's in Endless Street, 30s. from a corner tenement, with a shop (*or* shops) and cottages, of John Wootton in Culver Street, and 20s. from Robert Bowyer's tenement in Wineman Street. All the land,

tenements, and rent devised to Edith are to be held by her for life for finding a
chaplain to celebrate mass in St. Edmund's church for the 20 years following
Richard's death on behalf of his soul the souls of others. On Edith's death all,
except the tenements which John Shute and John Brewer hold, should remain to
Richard's executors, their executors, or subsequent executors to be sold. The
money received from the sale should be laid out, on celebrating masses, repairing
ways, giving alms to paupers, and doing other charitable deeds, on behalf of
Richard's soul, Edith's soul, and the souls of others. On Edith's death the two
excepted tenements should remain for life to Richard's brother John, and after
John's death they should be sold by Richard's executors, their executors, or
subsequent executors. The money received from the sale should be laid out by
the executors on behalf of Richard's soul and the souls of others. Richard
appointed the land and tenements, with a shop (*or* shops), a cottage (*or* cottages),
and a garden (*or* gardens), called Staple Hall and the Dragon, in St. Martin's
Street, in which Edith holds an estate for life with reversion to Richard and his
heirs, to be sold by Richard's executors immediately after Edith's death. The
money received from the sale should be laid out in the way which seemed to the
executors healthiest for Richard's soul and the souls of others. Richard appointed
a tenement, with a corner shop attached to it, in Brown Street and Wineman
Street, in which Edith holds an estate for life with reversion to him and his heirs,
to be sold by his executors, their executors, or subsequent executors immediately
after Edith's death. The money received from the sale should be laid out, on
celebrating masses, repairing ways, giving alms, and doing other charitable deeds,
on behalf of Richard's soul, the souls of his wives, and the souls of others.
<u>Executors</u>: Edith, William Algar, and William Lord; overseers, John Mower and
John Harries, esq. <u>Proof</u>: on 6 October 1414 John Perch, a clerk, a registrar of the
court of Canterbury and a commissary of the archbishop of Canterbury, ordered
an inquiry into the validity of the will and into whether what was bequeathed
and devised by means of it lay in more than one diocese in the province of
Canterbury. Those deputed to inquire were Robert Brown, a canon of Salisbury,
Simon Sydenham, LL.D., the archdeacon of Salisbury, Nicholas Lord, an advocate,
and Richard Willesden, a public notary. In the church of St. Mary of the arches,
London, they were to pronounce on the validity and contents of the will on the
first lawful day of business after 19 October and were to produce an inventory
there in front of John Perch on 19 November. On 11 October, on the strength of
a commission perfected for him, the will was exhibited and proved in front of
Robert Brown in St. Anne's chapel above the east gate of the canons' close,
[Salisbury]. The administration of whatever was in the will, wherever it lay in the
province of Canterbury, was entrusted to Richard's relict Edith and William
Algar, reserving the power to entrust it to William Lord when he might come to
be admitted. The seal of the office of the dean of Salisbury and, at Robert's
request the seals of the officers, were affixed to the will. <u>Approved</u> at a court held
in front of the bailiff, the mayor, and other citizens; the seisin of the land,
tenements, shops, cottage(s), yard(s), rent, and gardens was released to Edith, the
legatee.

14 November 1414, at Salisbury

2226 By their deed Robert Newton, a clerk, and Walter Shirley, William Warin, and Walter Nalder, citizens of Salisbury, quitclaimed to William Phebis, a citizen of Salisbury, their right or claim, by reason of a grant of Robert Deverill or of any other right or title, to three conjoined shops, with a sollar (*or* sollars), in the street on the way to the upper bridge of Fisherton [*as in* **2224**]. Seals: those of the four who quitclaimed and the common and mayoral seals of the city. Named witnesses: the bailiff, the mayor, the coroners, the reeves, John Mower, William Walter, William Bishop, William Dowding, and the clerk

12 December 1414, at Salisbury

2227 Approval of the will of John Needler, a citizen of Salisbury, made on 21 June 1413. <u>Interment</u>: in St. John's chapel in St. Edmund's church. <u>Bequests</u>: 13s. 4d. to the fabric of the cathedral church; 13s. 4d. to the fabric of St. Edmund's church, 12d. to each collegiate chaplain present at his funeral rites and mass on the day of his burial, 6d. to each annual chaplain, 12d. to the deacon, and 6d. to the sacristan; 6s. 8d. to the fabric of St. Thomas's church; 3s. 4d. to the fabric of St. Martin's church; 20s. both to the Franciscans of Salisbury and the Dominicans of Fisherton present at his funeral rites and mass on the day of his burial; £20, a second-best belt, furnished with silver, with a dagger, a best standing silver piece with a cover, 12 silver spoons, a standing mazer with a cover, a coverlet, a tester of blue worsted, a pair of linen sheets, a lead vessel for making malt, a trestle table with a trestle (*or* trestles), and a large basin with a laver to his son Richard; 6d. to each of his godchildren; 1d. to each pauper coming to a distribution on the day of his burial; a silver bowl with a cover, and a brass pot containing 10 gallons, to his son William; a standing piece of silver with a cover and three lions, a round silver bowl with a cover, a plain piece of silver, all his *iudum* malt, all his wool, dyed and not dyed, all his woollen yarns, two furnaces and all the vessels for brewing, a scarlet cloak, and 100s. to his wife Alice; a belt furnished with silver and gilded to his daughter Amice; a brass pot and a basin with a laver to Alice Westbrook, his servant; a brass pot to Beatrice, his servant; a coverlet, a pair of linen sheets, and a brass pot to Robert, his servant; 40s. and a plain piece [?of silver] to John Cornish, fuller. John appointed the rest of his goods to be divided into three parts, one to his executors to be laid out on behalf of his soul and the souls of others, one to his wife Alice to pray for his soul, and one to his son Richard for the good and praiseworthy service given, and henceforward to be given, to him. His son William and daughter Amice should seek or demand nothing for their share of his goods beyond that bequeathed to them and should by no means implead or disturb the executors; if they, or either of them, did they would forfeit their legacies, and what was bequeathed to them should be laid out by John's executors for the salvation of John's soul and the souls of others. <u>Devises</u>: to his wife Alice for life a tenement, with shops, in which he dwelt, in Wineman Street between a shop of late Edmund Enfield's, now Richard Spencer's, on the west side and a tenement of late John Forest's, now Nicholas Melbury's, on the east side. After

Alice's death the tenement, with the shops, should be held for ever by John's son Richard and his issue, and if Richard were to die without issue it should be sold by John's executors or their executors. The money received from the sale should be laid out, on celebrating masses, giving alms to paupers, repairing ways and broken bridges, and doing other charitable deeds, on behalf of John's soul, Alice's soul, and the souls of others. John devised to his daughter Amice, the wife of Nicholas Melbury, for life a shop in Castle Street between William Brawt's tenement on the north side and a tenement which Robert Baker bought from John on the south side. On Amice's death the shop should remain for ever to John's son Richard and his issue, and if Richard were to die without issue it should be sold by John's executors. The money received from the sale should be laid out by the executors on the salvation of the souls mentioned above. John appointed the tenements and cottages in Nuggeston in which Robert Lord, Thomas Hain, Richard Gore, William Turner, Robert Pannett, and John Furmage dwell, with the gardens and racks, to be sold by his executors. From the money issuing from the sale the executors should find a chaplain to celebrate mass, for the six years following John's death, in St. Edmund's church on behalf of John's soul, the soul of an elder John Needler, his uncle, and the souls of Edith and Emme, of late his wives; or at least the executors should find four chaplains to celebrate mass in that church, on behalf of those souls, for one year following John's death if that could be done more conveniently. If anything remained it should be laid out by the executors on the elder of the bedridden destitute and poor and on other charitable deeds. Executors: his son Richard and John Cornish, and John charges them not to annoy, disturb, or implead his wife Alice; overseer, William Needler, to whom John bequeathed a silver pear. Proved on 3 April 1414 in front of John Hulling, the subdean; the administration was entrusted to the executors. Approved at a court held in front of the bailiff, the mayor, and other citizens; the seisin of the tenements, shops, cottages, and gardens was released to the legatees.

26 December 1414, at Salisbury
2228 A deed of William Walter, John Lake, John Smith, a chaplain, and John Pilk, of Beckington, executors of Thomas Child, of late a citizen of Salisbury. Thomas devised to his wife Isabel the reversion of a tenement and shops when they fell due on the death of Margaret, the relict of William Godmanstone. The tenement and shops stand in Winchester Street, above the ditch, between Laurence Gowan's tenement on the west side and John Wishford's tenement, which William Sergeant holds, on the east side, and they are to be held for life by Isabel when they fell due. On Isabel's death the tenement, with the shops, should be sold by Thomas's executors, or the executors might sell the reversion in Isabel's lifetime if it could be done advantageously. The money received should be laid out on behalf of Thomas's soul and the souls of others. Margaret has died, Isabel in her celibate power has released her right or claim to the executors, and the fee of the tenement, with the shops, remains to the executors to be sold. By their deed, and on the strength of Thomas's will, the executors granted to John Bodenham, merchant, a citizen of Salisbury, the tenement, with the shops, to

be held for ever by him and his heirs and assigns as that which he bought from them in good faith for a sum of money to be laid out according to the terms of the will. Seals: those of the grantors and the common and mayoral seals of the city. Named witnesses: the bailiff, the mayor, the coroners, a reeve, John Mower, Walter Shirley, William Warin, Walter Nalder, William Dowding, and the clerk

2229 By his charter John, a son of John Camel, of late a citizen of Salisbury, granted to Walter Shirley, a merchant, a citizen of Salisbury, and his wife Joan two conjoined tenements in Brown Street, behind a tenement, in which Thomas Bleacher dwells, opposite a wide gate of that tenement, and which was formerly John Butterley's, between Roger Fadder's tenement on the south side and William Hoare's yard, with racks, on the north side. The tenements are to be held for ever by Walter and Joan and Walter's heirs and assigns. Clause of warranty. Seals: John's and the common and mayoral seals of the city. Named witnesses: the bailiff, the mayor, the coroners, the reeves, John Mower, William Warin, William Walter, Thomas Mason, draper, William Tull, and the clerk

2230 By his charter John Lake, a citizen of Salisbury, granted to John Wishford, a citizen of Salisbury, a tenement in New Street between a tenement of late Walter Orme's on the east side and a tenement of late that of John Baker, grocer, on the west side. The tenement was of late William Upton's, was acquired by John Lake from John Upton, a son and heir of William, and was afterwards the subject of a release of all his right or claim to it, with an obligation to warrant, by Thomas Upton, a clerk, to John Lake and his heirs and assigns. It is to be held for ever by John Wishford and his heirs and assigns. Clause of warranty. Seals: John Lake's and the common and mayoral seals of the city. Named witnesses: the bailiff, the mayor, the reeves, the coroners, John Mower, Walter Shirley, William Warin, Walter Nalder, William Dowding, and the clerk

2231 By their charter Nicholas Bell and Stephen Edington granted to William Phebis, weaver, three conjoined cottages, with a garden (*or* gardens), in Drake Hall Street between cottage property of late Thomas Southam's on the south side and cottage property of the vicars of the cathedral church on the north side; also four conjoined cottages, with a garden (*or* gardens), in the same street between cottage property of late Simon Belch's, now John Shad's, on the south side and Robert Play's cottage property, which John Ferrer, carter, of late held, on the north side. The seven cottages were of late held by Nicholas and Stephen, together with Thomas Child, deceased, by a grant of William Bishop and William Handley, a tailor, and, with the gardens, are to be held for ever by William and his heirs and assigns. Nicholas and Stephen release all their right or claim to the cottages, with the gardens, to William. Seals: those of Nicholas and Stephen and the common and mayoral seals of the city. Named witnesses: the bailiff, the mayor, the coroners, the reeves, John Mower, Walter Shirley, William Warin, Walter Nalder, William Dowding, and Henry Man

9 January 1415, at Salisbury
2232 By his charter Henry Man, a citizen of Salisbury, granted to Joan Warmwell, a daughter of the late William Warmwell, a citizen of Salisbury, a corner tenement,

which he acquired from John Whitmore, a clerk, in St. Martin's Street and Gigant Street between Joan's tenement and cottages on either side. The tenement is to be held for ever by Joan and her heirs and assigns. Clause of warranty. Seals: Henry's and the common and mayoral seals of the city. Named witnesses: the bailiff, the mayor, the coroners, the reeves, John Mower, Walter Shirley, William Warin, William Dowding, and the clerk

2233 A deed of Richard, a son, and an executor, of John Needler, of late a citizen of Salisbury, who appointed the conjoined tenements and cottages, with the gardens and racks, in Nuggeston, in which Robert Lord, Thomas Hain, Richard Gore, William Turner, Robert Pannett, and John Furmage dwell, between cottage property of late that of John Baker, grocer, on the west side and John Lake's tenement on the east side, to be sold by his executors. The money issuing from the sale should be spent on behalf of John's soul and the souls of others. Robert Warmwell and John Ruddock, citizens of Salisbury, have come to an agreement with Richard and have paid to him a sum of money, to the value of the tenements and cottages, for the tenements and cottages, with the gardens and racks, to be acquired by them. By his deed, and on the strength of John Needler's will, Richard granted the tenements and cottages, with the gardens and racks, to Robert and John to be held by them and their heirs and assigns as that which they bought from Richard for a sum of money to be spent according to the terms of the will. Seals: Richard's and the common and mayoral seals of the city. Named witnesses: the bailiff, the mayor, the coroners, the reeves, John Mower, Walter Shirley, William Warin, Walter Nalder, and the clerk

2234 By his charter [*dated to the Wednesday after the feast of St. Hilary (16 January) probably in error for the Wednesday before that feast (9 January)*] John Lake, a citizen of Salisbury, granted to Thomas Randolph and his wife Alice a rent of 40s. a year issuing from a messuage in Winchester Street, in which Richard Ryborough of late dwelt, between a tenement of late Nicholas Taylor's on the west [?*rectius* east] side and a tenement of late William Ferrer's on the west [?*east*] side. The rent was acquired by John from William Bishop, a citizen of Salisbury, and is to be held for ever by Thomas and Alice and their heirs and assigns. Seals: John's and the common and mayoral seals of the city. Named witnesses: the bailiff, the mayor, the coroners, the reeves, John Mower, Walter Shirley, William Bishop, William Dowding, and the clerk

23 January 1415, at Salisbury

2235 Approval of the will of Alice Heath made, in her chaste widowhood, on 14 September 1414. <u>Interment</u>: in St. Thomas's church, near the tomb of John Heath, of late her husband. <u>Bequests</u>: 13s. 4d. to the fabric of that church, 20s. to the rector for her forgotten tithes and lesser benefactions, 12d. to each chaplain, and 12d. each to the fraternity of the light of St. James, the fraternity of the light of St. Michael, the fraternity of the light of the high cross, and the fraternity of the light of St. Christopher; 6s. 8d. to the fabric of the church of Christchurch and 12d. to the fabric of the bridge; 20s. to the fabric of Homington church and 3s. 4d. to the parochial chaplain; 6s. 8d. to the fabric of the cathedral church and

6s. 8d. to the fraternity of the light of the high cross; 6s. 8d. to the fraternity of the light of the Holy Ghost in St. Martin's church; 12d. to each Franciscan friar of Salisbury, and to each Dominican friar of Fisherton, to pray for her soul; 6s. 8d., a silk kerchief, a red cape, and a red coverlet to Alice Weller, and 3s. 4d. to her son; 3s. 4d. to John, a son of Thomas Ward; a green bed, two blankets, two linen sheets, a mazer, a piece of silver, six silver spoons, a box, two kerchiefs, a best brass pot, a best pan, a basin with a laver, and £4 cash for her marriage to Alice Warrock; a piece of gilt from Spain, six silver spoons, a standing piece of silver with a cover, a bed of worsted, a tablecloth, with a towel, of diaperwork, a harnessed belt, a silver pyx, a silver cellar, a pair of linen sheets of 18 ells, and a bowl with a laver to Alice, a daughter of William Warin; 6s. 8d. to Richard Homington, and a red gown of a yellow colour (de luto) to his wife Joan; 10 marks for holding her obit and to be handed out among paupers; 3s. 4d. to each of her godchildren; 6s. 8d. to Henry Blackmoor; 6s. 8d. to the fabric of St. Cuthburga's church, Wimborne; half of her sheep, being in the keeping of John Porter, to the fabric of Homington church, for the maintenance of that church, and to find two candles at the high altar for celebrating mass and a torch at the tomb-shrine of Christ at Eastertide every year for ever, for the salvation of her soul, the soul of John, of late her husband, and the souls of others; a lead vessel, lying above the spinning-house ('Spyndynghous'), to the fabric of Homington church; a lead vessel for making malt to her executors to be sold, and Placid Day should be preferred to others in the purchase if he would give as much as any other; the other half of her sheep to John Porter to pray for her soul; a coverlet to John Weller; a coverlet to an elder John Porter; a tablecloth, with a towel, of diaperwork to a younger John Porter if he were to live, but otherwise to be disposed of by her executors on pious uses, and two boxes for making a stall (or stalls); 40s., of the debt which Placid Day owes to her, to William Warin; 40s. likewise to John Smith, a chaplain; her executors should levy the whole debt which Placid Day owes to her as quickly as possible and lay it out for the salvation of her soul and of the souls mentioned above; 3s. 4d. to the chaplain who read to her the sacraments of the holy church at her death and the indulgence granted to her by the pope; the rest of her goods to her executors to be disposed of for the salvation of her soul. Devise: to Alice Warrock, her servant, two conjoined shops in Carter Street, between a tenement, in which Nicholas Bell dwells on the, south side and a shop, which Placid Day holds, on the north side, to be held for ever by her and her issue. If Alice were to die without issue the shops should be sold by Alice Heath's executors, their executors, or subsequent executors. The money received from the sale should be laid out by the executors, on celebrating masses, giving alms to the poor, repairing ways and bridges, visiting the lame, the feeble, and the bedridden, and doing other charitable deeds, on behalf of Alice Heath's soul, the soul of John, of late her husband, and the souls of others. Executors: William Warin and John Smith, a chaplain. Proved on 18 October 1414 in front of John Hulling, the subdean; the administration was entrusted to the executors; the seal of the office of the subdean was affixed to the will on 20 October 1414. Approved: at a court held in front of the bailiff, the mayor, and other citizens; the seisin of the shops was released to Alice, the legatee.

2236 Approval of the will of John Castleton, a citizen of Salisbury, made on 10 September 1414. <u>Interment</u>: in St. John's chapel in St. Edmund's church, between Thomas Child's grave on the south side and the grave of John Needler, newly constructed, on the north side. <u>Bequests</u>: 3s. 4d. to the fabric of the cathedral church; 3s. 4d. both to the Franciscans of Salisbury and the Dominicans of Fisherton if they were to be present at his funeral rites and mass on the day of his burial; 10s. to the fabric of St. Thomas's church, 6s. 8d. to the rector for his forgotten tithes and lesser benefactions, 4d. to the deacon, and 2d. to the sacrist; 20d. to the fabric of St. Martin's church; 20s. to the fabric of St. Edmund's church; five sheep being in his keeping to Nicholas Gilbert; two *crees* of linen cloth to each of his servants serving him on the day on which his will was perfected, and beyond that 6s. 8d. to Marion, his servant, and to Edith Hancock cloth worth 6s. 8d. for a coat to be made for her at the discretion of his executors; 20s. to be handed out in halfpenny loaves to paupers on the day of his burial; 12 lb. wax from which five candles should be made and burned around his corpse in St. Thomas's church on the day of his burial; another 12 lb. wax to be burned around his corpse in St. Edmund's church on the day of his burial; 6d. to each chaplain of St. Thomas's church being present at his funeral rites in his house and in St. Thomas's church on the day of his burial and at his burial in St. Edmund's church, otherwise each should receive nothing; John remitted 6s. 8d. which the lord Nicholas Gifford owed to him in order that Nicholas should celebrate mass on behalf of his soul; 8d. to each collegiate chaplain in St. Edmund's church who comes to St. Thomas's church to carry his corpse to be buried in St. Edmund's church, 8d. to the deacon, 6d. to the sacrist, and 6d. to each annual chaplain; a sword to Henry Blackmoor; a gown to Simon Little, and he remits all the debt which Simon owes to him; 20s. and a brass pot, with a pan, to his kinsman John Brown, and a pot with a pan to that John's sister Agnes; 6s. 8d. to John Sexhampcote to pray for his soul; a harnessed belt, equipped with a pair of silver knives, to Walter Ward, a chaplain; a red book concerning the portrayal of the Old Testament and of the New; the rest of his goods to his wife Isabel to pray for his soul. <u>Devises</u>: to Isabel for life the tenement in which he dwelt, with a shop (*or* shops), cellars, and a garden, in Carter Street between William Tull's tenement on the south side and John Sampson's tenement on the north side. After Isabel's death the tenement, with the shop(s), cellars, and garden, should be sold by John's executors, their executors, or subsequent executors. The money received from the sale should be laid out, on celebrating masses, giving alms, repairing ways and broken bridges, and visiting paupers, the bedridden, the feeble, the lame, and the elderly in need, for the salvation of the souls of Thomas Castleton and his wife Maud, the souls of John and his wife Isabel, and the souls of others. John devised to Isabel a rent of 4s. a year, issuing from Robert Bowyer's cottages in Culver Street, to be held for ever by her and her heirs and assigns. He devised to John, a son of a younger Thomas Castleton, for life cottages in New Street, beyond Barnwell's cross, beside the city's ditch, and on the north side of the street, and after John's death to his own executors to be sold. The money received from the sale should be laid out, on pious uses and other charitable deeds, on behalf of the soul of John, the testator, and of other souls. John's executors should enfeoff Thomas Castleton, his father, in a [corner] tenement in St. Martin's Street between a tenement of late William Sall's on the south side and William Walter's tenement on the east side. They should also make an estate for Thomas in conjoined cottages in Shit Lane between William Walter's tenement on the north side and a corner tenement of late Alice Whitmore's on the south side. The cottages are to be held for ever by Thomas and his heirs and assigns on condition that he would pay to the executors £14 as quickly as possible, but if Thomas would not pay the £14 the executors should sell the cottages and John's estate in them to the highest bidder. The money received from the sale should be laid out on behalf of John's soul and the souls of others. Executors: his wife Isabel and John Lake. Proved on 27 November 1414 in front of an officer of the subdean; the administration was entrusted to Isabel, reserving the power to entrust it to John Lake when he might come to be admitted. Approved at a court held in front of the bailiff, the mayor, and other citizens; the seisin of the tenements was released to Isabel.

2237 Approval of the will of John Ettshall, a cordwainer, a citizen of Salisbury, made on 31 December 1413. Interment: in St. Thomas's church, beside the tomb of his daughter if that could be done; if not, in the church of the Dominicans of Fisherton beside the tomb of Maud, formerly his wife. Bequests: 6s. 8d. to the fabric of St. Thomas's church if he were to be buried there, 6s. 8d. to the high altar for his forgotten tithes if there were any, and 2d. to each chaplain present at his funeral rites; 3s. 4d. to the fabric of the cathedral church; 3s. 4d. both to the Franciscans of Salisbury and the Dominicans of Fisherton; 12d. to the hospital of the Holy Trinity, called Almshouse, of the renowned city; 12d. to the prisoners of the castle of Old Sarum if there were any; 1d. to each chaplain of the cathedral church, vicars and others, celebrating mass and in the close of that church, in St. Thomas's church, in St. Edmund's church, and in St. Martin's church, to each chaplain in de Vaux college and the hospitals of St. Nicholas and Holy Trinity, and to each chaplain of the Dominican friary at Fisherton and the Franciscan friary of Salisbury, to celebrate mass on behalf of his soul as soon after his death as it could be done conveniently; 20s. cash to Edith, his wife's sister; 30s. to be handed out, 3d. in bread to paupers coming to his gate and 2d. to the bedridden, on Fridays while the 30s. lasted; 20s. to John Looker; 20s. to John Hathaway if he would administer John's goods; 6s. 8d. to John Suffolk by the name of a stipend for the time he remained in service with him; 3s. 4d. to Agnes, his servant; 2s. to Joan Lacock, his servant; 6s. 8d. to the servants of his craft, who are called 'le remetireys', being on bonds on the day of his burial, to be enjoyed among themselves in his house when they wished after his burial; 6d. to each of his godchildren; the rest of his goods to his wife Agnes. Devises: to Agnes for life as dower a tenement, with a garden next to it, in which he dwelt and which he held by a feoffment of Margaret FitzRalph, in New Street between two shops of his own, with a cellar (or cellars), on the east side and a tenement which Walter Short and his wife Margaret hold for their life on the west side. Immediately after

Agnes's death the tenement, with the garden, should be sold by John's executors or their executors. The money raised from the sale should be laid out, on masses, alms, and other charitable deeds, on behalf of John's soul, the souls of Maud and Agnes, his wives, the soul of John Chandler, the souls of others. If Alice, with the assent of John's executors, without fraud or deceipt, wished to sell her estate in the tenement, with the garden, John appointed to Agnes half of the money received from the sale for her share and half to his executors to lay out on behalf of the souls mentioned above. John appointed the two shops, with the cellar(s), which he held by a feoffment of Bartholomew Goldsmith [otherwise Bartholomew Durkin, goldsmith: cf. *1057, 1297*], in New Street, between John's own tenement, in which he lived, on the west side and a tenement of the vicars of the cathedral church on the east side, to remain in Agnes's hand for holding yearly an obit for John, his former wife Maud, and John Chandler; also for praying for John Ettshall's soul, Maud's soul, and the soul of an elder John Chandler by name on the Sunday of every week in St. Thomas's church. After Agnes's death the two shops, with the cellar(s), should remain in the hands of John's executors for doing likewise. The shops, with the cellar(s), are to be held by Agnes for her life and by the executors for their life, and after their death should be sold by the executors of John's executors. The money received from the sale should be laid out, on masses and other charitable deeds, on behalf of John's soul, the souls of Maud and Agnes, his wives, and the souls of others. If, with the consent of Agnes and John's executors, the tenement, with the garden, were to be sold the two shops, with the cellar(s), should be sold with it. Agnes should have half the money received from the sale, and the other half should remain in the executors' hands for holding the obit for John and all those mentioned above yearly and doing other charitable deeds while the money lasted. If Agnes were to marry another man she should have the tenement, with the garden, and the two shops, with the cellar(s), if she would buy them as might anyone else. Executors: his wife Agnes and John Hathaway; overseer, John Looker. Witnesses: Walter Ward, a chaplain, and others. Proved on 8 March 1414 in front of John Hulling, the subdean; the administration was entrusted to the executors. Approved at a court held in front of the bailiff, the mayor, and other citizens; the seisin of the tenement, with the garden, and of the two shops, with the cellar(s), was released to Agnes, the legatee, then present in court.

2238 Approval of the will of Pauline, the wife of John Butler, mercer, made on 3 February 1414. Interment: in the graveyard of St. Edmund's church, in front of the west gate. Bequests: 3s. 4d. to the fabric of that church; the rest of her goods to her husband to pray for her soul. Devises: to her husband John a tenement in Wineman Street, in which she dwells, between William Chapman's tenement on the east side and a tenement of late William Warmwell's, now Joan River's, on the west side, to be held for ever by him and his heirs and assigns. Pauline appointed a cottage in Scots Lane, between Robert Linden's cottages on the west side and Robert Warmwell's tenement on the east side, to be sold by her executors. From the money issuing from the sale the expenses of her funeral, and of the burial of her corpse, should be met and her debts, and her husband's, should be paid.

Executors: her husband John and Hugh Richman, a chaplain, her son. Proved on 12 January 1415 in front of an officer of the subdean; the administration was entrusted to John, reserving the power to entrust it to Hugh when he might come to seek it. Approved at a court held in front of the bailiff, the mayor, and other citizens; the seisin of the tenement and the cottage was released to John Butler.

2239 By his deed [*dated to the Wednesday after the feast of the conversion of St. Paul (30 January) probably in error for the Wednesday before that feast (23 January)*] John Butler, mercer, of Salisbury, an executor of his late wife Pauline, on the strength of Pauline's will granted to Walter Shirley, a citizen of Salisbury, and his wife Joan a cottage in Scots Lane [*as in **2238***], which Pauline appointed to be sold by her executors. The cottage was held by Pauline by a devise of Robert Sexhampcote, of late her husband, who previously held it by a devise of Thomas Sexhampcote, of late a citizen of Salisbury, his brother, and it is to be held for ever by Walter and Joan and Walter's heirs and assigns as that which Walter bought from John in good faith for a sum of money to be laid out according to the terms of Pauline's will. Seals: John's and the common and mayoral seals of the city. Named witnesses: the bailiff, the mayor, the coroners, the reeves, John Mower, William Warin, Thomas Mason, Robert Warmwell, and the clerk

2240 By their writing John Shad, draper, and his wife Agnes, present in court, granted to William Phebis, a citizen of Salisbury, seven conjoined cottages, with a garden (*or* gardens), in Gigant Street and Nuggeston between a tenement of late William Sall's on the south side and a tenement of late Richard Knolle's on the east side. The cottages were acquired by John and Agnes from Laurence Groom and John Mitchell, chaplains, executors of William Buck, a chaplain, by means of an indented charter subject to a condition, and they are to be held for ever by William and his heirs and assigns. Seals: those of John and Agnes and the common and mayoral seals of the city. Named witnesses: the bailiff, the mayor, the coroners, the reeves, John Mower, Walter Shirley, William Warin, Walter Nalder, and the clerk

20 February 1415, at Salisbury

2241 By his indented charter William Warin, a citizen of Salisbury, granted to William Phebis, a citizen of Salisbury, a corner tenement, with a shop (*or* shops) and a cottage (*or* cottages) attached and next to it, in St. Martin's Street and Culver Street, between the cottage property of the provost of St. Edmund's church on the north side and cottage property now that of Thomas Hellier, a chaplain, on the west side, which, with rent and other cottages in the city, William Warin acquired from Walter Brown, of Oxford, an executor of his wife Margaret, the relict of Robert Play, formerly a citizen of Salisbury. The tenement, with the shop(s) and cottage(s), is to be held for ever by William Phebis and his heirs and assigns. Clause of warranty. The grant is made on condition that, if that William or another on his behalf were to pay to William Warin or his executors or assigns 20 marks at Salisbury on 25 December 1415, it would hold its full force. Clause to permit permanent repossession if William were to default on that

payment. Seals: those of the parties to the parts of the indented charter in turn
and the common and mayoral seals of the city. Named witnesses: the bailiff, the
mayor, the coroners, the reeves, John Mower, Walter Shirley, Walter Nalder, John
Becket, and the clerk

2242 By their deed William Bailiff, called Weston, and William at the lea,
executors of Margaret Godmanstone, the relict of William Godmanstone, a
citizen of Salisbury, on the strength of Margaret's will granted to John Sydenham,
a citizen of Salisbury, and his wife Cecily conjoined cottages, with a garden (*or*
gardens), in St. Martin's Street between John Becket's corner tenement, of late
that of John Baker, grocer, on the east side and a tenement of the scholars of de
Vaux college on the west side. The cottages, with the garden(s), with other land,
tenements, shops, cottages, racks, and gardens in the city, were appointed by
Margaret to be sold by her executors as soon after her death as it could be done
advantageously, and they are to be held for ever by John and Cecily and John's
heirs and assigns as that which John bought in good faith from the executors
for a sum of money to be laid out by them according to the terms of Margaret's
will. Seals: those of the grantors and the common and mayoral seals of the city.
Named witnesses: the bailiff, the mayor, the coroners, a reeve, John Mower,
Walter Shirley, William Warin, William Dowding, Walter Nalder, and the clerk

6 March 1415, at Salisbury

2243 By his charter [*dated to the Wednesday after the feast of St. Gregory (13 March)
probably in error for the Wednesday before that feast (6 March)*] Thomas Read, a
merchant, a citizen of Salisbury, granted to William Packing a corner tenement,
with shops and a cottage (*or* cottages) attached, in Endless Street and Chipper
Street between a cottage of late Sarah Pope's on the north side and a little trench
of running water beside William's tenement in Chipper Street on the east side.
The tenement, with the shops and cottage(s), was formerly Henry Pope's, was
held by Thomas by a devise of John Pope, a chaplain, and is to be held for ever
by William and his heirs and assigns. Clause of warranty. Seals: Thomas's and the
common and mayoral seals of the city. Named witnesses: the bailiff, the mayor,
the coroners, the reeves, John Mower, Walter Shirley, William Warin, William
Walter, Nicholas Harding, and the clerk

20 March 1415, at Salisbury

2244 By her deed Edith, the relict of Henry Pope, a citizen of Salisbury, in
her widowhood and full power quitclaimed to William Packing, a citizen of
Salisbury, and his heirs and assigns her right or claim, under the will of John Pope,
a chaplain, or otherwise, her right or claim to a corner tenement, with shops and
a cottage (*or* cottages) attached, and to any rent issuing from it, in Endless Street
and Chipper Street [*as in **2243***]. The tenement was of late Henry's. Seals: Edith's
and the common and mayoral seals of the city. Named witnesses: the bailiff, the
mayor, the coroners, the reeves, John Mower, William Warin, Walter Nalder,
Thomas Bleacher, and the clerk

15 May 1415, at Salisbury
2245 Approval of the will of John Dyer made on 23 February 1415. <u>Interment</u>: in the parish church of Longbridge Deverill. <u>Bequests</u>: 20 sheep to the fabric of that church, and 1 sheep to each light of the church; 40*d.* each to the fabric of the cathedral church and the fabric of St. Thomas's church; 100*s.*, if he would attend school, and a good bed, *viz.* a coverlet, two blankets, and a pair of linen sheets, to John Tisbury; 20 sheep to his daughter Alice; 12*d.* to each of his servants who were in his service at the time of his death if they were faithful, otherwise 6*d.*; 12*d.* to each of his godsons under the age of twelve; 32 marks for a respected priest to celebrate mass for the next four years on behalf of his soul and the souls of others, and for longer if that could be done conveniently by means of his executors, and on every day the priest should say the placebo and dirge with nine lessons in commendation in that [?Longbridge Deverill] church or graveyard; 40*s.* to Thomas [Wilcock], the vicar of Longbridge Deverill, for his work; the rest of his goods to his wife Ellen for her to dispose of on pious uses, *viz.* celebrating masses, handing out to paupers, and doing other charitable deeds, on behalf of his soul. <u>Devise</u>: to Ellen for life a tenement in Castle Street and all his tenements and rent in Longbridge Deverill. On Ellen's death the tenements should remain for ever to John's daughter Alice and her heirs and assigns. <u>Executors</u>: Thomas, the vicar of Longbridge Deverill, and Ellen. <u>Proved</u> at [Longbridge] Deverill on 9 April 1415 in front of an officer of the archdeacon of Salisbury; the administration was entrusted to the executors. <u>Approved</u> at a court held in front of the mayor, the bailiff, and other citizens; the seisin of the tenement in Salisbury was released to the legatee.
2246 By his charter John, a son of John Bodenham, of late a citizen of Salisbury, granted to John Wishford, a citizen of Salisbury, a corner tenement, called the Forge, with a shop on its north side and a sollar built above it, which he held by a devise of his father. The tenement stands in Minster Street and Winchester Street, opposite the 'Riole', between Thomas Marshall's shops, which William Hilary holds, on the north side and Thomas's shops, which were of late Adam Inways's, on the east side. It is to be held, with the shop and sollar, for ever by John Wishford and his heirs and assigns. Clause of warranty. Seals: John Bodenham's and the common and mayoral seals of the city. Named witnesses: the bailiff, the mayor, the coroners; a reeve, John Mower, Walter Shirley, William Warin, William Walter, William Bishop, John Becket, and the clerk

7 August 1415, at Salisbury
2247 By their writing Thomas Mason, draper, and John Parch quitclaimed to John 'Shorberd', carpenter, and his heirs and assigns their right or claim to conjoined cottages, with an empty ground and a portion of meadow, in Drake Hall Street between a garden (*or* gardens) or meadow formerly Walter Goss's, which Nicholas Melbury holds, on the north side and land formerly Robert of Ann's, now Roger Upton's, on the south side. The cottages, with the ground and meadow, were formerly those of William Guys and his wife Maud and were acquired by Thomas Mason John Parch, and John 'Shorberd' from James Green,

a chaplain. Seals: those of Thomas Mason and John Parch and the common and mayoral seals of the city. Named witnesses: the bailiff, the mayor, the coroners, the reeves, William Walter, Nicholas Harding, Richard Oword, Thomas Bower, and the clerk

4 September 1415, at Salisbury

2248 By his charter John 'Shorberd', carpenter, granted to John Bodenham, a merchant, a citizen of Salisbury, and his wife Joan conjoined cottages, with an empty ground and an area of meadow, in Drake Hall Street [*as in 2247*]. The cottages, with the ground and meadow, were acquired by John 'Shorberd' from James Green, a chaplain, who acquired them from Maud, the relict of William Guys, and are to be held for ever by John Bodenham and Joan and John's heirs and assigns. Clause of warranty. Seals: John 'Shorberd's' and the common and mayoral seals of the city. Named witnesses: the bailiff, the mayor, the coroners, a reeve, William Warin, William Dowding, Walter Nalder, John Becket, and the clerk

2249 By their deed John Dinton, a chaplain, and William Penton, executors of Nicholas, a son and heir of John Ball, of late a citizen of Salisbury, quitclaimed to Richard Christchurch, a merchant, a citizen of Salisbury, and his heirs and assigns their right or claim to [Ball's Place], a [corner] tenement of late John Ball's, of which Richard is possessed, with shops, a cottage (*or* cottages), a gate (*or* gates), a yard (*or* yards), gardens, and a dovecot, in Wineman Street and Brown Street between a tenement of late that of John Webb, of Woodlands, now Roger Fadder's, on the north side and a tenement of John Hain, loader, which Henry Louden, weaver, of late held, on the east side. Seals: those of John and William and the common and mayoral seals of the city. Named witnesses: the bailiff, the mayor, the coroners, the reeves, John Mower, William Warin, William Walter, Thomas Mason, Thomas Bower, and the clerk

2250 Approval of the will of John Purdy, a citizen of Salisbury, made on 1 August 1408. <u>Interment</u>: in the graveyard of St. Edmund's church. <u>Bequests</u>: 6*d.* to the fabric of the cathedral church; 3*s.* 4*d.* to the fabric of St. Edmund's church; 20*s.* to his daughter Amice, together with the 20*s.* which Agnes, his mother, bequeathed to her; 40*s.* to his daughter Edith likewise; 20*s.* should be laid out by his wife Cecily on behalf of the soul of his son John and the souls of others, for which sum the elder John is indebted to the younger John on account of a legacy of Agnes; the rest of his goods to Cecily to be disposed of on behalf of his soul and to pay his debts. <u>Devise</u>: to Cecily for life a tenement [in Endless Street: *cf. 2251*], in which he dwelt on the day on which his will was perfected, between a tenement of John Newman, hatter, on the south side and Robert Arnold's tenement on the north side. The tenement, with the reversion of it after Cecily's death, should be sold by Cecily or his executors, saving Cecily's estate and possession previously granted to her for life by John. From the money received from the sale John's debts should be paid by Cecily, and if anything remained it should be laid out on charitable deeds on behalf of his soul, the souls of Cecily and Agnes, and the souls of others as seemed best to Cecily. <u>Executors</u>: Cecily; overseers, John's brother Edmund, Thomas Dereham, and William Weston. <u>Proved</u>: on 11 August 1408 in front of an officer of the subdean; the administration was entrusted to the executor. <u>Approved</u> at a court held in front of the bailiff, the mayor, and other citizens; the seisin of the tenement was released to the legatee.

18 September 1415, at Salisbury
2251 By their writing William Horsebridge, weaver, and his wife Cecily, the relict of John Purdy, of late a citizen of Salisbury, granted to John Swift, ironmonger, a citizen of Salisbury, their right or claim, or Cecily's right or claim, for Cecily's life by John Purdy's devise, to a tenement in Endless Street [*as in* ***2250***]. The tenement is to be held for ever by John Swift and his heirs and assigns on the strength of the devise to Cecily. Seals: those of William and Cecily and the mayoral seal of the city. Named witnesses: the bailiff, the mayor, a coroner, the reeves, Walter Shirley, William Warin, William Bishop, Henry Man, and the clerk

16 October 1415, at Salisbury
2252 A deed of William Horsebridge, weaver, and his wife Cecily, the relict of John Purdy, of late a citizen of Salisbury, who devised to Cecily for life a tenement in Endless Street [*as in* ***2250***]. John appointed the tenement, after Cecily's death, to be sold by Cecily or her executors for the payment of his debts, and money which remained should be spent on behalf of his soul and the souls of others. John Swift, ironmonger, a citizen of Salisbury, has paid to Cecily a sum of money, the true value of the reversion of the tenement, to be spent according to the terms of John Purdy's will, William and Cecily have granted to him all Cecily's right or claim to the tenement, and by their deed William and Cecily granted the reversion to him. The tenement is to be held immediately by John and his heirs and assigns for ever. Seals: those of William and Cecily and the common and mayoral seals of the city. Named witnesses: the bailiff, the mayor, a coroner, the reeves, John Mower, Walter Shirley, William Warin, William Dowding, and the clerk

13 November 1415, at Salisbury
2253 Approval of the will of John Gilbert, a citizen of Salisbury, made on 29 May 1415. <u>Interment</u>: in the graveyard of St. Edmund's church, in front of the west gate. <u>Bequests</u>: 40*d.* to the fabric of that church, 40*d.* to the provost for his forgotten tithes, 12*d.* to the parochial chaplain to pray for his soul, 6*d.* to the deacon, and 4*d.* to the sacristan; 12*d.* to John Jakes, a chaplain; 6*d.* to Richard North, a chaplain; 6*s.* 8*d.* to the fabric of the cathedral church; the rest of his goods to his wife Margaret and his children for praying for his soul, to be disposed of on behalf of his soul. <u>Devises</u>: to Margaret for life the tenement [in Castle Street: *cf.* ***1728***] in which he dwelt and two tenements on the north side of it, all of which stand conjoined, beyond the bar, between a trench of water running under the bridge there on the south side and a tenement of the provost of St. Edmund's church on the north side. On Margaret's death the tenement in which John dwelt should remain for ever to his legitimate son John and his issue, if that

John were to die without issue it would remain for ever to the elder John's son William and his issue, if William were to die without issue it would remain for ever to the elder John's son Hugh and his issue, if Hugh were to die without issue it would remain for life to the elder John's bastard son John, and after that John's death it should be sold by the elder John's executors, their executors, or subsequent executors. The money received from the sale should be laid out, at the discretion of the executors who made the sale on the repair and maintenance of the ways leading from the bridge of Castle Street towards Old Sarum and on doing other charitable deeds. Also on Margaret's death another of the three tenements, that held by John Pickard between a tenement which John Smith holds and, on the north side, the provost's tenement, should remain for ever to William and his issue, if William were to die without issue it would remain for ever to the legitimate son John and his issue, if that John were to die without issue it would remain for ever to Hugh and his issue, and if Hugh were to die without issue it should be sold by the elder John's executors or subsequent executors under the oversight of the mayor for the time being. Of the money received from the sale half should be given to the collegiate chaplains of St. Edmund's church to pray for John's soul and the souls of others, and the other half should be given to the mayor and commonalty in aid and remission of their charges and tallages imposed on the city to have a memorial of him among them. Also on Margaret's death the third of the tenements, that in which John Smith, glover, dwells, should remain for ever to Hugh and his issue, if Hugh were to die without issue it would remain for ever to the legitimate son John and his issue, if that John were to die without issue it would remain for ever to William and his issue, if William were to die without issue it would remain for life to Joan Champions, if she were then living, and after Joan's death it should be sold by the elder John's executors or subsequent executors. Of the money received from the sale half should be given to the collegiate chaplains and half to the mayor and commonalty to pray and to have a memorial as stated above. Executors: his wife Margaret, his son John dwelling with him, and Thomas Farrant; John bequeathed 6s. 8d. to Thomas on condition that he would be a good friend and a faithful executor. Proved on 29 June 1415 in front of an officer of the subdean; the administration was entrusted to the executors. Approved at a court held in front of the bailiff, the mayor, and other citizens; the seisin of the tenements was released to the legatee.

27 November 1415, at Salisbury
2254 By their charter John Swift, ironmonger, and John Hellier, ironmonger, granted to Simon Sydenham, Edward Prentice, Robert Brown, Simon Membury, and Robert Wavendon, clerks, a tenement, which they held by a grant of William Duke, ironmonger, in Endless Street between a tenement of late Edmund Bramshaw's, now Thomas Farrant's, on the north side and a tenement of late John Fowle's, now John Camel's, on the south side. The tenement descended to William on the death of John Duke, his father, and is to be held for ever by the grantees and their heirs and assigns. Clause of warranty. Seals: those of John Swift and John Hellier and the common and mayoral seals of the city. Named

witnesses: the bailiff, the mayor, a coroner, the reeves, John Mower, William Walter, William Bishop, John Lewisham, Walter Nalder, and the clerk

11 December 1415, at Salisbury
2255 Approval of the will of Edward Fountain, weaver, of Salisbury, made on 4 October 1415. <u>Interment</u>: in the graveyard of the cathedral church, beside the cross opposite the west door. <u>Bequests</u>: 6*d*. to the fabric of the cathedral church; 12*d*. to the fabric of St. Thomas's church for his forgotten tithes; half a trental both to the Dominicans of Fisherton and the Franciscans of Salisbury; 12*d*. to Nicholas Whiting, carpenter; the rest of his goods to his wife Joan, his son Richard, and his daughter Alice. <u>Devises</u>: to Joan for life a tenement, with cottages and gardens, in New Street between Thomas Biston's tenement on the east side and a tenement of Walter Warwick, a chaplain, on the west side. Edward appointed the tenement, in which he dwelt, with the cottage in which Edith Brock dwells, and a garden lying all the way to the ditch behind the wall of the cathedral close, to be held on Joan's death by Richard and his issue for ever. If Richard were to die without issue the tenement, with the cottage and garden, would remain for ever to Alice and her issue. Edward appointed the cottage, with a garden next to it, in which John Jarvis, weaver, dwells, with the free ingress and egress as John now holds it, to be held on   Joan's death by Alice and her issue for ever. If Alice were to die without issue the cottage, with the garden, would remain for ever to Richard and his issue. If Richard and Alice were both to die without issue the land and tenement, with the gardens, should be sold by Edward's executors or their executors. The money received from the sale should be laid out, on celebrating masses and doing other charitable deeds, on behalf of Edward's soul, Joan's soul, and the souls of others. <u>Executors</u>: his wife Joan and Nicholas Whiting. <u>Proved</u> on 4 November 1415 in front of an officer of the subdean; the administration was entrusted to Joan, reserving the power to entrust it to Nicholas when he might come to seek it. <u>Approved</u> at a court held in front of the bailiff, the mayor, and other citizens; the seisin of the tenement and the cottages was released to the legatee.

25 December 1415, at Salisbury
2256 Approval of the will of Alice Ham, the relict of Thomas Ham, tailor, of Salisbury, made on 6 December 1415. <u>Interment</u>: in St. Edmund's church, opposite the altar of the Blessed Mary where the light of the tailors remains. <u>Bequests</u>: 6*s*. 8*d*. to the fabric of that church, 8*d*. to the high altar for her forgotten tithes, 5*s*. to Richard North, a chaplain, 12*d*. to David, the parochial chaplain, and 4*d*. to each collegiate chaplain present at her funeral rites and mass; 5*s*. [to be shared] among the Dominican friars of Fisherton to celebrate two trental masses on behalf of her soul; 5*s*. to the Franciscans of Salisbury likewise; 6*s*. 8*d*. for the repair and maintenance of two bridges, North bridge and South bridge, at Wareham; a rosary of amber beads, with a clasp, to the fabric of the church of the Blessed Mary, Wareham; 20*s*. to the daughter of John Ham, an apothecary, on condition that John would comply with Alice's executors and not trouble

them; 6*d.* to the fabric of the cathedral church; 6*s.* 8*d.* to the hospital of the Holy Trinity and to the ailing in it; 6*s.* 8*d.*, a brass pot, and a pan to Alice, her household servant; 20*s.* to her son Henry on condition that he would comply with her executors and not trouble them, and if he did he would not have his legacy; 20*s.* to Henry Romain, a chaplain; a coverlet powdered with lilies to Richard North; 20*d.* and a kerchief of cypress to Joan Titchfield; a furred gown of medley to Agnes Fulham; a gown with fur to her daughter Maud; a cloak with a green hood to Joan, her kinswoman; she remits the rent of one term to John at the wood; a brass pot of 2 gallons, a pan of 2 gallons, and a best coverlet to Cecily Stokes; 20*s.* to Hugh [Wareham], the prior of Sandleford; 20*s.* to William Harnhill, barber, one of her executors; the rest of her goods to her executors to be disposed of on behalf of her soul. <u>Devises</u>: she appointed to her executors a tenement in Gigant Street, between Thomas Messenger's tenement on the south side and a tenement of late Thomas Chaplin's on the north side, and a tenement, with a garden, in Gigant Street, of late Gilbert Skinner's, on the south side of John Lewisham's tenement. The two tenements are to be sold immediately after her death, except two conjoined shops next to one of them on its north side, on the street. Alice devised the two shops for life to her daughter Maud and appointed them, after Maud's death, to be sold by her own executors, their executors, or subsequent executors. The money received from the sale of the shops and the tenements should be laid out, on celebrating masses, repairing ways and bridges, giving alms to paupers, and doing other charitable deeds, on behalf of her soul, the soul of her husband Thomas, and the souls of others. <u>Executors</u>: her brother Hugh [Wareham], the prior, and William Harnhill. <u>Proved</u> on 20 December 1415 in front of an officer of the subdean; the administration was entrusted to the executors. <u>Approved</u> at a court held in front of the bailiff, the mayor, and other citizens; the seisin of the tenements and the shops was released to the legatees.

8 January 1416, at Salisbury
2257 By his deed Richard Harlwin, goldsmith, of Salisbury, an executor of Bartholomew Durkin, goldsmith, an executor of Agnes Northern, of late Bartholomew's wife, quitclaimed to Henry Harborough, a clerk, and his heirs and assigns his right or claim under Agnes's will or Bartholomew's will to a tenement, with shops, of late Agnes's, in the high street called Minster Street between a tenement of late Adam Countwell's, now John Spencer's, on the south side and a tenement, in which Richard dwells, beside the tenement on the north side. Seals: Richard's and the common and mayoral seals of the city. Named witnesses: the bailiff, the mayor, the coroners, the reeves, Walter Shirley, William Walter, Walter Nalder, John Becket, and the clerk
2258 A deed of Hugh [Wareham], the prior of Sandleford, and William Harnhill, barber, the executors of Alice Ham, the relict of Thomas Ham, tailor, of Salisbury. Alice appointed a tenement, with a garden, of late Gilbert Skinner's, in Gigant Street [*as in* **2256**], to be sold by her executors immediately after her death, except for two shops, next to the tenement on its north side, devised for life

to her daughter Maud. By their deed Hugh and William granted to William Whitcombe, Edmund of the river, and William Brawt the tenement, with the garden, together with the reversion of the shops when it fell due on Maud's death, to be held for ever by them and their heirs and assigns as that which they bought from Hugh and William for a sum of money for fulfilling Alice's will. Seals: those of Hugh and William and the common and mayoral seals of the city. Named witnesses: the bailiff, the mayor, the coroners, the reeves, John Mower, Walter Shirley, William Dowding, John Becket, and the clerk

2259 By their deed Hugh [Wareham], the prior of Sandleford, and William Harnhill, barber, the executors of Alice Ham, the relict of Thomas Ham, tailor, of Salisbury on the strength of Alice's will granted to Thomas Andrew, a clothier, of Salisbury, a tenement in Gigant Street between Thomas Messenger's tenement on the south side and a tenement of late Thomas Chaplin's on the north side. The tenement was acquired by Thomas Ham and Alice from John Wishford, a clerk, in fee simple, was appointed by Alice, who outlived Thomas, to be sold by her executors immediately after her death, and is to be held for ever by Thomas Andrew and his heirs and assigns. Clause of warranty. Seals: those of Hugh and William and the common and mayoral seals of the city. Named witnesses: the bailiff, the mayor, the coroners, the reeves, Walter Shirley, William Walter, William Bishop, William Dowding, and the clerk

22 January 1416, at Salisbury

2260 By his charter Richard Harlwin, goldsmith, granted to Henry Harborough, a clerk, William Boyton, called Bowyer, Stephen Edington, and William Hartshorn a tenement, in which he dwelt and which he acquired from John, a son of Joan, of late the wife of John Mildenhall, in the high street which is called Minster Street between a tenement of late William Northern's, now Henry Harborough's, on the south side and a tenement of late that of John Scammel [otherwise Camel], hatter, now Thomas Stabber's, on the north side. The tenement was of late John Pinnock's and is to be held for ever by the grantees and their heirs and assigns. Clause of warranty. Seals: Richard's and the common and mayoral seals of the city. Named witnesses: the bailiff, the mayor, the coroners, the reeves, John Mower, Walter Shirley, Walter Nalder, William Dowding, John Becket, and Thomas Mason

2261 By his charter William Ashley, a chaplain, a son and heir of William Ashley, of late a citizen of Salisbury, and his wife Isabel, granted to Nicholas Harding, Walter Shirley, and Stephen Edington, citizens of Salisbury, a tenement, which Thomas Messenger holds, in St. Martin's Street between a tenement, which John Ellis holds, on the west side and a tenement of late Thomas Bridgehampton's on the east side; also a tenement [in St. Martin's Street: *cf.* **1947**] which he acquired from John Gatcombe; also conjoined cottages and shops in [St. Martin's Street and] Brown Street between that tenement of late Thomas Bridgehampton's on the west side and a tenement, of late Thomas Chaplin's, which Margaret, the relict of Laurence Lane, holds, on the north side; also half a tenement, which was of late that of his mother Isabel, in Castle Street between a tenement of late John

Dogton's, now William Alexander's, on the south side and the other half of the tenement, which Joan, the wife of Robert Blake holds, on the north side. The tenements, shops, and cottages, and the half tenement, are to be held for ever by Nicholas, Walter, and Stephen and their heirs and assigns. Clause of warranty. Seals: William's and the common and mayoral seals of the city. Named witnesses: the bailiff, the mayor, the coroners, the reeves, John Mower, William Bishop, William Dowding, Thomas Mason, and William Tull

2262 By his letters of attorney William Ashley, a chaplain a son and heir of William Ashley, of late citizen of Salisbury, and his wife Isabel, appointed Walter Short and Roger Enterbush to surrender into the hand of Robert, the bishop of Salisbury, the seisin of a tenement, which Thomas Messenger holds, in St. Martin's Street, of a tenement [in St. Martin's Street: *cf. 1947*] which he acquired from John Gatcombe, of shops and cottages in St. Martin's Street and Brown Street, and of half a tenement in Castle Street [*as in 2261*] to the use of Nicholas Harding, Walter Shirley, and Stephen Edington, citizens of Salisbury. Seals: William's and the mayoral seal of the city

2263 By his charter John Mower, a citizen of Salisbury, granted to John Swift, ironmonger, a citizen of Salisbury, and his wife Christine a corner tenement, with shops and a gate, of late Thomas Britford's, in Castle Street and Chipper Street between a shop, of late that of William Buck, a chaplain, in which Alice Nutkin dwells, in Castle Street on the south side and William Tull's tenement, of late Thomas Burford's, in Chipper Street on the east side. The tenement was acquired by John Mower from William Buck, an executor of Thomas Britford, a citizen of Salisbury, and is to be held, with the shop and gate, for ever by John Swift and Christine and John's heirs and assigns. Clause of warranty. Seals: John Mower's and the common and mayoral seals of the city. Named witnesses: the bailiff, the mayor, a coroner, the reeves, Walter Shirley, William Walter, William Dowding, Thomas Mason, draper, and the clerk

2264 By his letters of attorney John Mower, a citizen of Salisbury, appointed Stephen Edington and Walter Short to surrender into the hand of Robert, the bishop of Salisbury, the seisin of a corner tenement, with shops and a gate, of late Thomas Britford's, in Castle Street and Chipper Street [*as in 2263*] to the use of John Swift, ironmonger, and his wife Christine. Seals: John Mower's and the mayoral seal of the city

5 February 1416, at Salisbury

2265 A copy of a charter of John Mower, of late a citizen of Salisbury. By his charter John, a citizen of Salisbury, granted to William Walter, Walter Shirley, Thomas Mason, draper, and John Swift, ironmonger, citizens of Salisbury, and to Henry Warin, a chaplain, of Salisbury, all his land, tenements, shops, cottages, rent, and reversions in the city, to be held for ever by them and their heirs and assigns. Clause of warranty. Seals: John Mower's and the common and mayoral seals of the city. Named witnesses: the bailiff, the mayor, a coroner, the reeves, William Bishop, Walter Nalder, Nicholas Harding, John Becket, and the clerk

18 March 1416, at Salisbury

2266 By their charter John Mower and William Walter, citizens of Salisbury, granted to William Cox, grocer, a citizen of Salisbury, and his wife Joan a corner tenement, of late that of William Hill, a merchant, called Glastonbury's Corner or Stratford's Corner, in Winchester Street and Gigant Street, between a tenement of late William Tenterer's, which John Parch now holds, on the west side and a tenement of late William Warmwell's in Gigant Street on the south side. The tenement is to be held for ever by William and Joan and William's heirs and assigns. Seals: those of John Mower and William Walter and the common and mayoral seals of the city. Named witnesses: the bailiff, the mayor, the coroners, the reeves, Walter Shirley, Walter Nalder, William Dowding, John Becket, Thomas Mason, and the clerk

29 April 1416, at Salisbury

2267 By his charter John Swift, ironmonger, a citizen of Salisbury, granted to Edward Burgh, an apothecary, and his wife Alice, a tenement, with a sollar, in which he of late dwelt and which he acquired from Thomas Sexton, in Minster Street near the graveyard of St. Thomas's church on its east side, [and] between John's own shop, with a sollar built above it, which was of late Bartholomew Durkin's, on the south side and a stile of the graveyard, beside a tavern, with a sollar, on the north side. The tenement, with the sollar, is to be held for ever by Edward and Alice and their heirs and assigns, to whom John released all his right or claim to it. Clause of warranty. Seals: John's and the common and mayoral seals of the city. Named witnesses: the bailiff, the mayor, a coroner, the reeves, Walter Shirley, William Walter, Thomas Mason, draper, John Lewisham, Robert Warmwell, and the clerk

13 May 1416, at North Charford

2268 By his deed John Stanley, a clerk, quitclaimed to Robert Smith and John Roper, clerks, and their heirs and assigns his right or claim to a chief tenement [*margin*: in Poultry], with shops, opposite the market place where poultry are sold, between Thomas Linford's tenement on the east side and Gunnore Bowyer's tenement on the west side, and to a cottage (*or* cottages), with a yard (*or* yards), in Castle Street beyond the bar, all which premises were held by all three clerks by a grant of John at the burgh. Seal: John Stanley's. Witnesses: John Popham, kt., Henry of Thorp, Thomas Merriott, Thomas Gilbert, Thomas Stabber, and Robert Bailiff

27 May 1416, at Salisbury

2269 By his charter Nicholas Harding, a citizen of Salisbury, granted to Richard Gage, John Parch, and John Ruddock, citizens of Salisbury, and to Robert Forest, of Salisbury, a tenement which Robert Play, ironmonger, of late held by a grant of William Bleacher, of Stoke Farthing (*Verdon*), and which Nicholas acquired for himself and his heirs in fee simple from Thomas Bleacher, an elder William Lord, Edmund Enfield, and a younger William Lord, executors of Robert, a citizen of Salisbury. The tenement stands in Endless Street between Nicholas Melbury's tenement on the south side and a tenement of late Robert Kirtlingstoke's, now John Lambard's, on the north side, and it is to be held for ever by the grantees. Clause of warranty. Seals: Nicholas Harding's and the common and mayoral seals of the city. Named witnesses: the bailiff, the mayor, the coroners, the reeves, Walter Shirley, William Walter, John Lewisham, Thomas Mason, draper, and the clerk

2270 By his letters of attorney Nicholas Harding, a citizen of Salisbury, appointed Stephen Edington, Walter Short, and Roger Enterbush to surrender into the hand of Robert, the bishop of Salisbury, a tenement, which he acquired [*as in 2269*], in Endless Street [*as in 2269*] to the use of Richard Gage, John Parch, and John Ruddock, citizens of Salisbury, and of Robert Forest, of Salisbury. Seal: Nicholas's

2271 By his deed Stephen Edington, a citizen of Salisbury, granted to Robert Warmwell, a citizen of Salisbury, a tenement, which he and John Smith, a chaplain, now dead, held by a grant of Richard Oword, a citizen of Salisbury, near the graveyard of St. Thomas's church on its north side, between a tenement of late William Godmanstone's, now that of John Swift, ironmonger, on the south side and a corner tenement of late that of John Chitterne, a clerk, opposite the market on the north side. The tenement is to be held for ever by Robert and his heirs and assigns. Seals: Stephen's and the common and mayoral seals of the city. Named witnesses: the bailiff, the mayor, the coroners, the reeves, Walter Shirley, William Dowding, Thomas Mason, Walter Nalder, and Thomas Bower

10 June 1416, at Salisbury
2272 By his deed Richard Oword, of Salisbury, quitclaimed to Robert Warmwell, of Salisbury, and his heirs and assigns his right or claim to a tenement, which Robert held by a grant of Stephen Edington, near the graveyard of St. Thomas's church on its north side [*as in 2271*]. Clause of warranty. Seals: Richard's and the common and mayoral seals of the city. Named witnesses: the bailiff, the mayor, the coroners, the reeves, Walter Shirley, William Bishop, John Becket, John Lewisham, William Tull, and the clerk

24 June 1416, at Salisbury
2273 By her charter Joan Warmwell, a daughter of William Warmwell, of late a citizen of Salisbury, granted to William Dowding, William Bower, and Robert Warmwell, citizens of Salisbury, and to Thomas Peasenhall, a chaplain, a tenement in Castle Street between a tenement in which Alice Bodenham dwells on the south side and a tenement of late John Justice's on the north side. The tenement was of late William Warmwell's and is to be held for ever by the grantees and their heirs and assigns. Clause of warranty. Seals: Joan's and the common and mayoral seals of the city. Named witnesses: the bailiff, the mayor, the coroners, the reeves, Walter Nalder, John Becket, Thomas Bower, Richard Gage, and the clerk

8 July 1416, at Salisbury

2274 By their indented charter William Dowding, William Bower, and Robert Warmwell, citizens of Salisbury, and Thomas Peasenhall, a chaplain, granted to Joan Warmwell, a daughter of William Warmwell, of late a citizen of Salisbury, a tenement, which they held by her grant, in Castle Street [*as in 2273*]. The tenement is to be held for life by Joan, after Joan's death should remain for ever to her daughter Margaret and Margaret's issue, and if Margaret were to die without issue would remain for ever to Joan and her heirs and assigns. Seals: those of the grantors and the common and mayoral seals of the city. Named witnesses: the bailiff, the mayor, the coroners, the reeves, Walter Shirley, William Walter, William Bishop, Thomas Mason, draper, and the clerk

2275 By their indented charter John Westbury, William Lord, and Thomas Dearing, executors of a younger Thomas Chaplin, granted to John Chandler, the dean of Salisbury, and Richard Holhurst, a clerk, a corner tenement or messuage, containing five dwelling houses, of late Thomas Chaplin's, in New Street and Brown Street between Joan River's tenement in Brown Street on the south side and the trench of water running through the hospital called Almshouse, beside the tenement, in New Street on the east side [*described slightly differently in 2278*]. The tenement or messuage is to be held for ever by John and Richard and their heirs and assigns on condition that, on every day through the year for ever, they find a chaplain to celebrate a mass of the Holy Trinity in the chapel of the Blessed Mary in the cathedral church on behalf of an elder Thomas Chaplin, his wife Joan, the younger Thomas Chaplin, and all the faithful departed. Seals: those of the grantors to the part of the charter remaining in the possession of John Chandler and Richard Holhurst, those of John and Richard to the part of the charter remaining in the possession of the grantors, and the common and mayoral seals of the city. Named witnesses: the bailiff, the mayor, a coroner, the reeves, Walter Shirley, William Walter, William Dowding, Walter Nalder, William Tull, and the clerk

2276 By his letters of attorney John Chandler, the dean of Salisbury, appointed John Grateley or Stephen Edington to receive the seisin of a corner tenement or messuage, containing five dwelling houses, of late Thomas Chaplin's, in New Street and Brown Street [*as in 2275*], according to the effect of an indented charter perfected for him and Richard Holhurst, a clerk, by John Westbury, William Lord, and Thomas Dearing, executors of a younger Thomas Chaplin. Seals: John Chandler's and the mayoral seal of the city

22 July 1416, at Salisbury

2277 By his charter William Tull, merchant, a citizen of Salisbury, granted to William Dowding, merchant, a citizen of Salisbury, three tenements, with shops and a cottage (*or* cottages). One tenement, with a shop (*or* shops), stands opposite the market place where grains are sold, between a tenement of late John Gatcombe's on the east side and John Judd's tenement on the west side; another, with a cottage (*or* cottages), stands in Carter Street, between a tenement of late John Castleton's on the north side and Richard at the mill's tenement on the

south side; the third, with a shop (*or* shops), stands in Carter Street, between a
tenement of late John Preston's on the south side and a shop of late Nicholas
Melbury's on the north side. The tenements, with the shops and cottage(s), are
to be held for ever by William Dowding and his heirs and assigns. Clause of
warranty. Seals: William Tull's and the common and mayoral seals of the city.
Named witnesses: the bailiff, the mayor, the coroners, the reeves, Walter Shirley,
William Walter, William Bishop, Thomas Mason, Thomas Bower, and the clerk
2278 By his deed William Alexander, of Salisbury, quitclaimed to John Chandler,
the dean of Salisbury, and Richard Holhurst, a clerk, and their heirs and assigns
his right or claim to a corner tenement or messuage, containing five dwelling
houses, of late Thomas Chaplin's, in New Street and Brown Street between Joan
River's tenement in Brown Street on the south side and the trench of water
running under the bridge in New Street on the east side [*described slightly differently
in 2275*]. Seals: William's and the common and mayoral seals of the city. Named
witnesses: the mayor, the coroners, the reeves, Walter Nalder, William Dowding,
William Bishop, John Becket, Thomas Mason, and the clerk
2279 By his deed John Judd, an executor of a younger Thomas Chaplin,
quitclaimed to John Chandler, the dean of Salisbury, and Richard Holhurst, a
clerk, and their heirs and assigns his right or claim to a corner tenement or
messuage, containing five dwelling houses, of late Thomas Chaplin's, in New
Street and Brown Street [*as in 2278*]. Seals: John Judd's and the common and
mayoral seals of the city. Named witnesses: the mayor, a coroner, the reeves,
Walter Shirley, William Walter, William Dowding, John Lewisham, William Tull,
and the clerk
2280 By her charter Joan, the relict of William River, a daughter and heir of
William Warmwell, of late a citizen of Salisbury, in her full power granted to
Thomas Slegge a rent of 6s. a year, which she was accustomed to receive, issuing
from a corner tenement, of late William Surr's, in Wineman Street and Culver
Street between a tenement formerly Thomas Pink's on one side, a tenement
formerly William Wild's on the other side, and a tenement (*or* tenements) of
late Gilbert Oword's on both sides. The rent is to be held for ever by Thomas
and his heirs and assigns. Clause of warranty. Joan also quitclaimed to Thomas
and his heirs and assigns her right or claim to the tenement. Seals: Joan's and the
common and mayoral seals of the city. Named witnesses: the bailiff, the mayor,
the coroners, the reeves, William Walter, William Dowding, Walter Nalder, John
Becket, Thomas Bower, and the clerk

26 August 1416, at Salisbury
2281 By their charter John Swift, ironmonger, a citizen of Salisbury, and his
wife Christine, appearing in court on that day, Christine by her pure will and
without fear or coercion, granted to William Shipton, a cordwainer, and his wife
Edith a tenement, in which William and Edith dwell, with the gutters from the
houses which are called Onesfall on the north side of the tenement, and the light
shining through a window on that side of the tenement and through windows
on the east side; also a conjoined shop, with a sollar, attached to the north side of

the tenement. The tenement and the shop stand in Castle Street between a shop of John and Christine, on the south side of an entrance to their chief tenement, which was formerly Thomas Britford's, on the north side and a shop of late that of the lord William Buck, in which Alice Nutkin dwells, on the south side, and the tenement extends as far as a garden of John and Christine on the east side. The tenement, with the shop, together with the chief tenement, were held by John and Christine by a grant of John Mower, a citizen of Salisbury, and, with the shop, gutters, and light, is to be held for ever by William and Edith and William's heirs and assigns. Clause of warranty. Seals: those of John and Christine and the common and mayoral seals of the city. Named witnesses: the bailiff, the mayor, a coroner, the reeves, Walter Shirley, William Walter, Thomas Mason, Robert Warmwell, and the clerk

27 August 1416, at Salisbury
2282 An indenture perfected between John Swift, ironmonger, and William Shipton, a cordwainer. A tenement, in which they dwell, in Castle Street is held by William and his wife Edith by a feoffment of John and his wife Christine. It has a window on the north side and two on the east side, through which light shines into it on the side of a tenement of John and Christine. To have the light without any hindrance of John and Christine or their heirs William granted for himself and his assigns that, within a year, he would cause the window on the north side of his tenement to be glazed and thereafter to be kept glazed. Within the year William would also cause the windows on the east side to be altered so that henceforward John and Christine and their assigns might suffer no damage through any defect of them. Seals: those of the parties to the parts of the indenture in turn and the mayoral seal of the city

2 September 1416, at Salisbury
2283 By his deed Thomas Upton, a clerk, a son and heir of John Upton, of late a citizen of Salisbury, granted to Walter Intborough, esq., and John Noble, a merchant, a rent of a pair of gauntlets a year issuing for the life of Reynold Glover from cottages, with a yard (*or* yards), in New Street between a tenement of late William Godmanstone's, now that of Henry Chubb, baker, on the east side and the river Avon on the west side, with the reversion of the cottages, with the yard(s), when it fell due on Reynold's death. The rent and the reversion are to be held for ever by Walter and John and their heirs and assigns. Clause of warranty. Thomas quitclaimed to Walter and John and their heirs and assigns the rent and the cottages, with the yard(s). Seals: Thomas's and the common and mayoral seals of the city. Named witnesses: the bailiff, the mayor, the coroners, the reeves, Walter Shirley, William Dowding, John Becket, Walter Nalder, and the clerk
2284 By his charter Reynold Kingsbridge, a clerk, a kinsman and heir of Geoffrey of Warminster, granted to Thomas Fellows and his heirs and assigns a tenement called Countwell's Inn, with shops and gardens next to it, in the high street called Minster Street, between a trench of water, running between that tenement and a tenement called Pinnock's Inn, on the south side and a tenement now that of

Henry Harborough, a clerk, formerly William Cockett's, on the north side, to be held for ever by him and his heirs and assigns. Clause of warranty, provided that the warranty extends only to the exclusion of Reynold and his heirs and not to the rent or value. Seals: Reynold's and the common and mayoral seals of the city. Named witnesses: the mayor, the bailiff, the coroners, the reeves, Walter Shirley, William Bishop, John Becket, Walter Nalder, and the clerk

2285 By his deed Reynold Kingsbridge, a son and heir of Alice Kingsbridge, a daughter of Edith, a daughter of Stephen, a son of Geoffrey of Warminster, quitclaimed to Thomas Fellows and his heirs and assigns his right or claim to a tenement called Countwell's Inn, with shops and gardens next to it, in the high street called Minster Street, [*as in* **2284**]. Clause of warranty, provided that the warranty extends only to the exclusion of Reynold and his heirs and not to the rent or value. Seals: Reynold's and the common and mayoral seals of the city. Named witnesses: the mayor, the bailiff, the coroners, the reeves, Walter Shirley, William Bishop, John Becket, Walter Nalder, and the clerk

2286 By his deed Reynold Kingsbridge, a clerk, a kinsman and heir of Geoffrey of Warminster, quitclaimed to Thomas Fellows and his heirs and assigns his right or claim to a tenement called Countwell's Inn [*from here the wording of the deed repeats that of* **2285**]. Seals: Reynold's and the common and mayoral seals of the city. Named witnesses: the mayor, the bailiff, the coroners, the reeves, Walter Shirley, William Bishop, John Becket, Walter Nalder, and the clerk

2287 By their charter Henry Popham, esq., and Stephen Popham, kt., a son and heir of Henry, granted to William Alexander, John at the burgh, and Thomas Pain, esqs., their land, tenements, shops, cottages, rent, and reversions in Salisbury, to be held for ever by them and their heirs and assigns. Clause of warranty. Seals: those of Henry and Stephen and the common and mayoral seals of the city. Named witnesses: the bailiff, the mayor, the coroners, the reeves, Walter Shirley, William Walter, Thomas Mason, draper, John Lewisham, and the clerk

16 September 1416, at Salisbury
2288 By his charter John Lake, of Salisbury, granted to Walter Intborough, esq., John Sparrow, and Roger Upton all his land, tenements, shops, cottages, rent, and reversions in Salisbury, to be held for ever by them and their heirs and assigns. Clause of warranty. Seals: John Lake's and the common and mayoral seals of the city. Named witnesses: the bailiff, the mayor, the coroners, the reeves, Walter Shirley, William Walter, William Bishop, John Becket, and the clerk

30 September 1416, at Salisbury
2289 By their tripartite charter William Alexander, John at the burgh, and Thomas Pain granted to Henry Popham, esq., the land, tenements, shops, cottages, rent, and reversions in Salisbury which they held by a grant of Henry and Stephen Popham, kt., a son and heir of Henry, to be held by Henry for life. On Henry's death the property should remain for ever to his son John and John's male issue, if John were to die without such issue it would remain for ever to Stephen and his male issue, and if Stephen were to die without such issue it would remain for ever

to Henry and his heirs. Seals: those of the grantors and the common and mayoral seals of the city. Named witnesses: the bailiff, the mayor, the coroners, the reeves, Walter Shirley, William Walter, William Bishop, Thomas Mason, draper, and the clerk

14 October 1416, at Salisbury
2290 By his deed William Whitcombe quitclaimed to Edmund of the river and William Brawt and their heirs and assigns his right or claim to a tenement, with a garden, which was of late Gilbert Skinner's, in Gigant Street on the south side of John Lewisham's tenement; also the reversion of two shops next to the tenement on its north side which William Goodall, barber, and his wife Maud hold for Maud's life. William Whitcombe, Edmund of the river, and William Brawt held the tenement, with the reversion, by a grant of Hugh [Wareham], the prior of Sandleford, and William Harnhill, barber, the executors of Alice, the relict of Thomas Ham. Seals: William Whitcombe's and the common and mayoral seals of the city. Named witnesses: the mayor, the bailiff, the coroners, the reeves, John Mower, Walter Nalder, William Dowding Thomas Mason, Robert Warmwell, and the clerk

28 October 1416, at Salisbury
2291 By his indented charter Nicholas Harding, a citizen of Salisbury, granted to Stephen Leonard, a fuller, and his wife Emme a tenement in Winchester Street between Nicholas's own tenement, in which Robert Hindon of late dwelt, on the west side and a tenement of late Richard Spencer's on the east side. The tenement measures 104 ft. 10 in. in length from the street to Nicholas's garden and 20 ft. 5 in. in width from Nicholas's tenement to that of late Richard's. It is to be held for ever by Stephen and Emme and Stephen's heirs and assigns on condition that, henceforward and for ever, they will discharge and keep harmless Nicholas and his heirs and assigns in respect of Robert Ashley, a son of the late Edith Ashley, and his heirs and assigns concerning rent henceforward demanded by Robert and his heirs or assigns from Nicholas or his heirs or assigns from a tenement of Nicholas, with a garden (*or* gardens) adjacent, in Gigant Street between a tenement of late John Ashley's on the south side and a tenement of Nicholas's own on the north side. If Nicholas, or his heirs or assigns in that tenement in Gigant Street or in any part of it, were to be distrained upon by Robert or his heirs or assigns for that rent, because the discharge relating to it was ineffective, Nicholas and his heirs and assigns might enter on the tenement in Winchester Street granted to Stephen and Emme, take back possession, and keep Nicholas's former estate. Clause of warranty. Seals: those of the parties to the parts of the charter in turn and the common and mayoral seals of the city. Named witnesses: the bailiff, the mayor, the coroners, the reeves, Walter Shirley, William Walter, John Lewisham, Thomas Read, a merchant, William Cox, and the clerk

11 November 1416, at Salisbury
2292 By their deed Alice, the relict, and an executor, of John Becket, a citizen

of Salisbury, and Henry Man, William Bishop, and William Alexander, her co-executors, on the strength of John's will granted to William Phebis, a citizen of Salisbury, a corner tenement, with shops and a garden next to it, in St. Martin's Street and Freren Street, between John Sydenham's cottages, of late Margaret Godmanstone's, on the west side and William Phebis's cottages, of late William Warmwells's, on the south side [*margin*: Tyrell's land at Friars bridge]. The tenement, with the shops and garden, are to be held for ever by William Phebis and his heirs and assigns as that which William bought from the executors in good faith for a sum of money to be laid out on the salvation of John Becket's soul. Seals: those of the grantors and the common and mayoral seals of the city. Named witnesses: the bailiff, the mayor, the coroners, the reeves, William Warin, William Walter, William Dowding, John Lewisham, and the clerk

25 November 1416, at Salisbury
2293 By her charter Agnes, the relict of Walter Orme, of late a citizen of Salisbury, granted to the master John Chandler, a clerk, Roger Purton, John Saunders, and Hugh Palfrey a tenement, with shops, formerly called Tarrant's Inn, in Minster Street between a tenement of late William Pickard's, now that of Thomas Cardmaker, of Warminster, on the north side and a tenement of late Reynold Glover's, now Thomas Cardmaker's, on the south side; also a garden, with a rack (*or* racks) built in it, in Freren Street beside cottage property of late Edmund Enfield's, afterwards Richard Spencer's, and between a garden of late Agnes Bodenham's on one side and a garden of late Richard Cook's on the other side. The tenement, with the shops, and the garden, with the rack(s), were held by Agnes in fee simple by a devise of Walter and are to be held for ever by the grantees and their heirs and assigns. Clause of warranty. Seals: Agnes's and the common and mayoral seals of the city. Named witnesses: the bailiff, the mayor, the coroners, the reeves, William Warin, William Bishop, Thomas Mason, draper, Walter Nalder, and the clerk

9 December 1416, at Salisbury
2294 By his charter Thomas Chaffin, called Cardmaker, of Warminster, granted to John Paul, esq., a tenement in Minster Street between a tenement of later Walter Orme's on the south side and a tenement which Robert Reading holds on the north side. The tenement was held by Thomas by a grant of William Dowding, a citizen of Salisbury, and is to be held for ever by John and his heirs and assigns. Clause of warranty. Seals: Thomas's and the common and mayoral seals of the city. Named witnesses: the bailiff, the mayor, the coroners, the reeves, William Warin, William Walter, Walter Nalder, Henry Man, John Wishford, and the clerk

23 December 1416, at Salisbury
2295 Approval [*dated to the Wednesday before the feast of St. Thomas the Apostle (16 December) probably in error for the Wednesday after that feast (23 December)*] of the will of John Becket, a citizen of Salisbury, made on 24 September 1416. Interment:

in St. Thomas's church, near the image of the prior of Bridlington by the seat in which he was accustomed to sit. <u>Bequests</u>: 20s. to the fabric of that church, 6s. 8d. to the high altar for his forgotten tithes, 2s. 6d. each to the parochial chaplain, to the lord Edward Croll, the lord Nicholas Wight, and Nicholas Gifford, a chaplain of that church, to celebrate mass on behalf of his soul, 6d. to each other chaplain to pray for his soul, 4d. to the deacon, and 4d. to the sacristan; 3s. 4d. each to the fabric of the cathedral church, the fabric of St. Edmund's church, and the fabric of St. Martin's church; 6s. 8d. to the Franciscans of Salisbury; 6s. 8d. to the Dominicans of Fisherton to pray for his soul; 20s. each to the fabric of Shrivenham church and the fabric of East Ilsley church; a black tunic furred with polecat to William Pusey, and a low piece of silver, with a cover, and a violet tunic furred with red pullen to his wife Margaret, John's sister; a tunic with the fur of otter to Thomas Benford, and a low piece of silver to his wife Tamsin, John's sister; 40s. to each of his executors for executing his will; the rest of his goods to his executors to be laid out on repairing ways, celebrating masses, giving alms, and in other ways. <u>Devises</u>: he appointed to his executors all his land and tenements, with their conjoined appurtenances, on the way to St. Martin's church, between a gate of the meadow called Bug moor on the north side and cottages of William Harnhill, barber, on the south side; also a tenement, in which John Hogman dwells, in Winchester Street between a tenement of John's own, in which Nicholas Blanchard dwelt, on the west side and a tenement of the mayor and commonalty on the east side; also a corner tenement, opposite the Franciscans of Salisbury, with a shop, at the north end of Freren Street; also a garden in Freren Street beside Henry Southwick's garden; also shops, opposite a corner shop in which John Swift dwells, on the way to the New Inn, between a tenement in which Edward Potticary dwells, opposite the cross where poultry are sold, on the west side and Gunnore Bowyer's shop on the south side; also all his land and tenements in Southampton; also a tenement, in which John Shaftesbury dwells, with a garden next to it, in New Street between Joan River's tenement on the west side and a tenement, in which John himself dwelt, on the east side. Those premises are to be sold immediately after his death. From the money received from the sale his debts should be paid, and if anything were to remain it should be laid out by the executors on behalf of John's soul and the souls of others. John devised to his wife Alice a tenement in Winchester Street, in which Nicholas Blanchard of late dwelt, between the tenement in which John Hogman dwells on the east side and Thomas Bonham's tenement, in which Thomas Slegge dwells, on the west side; also the tenement in which John himself dwelt, with an adjacent garden, in New Street between another of John's tenements on the west side and John Derby's tenement on the east side. The tenement in which Nicholas Blanchard of late dwelt is to be held by Alice for life. The tenement in which John himself dwelt, with the garden, is to be held by Alice for life and, after her death, by her executors for two years. After Alice's death the tenement in which Nicholas Blanchard of late dwelt should remain for ever to the mayor and commonalty and their successors, in aid of their tallage and other charges, to pray for John's soul, Alice's soul, and the souls of others, and to hold John's obit yearly among them. A tenement, which Simon Tredinnick of late held, [in Winchester Street: cf. *816, 1895*], above the ditch, between shop property of the 'Riole' on the west side and William Alexander's tenement on the east side, and a tenement, in which William Debden dwells, in New Street between John Wishford's tenement on the east side and John Hathaway's tenement on the west side, in each case immediately after Alice's death, and the tenement, with the garden, in which John Becket himself dwelt, in that case immediately after Alice's death and the term of two years, should remain for ever to John's bastard son John and that John's male issue. If that John were to die without such issue all the tenements, shops, and gardens, except the tenements and shops which the elder John appointed for sale and the discharge of his debts, and except for the tenement which he appointed, after Alice's death, to the mayor and commonalty, would remain for ever to William Durkin and his male issue, if William were to die without such issue they would remain for ever to John Durkin and his male issue, and if that John were to die without such issue they would remain for ever to John Becket's direct heirs on condition that they would find a chaplain to celebrate mass daily for ever in the church of Shrivenham on behalf of the soul of Walter Becket, John's father, of John's soul, and of the souls of others. John appointed the reversion of two shops, which John Swift, ironmonger, and William Halstead hold, at the west end of Butcher Row, in which his wife Alice, enfeoffed jointly with him, holds an estate for her life, to be sold by his executors, their executors, or subsequent executors. From the money received from the sale his debts should be paid. Executors: his wife Alice, William Bishop, Henry Man, and William Alexander. Proved at London on 27 October 1416 in front of John Estcourt, B.L., a general examiner of the court of Canterbury and a general commissary of Henry [Chichele], the archbishop of Canterbury. *John declared that John Becket was well known to have held goods in various dioceses of the province of Canterbury and that therefore the proving, recording, and approval of his will, the entrusting and administration of his goods, and the administration of the account, audit, discharge, and release, was the prerogative of the archbishop's court of Canterbury. John pronounced the will to be lawful. William Alexander, an executor named in it, was sworn by means of a corporal oath to make an inventory of all John Becket's goods, pertaining to his will and in the province of Canterbury, to show it to John, and, except for John Becket's funeral expenses, not to administer those goods. The result was set forth and the administration of the goods contained in the inventory was entrusted to William.* Approved at a court held in front of the bailiff, the mayor, and other citizens; the seisin of the land, tenements, cottages, gardens, and shops was released to the legatees.

2296 By his indented deed Thomas Chaffin, called Cardmaker, of Warminster, granted to John Paul, esq., a rent of 25s. a year to be received for ever by him and his heirs and assigns from a tenement, which Robert Reading holds [of Thomas: *cf. 2077*] in Minster Street between John's tenement, which he acquired from Thomas, on the south side and a tenement of late Thomas Chaplin's, which John Lake of late held, on the north side. Clause to permit entry on the tenement if the rent were to be in arrear, distraint, and the keeping of distresses until the unpaid rent was recovered. The grant was made on condition that, if Thomas Chaffin or his heirs or assigns were to discharge for ever the tenement which John acquired from Thomas against the scholars of de Vaux college from a rent of 25s. a year, if such rent were to be demanded and levied there without fraud and collusion, the present deed would be void. If Thomas or his heirs or assigns did not pay for a distress, if any were to be taken in John's tenement by the scholars, and if John and his heirs and assigns did not keep their immunity from loss, John and his heirs and assigns might enter on Thomas's tenement [held by Robert Reading], charged as above, and distrain and keep distresses until the distress thus taken for the rent was restored to John or his heirs or assigns. Seals: those of the parties to the parts of the charter in turn and the common and mayoral seals of the city. Named witnesses: the bailiff, the mayor, the coroners, the reeves, William Warin, William Bishop, William Dowding, Thomas Mason, and the clerk

2297 By his charter John Salisbury, weaver, of Salisbury, granted to William Westbury a [corner] messuage in St. Martin's Street between Walter Burton's tenement on the east side and cottages of the provost of St. Edmund's church on the north side [*margin*: ?Batt's corner house]. The messuage was held by John by a devise of his wife Christine and is to be held for ever by William and his heirs and assigns. Clause of warranty. Seals: John's and the common and mayoral seals of the city. Named witnesses: the mayor, the coroners, the reeves, William Warin, William Walter, William Dowding, Walter Nalder, Robert Warmwell, and the clerk

6 January 1417, at Salisbury

2298 Approval of the will of Thomas Chaplin, a son and heir of Thomas Chaplin, of late a citizen of Salisbury, made on 29 November 1415. Interment: in the cathedral church. Bequests: 20s. to the fabric of that church; 13s. 4d. to the fabric of St. Thomas's church; 6s. 8d. each to the fabric of St. Edmund's church and the fabric of St. Martin's church; 6s. 8d. to the almshouse of the Holy Trinity, and 13s. 4d. to be handed out among the ailing and sick in it; 2d. to each sick person, of both sexes, bedridden in St. Nicholas's hospital; 50s. both to the convent of the Franciscans of Salisbury and the Dominican friars of Fisherton to be handed out among the friars equally to pray for the souls of his parents Thomas and Joan, his own soul, the soul of Joan, of late his wife, and the souls of others; 10 marks to William Hindon, a Franciscan friar, to pray for his soul especially and for the souls mentioned above; 12d. to each canon of the cathedral church present at his funeral rites and mass on the day of his burial; 8d. to each vicar, 6d. to each chantry chaplain, 3d. to each chorister and acolyte, 8d. each to the subdean and the succentor, 20d. to the two sacristans and 8d. to their boys; 8d. to each chaplain celebrating mass in St. Thomas's church, St. Edmund's church, or St. Martin's church to pray for his soul; 8d. each to John Martin and William Priest, chaplains of de Vaux college; 100s. in bread to be handed out among paupers on the day of his burial; a gown of black worsted with the fur of squirrel on it, a gown of russet with the fur of foins on it, and 40s. to Edmund Friday; 40s. to the fabric of Fordingbridge church, and 6s. 8d. to the vicar to pray in the pulpit of that church for his soul and the soul of Joan, of late his wife, on every Sunday

for the year following Thomas's death; 40s. to John Holm, his servant; a silver
bowl, with a cover, with a chaplet to John Chandler, the dean of Salisbury; 40s.
to the master Nicholas Winbolt; 40s. to John Draper, a clerk; 6s. 8d. to Robert
Carpenter, a matins chaplain of the cathedral church; 12d. to John Messenger, the
parochial chaplain of St. Thomas's church; 40s. to each of his executors vigorously
taking on the burden of the administration of his will; the rest of his goods to his
executors to pay his debts and to dispose of on pious uses. <u>Devises</u>: he appointed
to Richard Holhurst, William Hendy, and Laurence Groom, chaplains, a [corner]
tenement, with shops, in Carter Street between his own tenement, in which John
Clark, taverner, dwells, on the north side and a tenement of late John Ashley's
on the east side, of which tenement three of the shops stand in New Street.
The tenement, with the shops, is to be held for ever by Richard, William, and
Laurence and their heirs and assigns on condition that, if within the two years
following Thomas's death the tenement, with the shops, could be appropriated
to the dean and chapter of Salisbury for finding a chaplain to celebrate mass daily
at the altar of the Holy Trinity in that church on behalf of Thomas's soul, the
souls of his parents Thomas and Joan, the soul of Joan, of late his wife, and the
souls of others, such an appropriation should be made. If not, the tenement, with
the shops, should be sold by Richard, William, and Laurence with the oversight
of John Chandler, the dean. The money issuing from the sale should be applied
to the finding of a chaplain to celebrate mass on behalf of those souls, under the
oversight and order of John Chandler, as long as it might last and not otherwise.
Thomas appointed to Nicholas Winbolt and John Draper, clerks, two tenements
in Gigant Street between Agnes Lea's tenement on the north side and a tenement
of late William Godmanstone's on the south side. The tenements are to be held
for ever by Nicholas and John and their heirs and assigns on condition that, if
within the two years following Thomas's death they could be appropriated to
the chaplains and scholars of de Vaux college for holding an obit each year in the
chapel of the college for Thomas, Joan, formerly his wife, and his parents Thomas
and Joan, such an appropriation should be made. Otherwise the tenement should
be sold by Nicholas and John. The money issuing from the sale should be handed
over to the chaplains and scholars to hold the obit, under the oversight and order
of John Chandler, as long as it might last. Thomas devised to Thomas Cofford,
his kinsman, and his wife Alice, a tenement, with shops, in which John Clark,
taverner, dwells, in Carter Street between a tenement of Robert Newport, tailor,
on the north side and Thomas Chaplin's own tenement, appointed as above, on
the south side. The tenement, with the shops, is to be held by Thomas and Alice
for their life and the life of the one of them living longer, is to be maintained
and repaired in all things necessary in that period, and after the death of Thomas
and Alice should be sold by Thomas Chaplin's executors, or their executors, with
the assent of John Chandler if he were living. The money issuing from the sale
should be laid out on pious uses on behalf of Thomas Chaplin's soul and the souls
mentioned above. Thomas devised to William Harvey, his servant, a rent of 20s. a
year issuing from a tenement, in the market place opposite where grains are sold,
which was of late John Gatcombe's. The rent is to be held by William for life, and

after his death should sold by Thomas's executors, or their executors, with the assent of John Chandler if he were living. The money issuing from the sale should be laid out on pious uses on behalf of Thomas's soul and the souls mentioned above. Thomas appointed the tenement in which of late Laurence Lane dwelt, and all his other tenements, rent, and possessions in Salisbury, to be sold as soon as possible after his death by his executors, or their executors, with the oversight and assent of John Chandler. From the money issuing from the sale two chaplains, one in the cathedral church and the other in St. Thomas's church, should be found to celebrate mass on behalf of his soul and the souls mentioned above as long as the money might last. No sale of Thomas's tenements, nor payment to any of his creditors or others, should be made without the assent and will of John Chandler in whom, as others, he trusts especially. <u>Executors</u>: John Westbury, William Lord, John Judd, and Thomas Dearing; overseer, John Chandler. <u>Proved</u> on 13 January 1416 in front of Simon Sydenham, the archdeacon of Salisbury, on the strength of a commission perfected for him by John Estcourt, B.L., a general examiner of the court of Canterbury, a general commissary of Henry [Chichele], the archbishop of Canterbury; the administration was entrusted to John Westbury, reserving to John Estcourt the power to entrust it to William Lord, John Judd, and Thomas Dearing when they might come to seek it. <u>Approved</u> at a court held in front of the bailiff, the mayor, and other citizens; the seisin of the land, tenements, and rent was released to the legatees.

2299 By their charter Edmund of the river and William Brawt granted to William Shilling a tenement, with a garden, which was of late Gilbert Skinner's, with the reversion of two shops next to it on its north side, which Maud, the wife of William Goodall, holds for life, when it fell due on Maud's death. The tenement, with the garden and shops, stands in Gigant Street on the south side of John Lewisham's tenement, was held, with the reversion, by Edmund of the river and William Brawt by a grant of Hugh [Wareham], the prior of Sandleford, and William Harnhill, barber, the executors of Alice, the relict of Thomas Ham, tailor, and is to be held, with the reversion, for ever by William Shilling and his heirs and assigns. Clause of warranty. Seals: those of Edmund of the river and William Brawt and the common and mayoral seals of the city. Named witnesses: the bailiff, the mayor, the coroners, the reeves, William Warin, William Walter, Nicholas Harding, John Lewisham, and the clerk

20 January 1417, at Salisbury
2300 By their deed Hugh [Wareham], the prior of Sandleford, and William Harnhill, barber, the executors of Alice, the relict of Thomas Ham, tailor, of Salisbury, quitclaimed to William Shilling and his heirs and assigns their right or claim by reason of Alice's will or otherwise to a tenement, with a garden, which was of late Gilbert Skinner's, with the reversion of two shops next to it when it fell due on the death of Maud, the wife of William Goodall, in Gigant Street [*as in 2299*]. The tenement, with the reversion, was acquired by William Shilling from Edmund of the river and William Brawt. Clause of warranty. Seals: those of the grantors and the common and mayoral seals of the city. Named witnesses:

the bailiff, the mayor, the coroners, the reeves, William Walter, John Lewisham, Walter Nalder, Thomas Bower, and the clerk

2301 A deed of William Goodall, barber, and his wife Maud. William Shilling acquired from Edmund of the river and William Brawt for himself and his heirs and assigns for ever a tenement, with a garden, which was of late Gilbert Skinner's, with the reversion of two shops next to it when it fell due on Maud's death, in Gigant Street [*as in 2299*]. At a court held on that day, and by their deed, William Goodall and Maud granted to William Shilling the right of Maud to the two shops, or to the tenement, to be held by him according to the force and effect of a devise in the will of Alice, the relict of Thomas Ham, tailor, Maud's mother. Seals: those of William Goodall and Maud and the common and mayoral seals of the city. Named witnesses: the bailiff, the mayor, the coroners, the reeves, William Walter, John Lewisham, John Bodenham, William Cox, Thomas Read, and the clerk

3 February 1417, at Salisbury

2302 By his charter John Mower, a citizen of Salisbury, granted to John Conge, a clerk, Walter Shirley, a merchant, and Henry Warin, William Spicer, and Robert Priest, chaplains, a cottage, with an empty plot of land, in Martin's Croft and Gigant Street towards St. Edmund's church, between cottage property of late Hugh Winterbourne's on the north side and cottage property of late of that church on the south side. The cottage, with the plot of land, was held by John Mower, together with Robert Ragenhill, a clerk, and Richard Spencer, by a grant of John Lake and is to be held, with the land, for ever by the grantees and their heirs and assigns. Seals: John Mower's and the common and mayoral seals of the city. Named witnesses: the bailiff, the coroners, the reeves, William Warin, William Walter, Thomas Mason, John Lewisham, Nicholas Harding, and the clerk

2303 By his letters of attorney John Mower, a citizen of Salisbury, appointed Walter Short and John Butler to surrender into the hand of Robert, the bishop of Salisbury, the seisin of a cottage, with an empty plot of land, in Martin's Croft and Gigant Street [*as in 2302*] to the use of John Conge, a clerk, Walter Shirley, a merchant, and Henry Warin, William Spicer, and Robert Priest, chaplains. Seals: John Mower's and the mayoral seal of the city

17 February 1417, at Salisbury

2304 By his deed Roger Upton, a son of the late John Upton, a citizen of Salisbury, and a kinsman and heir of John Homes, of late a citizen of Salisbury, quitclaimed to Walter Nalder and his heirs and assigns his right or claim to two messuages, with yards and two racks built in them, in Castle Street, beyond the bar, between cottage property of late John Homes's on the south side and cottage property of late Walter Chippenham's on the north side. Walter Nalder acquired the messuages, with the yards, under the name of a toft or garden, from John Chandler, of late a citizen of Salisbury. Seals: Roger's and the common and mayoral seals of the city. Named witnesses: the bailiff, the mayor, the coroners, the reeves, William Warin, William Walter, William Dowding, Thomas Mason, and the clerk

25 February 1417, at Salisbury
2305 An indenture recording an agreement between Walter Nalder, a citizen of Salisbury, on one side and Roger Upton, a kinsman and heir of John Homes, on the other side, concerning the building of a latrine and the ground on which it was built. [Walter] granted the ground and latrine to Roger and his heirs for ever. For that Roger granted to Walter and his heirs and tenants for ever an easement in respect of the latrine, with free ingress and egress as often as necessary. The latrine stands, in Castle Street on the river bank (*super ripam*), within Roger's tenement on the south side of Walter's tenement. Walter and Roger and their heirs will repair and maintain it at their own expense for ever. Clause of warranty in respect of the easement. Seals: those of the parties to the parts of the indenture in turn and the mayoral seal of the city

3 March 1417, at Salisbury
2306 A deed of John Little, an executor of John Amesbury, of late a citizen of Salisbury. John Amesbury devised to his wife Cecily for life two tenements in Culver Street. One tenement stands between a gate of a tenement then Robert Beechfount's on the south side and cottage property then Thomas Hill's, now that of John Brown, [a household servant] of the college [of St. Edmund's church], on the north side, and the other stands beside a yard of late Walter at the burgh's on the north side. On Cecily's death the tenements should remain for ever to John Amesbury's son John and to that John's issue, if that John were to die without issue they would remain for ever to the elder John's daughter Agnes and her issue, and if Agnes were to die without issue they should remain to the elder John's executors to be sold. The money received from the sale should be laid out on behalf of that John's soul and the souls of others mentioned in his will. Cecily has died, the younger John and Agnes have died without living issue, and all the elder John's executors have died except John Little, so that the sale of the tenements pertains to that John alone. By his deed and on the strength of John Amesbury's will John Little granted to John Conge, a clerk, Walter Shirley, a merchant, a citizen of Salisbury, and Henry Warin and William Spicer, chaplains, the two tenements, to be held for ever by them and their heirs and assigns as that which John Little sold to them for a sum of money to be laid out according to the will. Seals: John Little's and the common and mayoral seals of the city. Named witnesses: the bailiff, the coroners, the reeves, William Warin, William Walter, Thomas Mason, John Lewisham, Nicholas Harding, and the clerk
2307 A deed of Nicholas Lord, a clerk, and William Chandler, executors of John Newman, hatter, of late a citizen of Salisbury, an executor of Edith, the relict, and an executor, of William Newman, of late a citizen of Salisbury. William Newman devised to Edith for life a tenement in Endless Street between a tenement then Hugh Langford's on the south side and a tenement then William's on the north side. On Edith's death the tenement was to remain for ever to John, the son

of Henry Newman, William's brother, and John's issue, and if John were to die without issue, it should be sold by his own executors, their executors, or subsequent executors. The money issuing from the sale should be laid out on behalf of William's soul and the souls of others mentioned in his will. John, the son of Henry Newman, outlived Edith and has died without living issue so that, by the rigour of William's will, the sale of the tenement pertains to Nicholas Lord and William Chandler. Reynold Wishford has paid to Nicholas and William a sum of money to acquire the tenement for himself and his wife Joan and, on the strength of William Newman's will, Nicholas and William granted the tenement to them to be held for ever by them and their heirs and assigns as that which they bought from Nicholas and William in good faith for that sum of money to be laid out on the salvation of the souls mentioned above. Seals: those of Nicholas Lord and William Chandler and the common and mayoral seals of the city. Named witnesses: the bailiff, the mayor, the coroners, the reeves, William Warin, William Walter, Walter Nalder, Thomas Mason, and the clerk

17 March 1417, at Salisbury
2308 By his deed Robert Warmwell quitclaimed to Reynold Wishford and his wife Joan and their heirs and assigns his right or claim to a tenement, of late that of John Newman, hatter, in Endless Street [*as in 2307*]. Seals: Robert's and the common and mayoral seals of the city. Named witnesses: the bailiff, the mayor, the coroners, the reeves, William Warin, William Walter, William Bishop, William Dowding, Thomas Mason, draper, and the clerk
2309 By his charter Walter Nalder, a citizen of Salisbury, granted to William Warin, a citizen of Salisbury, Thomas Ringwood and William Walter two conjoined cottages in Castle Street, extending from the street all the way to the river Avon, between cottage property of late Ellis Homes's beyond the bar on the south side and cottage property of late Walter Chippenham's on the north side. The cottages are to be held for ever by the grantees and their heirs and assigns. Clause of warranty. Seals: Walter's and the common and mayoral seals of the city. Named witnesses: the bailiff, the mayor, the coroners, the reeves, William Dowding, William Bishop, Thomas Mason, Robert Warmwell, William Fewster, and the clerk

14 April 1417, at Salisbury
2310 By his charter Philip Wanstrow, carpenter, granted to William Basket, weaver, a garden, which he acquired from Thomas Manning, in Brown Street between William Slegge's tenement, formerly John Luckham's, on the south side and a tenement of late Robert Newport's, now Henry Prettyjohn's, on the north side, except a gutter [called] Onesfall of William Slegge's house. The garden runs in length from the street as far as the trench of running water at the end of it and, except for the gutter, is to be held for ever by William Basket and his heirs and assigns. Clause of warranty. Seals: Philip's and the common and mayoral seals of the city. Named witnesses: the bailiff, the mayor, the coroners, the reeves, William Warin, William Walter, Nicholas Harding, John Bodenham, and the clerk

2311 By his charter Nicholas Melbury, a citizen of Salisbury, granted to John Mower, a merchant, a citizen of Salisbury, a tenement in Endless Street between John's tenement on the south side and a tenement of late Nicholas Harding's on the north side. The tenement was held by Nicholas by a sale of Thomas Bleacher, ironmonger, an executor of Robert Play, a citizen of Salisbury, and is to be held for ever by John and his heirs and assigns. Clause of warranty. Seals: Nicholas's and the common and mayoral seals of the city. Named witnesses: the bailiff, the mayor, the coroners, the reeves, William Warin, William Walter, Thomas Mason, Edward Frith, and the clerk

2312 By his letters of attorney Nicholas Melbury, a citizen of Salisbury, appointed John Swift and John Butler, citizens of Salisbury, to surrender into the hand of Robert, the bishop of Salisbury, the seisin of a tenement in Endless Street [*as in 2311*] to the use of John Mower, a merchant, a citizen of Salisbury. Seals: Nicholas's and the mayoral seal of the city

2313 By his letters of attorney, John Mower, a merchant, a citizen of Salisbury, appointed Henry Warin, a chaplain, Richard Hooper, and Stephen Edington to receive the seisin of a tenement in Endless Street [*as in 2311*] according to the effect of a charter perfected for him by Nicholas Melbury. Seals: John's and the mayoral seal of the city

2314 By his charter William Lord, of Salisbury, granted to John Purvis and John Warbleton a messuage, with shops, a cottage (*or* cottages), a yard (*or* yards), and racks, in Carter Street between John Wishford's tenement on the south side and William Tull's tenement on the north side. The premises were of late held by Richard Oword and William Lord by a grant of Richard at the mill, of Salisbury, and are to be held for ever by John Purvis and John Warbleton and John Warbleton's heirs and assigns. Seals: William Lord's and the common and mayoral seals of the city. Named witnesses: the bailiff, the mayor, the coroners, the reeves, William Warin, William Bishop, William Dowding, Robert Warmwell, and the clerk

2315 By their letters of attorney John Purvis and John Warbleton appointed John Osgood, John Hampton, or a younger John Pope, a merchant, to receive from Robert, the bishop of Salisbury, the seisin of a messuage, with shops, a cottage (*or* cottages), and racks in Carter Street [*as in 2314*] according to the effect of a charter perfected for them by William Lord. Seals: those of John Purvis and John Warbleton and the mayoral seal of the city

2316 By their charter William Algar, a clerk, and William Lord, of Salisbury, executors of Richard Spencer, of late a citizen of Salisbury, and William Cambridge, grocer, a citizen of London, and his wife Edith, she being their co-executor, on the strength of Richard's will granted to John Purvis, a citizen of London, and John Warbleton a [chief: *cf. 2225*] tenement, in which Richard dwelt, in Winchester Street between a tenement of late Nicholas Harding's on the west side and Robert Ashley's tenement on the east side; also a sixth part of two tenements and 11 shops, of late John Thorburn's, [on a corner: *cf. 2225*] in the same street between William Hoare's tenement on the west side and a tenement of the dean and chapter of Salisbury [in Brown Street: *cf. 2376*] on the north side;

also two tenements, with a rack (*or* racks) and gardens, in Gigant Street between Richard Weston's tenement on the south side and William Hoare's garden on the north side; also a yard, with a rack (*or* racks), of late that of Robert Goyland, tucker, in Gigant Street between a toft of the provost of St. Edmund's church on the south side and John Judd's yard on the north side; also two tenements in Rolleston and Brown Street, of which John Shute holds one and John Brewer holds the other, between cottage property of the provost of St. Edmund's church on the north side and a yard of late Adam White's on the east side; also two conjoined tenements, called Staple Hall and the Dragon, with a shop (*or* shops), a cottage (*or* cottages), and a dovecot, in St. Martin's Street between Agnes Lea's tenement on the west side and a tenement formerly Adam Teffont's on the east side; also two tenements, one of which, with a shop (*or* shops), stands in Brown Street and is dwelt in by John Hampton, and the other of which, with a shop (*or* shops), is a corner tenement in Brown Street and Wineman Street, standing conjoined between Thomas Bonham's cottage property on the south side and a tenement of late John Needler's on the east side; also a cottage, with a rack (*or* racks) and a garden, which Walter Taylor holds, in Rolleston between cottage property of late Margaret Godmanstone's on the north side and cottage property of the provost of St. Edmund's church on the south side; also ... [*omitted from MS.*] opposite the Guildhall between William Cheese's shop on the north side and William Hoare's shop property on the south side; also the reversion of a sollar built above William Cheese's shop; also the reversion of a shop, which John Camel holds, between William Cheese's shop on the south side and Nicholas Harding's tenement on the north side; also a rent of 40s. issuing from a [corner] tenement, of late John Little's, in Endless Street between Nicholas Baynton's tenement on the west side and a tenement of a younger John Shute on the north side; also a rent of 30s. issuing from a corner tenement, with a shop (*or* shops) and a cottage (*or* cottages), now John Wootton's, in Winchester Street between a garden of late William Sall's on the south side and a tenement of an elder John Pope on the west side; also a rent of 20s. issuing from Robert Bowyer's tenement in Wineman Street between a tenement of late Gilbert Oword's on the east side and a tenement of late William Mercer's on the west side. All those premises, rents, and reversions are to be held by John Purvis and John Warbleton and John Warbleton's heirs. Seals: those of the grantors and the common and mayoral seals of the city. Named witnesses: the bailiff, the mayor, the coroners, the reeves, William Warin, William Bishop, William Dowding, Robert Warmwell, and the clerk

2317 By their letters of attorney William Cambridge, grocer, a citizen of London, and his wife Edith, an executor of Richard Spencer, of late a citizen of Salisbury, appointed a younger John Pope, John Tidworth, or Thomas Cofford to surrender into the hand of Robert, the bishop of Salisbury, together with William Algar, a clerk, and William Lord, of Salisbury, Edith's co-executors, the seisin of 25 messuages, 12 shops, 4 tofts, 1 dovecot, 4 gardens, a sixth part of 2 tenements and 11 shops of late John Thorburn's, and rent of £4 10s. to the use of John Purvis, a citizen of London, and John Warbleton, or to deliver the seisin to them. Seals:

those of William and Edith and the mayoral seal of the city

2318 By their letters of attorney John Purvis, a citizen of London, and John Warbleton appointed John Osgood or Thomas Moore to receive from Robert, the bishop of Salisbury, or from William Algar, a clerk, and William Lord, of Salisbury, executors of Richard Spencer, of late a citizen of Salisbury, and William Cambridge and his wife Edith, she being a co-executor of William Algar and William Lord, the seisin of 25 messuages etc. [*as in* **2317**] according to the effect of a charter perfected for them by William Algar, William Lord, and William Cambridge and Edith. Seals: those of John Purvis and John Warbleton and the mayoral seal of the city

28 April 1417, at Salisbury

2319 By his indented charter Thomas Read, a merchant, a citizen of Salisbury, granted to William Panter and his wife Agnes a tenement, with a garden, in which Christine Handley dwells, in Gigant Street between a tenement of late William Warmwell's on the north side and cottage property of late Thomas Eyre's, now John Bromley's, on the south side. The tenement, with the garden, is to be held by William and Agnes and their assigns for the life of William and Agnes, and by the executors or assigns of William and Agnes for the year following the death of the longer lived of William and Agnes. On the death of William and Agnes and after the year the tenement, with the garden, should remain to God and the hospital of the Holy Trinity called Almshouse for the maintenance of the hospital and of the paupers and the ailing in it, to be held for ever to pray for the soul of Robert Churchman, a chaplain, after he had died, the souls of William and Agnes, and the souls of others recommended by the paupers and the ailing. Clause of warranty. Seals: Thomas's and the common and mayoral seals of the city to the two parts of the charter, one part of which remains in the possession of William and Agnes and the other in the possession of the hospital and the masters or keepers of it. Named witnesses: the bailiff, the mayor, the coroners, the reeves, William Warin, William Bishop, William Dowding, Thomas Mason, and the clerk

2320 By her charter Agnes, the relict of Walter Orme, of late a citizen of Salisbury, granted to John Sherborne, a clerk, a tenement, with an adjacent shop (*or* adjacent shops), which she held in fee simple by a devise of John Sprot, her husband, in New Street, on the way towards the lower bridge of Fisherton, between shop property of late Thomas Knoyle's on the east side and a tenement of late Richard Monk's, now John Wishford's, on the west side. The tenement, with the shop(s), is to be held for ever by John Sherborne and his heirs and assigns. Clause of warranty. Seals: Agnes's and the common and mayoral seals of the city. Named witnesses: the bailiff, the mayor, the coroners, the reeves, William Warin, William Dowding, Walter Nalder, Henry Man, and the clerk

2321 By their deed Richard at the mill and Richard Oword quitclaimed to John Purvis and John Warbleton and the heirs and assigns of John Warbleton their right or claim to a messuage, with shops, a cottage (*or* cottages), and racks, which John Purvis and John Warbleton held by a grant of William Lord, of Salisbury, in

Carter Street [*as in 2314*]. Clause of warranty perfected by Richard at the mill. Seals: those of Richard at the mill and Richard Oword and the common and mayoral seals of the city. Named witnesses: the bailiff, the mayor, the coroners, the reeves, William Warin, William Dowding, Thomas Mason, Walter Nalder, William at the lea, and the clerk

12 May 1417, at Salisbury
2322 By her deed Agnes, the relict of Walter Orme, a citizen of Salisbury, quitclaimed to John Sherborne, a clerk, and his heirs and assigns her right or claim to a tenement, with an adjacent shop (*or* adjacent shops), which of late she held by a devise of John Sprot, her husband, in New Street [*as in 2320*]. Seals: Agnes's and the mayoral seal of the city. Named witnesses: the bailiff, the mayor, the coroners, and others as above [*in 2320*]

23 June 1417, at Salisbury
2323 By his charter Thomas Biston, a citizen of Salisbury, granted to William Halstead, butcher, and his wife Maud a tenement [*margin*: Warr's House], with a yard, which he acquired from Margery Justice, in Winchester Street between a tenement of late William Isaac's beside the ditch on the east side and cottage property of late John [Upton's: *cf. 1954*] on the west side. The yard extends as far as William Lord's yard on the south side. The tenement, with the yard, is to be held for ever by William Halstead and Maud and their heirs and assigns. Clause of warranty. Seals: Thomas's and the common and mayoral seals of the city. Named witnesses: the bailiff, the mayor, the coroners, the reeves, William Warin, William Bishop, William Dowding, Thomas Mason, John Lewisham, and the clerk
2324 By his charter [*the witnessing of the charter is dated to the Wednesday after the feast of St. Leo in the 5th year of the reign of Henry V (30 June 1417), possibly in error for the Wednesday before that feast in that year (23 June 1417); what appears to be the date at which the charter was otherwise perfected is given as 16 April 1417*] William Shilling granted to Richard Heathwolf, of Coate (*Cotyes*), in Bishop's Cannings hundred, a tenement, with a garden, of late Gilbert Skinner's, which William acquired from the executors of Alice, the relict of Thomas Ham, tailor. The tenement stands in Gigant Street between John Lewisham's tenement on the north side and a tenement of late Thomas Chaplin's, now William Alexander's, on the south side and, with the garden, is to be held for ever by Richard and his heirs and assigns. Clause of warranty. Seals: William's and the common and mayoral seals of the city. Named witnesses: the bailiff, the mayor, the coroners, the reeves, William Warin, William Walter, Nicholas Harding, John Lewisham, and the clerk

15 September 1417, at Salisbury
2325 By his charter John Swift, ironmonger, a citizen of Salisbury, granted to William Phebis, a citizen of Salisbury, a cellar, with a sollar built above it, in Minster Street, near the graveyard of St. Thomas's church, between a stile of the graveyard on the south side and John's shops, which were formerly Richard of Tidworth's, on the north side. The cellar, with the sollar, by the name of two

shops, was held jointly by John and his wife Christine, now dead, by a grant of Thomas Sexton and James Brock, smith, and is to be held for ever by William and his heirs and assigns. Clause of warranty. Seals: John's and the common and mayoral seals of the city. Named witnesses: the bailiff, the mayor, a coroner, the reeves, William Warin, William Bishop, William Dowding, Thomas Mason, draper, Robert Warmwell, and the clerk

13 October 1417, at Salisbury
2326 By his deed Thomas Felix, a clerk, quitclaimed to John Purvis, a citizen of London, and John Warbleton and the heirs and assigns of John Warbleton his right or claim to a corner tenement, with adjacent shops, which Richard Spencer, of late a citizen of Salisbury, built from new in Wineman Street and Brown Street between a tenement formerly Richard Aubin's, of late John Needler's, on the east side and a tenement formerly Richard Tropenell's, of late Richard Spencer's, in which John Hampton dwells, in Brown Street on the south side. Clause of warranty. Seals: Thomas's and the common and mayoral seals of the city. Named witnesses: the mayor, the bailiff, the coroners, the reeves, William Warin, William Bishop, William Dowding, Walter Nalder, and the clerk
2327 By his charter Walter Nalder, draper, a citizen of Salisbury, granted to Walter Shirley, a citizen of Salisbury, and his wife Joan a tenement, which he acquired from William Buck, a chaplain, and an elder John Chandler, and which was of late that of John Wallop, draper, and previously that of John Britford, a citizen of Salisbury. The tenement stands in Castle Street between Water Lane, near Scots Lane, on the south side and Walter Shirley's tenement on the north side, and it is to be held for ever by Walter and Joan and their heirs and assigns. Clause of warranty. Seals: Walter Nalder's and the common and mayoral seals of the city. Named witnesses: the bailiff, the coroners, the reeves, William Warin, William Bishop, William Dowding, John Lewisham, Robert Warmwell, and the clerk

27 October 1417, at Salisbury
2328 Approval of the will of William Walter, a merchant, a citizen of Salisbury, made on 21 May 1417. Interment: in the chapel of the Blessed Mary in St. Edmund's church, at the head of Richard Leach, beside the tomb of his wife Parnel. Bequests: William remits to that church the debt which is owed to him for the bells hanging in the timber there; 40s. more to the fabric of that church, 13s. 4d. to the provost and the high altar for his forgotten tithes and benefactions not made, 2s. 6d. to the parochial chaplain to pray for his soul among other prayers on feast days, 8d. to each other collegiate chaplain, 6d. to each other annual chaplain and chantry priest, 2s. to the fraternity of the Holy Cross, 12d. to the fraternity of the Blessed Mary of the art of the weavers, and 6d. each to the deacon and the sacristan; 40d. to the fabric of the cathedral church; 20d. each to the fabric of St. Thomas's church and the fabric of St. Martin's church; ½ mark to the paupers in the Almshouse; 2d. to each ailing bedridden person in St. Nicholas's hospital; 2s. to the prisoners in the Guildhall, to be divided among

them, to pray for his soul; 60s. to paupers and ailing bedridden people to be visited each week by his executors, to be divided among them in small amounts as long as that money might last by the week; 10s. both to the Franciscans of Salisbury and the Dominicans of Fisherton to pray for his soul; 20 marks to the fabric of the church of Alderton, near Towcester, the church in which he was baptized, and a pair of vestments and a missal to be kept there for praying there for his soul and the souls of others; a piece of silver, with a cover, and 20s. to his sister Alice; a best striped tunic, with a hood, and 20s. to his brother Henry; 40s. to be divided among the progeny of his brother and sister; a tunic with a hood, of William's use, and 30s. to Robert Chapman, his household servant, for his good service; a tunic with a hood, of William's use, and 20s. to Richard Lavington, his household servant; a tunic with a hood, of William's use, and 13s. 4d. to John Spadard, his household servant; a tunic with a hood, of William's use, and 6s. 8d. to John Sirman, his household servant, and William remits to John the debt which John owes to him; 6s. 8d. to Nicholas Abingdon, and William remits to Nicholas the debt which Nicholas owes to him; a tunic with a hood, of William's use, and 10s. to Simon Lavington, of late his household servant; 40s. to William Isaac, his household servant, so that he would attend on William's executors for the levying of debts to William and act in other affairs of the executors, having regard to things pending between him and William; 60s. over and above the stipend owed to her, two blankets, a pair of linen sheets, a coverlet with a tester, a basin with a laver, a tablecloth with a towel, a brass pot with a pan, two silver spoons, a candlestick of latten, a best gown, with fur, with a hood, and a pair of *pyn*... of the same style, of late his wife's, to Agnes, his household servant for her good service and praiseworthy diligence; a piece of silver to Agnes, a daughter of William Warin, his goddaughter; £20 to improve the ways in Drake Hall Street and beneath the park of Clarendon where, at the discretion of his executors, there was the greatest need; £10 to have the appropriation of six boys in the college of St. Edmund's church to perform divine service in that church for ever to pray for William's soul and the souls of others, if such an appropriation could be made; 40s. to be divided among poor canons of the house of Stavordale, Somerset; 60s. to each of his executors, and 60s. to their overseer; the rest of his goods to his executors to be disposed of on behalf of his soul and the souls of others according to their sound conscience, and he charges them to administer his will with their unanimous assent and will and without trouble and division. Devises: he appointed to his executors a corner tenement, with shops, a cottage (*or* cottages), and a garden (*or* gardens), of late Thomas Shove's, in New Street and Gigant Street, as also in St. Martin's Street, as the boundaries define it; also a tenement, in which John Clark, mercer, dwells, in Winchester Street opposite Bull Hall, between a corner tenement now Thomas Plummer's on the west side and Thomas Bonham's tenement on the east side; also cottages, with a garden (*or* gardens) and a dovecot, in Culver Street between cottages of the hospital of the Holy Trinity called Almshouse on the north side and cottage property of late Thomas Knoyle's on the south side. Those premises, except a cottage, with a garden, one of the cottages in Culver Street, which Isabel Carpenter of late held, should be sold immediately after William's death, when it could be done advantageously, if William's executors were living or otherwise by their executors. The money received should be laid out, among poor priests and laymen, among Franciscans and Dominicans, on celebrating masses and performing other divine services, among poor girls about to be married, among bedridden paupers to be visited, and on bestowing woollen clothes, linen clothes, and shoes on beggars, to pray for his soul and the souls of others and on doing other charitable deeds on behalf of those souls. William devised to Robert Chapman, his household servant, and his wife Maud the cottage in Culver Street excepted above, with an adjacent garden, which Isabel Carpenter of late held, to be held by them for their life and the life of the one of them living longer. On the death of Robert and Maud the cottage, with the garden, should be sold by William's executors if they were then living, by their executors, or by subsequent executors. The money received from the sale should be laid out by the executors, in the way described above, on behalf of William's soul and the souls of others. William devised to William Warin, one of the feoffees named with him in the acquisition of a tenement, shops, and a cottage (*or* cottages), of late those of John Thorburn, called Taylor, his share of the tenement, shops, and cottage(s), in Winchester Street [and Brown Street: *cf.* ***2225, 2316, 2376***], whether that part might be in common or divided. That share is to be held for ever by William Warin and his heirs and assigns to be disposed of, when the sum of money for that part shall have come to him and William's other executors, according to the terms assigned to the executors. William devised to Walter Shirley, the mayor, and the commonalty in aid and relief of their burdens, a tenement, which Richard Coof, draper, holds, opposite the market place where grains are sold, between Nicholas Melbury's tenement, in which John Shad dwells, on the west side and a tenement of the dean and chapter of Salisbury on the east side, to be held for ever by the mayor and commonalty and their successors. It is intended that the mayor and commonalty should help William's executors in their actions and pray for William's soul and the souls of others in their prayers for benefactors; the mayor and commonalty should hold William's obit yearly in St. Edmund's church, and the obit is to be overseen by the provost of that church and observed yearly without interruption. If the obit were not observed the provost should receive, for the year in which it was not observed, 20*s.* from the tenement with which he should hold the obit if it were held within eight days after the customary day. William devised to John Marshall, a dyer, one of his executors, a tenement built as two dwelling houses, of late newly built, which he acquired from Thomas Castleton, a citizen of Salisbury, at the north end of the street of Rolleston, on the way to St. Edmund's church. The tenement is to be held for ever by John and his heirs and assigns paying £50 for it, *viz.* by spending 4 marks a year by his own hand, if he were to live so long, from which William, William's kinsman dwelling with him, should be paid for at school, until he was of the age to become a priest if he wished, and be governed by John. If William were unwilling to be governed in good order in his minority, or were to die a minor, the money provided for him for the rest of the period, and all the other money remaining in John's hand, should be laid out by John, as an executor of the elder William, in the way mentioned above on behalf of the elder William's soul and the souls of others, if John were to live so long. In that manner the £50 should be paid and spent. If, meanwhile, John Marshall were to die the money should be laid out in the same manner by William's other executors. Executor: William Warin, a citizen of Salisbury, William Lord, and John Marshall; overseer, Thomas Ringwood, esq. Proof. By a commission of John Estcourt, B.L., a general examiner of the court of Canterbury and a commissary general of Henry [Chichele], the archbishop of Canterbury, Simon Sydenham, the archdeacon of Salisbury, and Nicholas Lord, B.L., of Salisbury, were to take on the proving of the will and the entrusting of the administration to the executors. On 5 September 1417 the will was proved in front of Simon on the strength of that commission; the administration was entrusted to William Warin, William Lord, and John Marshall. Approved at a court held in front of the mayor, the bailiff, and other citizens; the seisin of the tenements was released to the legatees.

2329 By his writing Stephen Edington granted to Richard Oword and his wife Alice a tenement, with a shop (or shops) and a cellar (or cellars), which John Smith, a chaplain, now dead, and Stephen held jointly by a grant of that Alice, the relict of William Bailey, draper, of Salisbury, in Castle Street between a tenement of late Thomas Bowyer's on the south side and a tenement of late that of John Dyer, of Longbridge Deverill, on the north side. The tenement, with the shop(s) and cellar(s), is to be held for ever by Richard and Alice and their heirs and assigns. Seals: Stephen's and the common and mayoral seals of the city. Named witnesses: the mayor, the coroners, the reeves, William Warin, William Bishop, William Dowding, Walter Nalder, and Robert Warmwell

24 November 1417, at Salisbury
2330 Approval of the will of John Wilmington, of Fisherton Anger, made on 24 August 1415. Interment: in the graveyard of St. Clement's church, Fisherton, beside the tomb of his wife Christine. Bequests: 40*d.* to the fabric of the cathedral church; 40*d.* both to the Dominicans of Fisherton and the Franciscans of Salisbury to be present at his funeral rites and to pray for his soul; 13*s.* 4*d.* to John Catlin, the rector of Fisherton, for forgotten and withheld tithes; the rest of his goods to his wife Agnes and his children to be shared among them equally. Devises: to Agnes for life four conjoined cottages in Gigant Street between cottage property of the college of St. Edmund's church on the north side and a tenement of a younger John Pope, on a corner of the street, on the south side. On Agnes's death the cottages should revert to the maintenance of his children, and if his children were to die in Agnes's lifetime the cottages should be sold by Agnes. The money received from the sale should be laid out, on charitable deeds, on behalf of his soul, the souls of his wives Christine and Agnes, and the souls of others. John devised to his son Thomas the rent in the borough of Shaftesbury, which he held by a grant of Nicholas at the pit and Parnel, the relict of an elder John Gowan, to be held for ever by him and his heirs and assigns. Executors: his wife Agnes and Gillian, Agnes's mother, the wife of John Judd, of Salisbury; overseer, John Judd. Witnesses: John Gatlin, William, the chaplain of a chantry in the church

of Fisherton, John Green, and others. <u>Proved:</u> on 23 October 1415 in front of an officer of the archdeacon of Salisbury; the administration was entrusted to Agnes, reserving the power to entrust it to Gillian when she might come to seek it. <u>Approved</u> at a court held in front of the mayor, the bailiff, and other citizens; the seisin of the cottages was released to the legatees.

5 January 1418, at Salisbury
2331 A deed of Robert Poynant and his wife Emme, the relict, and an executor, of John Barrett, of late a citizen of Salisbury, and of Nicholas Harding, Emme's co-executor. John devised to Emme for life a tenement, with shops, in which he then dwelt, in Winchester Street between a tenement then Robert Deverill's on the east side and a tenement then Stephen Brown's on the west side. After Emme's death the tenement was to be sold by John's executors. The money received from the sale should be laid out on behalf of John's soul and the souls of others mentioned in his will. By their deed Robert and Emme, and Nicholas, granted to John Jakes, a chaplain, the tenement and all Emme's right and estate in it. The tenement is to be held for ever by John and his heirs and assigns. Seals: those of Robert, Emme, and Nicholas and the common and mayoral seals of the city. Named witnesses: the mayor, a coroner, the reeves, Walter Shirley, William Warin, William Dowding, Thomas Mason, draper, and the clerk
2332 By his letters of attorney Nicholas Harding, an executor of John Barrett, of late a citizen of Salisbury, appointed Stephen Edington and Walter Short to surrender into the hand of John, the bishop of Salisbury, together with Robert Poynant and his wife Emme, she being Nicholas's co-executor, the seisin of a tenement, with shops, in Winchester Street [*as in 2331*] to the use of John Jakes, a chaplain. Seals: Nicholas's and the mayoral seal of the city
2333 Approval of the will of Richard Falconer, called Leach, made on 4 January 1411. <u>Interment</u>: in the chapel of the Blessed Mary in St. Edmund's church. <u>Bequests</u>: 20*s.* to the fabric of that church, 6*s.* 8*d.* to the provost for his forgotten tithes and lesser benefactions, 6*d.* to each chaplain present at his funeral rites, and 4*d.* each to the deacon and the sacristan; 20*s.* to the fabric of the cathedral church; 6*s.* 8*d.* to the fabric of St. Thomas's church; 40*d.* to the fabric of St. Martin's church; 6*s.* 8*d.* both to the Dominicans of Fisherton and the Franciscans of Salisbury to pray on behalf of his soul and the souls of others; 4*d.* to each ailing and bedridden person in the city; the rest of his goods to his wife Alice. <u>Devises</u>: to Alice for life all his land and tenements in the city. On Alice's death a tenement in Poultry should remain for ever to Gunnore Bowyer and her heirs, paying for it 20 marks to be laid out by Richard's executors on behalf of his soul and the souls of others. Also on Alice's death a tenement in the high street called Minster Street should remain for life to William Ferrer, of Hungerford, and on William's death it should remain to Richard's executors or their executors to be sold. The money received from the sale should be laid out on behalf of the souls mentioned above. Also on Alice's death a cottage in Culver Street should remain for life to Gillian, Richard's servant, and after Gillian's death that cottage, with all the [other] land and tenements on Alice's death, should remain to Richard's

executors to be sold. The money received from the sale should be laid out on behalf of the souls mentioned above. <u>Executors</u>: his wife Alice, John Jakes, a clerk, and William Lord. <u>Proved</u> on 10 June 1414 in front of John Hulling, the subdean; the administration was entrusted to John Jakes and William Lord, reserving the power to entrust it to Alice when she might come to seek it. Afterwards, on that same day, Alice appeared and the administration was entrusted to her. <u>Approved</u> at a court held in front of the bailiff, the mayor, and other citizens; the seisin of the land and tenements was released to the legatees. Because Gunnore Bowyer, William Ferrer, and Gillian, and John Jakes and William Lord, appeared in court, Alice then being dead, the seisin of the land and tenements was released to them according to the particulars of the will.

19 January 1418, at Salisbury
2334 An indented deed of John Jakes, a chaplain, and William Lord, executors of Richard Falconer, called Leach, of late a citizen of Salisbury. Among his other tenements Richard devised to his wife Alice for life a tenement [opposite the cross where poultry are sold: *cf. 2352*], called Oatmeal Corner, and two conjoined tenements, in Wineman Street between a corner tenement of William Lord and his wife Joan on the east side and Nicholas Melbury's tenement on the west side, under the name of all his land and tenements in the city. On Alice's death the three tenements should be sold by Richard's executors. The money received from the sale should be laid out on behalf of Richard's soul, Alice's soul, and the souls of others. John Cubble, of Ford, in Mottisfont parish, and William at the well, of West Tytherley, bought the three tenements from John Jakes and William Lord for 200 marks, of which £40 was paid in advance and 140 marks is to be paid as described below. By their deed and on the strength of Richard's will John Jakes and William Lord granted to John Cubble and William at the well the three tenements to be held for ever by them and their heirs and assigns on condition that, if the grantees were to pay to them or their heirs 20 marks cash at Michaelmas 1418 and 20 marks at Michaelmas for each of the following six years, the grant would remain valid. Clause to permit permanent repossession if a payment were defaulted on for 15 days after any Michaelmas. Seals: those of the grantors and the grantees to the parts of the deed in turn and the common and mayoral seals of the city. Named witnesses: the mayor, the bailiff, a coroner, the reeves, Walter Shirley, William Warin, William Dowding, John Lewisham, Thomas Mason, Walter Nalder, and the clerk
2335 A deed of William Warin, a citizen of Salisbury, William Lord, and John Marshall, dyer, executors of William Walter, a merchant, of late a citizen of Salisbury. William appointed to his executors, among other tenements, a tenement, in which John Clark, mercer, dwells, in Winchester Street, opposite Bull Hall, between Thomas Plummer's corner tenement on the west side and Thomas Bonham's tenement on the east side, to be sold when that could be done advantageously. The money received from the sale should be laid out by the executors on behalf of William's soul and the souls of others mentioned in his will. Thomas Bower, draper, a citizen of Salisbury, has paid to the executors a sum

of money agreed among them for the tenement to be held by him immediately, and by their deed the executors granted it to him to be held for ever by him and his heirs and assigns as that which he bought from them in good faith for William Walter's will to be carried out in that matter. Seals: those of the grantors and the common and mayoral seals of the city. Named witnesses: the bailiff, the mayor, a coroner, the reeves, Walter Shirley, William Dowding, Thomas Mason, Nicholas Harding, John Lewisham, and the clerk

2 February 1418, at Salisbury
2336 By his charter John Jakes, a chaplain, granted to Robert Poynant and his wife Emme a tenement, with shops and a gate, which he acquired from the executors of John Barrett, of late a citizen of Salisbury, in Winchester Street between a tenement of late Robert Deverill's on the east side and a tenement of late Stephen Brown's on the west side; the gate extends as far as Culver Street. The tenement, with the shops and gate, is to be held for ever by Robert and Emme and Robert's heirs and assigns. Clause of warranty. Seals: John Jakes's and the common and mayoral seals of the city. Named witnesses: the bailiff, a coroner, the reeves, Walter Shirley, William Warin, William Dowding, Thomas Mason, John Lewisham, and the clerk

16 March 1418, at Sailsbury
2337 By his deed Nicholas Melbury, of Newtown, near Old Sarum castle, of late a citizen of Salisbury, quitclaimed to John Shad, draper, and his wife Agnes and John's heirs and assigns his right or claim to a tenement, which John and Agnes hold, in which they dwell, and which they hold by Nicholas's grant for a term of eight years from 1 January 1417, the date of an indenture perfected between them. The tenement stands, opposite the market place where grains are sold, between John Gatcombe's tenement on the west side and a tenement of late William Walter's, in which Richard Coof, draper, dwells, on the east side. Clause of warranty. Seals: Nicholas's and the common and mayoral seals of the city. Named witnesses: the bailiff, the mayor, a coroner, the reeves, William Warin, William Dowding, Thomas Mason, Robert Warmwell, Richard Coof, and the clerk
2338 By his charter John Chandler, a son and heir of an elder John Chandler, of late a citizen of Salisbury, granted to John Giles, of Winchester, a tenement in Winchester Street, opposite the trench of running water [*margin*: above the ditch], between a tenement of late John Ashley's on the east side and a tenement of late Thomas Knoyle's on the west side. The tenement was of late held by John Fowle and the elder John Chandler, who outlived John Fowle, together by a grant of John Bodenham, of late a citizen of Salisbury, and his wife Alice, and it is to be held for ever by John Giles and his heirs and assigns, to whom the younger John Chandler quitclaimed his right or claim to it. Seals: the younger John Chandler's and the common and mayoral seals of the city. Named witnesses: the bailiff, the mayor, a coroner, the reeves, Walter Shirley, William Warin, William Bishop, William Dowding, Thomas Mason, draper, and the clerk
2339 By his charter Nicholas Melbury, of Newtown, near Old Saum castle, of

late a citizen of Salisbury, granted to John Shad, draper, and his wife Agnes a tenement in Wineman Street between a tenement of late John Needler's, which Richard Needler now holds, on the west side and a tenement of late Richard Leach's, now John Cubble's, on the east side; also a tenement, which John Shad and Agnes of late held for a term of years by Nicholas's grant, opposite the market place where grains are sold [*as in 2337*]. The tenements are to be held for ever by John and Agnes and John's heirs and assigns. Clause of warranty. Seals: Nicholas's and the common and mayoral seals of the city. Named witnesses: the bailiff, the mayor, a coroner, the reeves, Walter Shirley, William Warin, William Dowding, John Lewisham, William Tull, and the clerk

2340 By his letters of attorney Nicholas Melbury, of Newtown, near Old Sarum castle, of late a citizen of Salisbury, appointed a younger John Pope, draper, Roger Enterbush, and Richard Beard, tailor, to surrender into the hand of John, the bishop of Salisbury, the seisin of two tenements, one in Wineman Street [*as in 2339*] and one opposite the market place where grains are sold [*as in 2337*], to the use of John Shad, draper, and his wife Agnes. Seals: Nicholas's and the mayoral seal of the city

30 March 1418, at Salisbury

2341 By his deed John Jakes, a chaplain, quitclaimed to John Cubble, of Ford, in Mottisfont parish, and William at the well, of West Tytherley, and their heirs and assigns his right or claim to three tenements, which John and William held by a grant of him and William Lord, executors of Richard Falconer, called Leach. One tenement [opposite the cross where poultry are sold: *cf. 2352*] is called Oatmeal Corner; the other two stand conjoined in Wineman Street [*as in 2334*]. Seals: John Jakes's and the common and mayoral seals of the city. Named witnesses: the bailiff, the mayor, a coroner, the reeves, Walter Shirley, William Dowding, Thomas Mason, Robert Poynant, Thomas Bower, and the clerk

2342 By his charter Nicholas Harding, a citizen of Salisbury, granted to Thomas Mason, draper, Walter Shirley, Walter Nalder, William Lord, Stephen Edington, and Richard Weston, citizens of Salisbury, and Richard Gater a tenement in Minster Street between a tenement of late Thomas Gilbert's on the north side and a tenement of late Edmund Cofford's on the south side; also a messuage in Chipper Street between William Purchase's tenement on the west side and a tenement of late Roger Stapleford's on the east side; also two conjoined tenements in Minster Street, which is called Castle Street, between a tenement of late Walter Chippenham's, called the Cage, on the south side and a tenement of late Philip of Bristol's on the north side. The tenements and the messuage are to be held for ever by the grantees and the heirs and assigns of Walter Shirley, Walter Nalder, William Lord, Stephen Edington, Richard Weston, and Richard Gater. Seals: Nicholas's and the common and mayoral seals of the city. Named witnesses: the bailiff, the mayor, a coroner, the reeves, William Warin, William Dowding, William Bishop, John Lewisham, and William Packing

2343 By his letters of attorney Nicholas Harding, a citizen of Salisbury, appointed Roger Enterbush, Walter Short, and Robert Wolf, of Salisbury, to surrender into the hand of John, the bishop of Salisbury, the seisin of a tenement in Minster Street [*as in* **2342**], a messuage in Chipper Street [*as in* **2342**], and a tenement [?*rectius* two conjoined tenements: *cf.* **2342**] in Minster Street, which is called Castle Street, [*as in* **2342**], to the use of Thomas Mason, draper, Walter Shirley, Walter Nalder, William Lord, Stephen Edington, and Richard Weston. Seals: Nicholas's and the mayoral seal of the city

2344 By his charter John, a son of John Preston, grocer, of Salisbury, and his wife Clarice, granted to Edith New and Walter Messenger all his land, tenements, rent, services, and reversions in Salisbury, to be held for ever by them and Walter's heirs and assigns. Clause of warranty. Seals: John's and the common and mayoral seals of the city. Named witnesses: the bailiff, the mayor, a coroner, the reeves, William Warin, William Bishop, William Dowding, Walter Nalder, William at the lea, and the clerk

2345 By his letters of attorney John, a son of John Preston, grocer, of Salisbury, and his wife Clarice, appointed John Deverill to surrender into the hand of John, the bishop of Salisbury, the seisin of his land, tenements, rent, services and reversions in Salisbury to the use of Edith New and Walter Messenger. Seals: John's and the mayoral seal of the city

2346 By his charter John Swift, ironmonger, a citizen of Salisbury, granted to John Machin, weaver, and his wife Alice a tenement, which he lately acquired from William Horsebridge and his wife Cecily, the relict of John Purdy, in Endless Street between a tenement of late that of John Newman, hatter, on the south side and a tenement of late Robert Arnold's, now Peter Daw's, on the north side. The tenement is to be held for ever by John and Alice and John's heirs and assigns. Clause of warranty. Seals: John Swift's and the common and mayoral seals of the city. Named witnesses: the bailiff, the mayor, the reeves, Walter Shirley, William Warin, Thomas Mason, Edward Frith, Richard Gage, and the clerk

25 May 1418, at Salisbury

2347 By their indented charter Edward Furmage [?*otherwise* Cheese: *cf.* **1522**] and his wife Agnes granted to John Lush, of Upton, a corner tenement called Cheese Corner, with a cellar, a shop (*or* shops), and a sollar (*or* sollars), and with a shop, beside the cellar on the north side of it and beside John Camel's shop, opposite the corner tenement called Dyne's Corner, to be held for ever by them and their heirs and assigns. Clause of warranty. The grant was perfected on condition that, if Edward and Agnes, their heirs or executors, or anyone in their name within the following 30 years, in the presence of lawful men, were to pay to John Lush, his executors, or assigns the £30 formerly paid to Edward and Agnes for the tenement, it would be utterly quashed and Edward and Agnes and their heirs and assigns might re-enter on the tenement, with the cellar, shops, and sollar(s), take back possession, and keep their former estate for themselves and their heirs for ever. If Edward and Agnes or their heirs were not to pay the £30 within the 30 years the grant would keep its validity. Seals: those of the parties to the parts of the charter in turn and the common and mayoral seals of the city. Named witnesses: the bailiff, the mayor, a coroner, the reeves, Walter Shirley, William

Warin, William Bishop, Thomas Mason, William Packing, and the clerk

2348 By his deed William, a son and heir of Robert Blake and his wife Joan, a daughter of John Fosbury and his wife Agnes, a daughter and heir of Gilbert Dubber and a sister and heir of Gilbert's daughter Joan, quitclaimed to John Hain, loader, and his heirs and assigns his right or claim to a messuage, with half a yard, in Scots Lane between a messuage formerly John Russell's, now John Hain's, on the east side and a tenement of late Robert Hazelbury's, now Thomas Durnford's, on the west side; also his right or claim to the other half of the yard, which Thomas Durnford holds, beside Scots Lane between the half which John Hain held by a grant of Robert Blake and Joan, William's mother, on one side and a yard, which Richard Rivers formerly held, on the other side. Clause of warranty. Seals: William's and the common and mayoral seals of the city. Named witnesses: the bailiff, the mayor, a coroner, the reeves, Walter Shirley, William Warin, Thomas Mason, Walter Nalder, Robert Warmwell, and the clerk

2349 By their charter Alice, the relict, and an executor, of John Becket, and William Bishop, William Alexander, and Henry Man, her co-executors, on the strength of John's will granted to John Sydenham, a citizen of Salisbury, and his wife Cecily a tenement, with a small garden, and with a house, with a sollar built above it, within the tenement, in which John Hogman dwells, in Winchester Street beside a trench of running water, between a tenement of late John Becket's, which Alice holds for her life and which Nicholas Blanchard of late held, on the west side and a tenement, which John Parch holds, on the east side. The tenement was appointed by John Becket, among his other tenements, shops, and cottages, to be sold by his executors. It is to be held, with the garden and its other appurtenances, by John Sydenham and Cecily for their life, on the death of John and Cecily should remain for ever to Richard Bridge and his wife Agnes, the daughter of John and Cecily, and their joint issue, and if Richard and Agnes were to die without such issue would remain for ever to John Sydenham and his heirs and assigns. Seals: those of the grantors and the common and mayoral seals of the city. Named witnesses: the bailiff, the mayor, a coroner, the reeves, Walter Shirley, William Warin, William Dowding, Walter Nalder, Nicholas Harding, and the clerk

22 June 1418, at Salisbury

2350 By his deed Walter Nalder, a merchant, a citizen of Salisbury, quitclaimed to Edmund Purdy, weaver, and his heirs and assigns his right or claim to a tenement, in which Edmund dwells, and which he and Walter acquired jointly from John Lewisham, an executor of John Drury, of late a citizen of Salisbury, in Castle Street, beyond the bar, between John Starr's tenement on the south side and John Shipton's tenement on the north side. Seals: Walter's and the common and mayoral seals of the city. Named witnesses: the bailiff, the mayor, a coroner, the reeves, Walter Shirley, William Warin, Thomas Mason, William Fewster, John Noble, and the clerk

2351 By his charter John Shipton, dubber, granted to John Noble, a merchant, of Salisbury, and William Shilling a tenement, in which he dwelt, in Castle Street, beyond the bar, between a tenement now Edmund Purdy's on the south side and a tenement of late John Upton's on the north side, extending from the street to the river Avon. The tenement is to be held for ever by John and William and their heirs and assigns. Clause of warranty. Seals: John Shipton's and the common and mayoral seals of the city. Named witnesses: the bailiff, the mayor, a coroner, the reeves, Walter Shirley, William Warin, Thomas Mason, draper, William Fewster, Richard Gage, and the clerk

6 July 1418, at Salisbury
2352 By their charter John Cubble, of Ford, in Mottisfont parish, and William at the well, of West Tytherley, granted to William at the lea, a merchant, of Salisbury, three tenements which they acquired from John Jakes, a chaplain, and William Lord, the executors of Richard Falconer, called Leach, a citizen of Salisbury. One tenement, called Oatmeal Corner, stands opposite the cross where poultry are sold, and the other two stand conjoined in Wineman Street between William Lord's corner tenement, of late that Richard Leach's, on the east side and a tenement of late Nicholas Melbury's, now John Shad's, on the west side. The three are to be held for ever by William at the lea and his heirs and assigns. Clause of warranty. Seals: those of John Cubble and William at the well and the common and mayoral seals of the city. Named witnesses: the bailiff, the mayor, a coroner, the reeves, Walter Shirley, William Warin, William Dowding, Thomas Mason, William Tull, and the clerk
2353 By his letters of attorney John Cubble, of Ford, in Mottisfont parish, appointed Thomas Messenger and Stephen Messenger, together with William at the well, of West Tytherley, to surrender into the hand of John, the bishop of Salisbury, the seisin of a tenement called Oatmeal Corner [*as in **2352***] and of two conjoined tenements in Wineman Street [*as in **2352***] to the use of William at the lea, a merchant, a citizen of Salisbury. Seals: John Cubble's and the mayoral seal of the city

26 October 1418, at Salisbury
2354 Approval of the will of Laurence Lane, a citizen of Salisbury, made on 14 March 1415. <u>Interment</u>: in St. Thomas's church, in the nave, opposite the cross. <u>Bequests</u>: 6s. 8d. to the fabric of that church so that his body might rest there, and 4d. to each chaplain to pray for his soul and to be present at his funeral rites and mass and the bearing of his corpse to the church; 2d. to each Franciscan friar of Salisbury and to each Dominican friar of Fisherton to be present likewise; there should be 12 candles, each weighing 1 lb., burned around his corpse during his funeral rites and mass; 12d. to the fabric of the cathedral church; a new tunic lined with blanket cloth to Thomas Young, tucker; all his other clothes and utensils should be handed out among his poor kinsmen; the rest of his goods, after an inventory was made of them, to his wife Margaret on condition that she would pay £20 for them, for which she should give security to his other executors; the £20 should be handed out at all events among his poor kinsman on behalf of his soul at the discretion of his executors; 20s. each to John Downton, draper, and

Thomas Biston, his executors. <u>Devises</u>: a tenement in Brown Street, between a tenement of late Thomas Bridgehampton's on the south side and a tenement of the scholars of de Vaux college on the north side, which he acquired from John Chandler and in which his wife Margaret held an estate for life, should, after Margaret's death, be divided into two parts by good and lawful men. Laurence appointed one half to an elder John Hurst, of Fordingbridge parish, his kinsman, to be held for ever by him and his issue. If John were to die without issue that half would remain for ever to the nearest heir of his blood and to his heirs, and so from blood on to blood. He appointed the other half to Laurence and Thomas, sons of William Glover, of Downton, kinsmen of Laurence Lane's wife, to be held for ever by them and the issue of them and either of them. If Laurence and Thomas, and the one of them living longer, were to die without issue that half would remain for ever to the nearest heir of their blood, and the blood of the one of them living longer, and so from blood on to blood without any right of sale or alienation. <u>Executors</u>: his wife Margaret, John Downton, and Thomas Biston. <u>Proved</u> on 3 April 1415 in front of John Hulling, the subdean; the administration was entrusted to the executors. <u>Approved</u> at a court held in front of the bailiff, the mayor, and other citizens; the seisin of the tenement was released to John Hurst and Thomas, a son of William Glover, of Downton, Thomas's brother Laurence being dead.

9 November 1418, at Salisbury
2355 Approval of the will of John Huish, weaver, of Salisbury, made on 15 August 1418. <u>Interment</u>: in the graveyard of St. Edmund's church, beside his daughter's grave. <u>Bequests</u>: 12*d.* to the fabric of that church, a trental to the provost to celebrate mass on behalf of his soul, and a trental to Henry [Clere], the parochial chaplain; 4*d.* to the fabric of the cathedral church; the rest of his goods to his executors to be laid out, in the way described below, on behalf of his soul. <u>Devise</u>: to his wife Agnes for life a tenement in Mealmonger Street between John Breamore's tenement on the north side and William Needler's tenement on the south side. After Agnes's death the tenement should be sold by John's executors or, if Agnes would be satisfied that it should be sold immediately after John's death, the reversion should be sold by the executors, with their unanimous assent and not otherwise. The money received from the sale should be laid out, on giving alms and doing various charitable deeds, on behalf of John's soul and the souls of others. <u>Executors</u>: his wife Agnes and William Mead. <u>Proved</u> on 7 November 1418 in front of John Pedwell, the subdean; the administration was entrusted to the executor, who then came before the subdean and were dismissed. <u>Approved</u> at a court held in front of the bailiff, the mayor, and other citizens; the ordering of the seisin of the tenement to Agnes was adjourned because she showed by a deed that she held an estate for her life in it on the strength of the acquisition by John, so that she was jointly enfeoffed with him.

23 November 1418, at Salisbury
2356 By their writing William Clark, fuller, and his wife Agnes, the relict of John

Huish, weaver, granted to John Machin, weaver, the estate which Agnes held for her life, on the strength of an acquisition by John Huish, in a tenement in Culver Street or Mealmonger Street between William Needler's tenement on the south side and John Breamore's tenement on the north side. The tenement, and Agnes's estate, are to be held, according to the terms of the acquisition, by John Machin and his heirs and assigns. Seals: those of William and Agnes and the common and mayoral seals of the city. Named witnesses: the bailiff, the mayor, the coroners, the reeves, William Warin, William Bishop, Nicholas Harding, Walter Nalder, William Tull, and the clerk

2357 By their deed John Vincent, weaver, and his wife Edith, a kinswoman of the late William Ashley, a chaplain, quitclaimed to Walter Shirley and Nicholas Harding, citizens of Salisbury, and their heirs and assigns the right or claim which they, or Edith, might have on the strength of William's will or otherwise to a tenement, in which Walter and Nicholas are enfeoffed and in which Robert Hindon of late dwelt, in St. Martin's Street between Thomas Bridgehampton's tenement on the west side and a shop or cottage of Walter and Nicholas on the east side. Seals: those of John and Edith and the common and mayoral seals of the city. Named witnesses: the bailiff, the mayor, the coroners, the reeves, William Warin, William Bishop, Thomas Mason, William Dowding, Robert Warmwell, and William Tull

7 December 1418, at Salisbury
2358 A deed of William Clark, fuller, and his wife Agnes, the relict, and an executor, of John Huish, weaver, and William Mead, Agnes's co-executor. In his will John appointed a tenement in Culver Street or Mealmonger Street [*as in **2356**] to be sold by his executors. The money received from the sale should be laid out by the executors on behalf of his soul and the souls of others mentioned in his will. John Machin, weaver, has paid a sum of money to have the reversion of the tenement for himself and his heirs for ever, of late he acquired the estate which Agnes held for her life in the tenement, and he stands possessed of it. By their deed William Clark and Agnes, and William Mead, on the strength of John Huish's will granted to John Machin the tenement and the reversion, to be held for ever by him and his heirs and assigns. Seals: those of the grantors and the common and mayoral seals of the city. Named witnesses: the bailiff, the mayor, the coroners, the reeves, Walter Shirley, William Warin, William Bishop, Walter Nalder, Robert Warmwell, and the clerk

21 December 1418, at Salisbury
2359 By his charter John Machin, weeaver, granted to William Clark, fuller, and his wife Agnes a tenement, which was of late that of John Huish, weaver, in Culver Street or Mealmonger Stret [*as in **2356**]. The tenement was acquired by John from John Huish's executors and is to be held for ever by William and Agnes and William's heirs and assigns. Seals: John's and the common and mayoral seals of the city. Named witnesses: the bailiff, the mayor, the coroners, the reeves, Walter Shirley, William Warin, Thomas Mason, Thomas Bower, and the clerk

2360 By his deed John, a son of John Forest, of late a citizen of Salisbury, quitclaimed to Nicholas Harding, a citizen of Salisbury, and his heirs and assigns his right or claim to a tenement, with a garden, in which he dwells and in which his father of late dwelt, in Wineman Street between a tenement of John Hain, loader, on the west side and cottage property of late John Prentice's, now William Penton's, on the east side. The younger John Forest acquired the tenement from Nicholas and from Robert Forest, now dead, on a condition, not complied with, that various sums of money were paid, for the lack of which payment Nicholas has the right to re-enter on the tenement and take back possession. Clause of warranty. Seals: John Forest's and the common and mayoral seals of the city. Named witnesses: the bailiff, the mayor, the coroners, the reeves, Walter Shirley, William Warin, William Bishop, Thomas Mason, Robert Warmwell, and the clerk

4 January 1419
2361 By his charter Nicholas Harding, a citizen of Salisbury, granted to John Forest, weaver, of Salisbury, and his wife Agnes a tenement, in which John and Agnes dwell and which Nicholas held by John's grant, in Wineman Street, [*as in 2360*], to be held for ever by John and Agnes and their heirs and assigns. Seals: Nicholas's and the common and mayoral seals of the city. Named witnesses: the bailiff, the mayor, the coroners, the reeves, William Warin, William Dowding, Thomas Mason, William Tull, Thomas Bower, and the clerk
2362 By his letters of attorney Nicholas Harding, a citizen of Salisbury, appointed Stephen Edington and Walter Short to surrender into the hand of John, the bishop of Salisbury, the seisin of a tenement in Wineman Street [*as in 2360*] to the use of John Forest, weaver, and his wife Agnes. Seals: Nicholas's and the mayoral seal of the city

18 January 1419, at Salisbury
2363 By their indented deed Walter Shirley, Thomas Mason, draper, and John Swift, ironmonger, citizens of Salisbury, and Henry Warin, a chaplain, granted to Richard Gater, fuller, a corner tenement, with an adjacent yard (*or* adjacent yards), in Endless Street between Thomas Bleacher's tenement on the south side and Chipper Street on the north side. The tenement, with the yard(s), was of late that of John Mower, a citizen of Salisbury, and, with other land, tenements, shops, cottages, rent, and reversions in the city, was held by the grantors and William Walter, now dead, by a grant of John Mower. It extends in length from Endless Street as far as Brown Street. It is to be held, with the yard(s), for ever by Richard and his heirs and assigns on condition that, if he, his executors, or anyone in his name were to pay to William Warin, a citizen of Salisbury, or to the grantors, any one of them, or their assigns, in the following four years £20 cash a year, £10 on 24 June and £10 at Christmas or within 15 days of each date, the charter would keep its validity. Clause to permit permanent repossession if a payment were defaulted on. Seals: those of the parties to the parts of the deed in turn and the common and mayoral seals of the city. Named witnesses: the bailiff,

the mayor, a coroner, the reeves, William Bishop, William Dowding, Walter
Nalder, Robert Warmwell, Henry Man, and the clerk

2364 An indented deed of William Needler, a citizen of Salisbury, and his wife
Isabel, the relict, and an executor, of John Castleton, of late a citizen of Salisbury.
John devised to Isabel and her heirs and assigns for ever rent of 4s. a year issuing
from two cottages, of late those of Robert Bowyer, weaver, in Culver Street
between cottage property of late Gilbert Oword's on the north side and cottage
property of late John Mower's on the south side. John devised to Isabel for life
a tenement, with a shop (*or* shops), a cellar (*or* cellars), and a garden in Carter
Street, in which John then dwelt, between William Tull's tenement on the south
side and John Sampson's tenement on the north side. He appointed the tenement,
and the reversion of two cottages, with gardens, in New Street, beside the city's
ditch, on the north side of the street, when it fell due on the death of John, a
son of a younger Thomas Castleton, to be sold by his executors on Isabel's death.
The money received from the sale should be laid out on behalf of his soul and
the souls of others mentioned by him. John appointed that his executors should
enfeoff Thomas, his father, and Thomas's heirs and assigns for ever in a [corner]
tenement, of late Thomas Focket's, in St. Martin's Street, between a tenement,
then William Sall's, beside a trench on the west [?*rectius* south: *cf.* ***2236***] side and
a tenement, then William Walter's, on the east side, on condition that Thomas
would pay £14 cash to the executors. He also appointed that Thomas and his
heirs and assigns should hold for ever a feoffment perfected by Isabel and other
feoffors of 21 acres, of late Thomas Focket's, in the fields of Stratford, near Old
Sarum castle. In Hilary term 1419 Isabel and William, in the king's court, levied
a fine by which they acknowledged the right of Thomas to the tenement and its
appurtenances, by the name of four messuages, [21 acres, and rent of 4s.: *Feet of
Fines 1377–1509* (WRS xli, p. 80)], as that which the elder Thomas and William
Bishop held by their gift. By their deed, therefore, William and Isabel, she as an
executor of John Castleton, granted to Thomas Castleton and William Bishop,
citizens of Salisbury, all the land and tenements, with the shops, cottages, gardens,
rent, and reversions mentioned above, and Isabel's estate in them, to be held for
ever by them and their heirs and assigns, to whom William and Isabel quitclaimed
their right or claim, or Isabel's right or claim, to them. Seals: those of William
and Isabel to the part of the deed in the possession of Thomas and William,
those of Thomas and William to the part in the possession of William and Isabel,
and the common and mayoral seals of the city to both parts. Named witnesses:
the bailiff, the mayor, the coroners, the reeves, Walter Shirley, William Warin,
William Dowding, Walter Nalder, and the clerk

1 February 1419, at Salisbury

2365 A deed of William Bailiff, called Weston, and William at the lea, executors
of Margaret Godmanstone, the relict of William Godmanstone, a citizen of
Salisbury. In general words in her will Margaret appointed all her land, tenements,
shops, cottages, gardens, yards, rent, and reversions in the city, with the exception
of one cottage, to be sold by her executors after her death when it could be done

advantageously. Two of the cottages stand conjoined, with a yard, in Brown Street or Rolleston between cottage property of late Richard Spencer's, now William Cambridge's, on the south side and a yard of the provost of St. Edmund's church, on a corner beside the way which leads towards that church, on the north side; the yard extends in length as far as John Judd's yard opposite the church's graveyard. John Hain, loader, has paid a sum of money to the executors for the cottages, with the yard, to be held by him, and the executors, with their unanimous assent and on the strength of Margaret's will, granted them to him to be held for ever by him and his heirs and assigns as that which he bought from them in good faith to fulfil the will. Seals: those of William Bailiff and William at the lea and the common and mayoral seals of the city. Named witnesses: the bailiff, the mayor, the coroners, the reeves, Walter Shirley, William Warin, Thomas Mason, draper, Robert Warmwell, Thomas Bower, and the clerk

2366 By his letters of attorney William at the lea, an executor of Margaret Godmanstone, the relict of William Godmanstone, of late a citizen of Salisbury, appointed John Jakes, a chaplain, or Stephen Edington to surrender, with William Bailiff, called Weston, his co-executor, into the hand of John, the bishop of Salisbury, the seisin of two conjoined cottages, with a yard, in Brown Street, called Rolleston, [as in **2365**], to the use of John Hain, loader. Seals: that of William at the lea and the mayoral seal of the city

2367 By his deed William Shilling quitclaimed to John Noble, a citizen of Salisbury, and his heirs and assigns his right or claim to a tenement, with a garden, which he and John held jointly by a grant of John Shipton, dubber, in Castle Street, beyond the bars, between Edmund Purdy's tenement on the south side and Gunnore Bowyer's tenement on the north side. Seals: William's and the common and mayoral seals of the city. Named witnesses: the bailiff, the mayor, the coroners, the reeves, William Warin, Thomas Mason, Robert Warmwell, William Fewster, and the clerk

15 February 1419, at Salisbury

2368 By his deed Laurence Drew, weaver, quitclaimed to John Noble, a citizen of Salisbury, and his heirs and assigns his right or claim to a tenement, with a garden, of late that of John Shipton, dubber, which John Noble and William Shilling of late held by John Shipton's grant, in Castle Street, beyond the bars, [as in **2367**]. Seals: Laurence's and the common and mayoral seals of the city. Named witnesses: the bailiff, the mayor, the coroners, the reeves, Walter Shirley, William Warin, Thomas Mason, William Fewster, Richard Gage, and the clerk

2369 By his charter William Packing, of Crawley, granted to Thomas Randolph, of Salisbury, and his wife Alice a corner tenement, and all his other land, tenements, shops, cottages, gardens, yards, rent, and reversions in the city, in Endless Street and Chipper Street [Chipper Lane *in* **2572**], between Peter Daw's tenement in Endless Street on the north side and John Parch's tenement in Chipper Street on the east side, to be held for ever by Thomas and Alice and their heirs and assigns. Clause of warranty. Seals: William's and the common and mayoral seals of the city. Named witnesses: the bailiff, the mayor, the coroners, the reeves, Walter Shirley,

William Warin, William Bishop, William Dowding, and the clerk. [cf. *2572*]

29 March 1419, at Salisbury
2370 A deed of John Jakes, a clerk, and William Lord, the executors of Richard Falconer, called Leach. In his will Richard appointed, after the death of his wife Alice, a cottage, with a yard (*or* yards), to be held for life by Gillian, his servant. The cottage stands in Culver Street, which is called Mealmonger Street, between cottages of late David Fletcher's, afterwards William Coventry's, and now those of Henry Harborough, a clerk, on the north side and cottage property of late Robert Ashley's, which Thomas Randolph now holds, on the south side. On Gillian's death it should remain to the executors to be sold. The money received from the sale should be laid out on behalf of Richard's soul. Because it is well known to John and William that John Collingbourne, fuller, acquired for himself from Gillian her estate in the cottage, with the yard (s), wishing to acquire from them the reversion of it for his estate, and because they were willing to sell the reversion to him for a sum of money paid to them, by their deed they, on the strength of Richard's will, granted to him the reversion, when it fell due, to be held for ever by him and his heirs and assigns. John and William quitclaimed to John Collingbourne and his heirs and assigns their right or claim to the cottage, with the yard(s), on the strength of the will or otherwise. Seals: those of John and William and the common and mayoral seals of the city. Named witnesses: the bailiff, the mayor, the coroners, the reeves, Walter Shirley, William Warin, William Dowding, Thomas Mason, and the clerk

12 April 1419, at Salisbury
2371 By his deed William Weston, called Bailiff, an executor of Margaret Godmanstone, the relict of William Godmanstone, a citzen of Salisbury, granted to Gilbert Tanner and his wife Marion a rent of 13*s*. 4*d*. a year issuing from a corner tenement or cottage, with a portion of land for a garden, which John Mason, weaver, and his wife Alice hold for their life by Margaret's grant, in Brown Street between another tenement or cottage of late Margaret's beside it on the south side and the street of Chipper Street, called Shit Lane, on the north side, with the reversion of the tenement or cottage, and the portion of land, when it fell due on the death of John and Alice; also the reversion of another tenement or cottage, with adjacent land appointed to it for a garden, which Edith, of late a servant of Margaret and now the wife of John Goss, and her daughter Alice hold for their life by Margaret's devise, beside, and on the south side of, the tenement or cottage mentioned above; also three conjoined cottages, with a yard (*or* yards) and racks, in Gigant Street, on a corner, opposite cottages of late those of William Buck, a chaplain, between William Hoare's yard on the south side and the street of Chipper Street, called Shit Lane, on the north side, and extending from Gigant Street as far as the tenement or cottage in Brown Street mentioned above. All those premises, the rent, and the reversion, with other land, premises, rent, and reversions, were appointed by Margaret to be sold by her executors and are to be held for ever by Gilbert and Marion and their heirs and assigns as that which they

bought in good faith from William Weston, the executor. Seals: William Weston's and the common and mayoral seals of the city. Named witnesses: the bailiff, the mayor, the coroners, the reeves, Walter Shirley, William Bishop, William Dowding, Thomas Mason, and the clerk

2372 By his deed John, the bishop of Salisbury, granted to William Hendy, Laurence Groom, Hugh Read, and Richard Tidling, chaplains, a tenement or messuage containing five conjoined dwelling houses, which he, under the name of John Chandler, the dean of Salisbury, and Richard Holhurst, a clerk, now dead, held by a grant of John Westbury, William Lord, and Thomas Dearing, executors of a younger John Chaplin. The messuage stands in New Street and Brown Street, on a corner, between a tenement of Joan, the relict of William River, in Brown Street on the south side and the trench of water running through the hospital of the Holy Trinity, called Almshouse, in New Street on the east side, and is to be held for ever by the grantees and their heirs and assigns. Seals: the bishop's and the common and mayoral seals of the city. Named witnesses: the bailiff, the mayor, the coroners, the reeves, Walter Shirley, William Warin, William Bishop, William Dowding, Thomas Mason, draper, and the clerk

18 April 1419, at Salisbury

2373 By his letters of attorney John, the bishop of Salisbury, appointed Gilbert Marshall, William Chandler, and Stephen Edington to deliver to William Hendy, Laurence Groom, Hugh Read, and Richard Tidling, chaplains, the seisin of a tenement or messuage, containing five dwelling house, in New Street and Brown Street [*as in 2372*]. Seal: the bishop's

26 April 1419, at Salisbury

2374 By his charter John Bodenham, a merchant, a citizen of Salisbury, granted to Richard Forster, of Stanton Drew, a tenement or messuage, of late Margaret Godmanstone's, and, conjoined, a tenement (*or* tenements), a shop (*or* shops), and a cottage (*or* cottages) adjacent to it, in Winchester Street, above the ditch, between Laurence Gowan's tenement on the west side and John Wishford's tenement, which Walter Sergeant holds, on the east side. The tenement or messuage, with the tenement(s), shop(s), and cottage(s), was acquired by John Bodenham from William Walter, John Lake, John Smith, a chaplain, and John Pilk, of Beckington, executors of Thomas Child, of late a citizen of Salisbury, and is to be held for ever by Richard Forster and his heirs and assigns. Clause of warranty. Seals: John Bodenham's and the common and mayoral seals of the city. Named witnesses: the bailiff, the mayor, the coroners, the reeves, Walter Shirley, William Warin, William Bishop, Thomas Mason, draper, Robert Warmwell, and the clerk

2375 By their charter John Bodenham, a citizen of Salisbury, and his wife Joan granted to Richard Gater, fuller, conjoined cottages, with a yard (*or* yards), vacant ground, and a portion of meadow, in Drake Hall Street between meadow or a yard, which Nicholas Melbury of late held, on the north side and a meadow of late Roger Upton's on the south side. The cottages, with the yard(s), ground, and meadow, were acquired by John and Joan from John 'Shorberd', carpenter, that John held them by a feoffment of James Green, a chaplain, James held them by a grant of Maud, the relict of William Guys, and they are to be held for ever by Richard and his heirs and assigns. Clause of warranty. Seals: those of John and Joan and the common and mayoral seals of the city. Named witnesses: the bailiff, the mayor, the coroners, the reeves, Walter Shirley, William Warin, Thomas Mason, draper, John Bromley, and the clerk

2376 By his deed William Bishop, a citizen of Salisbury, quitclaimed to William Warin, a citizen of Salisbury, and his heirs and assigns his right or claim to tenements, shops, cottages, and yards, of late those of John Thorburn, called Taylor, which Richard Spencer and William Walter, both now dead, William Warin, and he jointly acquired from John Cary. The premises stand conjoined in Winchester Street and Brown Street, on a corner, between a tenement of late William Hoare's in Winchester Street on the west side and a tenement of the dean and chapter of Salisbury in Brown Street on the north side. Seals: William Bishop's and the common and mayoral seals of the city. Named witnesses: the bailiff, the mayor, the coroners, the reeves, Walter Shirley, Walter Nalder, Thomas Mason, draper, Nicholas Harding, Robert Warmwell, and the clerk

10 May 1419, at Salisbury

2377 By his deed Henry Man, a citizen of Salisbury, quitclaimed to Richard Forster, of Stanton Drew, and his heirs and assigns his right or claim to a tenement or messuage with, conjoined, a shop (*or* shops) and a cottage (*or* cottages), of late Margaret Godmanstone's, in Winchester Street [*as in* **2374**], which Richard acquired from John Bodenham, a merchant, a citizen of Salisbury. Seals: Henry's and the common and mayoral seals of the city. Named witnesses: the bailiff, the mayor, the coroners, the reeves, Walter Shirley, William Warin, Walter Nalder, Thomas Mason, Robert Warmwell, and the clerk

2378 By his charter John Hain, loader, granted to John Judd, a citizen of Salisbury, and his wife Gillian two conjoined cottages, with a yard (*or* yards), which he acquired from William Bailiff and William at the lea, executors of Margaret Godmanstone, in Brown Street or Rolleston [*as in* **2365**], to be held for ever by John Judd and Gillian and John's heirs and assigns. Seals: John Hain's and the common and mayoral seals of the city. Named witnesses: the bailiff, the mayor, a coroner, the reeves, Walter Shirley, William Warin, William Bishop, Walter Nalder, Henry Man, and the clerk

2379 Approval of the will of William at the lea, fishmonger, of Salisbury, made on 22 December 1418. <u>Interment</u>: in St. Thomas's church according to the order of his executors. <u>Bequests</u>: 6*s*. 8*d*. to the fabric of the cathedral church; 13*s*. 4*d*. to the fabric of St. Thomas's church, 20*s*. to the rector for his forgotten tithes and lesser benefactions, 40*d*. to the parochial chaplain to pray for his soul, 6*d*. to each other chaplain present at his funeral rites and mass on the day of his burial, and 6*d*. each to the deacon and the sacristan; 40*d*. to the fabric of St. Edmund's church; 20*d*. to the fabric of St. Martin's church; 6*s*. 8*d*. both to the Franciscans of Salisbury and the Dominicans of Fisherton if they were to be present at his funeral rites and mass on the day of his burial; 6s. 8d. to the fabric of the church of Bramshaw; from the day of his death to the day of his anniversary 100s. should be handed out among paupers by his executors; 5 candles each weighing 3 lb. should be burned around his corpse on the day of his burial; 12 paupers should be clothed in white cloth to pray for his soul; 20s. to William Bailiff; a swaged piece [?of silver] to his daughter Margaret; £10, or the value at the discretion of his executors, to Christine, his servant, for her marriage, and 100s. or the value of it to Emme, his kinswoman, for her marriage, and William wished that Christine and Emme should serve his wife Christine until their marriage, otherwise they would not have their legacy; 10s. to Edith, his servant, appointed to her by his mother, 10s. so that she might pray for his soul, and cloth so that she could have a gown from it; cloth of Bruton russet sufficient for a gown to be made and 3s. 4d. to each of Maud and Rose, his sisters; his best gown, of the style of Salisbury, to William Well, his brother; he remitted to John Cross, his servant, the debt which he owes to him, and bequeathed to him a tunic which William himself used; his daughter Margaret should be content with £20 for her share received from the rest of his goods, should not demand more from his executors, and should not implead the executors, or any one of them, on account of her share, and if she did demand more than the £20, or implead or trouble the executors on any pretext, the executors might immediately enter on a tenement devised to her (viz. that which William acquired from Placid Day), sell it, and lay out the money issuing from the sale on pious uses for the salvation of William's soul; of the rest of his goods one part to his executors to be laid out with all speed on the salvation of his soul, the other part to his wife Christine to pray for his soul. Devises: to Christine a tenement, in which he dwelt, in Winchester Street between a tenement of late John Knottingley's on the east side and Robert Ashley's tenement on the west side, to be held for ever by her and her heirs and assigns; also to Christine two tenements, one in Wineman Street between John Collingbourne's tenement on the west side and William Lord's corner tenement on the east side, and the other at the end of Pot Row where vegetables and the flour of oats are sold, to be held for ever by her and her heirs and assigns. William devised to his daughter Margaret a tenement in Winchester Street between Richard Inkpen's corner tenement on the east side and a tenement of late John Knottingley's on the west side, to be held for ever by her and her heirs and assigns as fully as William acquired it from Placid Day; William wished that John Eastbury and his wife Amice should enjoy the estate for a term of seven years perfected for them by him. William devised to Christine for life a messuage, which he acquired from Thomas Bleacher, in New Street between a tenement of Nicholas Brown, a clerk, on the west side and John Sydenham's tenement on the east side. He appointed it on Christine's death to Margaret and her issue, and if Margaret were to die without issue it should be sold by his executors, if they were both living, or by the one of them living longer. The money issuing from the sale should be laid out on pious uses for the salvation of William's soul. If Margaret were to die without issue and both William's executors were then dead the messuage should be entered on by him who was the nearest heir of William's blood and held for ever by him and his issue, and so for ever from direct heir to direct heir of William's blood. Executors: his wife Christine and Thomas Messenger, to whom he bequeathed 60s. and a gown with a cloak. Proved on 17 February 1419 at London in front of John Estcourt, B.L., a general examiner of the court of Canterbury and a general commissary of Henry [Chichele], the archbishop of Canterbury; the administration was entrusted to the executors. Approved at a court held in front of the bailiff, the mayor, and other citizens; the seisin of the tenements and of the messuage was released to the legatee.

24 May 1419, at Salisbury
2380 By his charter John Wishford, a citizen of Salisbury, granted to Robert Gilbert, tanner, a citizen of Salisbury, a tenement, in which Robert of late dwelt, in Endless Street, between Edward Frith's tenement on the north side and a tenement of the chapter of choristers (*capituli cantar'*), of late Reynold Tidworth's, on the south side, to be held for ever by him and his heirs and assigns. Clause of warranty. Seals: John's and common and mayoral seals of the city. Named witnesses: the bailiff, the mayor, the coroners, a reeve, Walter Shirley, William Warin, William Bishop, Thomas Mason, draper, Richard Coof, and the clerk
2381 By his deed an elder John Pilk, of Beckington, an executor of Thomas Child, of late a citizen of Salisbury, on the strength of Thomas's will granted to Joan, a daughter of Alice Nutkin, of Salisbury, a tenement, with an adjacent cellar, in Pot Row between a tenement of late Nicholas Longstock's on the east side and shop property of late Thomas Stabber's on the west side. The tenement was appointed by Thomas Child to be sold after the death of his wife Isabel, now dead, by John and his other executors, now dead, and, with the cellar, is to be held for ever by Joan and her issue. If Joan were to die without issue it would remain for ever to Laurence Groom, a chaplain, her brother, and his heirs and assigns. Seals: John Pilk's and the common and mayoral seals of the city. Named witnesses: the bailiff, the mayor, the coroners, the reeves, Walter Shirley, William Warin, Thomas Mason, draper, Robert Warmwell, and the clerk
2382 By his indented charter John Wishford, a citizen of Salisbury, granted to Stephen Hart, weaver, tenements and messuages, with gardens, which he acquired from Edward Elion and Thomas Marlborough, executors of Joan, the relict, and an executor, of William Wootton, of late a citizen of Salisbury, in Nuggeston, on a corner opposite a croft, in Mealmonger Street, and extending as far as the street opposite the graveyard of St. Edmund's church *cf.* **2611**]. The premises are to be held for ever by Stephen and his heirs and assigns for a yearly rent of 38s. cash to be paid to John and his heirs and assigns for each of the following 20 years. For the 20 years Stephen and his heirs and assigns should maintain the premises in all things necessary at their own expense, without causing any destruction in that period, so that the rent would not be lost. Clause to permit permanent repossession if the rent were to be in arrear for 15 days or damage were done; alternatively, if John Wishford and his heirs and assigns were to prefer, to permit re-entry, distraint, and the keeping of distresses until the unpaid rent and other losses were recovered. Clause of warranty. Seals: those of the parties to the parts

of the charter in turn and the common and mayoral seals of the city. Named witnesses: the bailiff, the mayor, the coroners, the reeves, Walter Shirley, William Bishop, Thomas Mason, Robert Warmwell, Richard Gage, and the clerk

2383 By his deed Thomas Messenger, fuller, quitclaimed to Margaret, the wife of John Wylye, mercer, a daughter of William at the lea, of late a citizen of Salisbury, and her heirs and assigns his right or claim to a tenement, with a kitchen, a brewery, and a shop, extending to Carter Street, which Margaret holds in fee simple by William's devise. The tenement stands in Winchester Street, above the ditch, between Richard Inkpen's corner tenement, which William Chandler holds, on the east side and Reynold Barentine's tenement on the west side. Seals: Thomas's and the common and mayoral seals of the city. Named witnesses: the bailiff, the mayor, the coroners, the reeves, Walter Shirley, William Warin, Thomas Mason, draper, Walter Nalder, Henry Man, and the clerk

7 June 1419, at Salisbury

2384 Approval of the will of Thomas Hawes, a chaplain, made on 26 May 1419. Interment: in the chancel of St. Martin's church. Bequests: a silver spoon to the fabric of the cathedral church; a best brass pot to the fabric of St. Martin's church, a brass pot to the fraternity of the Holy Ghost in that church, a bow and 24 arrows to the deacon, a pickaxe, [and] a spade to the sacristan, and a green belt harnessed with the letters T to the light of St. Nicholas in that church; a silver spoon to John Went, a chaplain, to pray for his soul; a silver spoon to William Westage, a chaplain; a harnessed belt, two pieces of silver, and two mazers, which he has from Thomas, to William Spicer, a chaplain, to pray for his soul, and William might take back from Thomas's executors the porteous and missal which Thomas bought from him; a manual which begins *Bilexi* to the lord John Conge to pray for his soul; a processional to Thomas Read for the time in which he dwelt in St. Martin's parish, so that it should remain in St. Martin's church for pronouncing divine service to the parishioners; a porteous to John Dinton, a chaplain, so that he might pray for Thomas's soul and pay 26s. 8d. to his executors; Thomas remits to William Roope and his wife Agnes the rent which they owe to him; he remits to William Woodham 40d. of the rent which he owes to him; he gives to Edith Breamore 20d. of the rent of the term of the Nativity of St. John the Baptist; 2s. 6d. and a piece of iron called Baking iron to the Franciscans of Salisbury; 2s. 6d. to the Dominicans of Fisherton; a tablecloth and 6s. 8d. to Walter Nalder; 4d. to each chaplain of St. Thomas's church so that on the day of his burial they might recite funeral rites and a mass on behalf of his soul, and there should be no ringing; 4d. to each chaplain of St. Edmund's church and each *annilari* present at his funeral rites and mass on the day of his burial; the rest of his goods to his executors to be laid out on behalf of his soul and the souls of others. Devises: to Margaret Baker, his servant, for her life a cottage, with a garden attached to it, with free ingress and egress in respect of a latrine and water within that cottage and other of his cottages there. Thomas dwelt in the cottage, which stands in the street on the way to St. Martin's church, adjoining Thomas Glover's cottage, on the east side of two other cottages of Thomas's own. Thomas devised to Thomas

Blackmoor, his godson, to pray for his soul and for his maintrenance at school, the two other cottages, with a garden (*or* gardens) attached to them, in the street on the way to St. Martin's church, between the cottage devised to Margaret on the east side and William Harnhill's cottages on the north side. The cottages are to be held by Thomas for his life, rendering whatever rent, charges, and service is due to the chief lords and others in respect of all three cottages. Whoever of Margaret and Thomas Blackmoor were to live the longer should hold the three cottages for life. The three cottages immediately after the death of Margaret and Thomas, or the reversion of them in their lifetime if that were advantageous, should be sold by Thomas Hawes's executors. The money received from the sale should be laid out on pious uses for the salvation of his soul. Thomas appointed five conjoined cottages in St. Martin's Street, between Thomas Castleton's corner tenement on the west side and William Phebis's cottage property on the east side, to be sold by his executors. With the money received from the sale a chaplain should be appointed by his executors to celebrate divine service in St. Martin's church on behalf of the souls of his father Richard Hawes and his mother Alice and of his own soul for as long as the money might last. The chaplain should take possession of Thomas's vestments, chalice, and adornments in the time of his celebration, with the box in which they were kept. After the chaplain shall have completed the celebration of divine service Thomas bequeathed the box to Thomas Blackmoor, and appointed that the chaplain should celebrate divine service on behalf of Thomas Hawes's soul as long as the vestments, chalice, and adornments might last (*attingere*). <u>Executors:</u> Walter Nalder and Henry Blackmoor. <u>Proved</u> on 5 June 1419 in front of John Pedwell, the subdean; the administration was entrusted to the executors, who afterwards appeared, accounted with the subdean, and were dismissed. <u>Approved</u> at a court held in front of the bailiff, the mayor, and other citizens; the seisin of the cottages was released to the legatees.

2385 By his charter Thomas Bleacher, called Clark, ironmonger, of Salisbury, granted to Richard Gage and John Judd, citizens of Salisbury, a tenement, with shops and a gate, in which he dwelt, in Endless Street between a tenement of late John Mower's, now Richard Gater's, on the north side and a tenement of late Thomas Chancellor's, which Thomas Abbott now holds, on the south side. The tenement extends to Brown Street, where the gate stands between the same tenement of late John Mower's on the north side and a tenement of late Henry Popham's on the south side, and, with the shops and gate, was of late that of William Boyland, a citizen of Salisbury. It is to be held, with the shops and gate, for ever by Richard Gage and John Judd and their heirs and assigns. Clause of warranty. Seals: that of Thomas Bleacher, called Clark, and the common and mayoral seals of the city. Named witnesses: the bailiff, the mayor, a coroner, the reeves, Walter Shirley, William Warin, William Bishop, Thomas Mason, Robert Warmwell, and the clerk

21 June 1419, at Salisbury

2386 By his charter William Bishop, a merchant, a citizen of Salisbury, granted to William Warin, grocer, a citizen of Salisbury, and William Marnhill, a clerk, a tenement, with a garden at the end of it and three walls inclosing the garden, in which he dwells, in Winchester Street, above the ditch, between a tenement of late Thomas Knoyle's on the east side and a tenement, called the New Inn, of late William Ashton's on the west side. The garden, with the walls, lies between the gardens of those bordering tenements on the east and west, and on the south of it lies the garden of a tenement of late John Beacock's. The tenement, with the garden and walls, is to be held for ever by William Warin and William Marnhill and their heirs and assigns. Clause of warranty. Seals: William Bishop's and the common and mayoral seals of the city. Named witnesses: the bailiff, the mayor, the coroners, the reeves, Walter Shirley, Thomas Mason, Walter Nalder, Nicholas Harding, Robert Warmwell, and the clerk

5 July 1419, at Salisbury
2387 By their deed Walter Nalder and Henry Blackmoor, the executors of Thomas Hawes, a chaplain, on the strength of Thomas's will granted to Robert Gilbert, tanner, five conjoined cottages in St. Martin's Street between Thomas Castleton's corner tenement on the west side and William Phebis's cottage property on the east side. The cottages were appointed by Thomas to be sold by his executors, and they are to be held for ever by Robert and his heirs and assigns as that which Robert finally bought from the executors for a sum of money to be laid out by them according to Thomas's will. Seals: those of Walter and Henry and the common and mayoral seals of the city. Named witnesses: the bailiff, the mayor, the coroners, a reeve, Walter Shirley, William Warin, William Bishop, Thomas Mason, John Bromley, and the clerk
2388 By their charter John Wylye, mercer, and his wife Margaret, a daughter of William at the lea, of late a citizen of Salisbury, appearing in court, granted to Thomas Messenger, fuller, and John Bonjou a tenement, with a kitchen, a brewery, and a shop, extending to Carter Sreet, in Winchester Street, above the ditch, [*as in 2383*]. The tenement, with the kitchen, the brewery, and the shop, is to be held for ever by Thomas Messenger and John Bonjou and their heirs and assigns. Clause of warranty. Seals: those of John Wylye and Margaret and the common and mayoral seals of the city. Named witnesses: the bailiff, the mayor, the coroners, the reeves, Walter Shirley, William Warin, William Bishop, Henry Man, Thomas Bower, and the clerk
2389 By their charter Thomas Messenger, fuller, and John Bonjou granted to John Wylye, mercer, and his wife Margaret, a daughter of the late William at the lea, a tenement with, adjacent, a kitchen, a brewery, and a shop, extending to Carter Street, in Winchester Street, above the ditch, [*as in 2383*]. The tenement was held by Thomas and John by a grant of John and Margaret and, with the kitchen, the brewery, and the shop, is to be held for ever by John and Margaret and their heirs and assigns. Seals: those of Thomas Messenger and John Bonjou and the common and mayoral seals of the city. Named witnesses: the bailiff, the mayor, the coroners, the reeves, Walter Shirley, William Warin, William Bishop, Thomas Mason, Henry Man, and the clerk
2390 By his charter Richard Ferrer granted to John Wishford, a citizen of

Salisbury, a corner shop or tenement, in which Richard of late dwelt and which he held by a devise of his wife Cecily, opposite the market place, at its west end, on the way to Castle Street, to be held for ever by John and his heirs and assigns. Clause of warranty. Seals: Richard's and the common and mayoral seals of the city. Named witnesses: the bailiff, the mayor, the coroners, the reeves, Walter Shirley, William Warin, Thomas Mason, Robert Warmwell, Richard Oword, and the clerk

2391 By their charter John Shad, draper, and his wife Agnes, appearing in court, granted to John Curtis, draper, cottages, with gardens, which they acquired from John Prentice, a clerk, a son of John Prentice, of late a citizen of Salisbury. The cottages stand in Culver Street, between cottage property of late Thomas Knoyle's on the north side and John Camel's cottage property, of late Richard Spencer's, on the south side, and, with the gardens, are to be to be held for ever by John Curtis and his heirs and assigns. Clause of warranty under the name of John Shad. Seals: those of John Shad and Agnes and the common and mayoral seals of the city. Named witnesses: the bailiff, the mayor, the coroners, the reeves, Walter Shirley, William Warin, Thomas Mason, Walter Nalder, and the clerk

2392 By their charter Roger Purton, John Saunders, and Hugh Palfrey granted to Thomas Mason, draper, a citizen of Salisbury, and Laurence Groom, a clerk, a tenement, with shops, called Tarrant's Inn, in Minster Street, which is called High Street, between a tenement of Thomas Cardmaker, of Warminster, on either side; also a garden, with a rack built in it, in Freren Street beside a yard of late Richard Spencer's. The tenement, with the shops, and the garden were held by the grantors and John Chandler, now the bishop of Salisbury, by a grant of Agnes, the relict of Walter Orme, a citizen of Salisbury, and are to be held by Thomas and Laurence and their heirs and assigns, to whom the grantors quitclaimed their right or claim to them. Seals: those of the grantors and the common and mayoral seals of the city. Named witnesses: the bailiff, the mayor, the coroners, the reeves, Walter Shirley, William Warin, Walter Nalder, Henry Man, Richard Coof, and the clerk

2393 By their letters of attorney Roger Purton, John Saunders, and Hugh Palfrey appointed Robert Wolf and William Chandler, of Salisbury, to surrender into the hand of John, the bishop of Salisbury, the seisin of a tenement, with shops, called Tarrant's Inn, in Minster Street, which is called High Street, [*as in 2392*], and the seisin of a garden, with racks built in it, in Freren Street, [*as in 2392*], to the use of Thomas Mason, draper, a citizen of Salisbury, and Laurence Groom, a clerk. Seals: those of the grantors and the mayoral seals of the city

2394 By his charter William Slegge, a citizen of Salisbury, granted to John Bromley, a citizen of Salisbury, and William Sever a tenement in Brown Street between his own tenement, in which he dwells, on the north side and a tenement of late William River's on the south side; also three shops in Fishmonger Row between a tenement, with a cellar, of late Robert Kirtlingstoke's on the west side and shop property of late John Upton's on the east side. The tenement and the shops are to be held for ever by John and William and their heirs and assigns. Clause of warranty. Seals: William Slegge's and the common and mayoral seals of

the city. Named witnesses: the bailiff, the mayor, the coroners, the reeves, Walter
Shirley, William Warin, Thomas Mason, draper, Robert Warmwell, and the clerk

16 August 1419, at Salisbury

2395 Approval of the will of William Fewster, a citizen of Salisbury, made on 9
June 1419. Interment: in St. Edmund's church. Bequests: 13*s.* 4*d.* to the fabric
of that church, 20*d.* to Henry Clere, the parochial chaplain, and 6*s.* 8*d.* to the
provost for his forgotten tithes; 6*s.* 8*d.* to the fabric of the cathedral church; 5*s.*
to the fabric of St. Thomas's church; 3*s.* 4*d.* both to the Dominicans of Fisherton
and the Franciscans of Salisbury; 3*s.* 4*d.* to be handed out among paupers in the
almshouse of the Holy Trinity; 12*d.* to each of his godchildren; 20*s.* to John
Judd; 13*s.* 4*d.* each to John Saunders and William Chandler; £10 for his funeral
expenses, of which 40*s.* should be spent among his neighbours for eating; 40*s.* to
be handed out among paupers on his behalf; a gown of new cloth to each of his
servants; 20*s.* to Edith, his servant; 6*s.* 8*d.* to John 'Fyrlyfa'; 10*s.* and a gown to
John, a son of John Teffont, of Bristol; a gown with a hood to William Fewster,
of late his apprentice; 12*d.* to each paralytic in the city; a green gown to the lord
John of Stratford if he were to survive him; a gown with a hood each to John
Manningford, William Phelps, William's own servant Adam, and William Taylor;
a gown with a hood of the livery of William Warin to Philip Baron; the rest of
his goods to his wife Edith to be laid out on behalf of his soul. Devises: to Edith
a tenement, with a shop (*or* shops) and a cottage (*or* cottages) attached, in which
he dwelt, in Castle Street between William Lord's tenement on the south side
and a common trench running under the bridge there on the north side. The
tenement, with the shop(s) and cottage(s), should be held for life by Edith and
her assigns, and on her death it should remain for life to John Saunders, when
he might be commissioned by the bishop of Salisbury. As quickly as it could be
done John should cause 200 masses a year to be celebrated, 100 at Michaelmas
and 100 at Easter, during his life on behalf of William's soul, Edith's soul, the souls
of others. In the lifetime of Edith, or in his own lifetime, when it might seem
advantageous to him to do it, John might sell the reversion of the tenement, with
the shop(s) and cottage(s). The money received from the sale should be laid out
by John, according to his wise conscience, on doing charitable deeds on behalf
of William's soul, Edith's soul, and the souls of others. If the sale were not made
in John's lifetime it should be made by John's executors, who should lay out the
money received from it in the way described above. William devised to Edith and
her heirs and assigns for ever a tenement, with four cottages next to it, in New
Street between the bridge or the river Avon on the west side and a tenement of
the scholars of de Vaux college on the east side. Executors: his wife Edith, the
principal executor, John Saunders, and William Chandler. Proved on 22 July
1419 in front of John Pedwell, the subdean; the administration was entrusted to
the executors, who afterwards appeared, accounted with an officer, and were
dismissed. Approved at a court held in front of the bailiff, the mayor, and other
citizens; the seisin of the tenements, cottages, and shop(s) was released to the
legatee.

27 September 1419, at Salisbury

2396 By his charter Richard Weston, weaver, of Salisbury, granted to John Weston, of Bristol, his elder son, two cottages, which, by the name of a tenement, he acquired from Richard Jewell, of Salisbury, in Gigant Street between a tenement of late Robert Godmanstone's, now that of William Cambridge, of London, on the north side and a gate of a garden of late John Ball's on the south side. The cottages are to be held for ever by John and his heirs and assigns. Clause of warranty. Seals: Richard's and common and mayoral seals of the city. Named witnesses: the bailiff, the mayor, the coroners, the reeves, Walter Shirley, William Warin, Walter Nalder, Thomas Bower, William Stout, and the clerk

25 October 1419, at Salisbury

2397 By her charter Agnes, the relict of a younger John Forest, of Salisbury, granted to George Westby and William Penton, dyer, a tenement in Wineman Street, between a tenement of John Hain, loader, on the west side and William's cottage property on the east side, to be held for ever by them and their heirs and assigns. Clause of warranty. Seals: Agnes's and the common and mayoral seals of the city. Named witnesses: the bailiff, the mayor, the coroners, the reeves, William Bishop, Walter Nalder, Nicholas Harding, Thomas Bower, Richard Coof, and the clerk

8 November 1419, at Salisbury

2398 By his charter Nicholas Brown, a clerk, granted to Stephen Edington and John Brown, of the college of St. Edmund's church, a tenement in New Street, between a corner tenement, which Thomas Eyre of late held, on the west side and a tenement of late Thomas Bleacher's on the east side, to be held for ever by them and their heirs and assigns. Clause of warranty. Seals: Nicholas's and the common and mayoral seals of the city. Named witnesses: the bailiff, the mayor, the coroners, the reeves, Walter Nalder, Henry Man, Thomas Bower, John Bromley, and Richard Coof

2399 Approval of the will of William Dowding, draper, made on 18 April 1419. <u>Interment</u>: in St. Thomas's church. <u>Bequests</u>: 20s. to the fabric of that church, 20s. to the rector for his forgotten tithes and lesser benefactions, 6s. 8d. to John Enford, a chaplain there, 12d. to each other chaplain to pray for his soul, 8d. to the deacon, and 4d. to the sacristan; 6s. 8d. each to the fabric of the cathedral church, the fabric of St. Edmund's church, and the fabric of St. Martin's church; 6s. 8d. both to the Franciscans of Salisbury and the Dominicans of Fisherton to pray for his soul; 3s. 4d. both to the paupers of the hospital of the Holy Trinity called Almshouse and to the prisoners in the Guildhall; 12 silver spoons and a large brass pot to his daughter Alice; his share in a ship called *Catherine [of] Salisbury*, if it were to survive and return to England, to William Tull, Alice's husband, otherwise to his executors to be sold. The money issuing from the sale should be laid out on behalf of his soul. William bequeathed 40s. to the mayor and commonalty of the city, for their common aid, to pray for his soul; 6s. 8d.

to Stephen Edington; 3s. 4d. to William, his godson, a son of George Westby;
a horse called Ambler (*Ambuler*) to George [Lowthorpe], the treasurer of the
cathedral church; 10 marks to be handed out among paupers at the discretion of
his executors; 6s. 8d. to Hugh, a Dominican friar, a son of Walter Trown, baker,
to pray for his soul; the rest of his goods to his wife Christine to provide for his
burial, to be laid out according to her conscience on behalf of his soul, and to
find a chaplain to celebrate on behalf of his soul, and the souls of others, in St.
Thomas's church for the year after his death, and for following years if it could
be continued longer, at Christine's discretion. Devises: to Christine for life a
tenement, in which Walter Mead, weaver, dwells, in Gigant Street, on the way
to St. Edmund's church, between William Stout's tenement on the south side
and Robert Poynant' tenement on the north side. After Christine's death the
tenement should be sold by William's executors, if they were then alive, by one of
them, or by their executors; at all events the reversion might be sold in Christine's
lifetime if that seemed best to her. The money received from the sale should be
laid out, on celebrating masses, giving alms, and doing other charitable deeds, by
the executors at their discretion on behalf of William's soul, Christine's soul after
she had died, and the souls of others. William devised to William Tull and his
wife Alice and their joint issue for ever the tenements, shops, cottages, yards, and
gardens in the city which he held by that William's grant. If William and Alice
were to die without such issue the premises should be sold by William Dowding's
executors, if they were then living, and, if not, by their executors or subsequent
executors. The money received from the sale should be laid out to give financial
help to a chaplain to celebrate mass on behalf of the souls of William Tull and
Alice and the souls of those mentioned above, and in doing other charitable
deeds at the discretion of the executors. William appointed a tenement, in which
he dwelt, in Winchester Street, above the ditch, between William Alexander's
tenement on the west side and John Woodhay's tenement on the east side, to
remain, after the death of his wife Christine, for ever to his daughter Alice,
the wife of William Tull, and her issue. If Alice were to die without issue the
tenement should be sold by William Dowding's executors, if they were then
living, or by their executors or subsequent executors. The money received from
the sale should be laid out in the way appointed above concerning the sale of the
other tenements. William devised to Thomas Read, a merchant, the reversion
of a tenement, in which Thomas and his wife Cecily dwell and in which Cecily
holds an estate for her life; William acquired the reversion, when it fell due on
Cecily's death, from the executors of John Courtman. The tenement stands in
Winchester Street between Thomas Knoyle's corner tenement on the west side
and a tenement of late Edmund Cofford's on the east side. The reversion, and the
tenement when it fell due on Cecily's death, is to be held for ever by Thomas
Read and his heirs and assigns. Executors: his wife Christine, William Tull, and
Thomas Read. Proved on 14 May 1419 in front of Simon Sydenham, the dean
of Salisbury, deputed a commissary of John Estcourt, B.L., a general examiner
of the court of Canterbury and a general commissary of Henry [Chichele], the
archbishop of Canterbury; on the strength of John's commission Simon entrusted

the administration to Christine and Thomas. Approved at a court held in front of the bailiff, the mayor, and other citizens; the seisin of the tenements was released to Christine, a legatee, reserving the right of William Tull, a legatee, having not yet appeared, his wife Alice being dead.

22 November 1419, at Salisbury
2400 Approval of the will of [*margin*: a younger] Thomas Stalbridge, a citizen of Salisbury, made on 22 August 1419. Interment: in the graveyard of St. Edmund's church. Bequests: 12*d*. each to the fabric of the cathedral church and the fabric of St. Edmund's church; 6*d*. both to the Franciscans [of Salisbury] and the Dominicans of Fisherton Anger; 6*d*. each to Richard Curtis, John Purdy, Robert Ferrer, John Watts, and William, a cordwainer; the rest of his goods to his wife Alice to pray for his soul. Devises: to Alice for life as dower a chief tenement, in which he dwelt, opposite the market place where grains are sold, between Thomas Garbett's tenement on the west side and John Bodenham's tenement on the east side. After Alice's death the tenement should be held for ever by Thomas's son Richard and Richard's issue, and if Richard were to die without issue it would remain for ever to the child being in Alice's womb and, if the child were to live, to the issue of that child; in default of issue the tenement would remain to the direct heirs of Thomas's blood. Thomas devised to Richard and his issue for ever cottages in New Street and Culver Street between a tenement of the hospital of the Holy Trinity in New Street on the west side and cottage property of late John Amesbury's in Culver Street on the north side. If Richard were to die without issue the cottages would remain to the direct heirs of Thomas's blood. Executor: his wife Alice. Proved on 10 October 1419 in front of an officer of the subdean; the administration was entrusted to Alice, who at length appeared, accounted with an officer, and was dismissed. Approved at a court held in front of the bailiff, the mayor, and other citizens; the seisin of the tenement and the cottages was released to the legatees.
2401 Approval of the will of Robert Stonard, a baker, a citizen of Salisbury, made on 1 September 1419. Interment: in the graveyard of St. Edmund's church, on the north side of the church. Bequests: 12*d*. to the fabric of the cathedral church; 40*d*. to the provost of St. Edmund's church, 6*s*. 8*d*. to the fabric, 4*d*. to each chaplain, and 4*d*. to the deacon; 12*d*. each to the fabric of St. Martin's church and the fabric of St. Thomas's church; 12*d*. to the lord Henry Clere; 40*d*. to be handed out in bread among paupers being in the almshouse of the Holy Trinity on the three days immediately after his death; 6*s*. 8*d*. and a rosary of amber beads to Alice, his mother; 6*s*. 8*d*. to John Stonard, an apprentice of John Ashford; 40*s*., a belt harnessed with silver, three silver spoons, a piece of silver, a brass pot with a capacity of 3 gallons, a brass ewer, a brass pan, a candlestick, and a basin with a laver to his daughter Joan; 40*s*., a silver belt, three silver spoons, a piece of silver, a brass pot with a capacity of 3 gallons, a brass ewer, a brass pan, a candlestick, and a basin with a laver to his daughter Alice; 13*s*. 4*d*. to his brother Nicholas; a gown of the livery (*lib'a*) of Salisbury, furred with white, to his brother John; a particoloured gown furred with a medley of Winchester, and a dagger harnessed

with silver to his brother William; a green furred gown to John Oakwood; 12*d*. to each of his godchildren; the rest of his goods to his wife Gillian to be laid out on behalf of his soul. Devises: to Gillian a tenement, in which he dwelt, in Castle Street between his own tenement, in which John Crop, skinner, dwells, on the south side and his own cottage, in which Richard White, weaver, dwells, on the north side; also to Gillian a tenement, which John Crop holds, in Castle Street between Walter Shirley's tenement on the south side and the tenement in which Robert himself dwells on the north side. The two tenements are to be held by Gillian and her assigns for her life. After her death the tenement in which Robert dwelt should remain for ever to his daughter Joan and her issue, and if Joan were to die without issue it would remain for ever to his daughter Alice and her issue, and if Alice were to die without issue it should be sold by Robert's executors, their executors, or subsequent executors. The money received from the sale should be laid out, on masses, alms, and doing other charitable deeds, on behalf of Robert's soul, Gillian's soul, and the souls of others. Also after Gillian's death the tenement in which John Crop dwells should remain for ever to Alice and her issue, if Alice were to die without issue it would remain for ever to Joan and her issue, and if Joan were to die without issue it should be sold by Robert's executors, their executors, or subsequent executors. The money received from the sale should be laid out on behalf of Robert's soul and the souls of those mentioned above. Robert appointed the cottage in which Richard White dwells, in Castle Street between the tenement in which Robert dwelt on the south side and cottage property of late John Needler's, now Nicholas Melbury's, on the north side to be sold by his executors immediately after his death. From the money received from the sale a chaplain should be found to celebrate mass in St. Edmund's church on behalf of Robert's soul and the souls of others, as long as the money might last. Executors: his wife Gillian and his brother Nicholas Stonard. Proved on 2 November 1419 in front of John Pedwell, the subdean; the administration was entrusted to the executors, who at length appeared, accounted with an officer, and were dismissed. Approved at a court held in front of the bailiff, the mayor, and other citizens; the seisin of the tenements and the cottage was released to the legatees.

2402 By his indented charter John Wishford, a citizen of Salisbury, granted to Henry Ham, draper, a tenement, which he acquired from William Dowding, in Wineman Street between a tenement of late Robert Body's on the east side and a tenement of late Dominic Uphill's, and of late William Sall's, on the west side. The tenement is to be held for ever by Henry and his heirs and assigns paying a rent of 40*s*. cash a year to John and his assigns for John's life. Clause to permit permanent repossession if the rent were to be in arrear for 15 days; alternatively, if John and his heirs and assigns were to prefer, to permit re-entry, distraint, and the keeping of distresses until the unpaid rent was recovered. Clause of warranty. Seals: those of the parties to the parts of the charter in turn and the common and mayoral seals of the city. Named witnesses: the bailiff, the mayor, the coroners, the reeves, Walter Shirley, William Warin, Thomas Mason, Thomas Bower, Richard Gage, and the clerk

2403 By his indented charter John Noble, a citizen of Salisbury, granted to Laurence Drew, weaver, and his wife Agnes a tenement, with an adjacent garden (*or* adjacent gardens), in Castle Street, beyond the bars, between Edmund Purdy's tenement on the south side and Gunnore Bowyer's tenement on the north side, to be held for ever by them and their joint issue. If Laurence and Agnes were to die without such issue the tenement, with the garden(s), would remain for ever to the direct heirs of the blood of whomever of Laurence and Agnes lived the longer. For the 10 years following the date of the charter a rent of 26s. 8d. cash a year should be paid to John and his heirs and assigns, and during that term Laurence and Agnes and their heirs and assigns should repair and maintain the tenement in all things necessary so that the rent would not be lost. Clause to permit re-entry if, during the 10 years, repairs and maintenance were not carried out or the rent were to be in arrear for a month, distraint, and the keeping of distresses until the unpaid rent was recovered. The grant was made on condition that, if Laurence or Agnes, their heirs, or anyone in their name were to pay to John, his executors, or his assigns £12 cash within the 10 years, and that to make such a payment they were not selling or mortgaging the tenement to anyone else, the charter would keep its force and effect and the rent of 26s. 8d. a year would cease. Clause to permit permanent repossession if Laurence or Agnes or their heirs were not to pay the £12 within the 10 years or if they were to fail to pay the rent and distresses sufficient for it could not be found in the tenement. Seals: those of the parties to the parts of the charter in turn and the common and mayoral seals of the city. Named witnesses: the bailiff, the mayor, the coroners, the reeves, Walter Shirley, Thomas Mason, Robert Poynant, Richard Gage, and the clerk

28 February 1420, at Salisbury
2404 By his deed Nicholas Harding, a citizen of Salisbury, quitclaimed to his son Thomas and Thomas's heirs and assigns his right or claim to a tenement, in which Thomas Hindon of late dwelt and which, by the rigour of the law, Nicholas recovered against John Wallop, of Salisbury, after the death of Alice, the wife of Thomas Hindon, as the right of his wife Agnes, the mother of his son Thomas and Alice's sister. The tenement stands, opposite the Guildhall, between William Moore's tenement on the north side and John Camel's tenement on the south side, and it is to be held for ever by Thomas Harding and his heirs and assigns. Seals: Nicholas's and the common and mayoral seals of the city. Named witnesses: the bailiff, the mayor, the coroners, the reeves, Walter Shirley, William Warin, Thomas Mason, draper, Thomas Bower, and the clerk

2405 By his letters of attorney Nicholas Harding, a citizen of Salisbury, appointed his son William, a clerk, and Stephen Edington to deliver to his son Thomas the seisin of a tenement, in which Thomas Hindon, a citizen of Salisbury, of late dwelt, opposite the Guildhall [*as in* **2404**], or to surrender the seisin of it into the hand of John, the bishop of Salisbury, to the use of Nicholas's son Thomas. Seals: Nicholas's and the mayoral seal of the city

2406 By their deed Richard Mill and his wife Christine granted to William Sutton, of Houghton, the estate which Christine held for her life by a devise of Robert Way, of late her husband, in two conjoined shops in Minster Street, which is called the high street, between a tenement formerly Robert Russell's on the north side and a tenement of late Dominic Uphill's on the south side. The shops, and Christine's estate in them, are to be held by William and his heirs and assigns according to the effect of Robert's will. Seals: those of Richard and Christine and the mayoral seal of the city. Named witnesses: the bailiff, the mayor, the coroners, the reeves, Walter Shirley, William Warin, Thomas Mason, Thomas Bower, and the clerk

13 March 1420, at Salisbury

2407 By their deed Gillian, the relict, and an executor, of Robert Stonard, a baker, of late a citizen of Salisbury, and Nicholas Stonard, a chaplain, her co-executor, on the strength of Robert's will granted to Edward Gilbert, dubber, a citizen of Salisbury, a messuage, which Robert acquired from John Needler, of late a citizen of Salisbury, with the ground and the length and breadth as John acquired it from John Waite, hosier, and his wife Maud. The messuage stands in Castle Street, between Gillian's tenement, of late Robert's, on the south side and cottage property of late John Needler's, now that of Nicholas Melbury and his wife Amice, on the north side, was appointed by Robert to be sold by his executors immediately after his death, and, with the ground, is to be held for ever by Edward and his heirs and assigns as that which Edward bought from Gillian and Nicholas in good faith for Robert's will to be carried out. Seals: those of Gillian and Nicholas and the common and mayoral seals of the city. Named witnesses: the bailiff, the mayor, the coroners, the reeves, Walter Shirley, William Warin, William Bishop, Thomas Mason, Robert Poynant, and the clerk

2408 By their charter John Morris and his wife Edith, the relict of William Fewster, a citizen of Salisbury, granted to Robert Gilbert, tanner, and John Shad, draper, a tenement, with an adjacent shop (*or* adjacent shops), in New Street, beside the lower bridge of Fisherton, between a tenement of the scholars of de Vaux college on the east side and a trench of running water beside the river on the west side. William and Edith held the tenement jointly in fee simple by a grant of William Sall, a citizen of Salisbury, and it is to be held for ever by Robert Gilbert and John Shad and their heirs and assigns. Clause of warranty. Seals: those of John Morris and Edith and the common and mayoral seals of the city. Named witnesses: the bailiff, the mayor, the coroners, the reeves, Walter Shirley, William Warin, Thomas Mason, Walter Nalder, Henry Man, and the clerk

27 March 1420, at Salisbury

2409 A deed of Richard Mill, of Salisbury, and his wife Christine, the relict, and an executor, of Robert Way, a skinner, of Salisbury. Robert devised to Christine for life two conjoined shops, with a sollar (*or* sollars), in Minster Street [*as in* **2406**]. On Christine's death the shops should remain to Robert's son John and daughters Edith and Margery for their life and the life of the one of them living longest, and after the death of John, Edith, and Margery they should be sold by Robert's executors. John, Edith, and Margery have died, William Sutton has acquired Christine's estate in the shops, and by their deed Richard and Christine, she as Robert's executor, granted the shops to William to be held for ever by him and his heirs and assigns as that which he acquired from them for Robert's will to be carried out. Seals: those of Richard and Christine and the common and mayoral seals of the city. Named witnesses: the bailiff, the mayor, the coroners, the reeves, Walter Shirley, William Warin, Thomas Mason, draper, Thomas Bower, and the clerk

2410 By their deed Robert Gilbert, tanner, and John Shad, draper, granted to John Morris and his wife Edith a tenement, with an adjacent shop (*or* adjacent shops), which they held by a grant of John and Edith, in New Street, beside the lower bridge of Fisherton, [*as in **2408***]. The tenement, with the shop(s), is to be held for ever by John and Edith and their heirs and assigns. Seals: those of Robert Gilbert and John Shad and the common and mayoral seals of the city. Named witnesses: the bailiff, the mayor, the coroners, the reeves, Walter Shirley, William Warin, William Bishop, Henry Man, Richard Gage, and the clerk

20 May 1420, at Salisbury
2411 A deed of William Harnhill, barber, and his wife Alice. Thomas Castleton, a citizen of Salisbury, granted to William and Alice a shop, with a sollar built above it, opposite the market place where fleeces are sold, between a shop, which Richard Stone holds, on the south side and a shop formerly Thomas Goodyear's on the north side; also a house, called the Cellar, within the shop, the easement of a well for water to be drawn from it, and the easement of a latrine with free ingress and egress in respect of it through Thomas Castleton's chief tenement. Those premises and easements were to be held by William and Alice for their life and the life of the one of them living longer, as is shown in an indenture dated 1 October 1393, and by their deed William and Alice surrendered their estate or right in them to Thomas Castleton and his heirs and assigns. Seals: those of William and Alice and the mayoral seal of the city. Named witnesses: the bailiff, the mayor, the coroners, the reeves, William Warin, Walter Shirley, William Bishop, Walter Nalder, Thomas Mason, Henry Man, and Richard Coof

22 May 1420, at Salisbury
2412 By his indented charter Thomas Castleton, mercer, granted to William Harnhill, barber, of Salisbury, a tenement, with shops next to it, opposite the market place where fleeces are sold, between a tenement formerly John Sherborne's, now William Bowyer's, on the north side and a tenement of late Peter Bennett's, now that of the dean and chapter of Salisbury, on the south side. The tenement, with the shops, was acquired by Thomas from Nicholas Taylor, draper, a citizen of Salisbury, and is to be held for ever by William and his heirs and assigns paying to Thomas, his heirs, and his executors £20 a year for each of the seven years following 24 June 1420, £10 at Christmas and £10 on 24 June, and £13 6s. 8d. in the eighth year. Clause to permit re-entry if a payment were to be in arrear for 15 days, distraint, and the keeping of distresses until the unmade payments were recovered; also, to permit permanent repossession if a payment

were to be in arrear for a month. Clause of warranty. Seals: those of the parties to the parts of the charter in turn and the common and mayoral seals of the city. Named witnesses: the bailiff, the mayor, the coroners, the reeves, William Warin, Walter Shirley, William Bishop, Walter Nalder, Thomas Mason, Henry Man, and Richard Coof

2413 Approval of the will of William Huggin, carpenter, made on 18 April 1420. <u>Interment</u>: in the graveyard of St. Thomas's church, near the north door. <u>Bequests</u>: 6*d*. to the high altar of that church for his forgotten tithes, a brass pot containing 7 gallons to the fabric, and 2*d*. each to six priests; a square to John of Coombe; an axe to Richard Purchase; the rest of his goods to his wife Alice. <u>Devises</u>: to Alice for life three cottages in New Street between John Sydenham's tenement on the west side and a tenement of late William West's on the east side. After Alice's death the cottages should be held by the almshouse of the Holy Trinity and once a year, in April, his obit should be held publicly and solemnly in that house for ever. <u>Executors</u>: his wife Alice and John Wareham, a clerk. <u>Proved</u> on 23 April 1420 in front of an officer of the subdean; the administration was entrusted to the executors. <u>Approved</u> at a court held in front of the bailiff, the mayor, and other citizens; the seisin of the tenement was released to the legatee.

5 June 1420, at Salisbury

2414 By their charter Laurence Groom and John Mitchell, chaplains, granted to Thomas Freeman, mercer, of Salisbury, and Joan, a daughter of Alice Nutkin, two shops, which Thomas Boughton, a cordwainer, of late held, in Castle Street between a tenement of John Shipton, a cordwainer, on the north side and Richard Chesham's shop on the south side. The shops were held by Laurence and John by a grant of Richard Jacob, a chaplain, and an elder John Chandler, and they are to be held for ever by Thomas and Joan and their heirs and assigns. Seals: those of the grantors and the common and mayoral seals of the city. Named witnesses: the bailiff, the mayor, the coroners, the reeves, Walter Shirley, William Warin, William Bishop, Walter Nalder, Thomas Mason, Henry Man, and the clerk

2415 A deed of Laurence Groom, a chaplain. Joan, a daughter of Alice Nutkin, of Salisbury, holds a tenement, with an adjacent cellar, in Pot Row, between Thomas Bower's tenement on the east side and John Spencer's shops on the west side, by a grant to her and her issue of an elder John Pilk, of Beckington, an executor of Thomas Child, of late a citizen of Salisbury. For the lack of issue of Joan the tenement should remain to Laurence and his heirs and assigns, as is contained in a charter dated 24 May 1419. By his deed Laurence granted to Thomas Freeman, mercer, a citizen of Salisbury, that, for the lack of issue of Joan, the tenement, with the cellar, would remain not to him but for ever to Thomas and his heirs. Laurence quitclaimed to Thomas and his heirs and assigns his right or claim to the tenement, with the cellar. Seals: Laurence's and the common and mayoral seals of the city. Named witnesses: the bailiff, the mayor, the coroners, the reeves, Walter Shirley, William Warin, William Bishop, Walter Nalder, Thomas Mason, Henry Man, and the clerk

19 June 1420, at Salisbury

2416 Approval of the will of Thomas Bridgehampton, a citizen of Salisbury, made on 1 May 1420. <u>Interment</u>: in the graveyard of the church of the Blessed Mary the Virgin, Andover. <u>Bequests</u>: 2*s*. to the fabric of that church, 12*d*. to the vicar, 6*d*. to each priest present at his funeral rites, 4*d*. to both parochial clerks, and 6*d*. to St. Swithun's, Winchester, the mother church; a basin with a cover, a best brass pan with six platters and six dishes of pewter, a small box with a brass candlestick, and 10 sheep from 20 bequeathed to him by John Dudand, as is contained in John's will, to his daughter Isabel; 20 [?*rectius* 10] of the same sheep, a small box, a brass pan bound with iron of late newly bought, two platters with two dishes of pewter, and a bowl with a cover to his daughter Alice; his best gown to John Forster; his second-best gown to Richard Forster; his best doublet and second-best hat to Adam at the grove; his best hat and his second-best doublet to William Pewsey; the rest of his goods to his wife Joan to be disposed of at her discretion. <u>Devises</u>: to Joan for life a chief messuage, with an adjacent garden beyond a trench of water appurtenant to the messuage, in Brown Street, between a tenement of late that of John Stoke, tailor, on the north side and a tenement of late John Basingstoke's on the south side, which Thomas held by a feoffment of Thomas Bridgehampton, his father, as is contained in the elder Thomas's will. On Joan's death the messuage, with the garden, should remain for ever to Thomas's daughter Isabel and her issue. Thomas devised to Joan for life a messuage, with a garden, in the same vill [?in St. Martin's Street: *cf.* **2261**] between William Ashley's tenement on the west side and John Messenger's messuage on the east side. On Joan's death that messuage, with the garden, should remain for ever to Thomas's daughter Alice and her issue. If Isabel or [?*rectius* and] Alice were to die in Joan's lifetime she, as Thomas's executor, should sell the tenements, with the gardens. The money received should be laid out by her, on pure marriages and doing other charitable deeds, on behalf of Thomas's soul and the souls of others; also for celebrating masses and handing out alms to paupers on behalf of his soul. Thomas appointed seven shops in Brown Street in [?*rectius* and] St. Martin's Street, beside a tenement formerly William Chard's on the south side, which his sister Joan holds for life, to be sold by his wife Joan, his executor, after that Joan's death, according to the will of Thomas, his father. <u>Executors</u>: his wife Joan, Alexander Smith, Thomas Harris, and Nicholas Cricklade. <u>Proved</u> at Winchester on 14 May 1420 in front of an officer of Winchester; the administration was entrusted to the executors. <u>Approved</u> at a court held in front of the bailiff, the mayor, and other citizens; the seisin of the tenements was released to the legatees.

2417 A deed of Laurence Groom and John Mitchell, chaplains, executors of William Buck, a chaplain. William appointed a rent of 12*s*. a year issuing from a tenement, of late Gillian Bold's, in Pot Row between Thomas Bower's shop on the east side and John Spencer's shops on the west side, to be sold by his executors. The money raised from the sale should be laid out on behalf of William's soul and the souls of others. By their deed, on the strength of William's will, Laurence and John granted the rent to Thomas Freeman, of Salisbury, to be held for ever by him and his heirs and assigns as that which he bought from them for a sum of money, reaching the full value of the rent, to be wholly laid out according to the terms of William's will. Laurence and John quitclaimed to Thomas and his assigns their right or claim to the tenement or the rent. Seals: those of Laurence and John and the common and mayoral seals of the city. Named witnesses: the bailiff, the mayor, the coroners, the reeves, Walter Shirley, William Warin, William Bishop, Henry Man, Richard Gage, and the clerk

2418 By his writing Nicholas Melbury quitclaimed to Robert Warmwell and Henry Man and their heirs and assigns his right or claim, on the strength of a statute merchant acknowledged to him and William Sall, now dead, by a younger John Bodenham, of Wilton, or on the strength of any other title, to a tenement, with shops and rooms, in which John Gatcombe, called Sergeant, of late dwelt, opposite the market place where grains are sold, between a tenement of late William Tull's on the west side and a tenement, in which John Shad dwells, on the east side. The tenement, with the shops and rooms, was held by Robert and Henry by a grant of John Bodenham, a son of the younger John Bodenham, and the younger John was seised of it in his demesne as of fee at the time of the acknowledgement. Seals: Nicholas's and the common and mayoral seals of the city. Named witnesses: the bailiff, the coroners, the reeves, Walter Shirley, William Warin, William Bishop, Henry Man, John Bromley, and the clerk

2419 By her deed Margaret Baker, otherwise Hutchins, granted to Henry Blackmoor the estate for life which she held in three cottages in the street on the way to St. Martin's church, between a cottage of late Thomas Glover's, previously Robert Harass's, on the east side and cottages or a tenement of William Harnhill, barber, on the north side. The cottages were held by Margaret by a devise of Thomas Hawes, otherwise Hellier, a chaplain, and are to be held for her life by Henry and his assigns or executors. Seals: Margaret's and the mayoral seals of the city. Named witnesses: the bailiff, the mayor, the coroners, the reeves, Walter Shirley, William Warin, and Thomas Mason

3 July 1420, at Salisbury
2420 By their charter John Swift, ironmonger, of Salisbury, and his wife Christine, appearing in court, granted to Robert Warmwell, a citizen of Salisbury, a tenement, in the street on the way to the upper bridge of Fisherton, between a tenement of late Nicholas Taylor's on the east side and a tenement of late that of Richard at the bridge, which John Crablane of late held, on the west side, to be held for ever by him and his heirs and assigns. Clause of warranty. Seals: those of John and Christine and the common and mayoral seals of the city. Named witnesses: the bailiff, a coroner, the reeves, Walter Shirley, William Warin, Thomas Mason, Henry Man, and John Bromley

31 July 1420, at Salisbury
2421 By his indented charter William Blake, of Salisbury, granted to Geoffrey Mansel, goldsmith, of Salisbury, a tenement in Castle Street, between William Alexander's tenement on the south side and a tenement of the provost of St. Edmund's church on the north side, to be held for ever by him and his heirs and

assigns. Clause of warranty. The grant was made on condition that, if William or his heirs or assigns were to pay to Geoffrey or his heirs or assigns £20 at Michaelmas 1423, together with the expenses and payments concerning the repair of the tenement imposed on Geoffrey or his heirs and assigns, such expenses and payments to be assessed at the order of four law-worthy men chosen from each side, the grant would be suspended and counted for nothing. In that case William and his heirs and assigns might enter on the tenement, take back possession, and keep their former estate in it. If William were to default on the payment of the £20, or not meet the expenses and payments, the grant would keep its force and effect. Seals: those of the parties to the parts of the charter in turn and the common and mayoral seals of the city. Named witnesses: the bailiff, the mayor, the reeves, Walter Shirley, William Warin, Walter Nalder, John Judd, and the clerk

14 August 1420, at Salisbury
2422 By their charter Robert Warmwell and Henry Man, citizens of Salisbury, granted to John Conge, a clerk, and William Warwick, of Salisbury, a rent of a rose a year issuing from a tenement of late John Gatcombe's, with the reversion of the tenement when it fell due on the death of John's relict Joan, except four shops in the tenement which John Bodenham, of Salisbury, holds for Joan's life. The tenement stands, opposite the market place [where grains are sold: *cf. 2418*], between a tenement of late William Tull's on the west side and a tenement, in which John Shad dwells, on the east side. The rent and the reversion are to be held for ever by John Conge and William Warwick and the heirs of William. Clause of warranty. Seals: those of Robert and Henry and the common and mayoral seals of the city. Named witnesses: the bailiff, the coroners, the reeves, Walter Shirley, William Warin, Walter Nalder, Thomas Mason, Robert Poynant, and the clerk

2423 By his deed John Bodenham, of Salisbury, granted to John Conge, a clerk, and William Warwick, of Salisbury, his estate in four shops in a tenement [opposite the market place where grains are sold: *cf. 2422*] in which Joan, the relict of John Gatcombe, dwells and which, by an indenture dated 13 August 1410 and by the name of four old shops or rooms, she granted to John Bodenham, a citizen of Salisbury, his father, for her life. The shops, and John Bodenham's estate in them, are to be held by John Conge and William Warwick, to whom, and to William's heirs, John Bodenham quitclaimed his right or claim to them and the tenement. Clause of warranty. Seals: John Bodenham's and the common and mayoral seals of the city. Named witnesses: the bailiff, the mayor, the coroners, the reeves, Walter Shirley, William Warin, Walter Nalder, Thomas Mason, Robert Poynant, Henry Man, and the clerk

2424 By his letters of attorney John Bodenham, of Salisbury, appointed William Lord or John Butler to surrender into the hand of John, the bishop of Salisbury, the seisin of four shops in a tenement [opposite the market place where grains are sold: *cf. 2422*] in which Joan, the relict of John Gatcombe, dwells and which, by an indenture [*as in 2423*], she granted to John Bodenham, a citizen of Salisbury, his father, for her life, to the use of John Conge, a clerk, and William Warwick, of Salisbury. Seals: John Bodenham's and the mayoral seal of the city

28 August 1420, at Salisbury

2425 Approval of the will of Stephen Edington, of Salisbury, made on 1 May 1420. Interment: in the graveyard of St. Edmund's church, beside the tomb of his father and mother, opposite the entrance to the college. Bequests: 6s. 8d. to the fabric of that church, 2s. 6d. to Henry [Clere], the parochial chaplain, to pray for his soul, the soul of the master Robert Ragenhill, and the souls of others, and 12d. to John Crosier, a chaplain of that church; 13s. 4d. to the fabric of St. Martin's church, and 2s. 6d. to William Spicer, the parochial chaplain; 20d. each to the fabric of the cathedral church and the fabric of St. Thomas's church; 40d. to the convent of the Franciscans of Salisbury, and 4d. to each friar of it to pray for his soul; 2d. to each poor friar in the convent of the Dominicans of Salisbury [*recte* Fisherton] at the discretion of his executors; 12d. to the lord Nicholas Gifford; 12d. to Hugh Howel, a chaplain in the Close; 20s. and a stone ring, which is called Calcidome and which he held by his gift, to John Mitchell, the rector at Wilton; a gown with fur and his smaller dagger to Thomas Brute, called Brandon, of Chalke, to whom he remits the debt, except 6s. 8d., which he is owed by him; 13s. 4d., a small piece of silver weighing 4¼ oz., and four silver spoons to Margery, the wife of Thomas Brute; a standing horn, furnished with silver feet, which is called Wassail, to his beloved Thomas Mason, draper, his intimate friend, a low silver piece with an inscribed cover to his wife Joan, and a piece of silver, without a cover, and three silver and gilt spoons to their daughter Edith, his goddaughter; 12d. to each of his other godchildren; for the seven years following his death his executors should provide 4d., in money or victuals, each week to paupers [?each pauper] of the hospital called Almshouse; a dagger, to be chosen from two, and worsted cloth for a doublet to be made from it to William Lord; his best russet cloak, with a red hood, and 40d. to William Moore, of Salisbury, and 6s. 8d. to his wife Susan; 13s. 4d. to Christine Cole; a brass pot and a pan, at the discretion of his executors, and 40d. to Lucy, his servant; a furred gown, at the discretion of his executors, to John, his household servant; he remits a quarter's rent to each of his tenants; he wished that Thomas Mason would pay the £20 which he lent to him in his parlour; the rest of his goods should be disposed of on behalf of his soul. Devises: to his wife Christine for life as dower a tenement, in which he of late dwelt, in St. Martin's Street if she would be content with that. If Christine would not be content with that the feoffees in a tenement [in Castle Street], in which he then dwelt, should enfeoff her for life in a single dwelling house from it, to be maintained and repaired at her own expense according to an indenture perfected in the matter, on pain of losing that house. Stephen appointed that his son William should hold for life shops next to the tenement in Castle Street together with, after Christine's death, the chief dwelling house of the tenement, except for the shops annexed to the gate of the tenement. The estate in that dwelling house having been perfected for Christine, the tenement in St. Martin's Street as her dower having been declined, William should hold for life the tenement in

St. Martin's Street, with the shops next to the tenement in Castle Street, except those annexed to the gate, paying a rent of 20s. a year to his brother John if John would live under good and moderate guidance. Clause to permit John to enter on the tenement and shops if the rent were to be in arrear for 15 days, distraint, and the keeping of distresses until the unpaid rent was recovered. On Christine's death the chief dwelling house of the tenement in Castle Street should remain to William for life, and after the death of William and Christine the tenement, with the shops, except the shops annexed to the gate, should remain to John for life if he would keep himself under good guidance. The shops annexed to the gate should remain to Margery, the wife of Thomas Brandon, and Christine Cole for their life or the life of the one of them living longer, maintaining them etc. On the death of Margery and Christine those shops should remain to William for life, and on William's death they should remain to John for life. On John's death the tenement and all the shops should remain to Stephen's feoffees and executors to be sold. The money received from the sale should be laid out by the feoffees and executors on behalf of his soul, the souls of William Knoyle and Edith, the relict of William Knoyle and formerly Stephen's wife, the souls of others. If Christine were to decline the dwelling house in Castle Street William should hold it with the shops next to the tenement for life, for the rent of 20s. a year to John, with the reversion of the tenement in St. Martin's Street. On William's death the dwelling house, with the shops, and the reversion should remain to John, and after John's death should remain to Stephen's feoffees and executors to be sold. The money received from the sale should be laid out on behalf of Stephen's soul and the souls of those mentioned above. Stephen appointed a tenement, which Robert Bramshaw holds, in Endless Street, opposite a tenement of late John Mower's, on the north side of a tenement of late William Duke's, which would revert to him because of Robert's lack of issue, to remain for ever to Edmund Friday and his heirs. Executors: Thomas Mason, William Lord, William Moore, and Stephen's son William. Approved at a court held in front of the bailiff, the mayor, and other citizens; the seisin of the tenements was released to the legatees.

2426 A deed of Robert Warmwell and Henry Man, citizens of Salisbury. John Bodenham devised to his son John four shops, by the name of four shops with a kitchen, a stable, and a portion of empty ground, within his tenement opposite the market place [where grains are sold: cf. *2418*] which was of late John Gatcombe's. The shops were to be held for ever by the younger John and his heirs and assigns paying 13s. 4d. [a year] to Joan, the relict of John Gatcombe, for her life, as it appears in a codicil of the elder John's will approved under the mayoral seal of the city. John Conge, a clerk, and William Warwick acquired those shops, with the kitchen, stable, and portion of land, under the name of four shops, from the younger John Bodenham, and by their deed Robert and Henry quitclaimed to John and William and William's heirs their right or claim to those shops. Seals: those of Robert and Henry and the common and mayoral seals of the city. Named witnesses: the bailiff, the coroners, the reeves, Walter Shirley, William Warin, Walter Nalder, Thomas Mason, Robert Poynant, and the clerk

2427 By their charter William Warin, grocer, a citizen of Salisbury, and William

Marnhill, a clerk, granted to William Bishop, a merchant, a citizen of Salisbury, a tenement, with an adjacent garden and three walls enclosing the garden, which they held by William's grant. The tenement stands in Winchester Street, above the ditch, between a tenement of late Thomas Knoyle's on the east side and a tenement of late William Ashton's, called the New Inn, on the west side, and, with the garden and walls, is to be held by William Bishop for life. On William's death it should remain, with the garden and walls, for ever to William Warner, of Poole, and his wife Edith, William's daughter, and their heirs. Seals: those of William Warin and William Marnhill and the common and mayoral seals of the city. Named witnesses: the bailiff, the mayor, the coroners, the reeves, Walter Shirley, Thomas Mason, Walter Nalder, Henry Man, John Bromley, and the clerk

9 October 1420, at Salisbury
2428 By their indented deed William Warin, a citizen of Salisbury, William Lord, and John Marshall, dyer, executors of William Walter, granted to Robert Poynant and Richard Gage, citizens of Salisbury, a corner tenement, with shops, cottages, gardens, and yards, of late Thomas Shove's, which William Walter acquired from Thomas and his wife Agace, in New Street, Gigant Street, and St. Martin's Street. William Phebis, a citizen of Salisbury, forfeited the tenement, with the shops, cottages, gardens, and yards, to William Warin, William Lord, and John Marshall according to a feoffment to him for a rent of £20 a year to be paid at the festival of Corpus Christi and not paid, as is contained in an indented charter dated at Salisbury on 25 May 1418. The tenement, with the shops, cottages, gardens, and yards, is to be held for ever by Robert and Richard and their heirs and assigns on condition that, if they or their heirs or executors were to pay to the grantors or to any one of them 20 marks at Michaelmas 1421, and 20 marks at Michaelmas in each of the four following years until 100 marks had been paid, the grant would keep its validity. Clause to permit permanent repossession if Robert and Richard were to default on any payment. Seals: those of the parties to the parts of the deed in turn and the common and mayoral seals of the city. Named witnesses: the bailiff, the mayor, the coroners, the reeves, Walter Shirley, William Bishop, Thomas Mason, Walter Nalder, Henry Man, John Bromley, and Robert Gilbert

23 October 1420, at Salisbury
2429 Approval of the will of Thomas Veal, mercer, of Salisbury, made on 14 September 1420. Interment: in the graveyard of St. Edmund's church. Bequests: 20*d.* to the fabric of the cathedral church; 6*s.* 8*d.* to the fabric of St. Edmund's church; 6*s.* 8*d.* to John Jakes, a chaplain; 6*s.* 8*d.* in bread to be handed out to paupers on the day of his burial; 6*s.* 8*d.* each to William Harnhill, barber, and his wife Alice; 40*d.* to Philip Brown; 6*s.* 8*d.* to John Clark, taverner; the rest of his goods to John Passenger, a chaplain. Devises: to John Passenger a tenement, with houses within it, a latrine, and a portion of garden next to the tenement and on its east side, which Thomas held by a grant of Thomas Castleton, a citizen of Salisbury. The tenement stands in St. Martin's Street, between a tenement of late that of Thomas Hawes, a chaplain, on the east side and Thomas Castleton's

tenement, on a corner in that street, on the west side, and, with the houses, latrine, and portion of garden, is to be held for ever by John and his heirs and assigns. Executors: John Passenger and William Harnhill. Proved on 16 October 1420 in front of John Pedwell, the subdean; the administration was entrusted to the legatees. Approved at a court held in front of the bailiff, the mayor, and other citizens; the seisin of the tenement, with the houses, latrine, and portion of garden, was released to the legatee.

18–24 November, 1420, at Westminster
2430 In a final agreement reached in the king's court in the week beginning 18 November 1420 in front of Richard Norton, Robert Hill, John Cockayne, John Preston, William Babington, and John Martin, justices, between Nicholas Stafford, a clerk, and Henry Swaff, plaintiffs, and John Spencer and his wife Alice, defendants, concerning two messuages and three shops in Salisbury [*described in* **2433**], John and Alice acknowledged the tenements to be the right of Henry, as that which Henry and Nicholas held by their gift, and for themselves and the heirs of Alice quitclaimed them to Nicholas and Henry and the heirs of Henry. Clause of warranty. For that acknowledgement, quitclaim, and warranty Nicholas and Henry gave 20 marks to John and Alice.

4 December 1420, at Salisbury
2431 A deed of Henry Blackmoor. Margaret Baker, otherwise Hutchins, granted to Henry the estate which she held in three cottages in the street on the way to St. Martin's church [*as in* **2419**]. She held the cottages for life by a devise of Thomas Hawes, a chaplain, and, because Thomas Blackmoor, a godson of Thomas, to whom Thomas devised two of the three cottages for life, has died before Margaret, by the terms of Thomas Hawes's will it pertained to Margaret to hold the three until the end of her life. By his deed Henry Blackmoor granted to John Hampton, grocer, and his wife Joan the estate which he held in the cottages for Margaret's life. The cottages, and Henry's estate in them, are to be held for Margaret's life by John and Joan and their assigns. Seals: Henry's and the common and mayoral seals of the city. Named witnesses: the bailiff, the mayor, the coroners, the reeves, Walter Shirley, William Warin, William Bishop, Thomas Mason, and John Bromley
2432 A deed of Walter Nalder and Henry Blackmoor, executors of Thomas Hawes, a chaplain. Thomas devised to Margaret Baker, his servant, for life a cottage, with a garden attached to it and with free ingress and egress in respect of a latrine and water within that cottage and two other of his cottages. The cottage stands in the street on the way to St. Martin's church, adjoining a cottage of late Thomas Glover's, on the east side of Thomas Hawes's other two cottages. Thomas devised to Thomas Blackmoor, his godson, for life, to pray for his soul and for that Thomas's maintenance at school, the two other cottages, between the cottage devised to Margaret on the east side and cottages of William Harnhill, barber, on the north side. Whoever of Margaret and Thomas Blackmoor were to live the longer should hold the three cottages for life. The three cottages immediately after the death of Margaret and Thomas, or the reversion of them

in their lifetime if that were advantageous, should be sold by Thomas Hawes's executors. The money received from the sale should be laid out on pious uses for the salvation of his soul. Thomas Blackmoor is dead, Margaret survives, and the reversion of the cottages pertains to the executors to be sold. By their deed Walter and Henry, wishing to fulfil Thomas Hawes's will and on the strength of it, granted to John Hampton, grocer, and his wife Joan the reversion of the three cottages, with the gardens. The cottages, when they fell due on Margaret's death, are to be held for ever by John and Joan and their heirs and assigns. Seals: those of Walter and Henry and the common and mayoral seals of the city. Named witnesses: the bailiff, the mayor, the coroners, the reeves, Walter Shirley, William Warin, Thomas Mason, William Bishop, and John Bromley

18 December 1420, at Salisbury
2433 By their charter Nicholas Stafford, a chaplain, and Thomas Swaff, goldsmith, granted to John Spencer, of Salisbury, two tenements, with sollars and cellars, and three conjoined shops in Pot Row between Robert Earl's shop on the west side and a shop of Thomas Freeman, mercer, on the east side. One of the tenements stands, opposite the market place where grains are sold, between John Judd's tenement on the east side and Robert Chamberlain's tenement on the west side. The other tenement, with the sollars and cellars, stands, in the high street [called Minster Street: *cf. 2257, 2333*], between a tenement of Henry Harborough, a canon of the cathedral church, on the south side and William Ferrer's shop, of late that of the master Richard Leach, on the north side. The tenements and the shops are to be held for ever by John Spencer and his heirs and assigns. Seals: those of Nicholas and Thomas and the common and mayoral seals of the city. Named witnesses: the bailiff, the mayor, the coroners, the reeves, Walter Shirley, William Warin, Walter Nalder, Thomas Mason, Robert Poynant, Robert Warmwell, John Bromley, and the clerk

1 January 1421, at Salisbury
2434 By his charter John Spencer, of Salisbury, granted to Thomas Freeman, mercer, three conjoined shops in Pot Row [*as in 2433*] which, with two tenements, with sollars and cellars, he himself held by a grant of Nicholas Stafford, a chaplain, and Henry Swaff, goldsmith. The shops are to be held for ever by Thomas and his heirs and assigns. Clause of warranty. Seals: John's and the common and mayoral seals of the city. Named witnesses: the bailiff, the mayor, the coroners, the reeves, Walter Shirley, William Warin, Walter Nalder, Thomas Mason, Robert Poynant, Robert Warmwell, John Bromley, and the clerk
2435 By his charter John Spencer, of Salisbury, granted to Thomas Freemen, mercer, of Salisbury, a tenement opposite the market place where grains are sold [*as in 2433*] which, with other land, tenements, sollars, and cellars, he himself held by a feoffment of Nicholas Stafford, a chaplain, and Henry Swaff, goldsmith. The tenement is to be held for ever by Thomas and his heirs and assigns. Clause of warranty. Seal: John's. Named witnesses: the bailiff, the mayor, the coroners, the reeves, Walter Shirley, William Warin, Walter Nalder, Thomas Mason, Robert

Poynant, Robert Warmwell, John Bromley, and the clerk

15 January 1421, at Salisbury
2436 By his charter William Harnhill, barber, of Salisbury, granted to John Conge, a chaplain, the provost of St. Edmund's church, and John Morris, a chaplain, a messuage, with shops, opposite the market place where fleeces are sold, between William Bowyer's tenement on the north side and a tenement of the dean and chapter of Salisbury on the south side. The messuage, with the shops, by the name of a tenement, was held by William by a feoffment of Thomas Castleton, a mercer, on pain of the payment, or non-payment, of £140, as is contained in an indented charter perfected between them. It is to be held, with the shops, for ever by John Conge and John Morris and their heirs and assigns. Clause of warranty. Seals: Willam Harnhill's and the common and mayoral seals of the city. Named witnesses: the bailiff, the mayor, the coroners, the reeves, Walter Shirley, William Warin, Walter Nalder, Thomas Mason, Robert Poynant, Robert Warmwell, John Bromley, and the clerk

29 January 1421, at Salisbury
2437 By his charter William Phebis, a citizen of Salisbury, granted to John Hampton, of Salisbury, seven conjoined cottages, with gardens, in Gigant Street and Nuggeston between a tenement of late William Sall's on the south side and a tenement of late Richard Knolle's on the east side. The cottages, with the gardens, were held by William by a grant of John Shad, draper, and his wife Agnes and are to be held for ever by John Hampton and his heirs and assigns. Clause of warranty. Seals: William's and the common and mayoral seals of the city. Named witnesses: the bailiff, the mayor, the coroners, the reeves, Walter Shirley, William Warin, Walter Nalder, Thomas Mason, Robert Poynant, Robert Warmwell, John Bromley, and the clerk
2438 By his deed [*dated to the Wednesday after the feast of the purification of the Blessed Mary (5 February) probably in error for the Wednesday before that feast (29 January)*] Laurence Groom, a chaplain, quitclaimed to John Hampton, of Salisbury, and his heirs and assigns his right or claim to seven conjoined cottages, with gardens, in Gigant Street and Nuggeston [*as in 2437*]. Seals: Laurence's and the common and mayoral seals of the city. Named witnesses: the bailiff, the mayor, the coroners, the reeves, Walter Shirley, William Warin, Walter Nalder, Thomas Mason, Robert Poynant, Robert Warmwell, John Bromley, and the clerk
2439 By their deed [*dated to the Wednesday after the feast of the purification of the Blessed Mary (5 February) probably in error for the Wednesday before that feast (29 January)*] Robert Poynant and Richard Gage, citizens of Salisbury, quitclaimed to John Hampton, of Salisbury, their right or claim to seven conjoined cottages, with gardens, in Gigant Street and Nuggeston [*as in 2437*]. Seals: those of Robert and Richard and the common and mayoral seals of the city. Named witnesses: the bailiff, the mayor, the coroners, the reeves, Walter Shirley, William Warin, Walter Nalder, Thomas Mason, Robert Warmwell, John Bromley, and the clerk

12 March 1421, at Salisbury
2440 Approval of the will of Edmund Purdy, a citizen of Salisbury, made on 14 November 1420. <u>Interment</u>: in the graveyard of St. Edmund's church. <u>Bequests</u>: 12*d*. to the fabric of that church, and 4*d*. to the high altar; 12*d*. to the fabric of the cathedral church; the rest of his goods to his wife Christine and his son John. <u>Devise</u>: to Christine a tenement, in which he dwelt, in Castle Street between a tenement of late John Shipton's, now John Noble's, on the north side and Edith Starr's cottage on the south side. The tenement is to be held for life by Christine and her assigns, and after her death is to be held for ever by Edmund's son John and his heirs and assigns. <u>Executors</u>: Christine and John. <u>Proved</u> on 20 November 1420 in front of an officer of the subdean; the administration was entrusted to the executors, who afterwards appeared, accounted with an officer, and were dismissed. <u>Approved</u> at a court held in front of the bailiff, the mayor, and other citizens; the seisin of the tenement was released to the legatees.
2441 Approval of the will of Roger Enterbush, of Salisbury, made on 18 August 1420. <u>Interment</u>: in the graveyard of St. Edmund's church, in front of the south door. <u>Bequests</u>: 2*s*. to the fabric of that church; 20*s*. to the fabric of the cathedral church; 5 lb. of wax, for candles to be burned around his corpse on the day of his burial; a striped gown to William Dinton; a gown with white stripes to his brother Robert; a blue gown to Edmund Witney; 3*s*. 4*d*. and four silver spoons to William Furber; 3*s*. 4*d*. and three silver spoons to John Durnford; the rest of his goods to his wife Agnes to pray for his soul. <u>Devises</u>: to Agnes the reversion of two conjoined cottages, in Mealmonger Street between William Mead's tenement on the south side and cottages of late Adam Dummer's on the north side, when it fell due on the death of Edmund Friday. The reversion, and the cottages when they fell due on Edmund's death, are to be held for ever by Agnes and her heirs and assigns. Roger appointed a cottage, with a garden, in New Street near Barnwell's cross, between William Reynold's tenement on the west side and Thomas Castleton's cottages on the east side, to be sold by his executors. The money received from the sale should be laid out by the executors on pious uses for the salvation of Roger's soul and the souls of others. <u>Executors</u>: William Furber and John Durnford. <u>Proved</u> on 28 September 1420 in front of an officer of the subdean; the administration was entrusted to the executors, who accounted with an officer and were dismissed. <u>Approved</u> at a court held in front of the bailiff, the mayor, and other citizens; the seisin of the cottages and the garden was released to the legatees.
2442 By his charter John Camel, of Salisbury, granted to Walter Short and Thomas Biston a corner tenement, with shops and cottages, in New Street between a tenement, which Thomas Farnborough holds, on the west side and the trench of running water, at the gridiron below the walls of the canons' close, on the south side, to be held for ever by them and their heirs and assigns. Clause of warranty. Seals: John's and the common and mayoral seals of the city. Named witnesses: the bailiff, the mayor, the coroners, the reeves, Walter Shirley, William Warin, Walter Nalder, Thomas Mason, Robert Poynant, John Wishford, Robert Warmwell, John Bromley, and the clerk

26 March 1421, at Salisbury

2443 By their charter Walter Short and Thomas Biston granted to John Camel, of Salisbury, and his wife Joan a corner tenement, with shops and cottages, in New Street, [*as in* **2442**], which they held by John's grant, to be held for ever by John and Joan and John's heirs. Seals: those of Walter and Thomas and the common and mayoral seals of the city. Named witnesses: the bailiff, the mayor, the coroners, the reeves, Walter Shirley, William Warin, Walter Nalder, Thomas Mason, Robert Poynant, Robert Warmwell, John Bromley, and the clerk

9 April 1421, at Salisbury

2444 By his charter John Sherborne, a clerk, granted to John Martin, a chaplain, John Hazard, John Manning, a chaplain, William Harding, and Richard Oliver the reversion of a tenement in New Street, between John Wishford's tenement on the west side and shops of late Thomas Knoyle's, now Robert Earl's, on the east side, when it fell due on the death of Agnes, the relict of Walter Orme, of late a citizen of Salisbury. The tenement is held by Agnes for her life, with reversion to John Sherborne and his heirs, by a grant of that John, and, when it fell due, is to be held for ever by the grantees and their heirs and assigns. Seals: John Sherborne's and the common and mayoral seals of the city. Named witnesses: the bailiff, the mayor, the coroners, the reeves, Walter Shirley, William Warin, Walter Nalder, Thomas Mason, Robert Poynant, Robert Warmwell, John Bromley, John Noble, and the clerk

2445 Approval of the will of Philip Marshall, a son and heir of Thomas Marshall, of Salisbury, made on 12 August 1420. <u>Interment</u>: in the graveyard of the parish church of Bishopstone. <u>Bequests</u>: 6*d*. each to the fabric of that church and the fabric of the chapel of Flamston, 8*d*. to the perpetual vicar of Bishopstone, and 2*d*. to each priest present at his funeral rites; 6*d*. to the fabric of the cathedral church; the rest of his goods to his wife Isabel. <u>Devises</u>: to Isabel the rent issuing from his inn, called the Horseshoe, otherwise Marshall's Inn, with two shops next to it, in the high street of the city [?Minster Street: *cf.* **1968, 2246**]. The inn, with the shops, is to be held by Isabel for life and, on her death, by Philip's daughter Cecily and her issue. If Cecily were to die without issue Philip appointed it to his brother John and his issue, and if John were to die without issue he appointed it to be sold, and [the money received from the sale] to be laid out on behalf of his soul and the souls of others, on the order of Nicholas Baynton, esq., his master, and William Charborough, goldsmith. Philip devised to Cecily the rent issuing from his [?corner] tenement [?in Winchester Street], which John Marshall, smith, holds, above a ditch, between John Wishford's tenement on the north side and a tenement formerly Thomas Knoyle's on the east side, to be held by her and her issue. If Cecily were to die without issue, which God forbid, the tenement and the rent from it would remain for life to his wife Isabel, and on Isabel's death the rent from the two tenements should be held by Philip's brother John and his issue. If that John were to die without issue, which God forbid, the tenement and the rent from it should be sold on the order of Nicholas Baynton and William

Charborough. The money received from the sale should be laid out in good faith, on celebrating masses and giving alms, on behalf of Philip's soul and the souls of others. Executors: his wife Isabel and William Charborough. Proved on 21 October 1420 in front of an officer of the archdeacon of Salisbury; the administration was entrusted to Isabel, reserving the power to entrust it to William when he might come to seek it, and afterwards Isabel appeared, accounted with an officer, and was dismissed. Approved at a court held in front of the bailiff, the mayor, and other citizens; the seisin of the tenements and the rent was released to the legatee.

18 June 1421, at Salisbury

2446 By his charter William Bailiff, called Weston, an executor of Margaret Godmanstone, the relict of William Godmanstone, formerly a citizen of Salisbury, on the strength of Margaret's will granted to William Child, draper, of Salisbury, and his wife Eleanor four cottages, with a yard and a rack, in Endless Street between John Hogman's tenement on the south side and a trench of running water on the north side. The cottages, with the yard and rack, extend from Endless Street as far as the garden, formerly the orchard, of the provost of St. Edmund's church on the east side. Margaret appointed them, with other land and tenements in the city, to be sold by her executors, and they are to be held for ever by William and Eleanor and William's heirs and assigns as that which William and Eleanor bought from William Bailiff in good faith for a sum of money reaching their true value. Seals: William Bailiff's and the common and mayoral seals of the city. Named witnesses: the bailiff, the mayor, the coroners, the reeves, Walter Shirley, William Warin, Walter Nalder, Thomas Mason, Robert Poynant, Robert Warmwell, John Bromley, and the clerk

2447 By their indented charter Edward Furmage [*?otherwise* Cheese] and his wife Agnes granted to John Beccles, a clerk, a corner tenement, called Cheese Corner, with a cellar, shops, and sollars, in Carter Street [and Winchester Street], opposite a corner tenement called Dyne's Corner, between John Hoare's tenement on the east side and that John's shop(s) on the north side; also a shop in Carter Street, opposite the Guildhall, between William Cambridge's shop(s) on the south side and John Camel's shop on the north side. The tenement, with the cellar, shops, and sollars, is to be held for ever by John Beccles and his heirs and assigns. Clause of warranty. The grant was made, and the warranty given, on condition that, if John or his executors or assigns were to hold the tenement, with the cellar, shops, and sollars, from 24 June 1421 for the following 30 years without being disturbed or troubled by Edward and Agnes or their heirs or any other in their name, Edward and Agnes and their heirs and assigns may, at the end of the 30 years, enter on those premises, take back possession, and keep them for themselves and their heirs and assigns for ever. If within the 30 years John Beccles or his executors or assigns were to be impleaded, troubled, or disturbed by Edward and Agnes or their heirs and assigns concerning the tenement, with the cellar, shops, and sollars, the charter would stand in its validity and effect. Seals: those of the parties to the parts of the charter in turn and the common and mayoral seals of the city. Named witnesses: the bailiff, the mayor, the coroners, the reeves, Walter Shirley, William Warin, Walter Nalder, Thomas Mason, Robert Poynant, Robert Warmwell, John Bromley, and the clerk

30 July 1421, at Salisbury
2448 By his charter William Westbury granted to John Hain, loader, of Salisbury, a [?corner] messuage in St. Martin's Street between Walter Burton's tenement on the east side and cottages of the provost of St. Edmund's church on the north side. The messuage was held by William by a grant of John Salisbury, weaver, of Salisbury, and is to be held for ever by John Hain and his heirs and assigns. Clause of warranty. Seals: William's and the common and mayoral seals of the city. Named witnesses: the mayor, the coroners, the reeves, Walter Shirley, William Warin, Walter Nalder, Thomas Mason, Robert Poynant, Robert Warmwell, John Bromley, and the clerk

27 August 1421, at Salisbury
2449 By his charter John Passenger, a chaplain, granted to Robert Gilbert, tanner, a citizen of Salisbury, a tenement, with houses, a latrine, and a portion of garden, in St. Martin's Street between Robert's cottages on the east side and a corner tenement of John Moore, baker, on the west side. The tenement, with the houses, latrine, and portion of garden, was held by John Passenger by a devise of Thomas Veal, mercer, of Salisbury, and is to be held for ever by Robert and his heirs and assigns. Clause of warranty. Seals: John Passenger's and the common and mayoral seals of the city. Named witnesses: the bailiff, the mayor, the coroners, the reeves, Walter Shirley, William Warin, Walter Nalder, Thomas Mason, Robert Poynant, Robert Warmwell, John Bromley, and the clerk

24 September 1421, at Salisbury
2450 By his charter John Spencer, of Salisbury, granted to Robert Warmwell, a citizen of Salisbury, and his wife Margaret a tenement, with sollars and cellars, in the high street [called Minster Street: *cf.* **2257, 2333**], between a tenement of Henry Harborough, a canon of the cathedral church, on the south side and William Ferrer's shop, of late that of the master Richard Leach, on the north side, which, with other tenements and shops in the city, he held by a grant of Nicholas Stafford, a chaplain, and Henry Swaff, goldsmith. A fine concerning the tenement was levied, in the king's court at Westminster in the octave of Martinmas 1420 in front of Richard Norton and his fellow justices, between Nicholas and Henry, plaintiffs, and John and his wife Alice, then living, defendants [*cf.* **2430**]. The tenement, with the sollars and cellars, is to be held for ever by Robert and Margaret and their heirs and assigns. Clause of warranty. Seals: John Spencer's and the common and mayoral seals of the city. Named witnesses: the bailiff, the mayor, the coroners, the reeves, Walter Shirley, William Warin, Walter Nalder, Thomas Mason, Robert Poynant, John Bromley, and the clerk
2451 By his charter Thomas Castleton, mercer, of Salisbury, granted to William Vivian, mercer, of Salisbury, a garden in Freren Street, on the east side of the

street, between William Cambridge's garden on the north side and the ditch of
Bug moor on the south side. The garden was bought by Thomas from William
Cambridge, a citizen of London, and his wife Edith, the relict, and an executor,
of Richard Spencer, and it is to be held for ever by William Vivian and his heirs
and assigns. Clause of warranty. Seals: Thomas's and the common and mayoral
seals of the city. Named witnesses: the bailiff, the mayor, coroners, the reeves,
Walter Shirley, William Warin, Walter Nalder, Thomas Mason, Robert Poynant,
Robert Warmwell, John Bromley, and the clerk

2452 By his letters of attorney Thomas Castleton, mercer, of Salisbury, appointed
William Lord or John Butler to surrender into the hand of John, the bishop of
Salisbury, the seisin of a garden in Freren Street [*as in* **2451**], which Thomas of
late bought [*as in* **2451**], to the use of William Vivian, mercer, of Salisbury. Seals:
Thomas's and the mayoral seal of the city

2453 By his writing Thomas Castleton, mercer, of Salisbury, quitclaimed to
John Moore, baker, and his heirs and assigns his right or claim to a cottage, with
a garden, in New Street, towards the east part of the street, between the street
on the south side and William Lord's garden on the north side. Seals: Thomas's
and the common and mayoral seals of the city. Named witnesses: the bailiff, the
mayor, the coroners, the reeves, Walter Shirley, William Warin, Walter Nalder,
Thomas Mason, Robert Poynant, Robert Warmwell, John Bromley, and the
clerk

22 October 1421, at Salisbury

2454 By his charter William Vivian, mercer, of Salisbury, granted to John
Mottisfont, a cordwainer, of Salisbury, and his wife Tamsin a garden in Freren
Street [*as in* **2451**]. The garden was held by William by a grant of Thomas
Castleton, mercer, of Salisbury, and is to be held for ever by John and Tamsin and
their heirs and assigns. Clause of warranty. Seals: William's and the common and
mayoral seals of the city. Named witnesses: the bailiff, the mayor, the coroners, the
reeves, Walter Shirley, William Warin, Walter Nalder, Thomas Mason, Robert
Poynant, Robert Warmwell, John Bromley, and the clerk

5 November 1421, at Salisbury

2455 By her charter Agnes, the relict of John Bedford, skinner, a daughter and
heir of Richard of Otterbourne, a public notary, now dead, in her widowhood
and full power granted to William Oving, chandler, of Salisbury, a tenement in
New Street between cottages of Thomas Upton, a clerk, on the west side and
an empty plot of Robert Netton, a chaplain, on the east side. The tenement
descended to Agnes in fee simple on the death of her father and is to be held
for ever by William and his heirs and assigns. Clause of warranty. Seals: Agnes's
and the common and mayoral seals of the city. Named witnesses: the bailiff,
the mayor, a coroner, the reeves, Walter Shirley, William Warin, Walter Nalder,
Thomas Mason, Robert Poynant, Robert Warmwell, Henry Man, William
Warwick, John Bromley, and the clerk

6 November 1421, at Salisbury

2456 By his writing Robert Bedford, a son and heir of John Bedford and his wife Agnes, quitclaimed to William Oving, chandler, of Salisbury, and his heirs and assigns his right or claim to a tenement in New Street [*as in 2455*], which was formrly that of Richard of Otterbourne, a public notary, his grandfather. Clause of warranty. Seals: Robert's and the common and mayoral seals of the city. Named witnesses: the bailiff, the mayor, the coroners, the reeves, Walter Shirley, William Warin, Walter Nalder, Thomas Mason, Robert Poynant, Robert Warmwell, William Warwick, John Bromley, and the clerk

19 November 1421, at Salisbury

2457 By his charter Richard Oword, a son, and an executor, of Gilbert Oword, of late a citizen of Salisbury, on the strength of Gilbert's will granted to Robert Chinchin a tenement in Wineman Street between a tenement of late that of Robert Bowyer, weaver, on the west side and a sometime toft of William Surr on the east side. The tenement was appointed by Gilbert to be sold by his executors after the death of his wife Alice, now dead, and it is to be held for ever by Robert and his heirs and assigns as that which Robert bought from Richard in good faith for a sum of money, reaching its true value, to be laid out wholly on behalf of Gilbert's soul and the souls of others according to the terms of Gilbert's will. Clause of warranty. Seals: Richard's and the common and mayoral seals of the city. Named witnesses: the bailiff, the mayor, a coroner, the reeves, Walter Shirley, William Warin, Walter Nalder, Thomas Mason, Robert Poynant, Robert Warmwell, Henry Man, John Bromley, and the clerk

2458 By his charter John Swift, ironmonger, a citizen of Salisbury, granted to Richard Gater, tucker, of Salisbury, a tenement in Minster Street between William Lord's tenement on the south side and Edward Potticary's tenement on the north side. The tenement was held by John by a grant of Richard Harlwin and is to be held for ever by Richard Gater and his heirs and assigns. Clause of warranty. Seals: John's and the common and mayoral seals of the city. Named witnesses: the bailiff, a coroner, the reeves, Walter Shirley, William Warin, Walter Nalder, Thomas Mason, Robert Poynant, Robert Warmwell, John Bromley, and the clerk

4 December 1421, at Salisbury

2459 A deed [*dated as above, although a date later than that of 2462 might have been expected*] of Robert Ogbourne. Gunnore, the relict of Thomas Boyton, bowyer, of late a citizen of Salisbury, holds for life by Thomas's devise a chief tenement in Minster Street, which is called Castle Street, [*as in 2462*], the reversion of which pertains to Thomas's executors to be sold. On the strength of Thomas's will William Lord, one of the executors, granted the reversion, when it fell due on Gunnore's death, to Robert and his heirs and assigns. Robert appointed Richard Read, a chaplain, to receive from Gunnore an attornment, by the name of seisin, on the strength of the grant of the reversion. Seals: Robert's and the mayoral seal of the city

17 December 1421, at Salisbury

2460 Approval of the will of Edmund Friday made on 10 October 1420. <u>Interment</u>: in the graveyard of St. Edmund's church, beside the tomb in which the corpse of Thomas Friday, his father, lies buried. <u>Bequests</u>: 6*d.* to the fabric of that church, and 10*s.* to Richard Curtis, a chaplain of it, to pray for his soul; 20*s.* to William Lord; a red coverlet, with two blankets, and a pair of linen sheets to Hugh Kingsbury, skinner; a green gown with fur to Edith Capps; two gowns, one lined with green and the other lined with blue motley to Hugh Capps; the rest of his goods to his executors to be laid out on behalf of his soul and the souls of others. <u>Devise.</u> John Judd acquired from him a corner tenement, with shops, cottages, and a yard (*or* yards), in Endless Street and Chipper Lane, between a tenement of late Stephen Shearer's, now that of the dean and chapter of Salisbury, on the south side and cottages of late William Tull's on the west side, to be held by John when it fell due on the death of Robert, a son of Edmund Bramshaw, by reason of Robert's want of issue; also the reversion of a rent of 38*s.* [a year] issuing from the tenement, with the shops, cottages, and yard(s). Let it be known to all men that, on account of the very great security of John Judd, the things which Edmund set in motion for John concerning the purchase of the tenement, with the shops, cottages, and yard(s), could be demanded to be duly carried out according to the effect of a charter perfected for John in the matter. Edmund appointed the tenement, with the shops, cottages, and yard(s), which by reason of Robert's want of issue would remain to him, to remain to John Judd and his heirs, together with the reversion of the rent of 38*s.*, to be held for ever by John and his heirs. <u>Executors</u>: Richard Curtis, a chaplain, and William Lord. <u>Proved</u> on 4 July 1421 in front of Alexander Sparrow, a bachelor, deputed a commissary by John, the bishop of Salisbury; the administration was entrusted to Richard, reserving the power to entrust it to William when he might come to be admitted. <u>Approved</u> at a court held in front of the bailiff, the mayor, and other citizens.

2461 By their charter John at the weir and his wife Joan, appearing at the court held on that day, granted to William Oving, chandler, of Salisbury, a toft, with a garden, in New Street, between William's tenement on the west side and a tenement of late John Stone's on the east side, to be held for ever by William and his heirs and assigns. Clause of warranty. Seals: those of John and Joan and the common and mayoral seals of the city. Named witnesses: the bailiff, the mayor, a coroner, the reeves, Walter Shirley, William Warin, Walter Nalder, Thomas Mason, Robert Poynant, Robert Warmwell, Henry Ham [?*rectius* Man], John Bromley, and the clerk

2462 By his charter William Lord, an executor of Thomas Boyton, bowyer, of late a citizen of Salisbury, on the strength of Thomas's will granted to Robert Ogbourne the reversion of a chief tenement in Minster Street, which is called Castle Street, between a tenement formerly that of William Bailiff, draper, now Richard Oword's, on the north side and a tenement which John Moore, baker, holds on the south side. Thomas appointed the tenement to be sold by his executors after the death of his wife Gunnore and the year following that, and after the death of William Boyton, now dead. When it fell due the reversion is to be held for ever by Robert and his heirs and assigns as that which he bought in good faith from Gunnore, as an executor of Thomas, and William for a sum of money, reaching its true value, to be wholly laid out according to the terms of Thomas's will. Seals: William's and the common and mayoral seals of the city. Named witnesses: the bailiff, the mayor, a coroner, the reves, Walter Shirley, William Warin, Walter Nalder, Thomas Mason, Robert Poynant, Robert Warmwell, Henry Man, and John Bromley

14 January 1422, at Salisbury

2463 By his charter Thomas Biston, a citizen of Salisbury, granted to an elder John Pope and his wife Christine, and to a younger John Pope, a tenement in Winchester Street between a tenement of the elder John on the east side and a tenement of Thomas Read, merchant, on the west side. The tenement was formerly that of John Monkton, some time since a citizen of Salisbury, and is to be held for ever by the grantees and their heirs and assigns. Clause of warranty. Seals: Thomas Biston's and the common and mayoral seals of the city. Named witnesses: the bailiff, the mayor, a coroner, the reeves, Walter Shirley, William Warin, Walter Nalder, Robert Poynant, Robert Warmwell, Henry Man, and John Bromley

28 January 1422, at Salisbury

2464 By their charter Thomas Mason, William Lord, and William Moore, executors of Stephen Edington, of late a citizen of Salisbury, on the strength of Stephen's will granted to Robert Watercombe, otherwise called Robert Chidley, and his wife Agnes a tenement in St. Martin's Street between a tenement of the vicars of the cathedral church on either side. The tenement was appointed by Stephen in his will to be sold by his executors after the death of his sons William and John, both dead, and is to be held for ever by Robert and Agnes and Robert's heirs and assigns. Seals: those of the grantors and the common and mayoral seals of the city. Named witnesses: the bailiff, the mayor, a coroner, the reeves, Walter Shirley, William Warin, Walter Nalder, Robert Poynant, Robert Warmwell, Henry Man, and John Bromley

2465 By his charter Richard, a son and heir of Edward Breamore, of Salisbury, granted to John Marshall, dyer, of Salisbury, a rent of 4s. 7d. a year issuing from a messuage in Minster Street between William Lord's tenement on the south side and a tenement of late Edward's on the north side; also the reversion of a tenement, when it fell due on the death of Edith, Richard's mother, in Minster Street between William Alexander's tenement on the south side and a tenement of John Durnford, dyer, on the north side. The rent and the reversion are to be held for ever by John Marshall and his heirs and assigns. Clause of warranty. Seals: Richard's and the common and mayoral seals of the city. Named witnesses: the bailiff, the mayor, a coroner, the reeves, Walter Shirley, William Warin, Walter Nalder, Thomas Mason, Robert Poynant, Robert Warmwell, John Bromley, and the clerk

2466 By his charter Thomas Castleton, a citizen of Salisbury, granted to Henry Man and Peter Daw, of Salisbury, a tenement in St. Martin's Street, between a bridge of the running water on the west side and a tenement of Robert Poynant and Richard Gage on the east side, to be held for ever by them and their heirs and assigns. Clause of warranty. Thomas also granted and released to Henry and Peter all his goods and chattels, movable and immovable. Seals: Thomas's and the common and mayoral seals of the city. Named witnesses: the bailiff, the mayor, a coroner, the reeves, Walter Shirley, William Warin, Walter Nalder, Thomas Mason, and the clerk

2467 By his letters of attorney Thomas Castleton, a citizen of Salisbury, appointed William Lord to surrender into the hand of John, the bishop of Salisbury, the seisin of a tenement in St. Martin's Street, [*as in 2466*], to the use of Henry Man and Peter Daw, of Salisbury. Seals: Thomas's and the mayoral seal of the city

25 March 1422, at Salisbury

2468 By his charter John Noble, a citizen of Salisbury, granted to John Upton cottages, with a yard (*or* yards), of late those of Reynold Glover, of Salisbury, which John Noble held by a grant of Thomas Upton, a clerk. The cottages stand in New Street, between a tenement of late William Godmanstone's, now that of Henry Chubb, baker, on the east side and the river Avon on the west side, and, with the yard(s), are to be held for ever by John Upton and his heirs and assigns. John Noble quitclaimed to John Upton and his heirs and assigns his right or claim to the cottages, with the yard(s). Seals: John Noble's and the common and mayoral seals of the city. Named witnesses: the bailiff, the mayor, a coroner, the reeves, Walter Shirley, William Warin, Walter Nalder, Robert Warmwell, Henry Man, and John Bromley

8 April 1422, at Salisbury

2469 By his writing Laurence Groom, a chaplain, an executor of John Oword, a chaplain and of late a vicar of the cathedral church, quitclaimed to Robert Chinchin, of Salisbury, and his heirs and assigns his right or claim to a tenement in Wineman Street between a tenement formerly Robert Bowyer's on the west side and a tenement of late William Surr's on the east side. Seals: Laurence's and the common and mayoral seals of the city. Named witnesses: the bailiff, the mayor, a coroner, the reeves, Walter Shirley, William Warin, Walter Nalder, Thomas Mason, Robert Warmwell, and the clerk

22 April 1422, at Salisbury

2470 By his charter John Judd granted to Edward Prentice, the precentor of the cathedral church, all his land, tenements, rent, services, and reversions, with cottages, yards, racks, and gardens, which, with John Lake and William Mercer, now dead, he held by a grant of William Coventry, and which were of late those of John Butterley, a citizen of Salisbury. The premises, opposite the graveyard of St. Edmund's church and in Nuggeston, are to be held for ever by Edward and his heirs and assigns. Seals: John Judd's and the common and mayoral seals of the city. Named witnesses: the bailiff, the mayor, the reeves, Walter Shirley, William Warin, Walter Nalder, Thomas Mason, Robert Warmwell, Henry Man, and John Bromley

2471 By their charter John Judd and William Alexander demised to Edward Prentice, the precentor of the cathedral church, premises [*as in* ***2470***], opposite the graveyard of St. Edmund's church and in Nuggeston, to be held for ever by Edward and his heirs and assigns. Seals: those of John and William. Named witnesses: the bailiff, the mayor, the reeves, Walter Shirley, William Warin, Walter Nalder, Thomas Mason, Robert Warmwell, Henry Man, and the clerk

2472 By her charter Olive, the relict of John Lake, of late a citizen of Salisbury, granted to Edward Prentice, the precentor of the cathedral church, two tenements in Minster Street, one in Cook Row between Thomas Harding's tenement on the south side and a shop of John Burgh [?at the burgh] on the north side, and the other, on the west side of the street, between William Fines's tenement on the north side and a tenement of Thomas Cardmaker, of Warminster, on the south side. The tenements were held by Olive by a devise of John Lake and are to be held for ever by Edward and his heirs and assigns. Clause of warranty. Seals: Olive's and the common and mayoral seals of the city. Named witnesses: the bailiff, the mayor, the coroners, the reeves, Walter Shirley, William Warin, Walter Nalder, Thomas Mason, Robert Warmwell, Henry Man, and the clerk

20 May 1422, at Salisbury

2473 By his writing Simon Membury, a canon of the cathedral church, quitclaimed to Edward Prentice, the precentor, his right or claim to premises [*as in* ***2470***], formerly those of John Butterley, of late a citizen of Salisbury, opposite the graveyard of St. Edmund's church and in Nuggeston; also his right or claim to two tenements in Minster Street [*as in* ***2472***], which Edward held by a grant of Olive, the relict of John Lake. Simon also released to Edward all manner of personal actions against him. Seals: Simon's and the common and mayoral seals of the city. Named witnesses: the bailiff, the mayor, the coroners, the reeves, Walter Shirley, William Warin, Walter Nalder, Thomas Mason, Robert Warmwell, Henry Man, and the clerk

21 May 1422, at Salisbury

2474 By his indented charter John Gould, a chaplain, granted to John Upton, a son of an elder John Upton, of late a citizen of Salisbury, a corner tenement, with shops, cottages, gardens, and a yard (*or* yards), in Winchester Street and Culver Street, between a tenement of late John Butterley's, now that of William Halstead, butcher, in Winchester Street on the east side and cottages of late Bartholomew Durkin's, now those of the hospital of the Holy Trinity, called Almshouse, in Culver Street on the south side, to be held for ever by him and his issue. If the younger John Upton were to die without issue the tenement, with the shops, cottages, gardens, and yard(s), would remain to John Gould, or his executors or their executors, to be sold. The money received from the sale should be laid out, according to the terms of a feoffment perfected by the elder John

Upton for Richard Upton, a chaplain, now dead, and John Gould, on behalf of the elder John Upton's soul and the souls of others. Seals: John Gould's and the common and mayoral seals of the city. Named witnesses: the bailiff, the mayor, the coroners, the reeves, Walter Shirley, William Warin, Walter Nalder, Thomas Mason, Robert Warmwell, Henry Man, and the clerk

2475 By his letters of attorney John Gould, a chaplain, appointed Walter Nalder and Walter Short to surrender into the hand of John, the bishop of Salisbury, a corner tenement, with shops, cottages, gardens, and a yard (*or* yards), in Winchester Street and Culver Street [*as in* **2474**] to the use of John, a son of John Upton, of late a citizen of Salisbury. Seals: John Gould's and the mayoral seal of the city

3 June 1422, at Salisbury

2476 By his indented charter Nicholas Upton granted to John Sydenham, of Salisbury, and his wife Cecily, and to Richard Bridge and his wife Agnes, a messuage with three conjoined shops in Carter Street between Robert Earl's cottages on the south side and cottages, which Thomas Hussey holds for his life of Nicholas, on the north side; also the reversion of [the] three cottages, with gardens, which Thomas holds for his life, between Richard Ecton's cottages on the north side and the shops granted to John and Cecily, and to Richard and Agnes, on the south side. The messuage, with the shops, and the reversion of the cottages, with the gardens, when they fell due, are to be held for ever by John and Cecily, and Richard and Agnes, and the joint issue of Richard and Agnes. If Richard and Agnes were to die without such issue the messuage, with the shops, and the reversion of the cottages, with the gardens, would remain for ever to John Sydenham's direct heirs. Clause of warranty. Seals: Nicholas's to both parts of the charter and the common and mayoral seals of the city. Named witnesses: the bailiff, the mayor, the coroners, the reeves, Walter Shirley, William Warin, Walter Nalder, Thomas Mason, Robert Warmwell, and the clerk

4 June 1422, at Salisbury

2477 By his writing Thomas Upton, a clerk, quitclaimed to John Sydenham, of Salisbury, and his wife Cecily, and to Richard Bridge and his wife Agnes, his right or claim to a messuage, with three conjoined shops, in Carter Street [*as in* **2476**]; also to the reversion of three cottages, with gardens, which Thomas Hussey holds for his life, [*as in* **2476**]. Seals: Thomas's and the common and mayoral seals of the city. Named witnesses: the bailiff, the mayor, the coroners, the reeves, Walter Shirley, William Warin, Walter Nalder, Thomas Mason, Robert Warmwell, and the clerk

17 June 1422, at Salisbury

2478 Approval of the will of Nicholas Baynton made on 12 January 1422. <u>Interment</u>: in the chapel of the Blessed Mary Magdalen at Faulston. <u>Bequests</u>: 6s. 8d. to the chaplain of that chapel; 6s. 8d. to the church of Bishopstone, and 3s. 4d. to the vicar; a porteous and 3s. 4d. to John Bullock, his chaplain; 3s. 4d. to Eleanor, his household servant; 20*d*. to each of his servants; 3*s*. 4*d*. to William Goldsmith; 6*s*. 8*d*. to the cathedral church; 6*s*. 8*d*. each to the churches of the two orders of friars at Salisbury; the rest of his goods to his wife Joan. Devise: to Joan, to be held for ever by her and her heirs and assigns, all his messuages, cottages, shops, tenements, reversions, rent, and services in Salisbury. Executors: Joan, his principal executor, and Thomas Garbett and John Gilbert, to each of whom he bequeathed 20*s*. for his work; overseer, [Simon Sydenham,] the dean of Salisbury. Proved on 7 February 1422 in the chapel of Faulston in front of John Fitton, a canon of the cathedral church, specially appointed a commissary for the purpose; the administration was entrusted to the executors, who consequently accounted with that commissary and were dismissed. Approved at a court held in front of the bailiff, the mayor, and others; the seisin of the tenements was released to the legatee.

2479 By their charter George Westby and William Penton, dyer, granted to Thomas Freeman and his wife Agnes, the relict of a younger John Forest, of Salisbury, a tenement in Wineman Street, between a tenement of John Hain, loader, on the west side and William's cottage property on the east side, to be held for ever by them and their heirs and assigns. Seals: those of George and William and the common and mayoral seals of the city. Named witnesses: the bailiff, the mayor, the coroners, the reeves, Walter Shirley, William Warin, Walter Nalder, Thomas Mason, Robert Warmwell, Henry Man, and the clerk

2480 By his charter John Hewet, of Longbridge Deverill, granted to William Alexander and Henry Man, [both] of Salisbury, and John Whitehorn a messuage, with shops and cottages, called Deverill's Inn, in Castle Street, opposite the market place where grains are sold, between Richard Oword's messuage on the south side and a cottage of Thomas Forster, dyer, on the north side. The messuage, with the shops and cottages, with other land, tenements, meadow, pastures, pasture rights, rent, services, and reversions which John Dyer, of Longbridge Deverill, held in Wiltshire, was held by John Hewet and an elder John Gowan, now dead, by John Dyer's grant, and it is to be held for ever by William Alexander, Henry Man, and John Whitehorn and their heirs and assigns. Clause of warranty. Seals: John Hewet's and the common and mayoral seals of the city. Named witnesses: the bailiff, the mayor, the coroners, the reeves, Walter Shirley, William Warin, Walter Nalder, Thomas Mason, Robert Warmwell, Thomas Bower, William Warwick, and the clerk

2481 By their charter Henry Man and Peter Daw, [both] of Salisbury, granted to John Moore, baker, of Salisbury, and his wife Isabel a tenement in St. Martin's Street, between a bridge of the running water on the west side and Richard Gage's tenement on the east side, to be held for ever by them and their heirs and assigns. Seals: those of Henry and Peter and the common and mayoral seals of the city. Named witnesses: the bailiff, the mayor, the coroners, the reeves, Walter Shirley, William Warin, Walter Nalder, Thomas Mason, Robert Warmwell, Henry Man, and the clerk

1 July 1422, at Salisbury
2482 Approval of the will of William Bower made on 30 March 1421. Interment:

in the graveyard of the church of Horton. <u>Bequests</u>: 12*d*. to the fabric of the cathedral church; 20*s*. to the fabric of Horton church, and 6*s*. 8*d*. to the vicar; 6*s*. 8*d*. to All Saints' church, Up Wimborne; 10*s*. and a vestment worth 20*s*. to the church of Knowlton; 6 ewes each to William Irish, to the daughter of Robert Dowge, and to William, a son of Robert Rill; 2 ewes to each of his godchildren, each of his servants, and Martin of [the] almshouse; 1 ewe to John Corset; 1 bu. of wheat to each pauper of Horton parish; 40 sheep each to Margaret Cornish and Robert Warmwell; a red cow to the wife of Robert Rill; a rosary of gold beads to Joan River; a gilt rosary and a gold ouch to the wife of Robert Warmwell; a red cow and a tod of black and white wool to Cecily, the wife of John Hobbs; 6 hoggasters to Richard Bishop; a loaf of bread to each person coming to his burial, the loaves to be ordered at three for a penny; 10 marks to the monks of Beaulieu out of a debt of 20 marks owed to William by the abbot; 6*s*. 8*d*. both to the Dominicans of Fisherton and the Franciscans of Salisbury; 500 masses should be celebrated on behalf of his soul on the three days immediately after his death; 6*s*. 8*d*. to two monks of Horton to pray for his soul; Robert Warmwell, his executor, should find a chaplain to celebrate mass in the church of Horton for seven years on behalf of his soul and the souls of others; 20*s*. to Gilham, his servant, and Gilham should remain in custody with his executor; a coverlet, two blankets, and two linen sheets to Alice Joiner; 6 ewes to John Bride; 1*d*. to each pauper coming to his burial; a coverlet, two linen sheets, and two blankets, and a blue and green gown, to Robert Rill; 40*d*. to John Bertram; 6*d*. to each chaplain coming to his burial; 40*d*. to Roger, a friar, of Cranborne; a gown of sendal and blue to both John Shepherd and Richard Bishop; a spinning wheel and a sheep to a daughter of John Buck, and a sheep to John's other daughter; a gown furred with beaver to John Cornish, three pairs of linen sheets, a rosary of silver beads, two beds, two testers, a tablecloth, and two altar cloths to his wife Margaret, and a brass pot to Margaret's daughter; 12*d*. to the wife of Robert Joiner; the rest of his goods to Robert Warmwell for him to dispose of on behalf of William's soul and the souls of others. <u>Devises</u> he appointed a corner tenement in Castle Street and Scots Lane, between George Goss's tenement on the south side and Robert Lyveden's tenement on the east side, to be sold by Robert Warmwell, his executor. The money received from the sale should be laid out on the salvation of William's soul and the souls of others. William devised to John Hobbs and his wife Cecily a tenement in St. Martin's Street, between a tenement of the provost of St. Edmund's church on the east side and a tenement of the vicars of the cathedral church on the west side, to be held for ever by them and their heirs and assigns. <u>Executor</u>: Robert Warmwell. <u>Proved</u> at Gussage on 12 October 1421 in front of an officer of the archdeacon of Dorset; the administration was entrusted to the executor. <u>Approved</u>: at a court held in front of the bailiff, the mayor, and other citizens; the seisin of the tenements was released to the legatees.

2483 Approval [*the approval is dated to the Wednesday after the feast of the translation of St. Thomas the Martyr (8 July) probably in error for the Wednesday before that feast (1 July)*] of the will of Joan Knolle made on 4 January 1422. <u>Interment</u>: in St. Thomas's church. <u>Bequests</u>: 6*s*. 8*d*.to the fabric of the cathedral church; 10*s*. to the fabric of St. Thomas's church, 6*d*. each to the deacon and the sacristan, and 12*d*. to the sacristan for making her tomb; 40*d*. each to the fabric of St. Edmund's church and the fabric of St. Martin's church; 6*s*. 8*d*. both to the Franciscans of Salisbury and the Dominicans of Fisherton; 20*d*. to the almshouse at Salisbury; 12*d*. both to the prisoners at Fisherton and the prisoners in the Guildhall; 6*s*. 8*d*. to the fabric of Netheravon church, and 12*d*. to the vicar; 12*d*. each to the fabric of Durrington church and the fabric of Fittleton church; 6*d*. to the paupers of St. Nicholas's hospital; 6*d*. to the fabric of St. Clement's church, Fisherton; 12*d*. each to the bridge of Upavon called Cat bridge and the bridge of Netheravon called Brewer bridge; 12*d*. for the repair of the way called Lud marsh; immediately after her death 100 masses should be celebrated on behalf of her soul; 60*s*. in money should be handed out to paupers by her executors on the day of her burial; on the same day her executors should provide five gowns to five paupers bearing five candles to her funeral rites and mass, and five pairs of shoes, and they should hand out five smocks to five needy wives; 4*d*. to each chaplain present at her funeral rites and mass, and 2*d*. to each clerk being there; 3*s*. 4*d*. to Nicholas Wight; 6*s*. 8*d*. to John Enford; 20*s*. to the master John Teffont; 3*s*. 4*d*. to John Teffont; 20*d*. to Joan, a daughter of John Judd; 4*d*. to each of her other godchildren; 12*d*. to Christine Stout and her children; the rest of her goods to William Knolle, her son, and his wife Agnes to pray for her soul. <u>Devises</u>: to William a tenement, in which she dwelt, in Wheeler Row between shops of late Simon Tredinnick's on the north side and Robert Ashley's tenement on the south side; also to William a tenement in Carter Street between John Sampson's shops on the south side and Henry Man's tenement on the north side; also to William a cottage in Nuggeston between cottages of late John Forest's on the east side and a corner cottage of John Hampton, grocer, on the west side. The tenements and the cottage are to be held for ever by William and his heirs and assigns. <u>Executors</u>: her son William and John Noble, her intimate friend. <u>Proved</u> on 16 June 1422 in front of John Pedwell, the subdean; the administration was entrusted to the executors, who at length appeared, accounted with an officer, and were dismissed. <u>Approved</u> at a court held in front of the bailiff, the mayor, and other citizens; the seisin of the tenements was released to the legatee.

26 August 1422, at Salisbury

2484 By their charter Thomas Mason, William Lord, and William Moore, the executors of Stephen Edington, of Salisbury, on the strength of Stephen's will granted to Robert Potter, a cordwainer, of Salisbury, the reversion of a shop, which Margery Brandon and Christine Cole hold for their life by Stephen's devise, in Castle Street between a chief tenement, in which Stephen dwelt, on the north side and a corner shop, of late Stephen's, on the south side. Stephen appointed the shop to be sold by his executors after the death of Margery and Christine, and after the death of his sons William and John, who are now dead, and it is to be held for ever, when it fell due on the death of Margery and Christine, by Robert and his heirs and assigns. Seals: those of the grantors and the common and mayoral seals of the city. Named witnesses: the bailiff, the mayor, the coroners, the reeves, Walter Shirley, William Warin, Walter Nalder, Robert Warmwell, Henry Man, William Warwick, and Thomas Bower

2485 By his charter Nicholas Stafford, a chaplain, an executor of Adam Countwell, of late a citizen of Salisbury, an executor of John Beeton, formerly a citizen of Salisbury, on the strength of John's will granted to Edward Gilbert, dubber, a citizen of Salisbury, a messuage in Castle Street between Edward's tenement on the south side and Thomas Farrant's tenement on the north side. John Beeton appointed the messuage, by the name of a tenement, in which he dwelt, to be sold by his executors or their executors, for want of issue of Thomas, Margaret, and Alice, his children, who have all died without issue, after the death of his wife Alice. The money received from the sale should be laid out, on celebrating masses, repairing ways, and doing other charitable deeds, on behalf of John's soul and the souls of others. The messuage is to be held for ever by Edward and his heirs and assigns as that which he bought from Nicholas in good faith for a sum of money, reaching its true value, to be laid out in the way specified above. Seals: Nicholas's and the common and mayoral seals of the city. Named witnesses: the bailiff, the mayor, the coroners, the reeves, Walter Shirley, William Warin, Walter Nalder, Thomas Mason, Robert Warmwell, Henry Man, William Warwick, and the clerk

2486 By their writing Agnes, the relict of Thomas Beeton, of Salisbury, [and] John Hellier, ironmonger, and Edward Potticary, executors of Thomas, quitclaimed to Edward Gilbert, dubber, a citizen of Salisbury, and his heirs and assigns their right or claim to a messuage in Castle Street [*as in 2485*]. The messuage was held by Edward by a grant of Nicholas Stafford, a chaplain, an executor of Adam Countwell, of late a citizen of Salisbury, an executor of John Beeton, formerly a citizen of Salisbury. Seals: those of Agnes, John, and Edward and the common and mayoral seals of the city. Named witnesses: the bailiff, the mayor, the coroners, the reeves, Walter Shirley, William Warin, Walter Nalder, Thomas Mason, Robert Warmwell, Henry Man, William Warwick, and the clerk

23 September 1422, at Salisbury

2487 By her charter Emme, the relict of Robert Poynant, of late a citizen of Salisbury, in her widowhood and full power granted to Robert Gilbert, tanner, of Salisbury, and Philip Gough, a chaplain, a tenement in Winchester Street between John Deverill's tenement on the east side and a tenement, which Hugh Andrew holds, on the west side. The tenement was held by Emme by a devise of Robert to her and her heirs and assigns for ever, and it is to be held for ever by Robert Gilbert and Philip Gough and their heirs and assigns. Clause of warranty. Seals: Emme's and the common and mayoral seals of the city. Named witnesses: the bailiff, the mayor, the coroners, the reeves, Walter Shirley, William Warin, Walter Nalder, Thomas Mason, Robert Warmwell, Henry Man, William Warwick, and the clerk

2488 By her letters of attorney Emme, the relict of Robert Poynant, of late a citizen of Salisbury, in her widowhood and full power appointed Henry Man to surrender into the hand of John, the bishop of Salisbury, the seisin of a tenement in Winchester Street [*as in 2487*] to the use of Robert Gilbert, tanner, of Salisbury, and Philip Gough, a chaplain. Seals: Emme's and the mayoral seal of the city

2489 A charter of Thomas Mason, William Lord, and William Moore, the executors of Stephen Edington, of Salisbury. Stephen devised to his wife Christine a chief tenement, in which he dwelt, in Castle Street between a shop, which Margery Brandon and Christine Cole hold for their life by Stephen's devise, on the south side and a shop, of late Stephen's, on the north side. The tenement was to be held by Christine for life as dower, and after her death was to remain severally to Stephen's sons William and John for their life. Also, Stephen devised to William and John shops next to the chief tenement, except the shop devised to Margery Brandon and Christine Cole, to be held by them severally for their life and the life of the one of them living longer. After the death of William and John the chief tenement and the shops, except the shop devised to Margery and Christine, were to remain to Stephen's executors to be sold. The money raised from the sale was to be laid out by the executors on behalf of Stephen's soul, the souls of William Knoyle, painter, and Edith, of late Stephen's wife, and the souls of others. The tenement, with the shops, stands, in Castle Street, between Thomas Mason's tenement on the north side and a tenement of late John Parch's on the east side. Stephen's relict Christine, and his sons William and John, are dead, so that it pertains to the executors to sell the chief tenement and the shops, except the shop devised to Margery Brandon and Christine Cole. Robert Potter, a cordwainer, of Salisbury, has paid to the executors a sum of money reaching the true value of the tenement and shops and, by their charter and on the strength of Stephen's will, the executors granted them to him, to be held for ever by him and his heirs and assigns as that which he bought from the executors in good faith for the sum of money to be wholly laid out according to the terms of the will. Seals: those of the executors and the common and mayoral seals of the city. Named witnesses: the bailiff, the mayor, the coroners, the reeves, Walter Shirley, William Warin, Walter Nalder, Robert Warmwell, Henry Man, William Warwick, and the clerk

2490 By his charter Robert Warmwell, a citizen of Salisbury, granted to John Swift, ironmonger, a citizen of Salisbury, and his wife Christine a tenement in the street on the way to the upper bridge of Fisherton [*as in 2420*], to be held for ever by them and their heirs and assigns. Clause of warranty. Seals: Robert's and the common and mayoral seals of the city. Named witnesses: the bailiff, the reeves, Walter Shirley, William Warin, Thomas Mason, Henry Man, John Bromley, and William Warwick

7 October 1422, at Salisbury

2491 By his indented charter John Wishford granted to Henry Man, a citizen of Salisbury, a tenement in New Street between a tenement of late Agnes Bodenham's, now Henry's, on the east side and a tenement of late that of Thomas Trubb, a chaplain, now Thomas Merriott's, on the west side. The tenement was held by John by a grant of William Wilton, formerly a citizen of London, and is to be held for ever by Henry and his heirs and assigns for paying a rent of

40s. a year to John and his assigns for John's life. Clause to permit re-entry if the rent were to be in arrear for 15 days, distraint, and the keeping of distresses until the unpaid rent and other losses were recovered; also, to permit permanent repossession if the rent were to be in arrear for a month. During John's life Henry should repair and maintain the tenement at his own expense so that the rent would not be lost. Clause to permit permanent repossession if the tenement were not thus repaired. Clause of warranty. Seals: those of the parties to the parts of the charter in turn and the common and mayoral seals of the city. Named witnesses: the bailiff, the mayor, the coroners, the reeves, Walter Shirley, William Warin, Walter Nalder, Thomas Mason, Robert Warmwell, and the clerk

2492 By his charter William Basket, weaver, of Salisbury, granted to William Oving, chandler, of Salisbury, a garden in Brown Street, between a tenement of late William Slegge's on the south side and a tenement of late Henry Prettyjohn's on the north side, except a gutter, called Onesfall, of a house of late William Slegge's. The garden extends in length from Brown Street as far as the trench of running water at the end of it on the east side. It was held by William Basket by a grant of Philip Wanstrow, carpenter, and, except for the gutter, is to be held for ever by William Oving and his heirs and assigns. Clause of warranty. Seals: William Basket's and the common and mayoral seals of the city. Named witnesses: the bailiff, the mayor, the reeves, Walter Shirley, William Warin, Walter Nalder, Thomas Mason, Robert Warmwell, Henry Man, and the clerk

2493 A charter of William Lord, an executor of Richard Falconer, called Leach. Richard devised to William Ferrer, of Hungerford, a tenement in the high street which is called Minster Street between Robert Warmwell's tenement on the south side and a tenement of the dean and chapter of Salisbury on the north side. The tenement was to be held for life by William when it fell due on the death of Richard's wife Alice, now dead, and on William's death it should remain to Richard's executors, or their executors, to be sold. The money raised from the sale should be laid out on behalf of the souls of Richard and Alice and the souls of others. William Warin, a citizen of Salisbury, has paid to William Lord a sum reaching the true value of the reversion. Considering that the will of any deceased person should be fulfilled quickly, in that the mercy of God may be quickly brought to the aid of those souls and the souls brought over to a place of refreshment, and so that the divine mercy of God might be brought quickly to help those souls, by his charter, on the strength of Richard's will, William Lord granted to William Warin the reversion of the tenement when it fell due on the death of William Ferrer, to be held for ever by him and his heirs and assigns. Seals: William Lord's and the common and mayoral seals of the city. Named witnesses: the bailiff, the mayor, the reeves, Walter Shirley, Walter Nalder, Thomas Mason, Robert Warmwell, and Henry Man

4 November 1422, at Salisbury

2494 By their charter Thomas Keech, of Marlborough, and his wife Isabel, the relict, and an executor, of Stephen Brown, grocer, of late a citizen of Salisbury, appearing in court granted to Hugh Andrew, of Salisbury, a tenement, with shops, in Winchester Street between a tenement of late Robert Poynant's on the east side and a corner toft, which Thomas Messenger holds, on the west side. The tenement was devised by Stephen to Isabel and her heirs for ever and, with the shops, is to be held for ever by Hugh and his heirs and assigns as that which he bought from Thomas and Isabel in good faith for a sum of money, reaching its true value, to be laid out entirely on behalf of Stephen's soul according to his will. Seals: those of Thomas and Isabel and the common and mayoral seals of the city. Named witnesses: the bailiff, the mayor, the reeves, Walter Shirley, Walter Nalder, Thomas Mason, Robert Warmwell, Henry Man, John Swift, William Warwick, and the clerk

2 December 1422, at Salisbury
2495 Approval of the will of Thomas Bower, a citizen of Salisbury, made on 24 September 1422. Interment: in the new aisle of St. Edmund's church, as one enters the chapel of the Blessed Mary, in front of his seat. Bequests: 3s. 4d. to the fabric of the cathedral church; 20s. to the fabric of St. Edmund's church, 13s. 4d. to the rector for his forgotten tithes and lesser benefactions, 3s. 4d. and 3 yd. of russet cloth of Bruton to the parochial chaplain, 2s. 6d. to each other collegiate chaplain to pray for his soul, and 4d. to each other annual chaplain; 3s. 4d. both to the Franciscans of Salisbury and the Dominicans of Fisherton Anger; 3s. 4d. to the fabric of St. Thomas's church; a chaplain should be appointed by his executors to celebrate mass in St. Edmund's church for seven years after his death on behalf of his soul and the souls of others; a halfpenny loaf to each pauper coming to a distribution on the day of his burial; a striped gown with the fur of otter to Robert Pile, his servant; a green striped gown with the fur of lamb to John Robbs, his apprentice; a blue striped gown with the fur of lamb to Peter, his apprentice; a brass pot of 3 gallons, a coverlet, two blankets, two linen sheets, and 40s. for her stipend to Cecily, his servant; six silver spoons to his daughter Margaret to pray for his soul; six silver spoons, a basin, a laver, and a bed to his son Edward; the rest of his goods to his wife Ellen. Devises: to Ellen for life two conjoined tenements in Castle Street between a tenement of Thomas Forster, dyer, on the south side and John Bodenham's tenement on the north side. After Ellen's death the tenement should be held for ever by Thomas's son Edward and Edward's issue. If Edward were to die without issue the tenements should be sold by John Noble, Thomas's executor, by his executors, or by subsequent executors. The money received from the sale should be laid out by his executor on pious uses for the salvation of his soul. Thomas also devised to Ellen for life a chief tenement, [Grandon's Corner, opposite the market place: *cf. 1219, 2015, 2017*], on a corner of Wineman Street, between a tenement of late Robert Poynant's in Wineman Street on the east side and a tenement of late William Bowyer's on the south side. After Ellen's death the tenement should be sold by John Noble or subsequent executors and, if it could be done advantageously for the salvation of Thomas's soul, the reversion of the tenement should be sold by the executor in Ellen's lifetime. The money issuing from the sale should be laid out by the executors, and by Ellen if she were living, on pious uses on behalf of Thomas's

soul and the souls of others. Thomas also devised to Ellen for life a tenement, with a cellar, in Pot Row between a tenement of Thomas Freeman, mercer, on the west side and Thomas Cardmaker's tenement on the east side. After Ellen's death the tenement, with the cellar, should be held for ever by Thomas Bower's daughter Margaret and her issue. After Margaret's death, if she were to die without issue, the tenement, with the cellar, should be sold by John Noble. The money received from the sale should be laid out on behalf of Thomas's soul. Thomas appointed two tenements, one in Winchester Street between Thomas Bonham's tenement on the east side and Isabel Plummer's tenement on the west side, and the other in the high street, opposite the cross where poultry are sold, between an empty plot of John at the burgh, esq., on the west side and a tenement of the provost of St. Edmund's church on the north side, to be sold by John Noble, his executor. The money issuing from the sale should be laid out by John Noble and Thomas's wife Ellen on the salvation of Thomas's soul and the souls of others. Executors: his wife Ellen and John Noble. Proved on 14 November 1422 in front of John Pedwell, the subdean; the administration was entrusted to the executors. Approved at a court held in front of the bailiff, the mayor, and other citizens; the seisin of the tenements was released to the legatees.

16 December 1422, at Salisbury
2496 By his charter John Chaffin, cardmaker, of Warminster, granted to John Paul, a furbisher, of Salisbury, a tenement in Minster Street, between a tenement called the Rose on the south side and Laurence Groom's tenement on the north side, to be held for ever by him and his heirs and assigns. Clause of warranty. Seals: John Chaffin's and the common and mayoral seals of the city. Named witnesses: the bailiff, the mayor, the reeves, Walter Shirley, Walter Nalder, Thomas Mason, Robert Warmwell, Henry Man, William Warwick, and the clerk
2497 By his charter Thomas Chaffin, cardmaker, of Warminster, granted to John Paul, furbisher, of Salisbury, and his wife Christine a tenement in Minster Street between a tenement called Pinnock's Inn on the north side and John Paul's tenement on the south side. Thomas held the reversion of the tenement, when it fell due on the death of Robert Reading, now dead, by a grant of Thomas Castleton, mercer, a citizen of Salisbury. The tenement is to be held for ever by John and Christine and John's heirs and assigns. Seals: Thomas's and the common and mayoral seals of the city. Named witnesses: the bailiff, the mayor, the reeves, Walter Shirley, Walter Nalder, Thomas Mason, Robert Warmwell, Henry Man, William Warwick, and the clerk
2498 By his charter Edward Prentice, the precentor of the cathedral church, granted to Thomas Randolph and his wife Alice two tenements in Minster Street, one in Cook Row between Thomas Harding's tenement on the south side and a shop of John Burgh [?at the burgh] on the north side, and the other on the west side of the street between William Fines's tenement on the north side and a tenement of Thomas Cardmaker, of Warminster, on the south side. The tenements were held by Edward by a grant of Olive, the relict of John Lake, of late a citizen of Salisbury, and are to be held for ever by Thomas Randolph

and Alice and their heirs and assigns. Clause of warranty. Seals: Edward's and the common and mayoral seals of the city. Named witnesses: the bailiff, the mayor, the reeves, Walter Shirley, Walter Nalder, Thomas Mason, Robert Warmwell, Henry Man, John Swift, John Bromley, and the clerk

30 December 1422, at Salisbury
2499 By his writing John Noble, of Salisbury, quitclaimed to Laurence Drew, weaver, of Salisbury, and his heirs and assigns his right or claim to a tenement, with an adjacent garden, in Castle Street, beyond the bars, between a tenement of late Edmund Purdy's on the south side and Gunnore Bowyer's tenement on the north side. Laurence and his wife Agnes, who died without issue, held the tenement, with the garden, by a grant of John to them and their joint issue, as is contained in an indenture perfected between them [*2403*]. Seals: John's and the common and mayoral seals of the city. Named witnesses: the bailiff, the mayor, the reeves, Walter Shirley, Walter Nalder, Thomas Mason, Robert Warmwell, Henry Man, and the clerk
2500 By their charter William Alexander, Henry Man, [both] of Salisbury, and John Whitehorn granted to John Bromley, a citizen of Salisbury, a messuage, with shops and cottages, called Deverill's Inn [*margin*: Hooper's House], in Castle Street, opposite the market place where grains are sold, between a messuage called Oword's Place on the south side and a cottage of Thomas Forster, dyer, on the north side. The messuage, with the shops and cottages, was held by William, Henry, and John by a grant of John Hewet, of Longbridge Deverill, and is to be held for ever by John Bromley and his heirs and assigns. Seals: those of the grantors and the common and mayoral seals of the city. Named witnesses: the bailiff, the mayor, the reeves, Walter Shirley, Walter Nalder, Thomas Mason, Robert Warmwell, John Swift, William Warwick, and the clerk

13 January 1423, at Salisbury
2501 By his charter Thomas Freeman, mercer, of Salisbury, granted to Hildebrand Elwell, grocer, a citizen of London, three conjoined shops in Pot Row between Robert Earl's shop on the west side and Thomas's own shop on the east side. The three shops were held by Thomas by a grant of John Spencer, of Salisbury, and are to be held for ever by Hulbrond and his heirs and assigns. Seals: Thomas's and the common and mayoral seals of the city. Named witnesses: the bailiff, the mayor, the reeves, Walter Shirley, Thomas Mason, Robert Warmwell, John Bromley, and the clerk
2502 Approval of the will of Agnes, the relict of John Lewisham, made on 30 June 1419. Interment: in St. Edmund's church, beside the grave and the place in which John's corpse lies buried, in front of the image of St. Lucy the Virgin. Bequests: 3s. 4d. to the fabric of the cathedral church; 6s. 8d. to the fabric of St. Edmund's church, and 6s. 8d. to the provost to pray for her soul; 2s. to the fabric of St. Martin's church; a red harnessed belt to Agnes, her goddaughter, a daughter of Richard Christchurch, if she were to live to her majority; if Agnes were to die before she reached her majority the belt should be sold by the elder Agnes's

executors and [the money received] laid out on pious uses; the belt should remain in the hands of those executors, or of their executors, and not delivered to the younger Agnes until she, at her majority, was approved of; a piece of silver, a mazer, six silver spoons, a basin with a laver, a brass pot, a metal pot, and six pewter vessels to Alice at the ford, her servant; a piece of silver to Henry Blackmoor; a smock and a gown, which Agnes used, to the wife of William Lake; 5 candles, each of wax weighing 3 lb., to be burned around her corpse on the day of her burial; 100s. to be handed out to paupers as bread on the day of her burial; 6s. 8d. both to the Franciscans of Salisbury and the Dominicans of Fisherton Anger if they were to be present at her funeral rites and mass on the day of her burial; the rest of her goods to her executors to be disposed of for the salvation of her soul. Devises: Agnes appointed two tenements in Wineman Street and Gigant Street [margin: Three Cups chequer], between Edith Mercer's tenement in Wineman Street on the east side and three cottages of her own in Gigant Street on the south side, to be sold by her executors immediately after her death. The money received from the sale should be laid out by her executors or their executors for the salvation of her soul, the souls of John Dacy, Hugh Hoare, and John Lewisham, her husbands, and the souls of others. Agnes devised to Alice at the ford, her servant, three conjoined cottages in Gigant Street, between a tenement of late Gilbert Skinner's on the south side and her own corner tenement on the north side, to be held for ever by Alice and her heirs and assigns. Agnes devised to John Butler the estate which she held in a cottage, with a yard, for a term of years by a demise of William Chapman, weaver, and his wife Margaret, to pray for her soul; the cottage stands in Wineman Street beside the ditch and the bars of the city. Executors: John Butler, a younger John Pope, and Alice at the ford. Proved on 30 October 1422 in front of John Pedwell, the subdean; the administration was entrusted to the executors. Approved at a court held in front of the bailiff, the mayor, and other citizens; the seisin of the tenements and the cottages, with the yard, was released to the legatees.

2503 By his indented charter John Wishford granted to John Moore, of Salisbury, two messuages, with shops. One, with shops, stands in Carter Street between a messuage of William Cambridge, of London, on the north side and Thomas Harding's tenement on the south side; the other, with shops, stands in the high street called Minster Street, between a shop of the scholars of de Vaux college on the north side and William Sutton's shop on the south side, and was held by John Wishford by a grant of Robert Russell, kt. Also John Wishford granted to John Moore a corner tenement, opposite the market place where grains are sold, between a tenement of late Agnes Lea's on either side. The two messuages, with the shops, and the tenement are to be held for ever by John Moore and his heirs and assigns, paying to John Wishford and his assigns for that John's life a rent of £11 11s. 4d. a year and rendering whatever rent and service is due to the chief lord of the city. Clause to permit re-entry on the two messuages, with the shops, and the tenement if the rent of £11 11s. 4d. were to be in arrear for 15 days, distraint, and the keeping of distresses until the unpaid rent and other losses were recovered; also, to permit permanent repossession if the rent were to be in arrear for a month. John Moore and his heirs should maintain and repair the premises in the lifetime of John Wishford at their own expense so that the rent would not be lost. Clause to permit permanent repossession if the premises were not thus repaired. Clause of warranty. Seals: those of the parties to the parts of the charter in turn. Named witnesses: the bailiff, the mayor, the reeves, Walter Shirley, Walter Nalder, Thomas Mason, Robert Warmwell, Henry Man, John Swift, John Bromley, and the clerk

2504 By his charter John Bromley, a citizen of Salisbury, granted to John Port, a merchant, and his wife Gillian a messuage, with shops and cottages, called Deverill's Inn [*margin*: Hooper's House] in Castle Street, opposite the market place where grains are sold, between [Oword's Place: *cf.* **2500**], a tenement of late Richard Oword's, on the south side and a cottage of Thomas Forster, dyer, on the north side. The messuage, with the shops and cottages, was held by John Bromley by a grant of William Alexander, Henry Man, [?both] of Salisbury, and John Whitehorn, and it is to be held for ever by John Port and Gillian and their heirs and assigns. Clause of warranty. Seals: John Bromley's and the common and mayoral seals of the city. Named witnesses: the bailiff, the mayor, the reeves, Walter Shirley, Walter Nalder, Thomas Mason, Robert Warmwell, Henry Man, John Swift, William Warwick, and the clerk

27 January 1423, at Salisbury

2505 By his indented charter John Wishford granted to William Oving, chandler, of Salisbury, a tenement [*margin*: 'Johnes'], with shops and cottages, in Winchester Street between Richard Forster's tenement on the west side and Laurence Gowan's tenement on the east side [*the tenement is described slightly differently in* **2558**]. The tenement, with the shops and cottages, is to be held for ever by William and his heirs and assigns, paying to John and his assigns for the following 20 years, if John were to live that long, a rent of £4 a year. William and his heirs should maintain and repair the premises in all things necessary at their own expense so that the rent would not be lost. Clause to permit re-entry if in John's lifetime the rent were to be in arrear for 15 days, distraint, and the keeping of distresses until the unpaid rent and other losses were recovered; also, to permit permanent repossession if in John's lifetime the rent were to be in arrear for a month or William were not to maintain the tenement, with the shops and cottages. If John were to die within the 20 years the payment of the rent would cease, for the rest of that period William and his heirs would pay to John's daughter Margaret, a nun of Wherwell abbey, 40s. a year if she were then living, and if Margaret were to die within the 20 years that payment would cease. Clause of warranty. Seals: those of the parties to the parts of the charter in turn and the common and mayoral seals of the city. Named witnesses: the bailiff, the mayor, the reeves, Walter Shirley, Walter Nalder, Thomas Mason, Robert Warmwell, Henry Man, John Swift, William Warwick, and the clerk

10 March 1423, at Salisbury

2506 By his indented charter John Teffont, of Salisbury, a son and heir of Parnel, the relict of Adam Teffont, John's father, granted to Robert Grim, weaver, of Salisbury, a cottage, with a garden, which John Harding, weaver, of late held, in Gigant Street between John Teffont's own cottages on the north side and a cottage of late that of John Hampton, brewer, on the south side. The cottage, with the garden, and with the cottages on the north side of it, was bought by Adam and Parnel from Thomas Hindon and his wife Alice for themselves and their heirs for ever, and all those cottages descended to John on the death of Parnel, who outlived Adam. The cottage, with the garden, is to be held for ever by Robert and his issue just as fully as John Harding held it, and if Robert were to die without issue it would revert for ever to John Teffont and his heirs. Clause of warranty. Seals: those of the parties to the parts of the charter in turn and the common and mayoral seals of the city. Named witnesses: the bailiff, the mayor, the reeves, Walter Shirley, Walter Nalder, Thomas Mason, Robert Warmwell, Henry Man, John Swift, John Bromley, and the clerk

7 April 1423, at Salisbury
2507 Approval of the will of Joan London, the wife of John London, mason, of Gloucester, made at Gloucester on 30 January 1423. Interment: according to the ecclesiastical law of burial in the conventual church of St. Peter, Gloucester. Bequests: 6d. to the mother church of Worcester; 6d. to the high altar of the church of the Blessed Mary in front of the door of Gloucester abbey for her forgotten tithes, 3d. to William Bridge, the vicar, having cure of her soul, 12d. to the light of the Holy Trinity, 6d. to each other light, 12d. towards the maintenance of the chaplain of the Holy Trinity, and 2d. to each of the two clerks; ½d. to each sick pauper of the hospital of St. Bartholomew, Gloucester; a lesser belt, a kerchief, a chest, a red hat with 'botuys', and a posnet to Catherine, a daughter of William Sawman; a kerchief of cypress to the wife of William Sawman; a cotton kerchief to the wife of John Sawman, of Wotton under Edge; a kerchief of Rennes (' Reynes'; ?Reims) to Agnes Smith; a russet gown to Isabel Dobbs; a russet coat to Eleanor Launder; a rosary of jet beads with silver-gilt gauds to Christine Penton; a green furred gown and her best cloak to Joan, the sister of her husband John; the rest of her goods to her executors to administer on behalf of her soul. Devises: William Penton should enfeoff her husband John in her land and meadow in Laverstock and Milford Pichard, in which William stands enfeoffed, to carry out her will; the land and meadow is to be held for ever by John and his heirs and assigns. Joan devised to John a tenement in Winchester Street between John Pope's tenement on the east side and Thomas Read's tenement on the west side. The tenement is to be held by John and his heirs and assigns on condition that he, one of her executors, or William Penton, her other executor, sell it and, from the money issuing from the sale, give 40s. to the fabric and maintenance of St. Martin's church; the rest of the money should be laid out by her executors, on masses and other charitable deeds, on behalf of the souls of John Monkton and Nicholas Monkton, her own soul, her husband's soul, and the souls of others. Joan devised to her husband John a yard, with houses and three racks on it, in Mealmonger Street. The yard was of late that of Edmund Cofford, Joan's

father, and, with the houses and racks, is to be held by John and his heirs and assigns. <u>Executors</u>: her husband John and William Penton. <u>Approved</u>, through John Cheddington and Nicholas Langley, both of Gloucester, at a court held in front of the bailiff, the mayor, and other citizens; the seisin of the tenement and the yard, with the racks, was released to the legatee.

8 April 1423, at Salisbury
2508 By their deed John London, mason, of Gloucester, and William Penton, dyer, of Salisbury, the executors of Joan, of late John's wife, quitclaimed to an elder John Pope and his wife Christine, a younger John Pope, and their heirs and assigns a tenement, or their right or claim to it, in Winchester Street between a tenement of the elder John Pope on the east side and a tenement of Thomas Read, merchant, on the west side. Seals: those of John London and William Penton and the common and mayoral seals of the city. Named witnesses: the bailiff, the mayor, the reeves, Walter Shirley, Walter Nalder, Thomas Mason, Robert Warmwell, Henry Man, John Swift, John Bromley, and the clerk

21 April 1423, at Salisbury
2509 Approval of the will of Maud, the relict of Henry Winpenny, made on 15 March 1423. <u>Interment</u>: in St. Thomas's church. <u>Bequests</u>: 20*d.* to the fabric of that church, 20*d.* to the high altar for her forgotten tithes and lesser benefactions, and 4*d.* to each chaplain present at her funeral rites and mass on the day of her burial; a gold ring to the fabric of the cathedral church; a best mazer and two silver spoons to William Gilbert, butcher; a flat piece of silver to John Hutchins; a piece of silver, with a cover, and an entire best bed to Alice Brit, her servant; a second-best coverlet, two second-best blankets, and two second-best linen sheets to Christine, her servant; a best brass pot and a best pan to Robert Robbs; a silver spoon and 2*s.* 6*d.* to John Summerham; 2*s.* 6*d.* each to the convent of the Franciscans of Salisbury and the convent of the Dominicans of Fisherton; a basin and a laver to Agnes, her servant; a linen sheet and a garment called Friend to Edith Guy; a silver spoon to John, a son of Adam Warin; a blue hat with six silver knobs to her daughter Isabel; a blue muslin to Agnes, her servant; a motley kirtle to Agnes Pierce; a gold ring each to Maud Coveland and Agnes Coveland; the rest of her goods to Alice Brit to find and give to her own daughter Alice Miller her needs of food and clothing in her misery in the time of her life. <u>Devise</u>: to Alice Brit, for her good and praiseworthy service devoted to Maud, a shop in Butcher Row, between Robert Earl's shop on the west side and a shop of Stephen Popham, kt., on the east side, to be held for ever by Alice and her heirs and assigns. For that devise Maud charges Alice, on peril of her soul, that she and her husband, to whom she might have been married, should find and give to Alice Miller, Maud's daughter, her needs of food and clothing during her lifetime. Alice Brit, every year for her own life, should cause the soul of Henry Winpenny to be commended in the pulpit of St. Thomas's church and hold Maud's obit yearly in that church. <u>Executors</u>: Alice Brit and William Halstead; overseer, John Summerham. <u>Proved</u> on 8 April 1423 in front of an officer of the subdean; the

administration was entrusted to Alice Brit, reserving the power to entrust it to
William Halstead when he might come to seek it. <u>Approved</u> at a court held
in front of the bailiff, the mayor, and other citizens; the seisin of the shop was
released to the legatee.

5 May 1423, at Salisbury
2510 By his indented charter Robert Warmwell, a citizen of Salisbury, granted
to Richard Gage, a citizen of Salisbury, a messuage [*margin*: Mr. Ayort house],
with shops and cellars, in Castle Street, opposite the market, between Gunnore
Bowyer's tenement on the south side and John Port's shops on the north side. The
messuage, with the shops and cellars, was of late held by Stephen Edington, now
dead, John Judd, who released his right in it to Robert, and Robert himself by
a grant of Richard Oword, and it is to be held for ever by Richard Gage and his
heirs and assigns. The grant to that Richard was perfected on condition that, if he
or his heirs or executors, or anyone else for him or them, were to pay to Robert or
his executors £10 a year at Christmas for the following eight years, until £80 had
been paid, the grant would hold its force and effect. Clause to permit permanent
repossession if Richard were to default for a month on any payment of £10.
Seals: that of Robert to the part of the charter remaining in the possession of
Richard Gage, that of Richard to the part remaining in the possession of Robert,
and the common and mayoral seals of the city. Named witnesses: the bailiff, the
mayor, the reeves, Walter Shirley, Walter Nalder, Thomas Mason, Henry Man,
John Swift, John Bromley, and the clerk
2511 By their charter Richard Coof, a citizen of Salisbury, and Walter Short,
executors of William Sall, of late a citizen of Salisbury, on the strength of
William's will granted to John Hampton, grocer, a citizen of Salisbury, a chief
tenement, with a garden, in Wineman Street between a corner tenement of late
William's on the east side and a tenement of late Thomas Bower's on the west
side; also the corner tenement, with shops and cottages, in Wineman Street [and
?Brown Street] between the chief tenement on the west side and a messuage of the
dean and chapter of Salisbury on the south side; also two conjoined cottages, with
gardens, in Nuggeston between Thomas Ferring's tenement on the east side and
William Knolle's cottage on the west side; also six conjoined cottages, with gardens,
in Culver Street between Robert Earl's cottage property on the south side and a
garden of late William Sall's on the north side; also the garden in Culver Street
between the six cottages on the south side and cottages of late John Wootton's on
the north side. The tenements, cottages, and gardens, with other land, tenements,
shops, cottages, gardens, rent, and reversions, were devised by William Sall to his
wife Emme for life and, after her death, to Richard and Walter, his executors, to be
sold. The tenements, cottages, and gardens are to be held for ever by John Hampton
and his heirs and assigns, paying to Richard and Walter and their heirs and assigns
£20 a year at Easter for the following eight years. Clause to permit re-entry if a
payment were to be in arrear for 15 days, distraint, and the keeping of distresses
until the unpaid money was recovered; also, to permit permanent repossession if a
payment were to be in arrear for a month. Seals: those of Richard and Walter and

the common and mayoral seals of the city. Named witnesses: the bailiff, the mayor, the reeves, Walter Shirley, Walter Nalder, Thomas Mason, Robert Warmwell, Henry Man, John Swift, John Bromley, and the clerk

19 May 1423, at Salisbury
2512 By his charter Richard Needler, of Salisbury, granted to William Chapman, tucker, of Salisbury, tenements and cottages, with gardens and racks, in Nuggeston between cottages of the mayor and commonalty on the west side and a tenement of late John Lake's on the east side. The tenements and cottages, with the gardens and racks, were held by Richard by a feoffment of Robert Warmwell and John Ruddock, now dead, of late a citizen of Salisbury, and are to be held for ever by William and his heirs and assigns. Clause of warranty. Seals: Richard's and the common and mayoral seals of the city. Named witnesses: the bailiff, the mayor, the reeves, Walter Shirley, Walter Nalder, Thomas Mason, Robert Warmwell, Henry Man, John Swift, John Bromley, and the clerk

24 June 1423, at Salisbury
2513 By their deed William Algar and Edward Russell, clerks, executors of the master Edmund Enfield, of late a citizen of Salisbury, for a sum of money paid to them in advance and to fulfil Edmund's will, quitclaimed to an elder John Westbury, William Westbury, Thomas Coates, and John Tidworth, and to William Westbury's heirs and assigns, their right or claim to a messuage, of late Edmund's, in St. Martin's Street, between a tenement of the vicars of the cathedral church on the east side and the gate and entrance to the Franciscans' church on the west side, extending to the friars' wall on the south and to the street on the north. William Algar's and Edward Russell's estate in the messuage is to be held for ever by John Westbury, William Westbury, Thomas Coates, and John Tidworth and by William Westbury's heirs and assigns. Seals: those of William Algar and Edward Russell and the common and mayoral seals of the city. Named witnesses: the mayor, the reeves, Walter Shirley, Thomas Mason, Henry Man, Robert Warmwell, and John Bromley

30 June 1423, at Salisbury
2514 By their charter Thomas Cowfold and his wife Amice granted to Henry Man, of Salisbury, a messuage in New Street between a shop of the abbot of Stanley on the west side and Thomas Merriott's tenement on the east side. The messuage was held by Amice by a devise of William Needler, her father, of late a citizen of Salisbury, and is to be held for ever by Henry and his heirs and assigns. Clause of warranty. Seals: those of Thomas and Amice and the common and mayoral seals of the city. Named witnesses: the bailiff, the mayor, the reeves, Walter Shirley, Walter Nalder, Thomas Mason, Robert Warmwell, John Swift, John Bromley, and the clerk

28 July 1423, at Salisbury
2515 By his charter Richard Gage, a citizen of Salisbury, granted to Robert

Gilbert, a citizen of Salisbury, a tenement in Castle Street between Robert's own tenement on the south side and a tenement of Edward Gilbert, dubber, on the north side. The tenement was held by Richard by a grant of Henry Berwick and is to be held for ever by Robert and his heirs and assigns. Clause of warranty. Seals: Richard's and the common and mayoral seals of the city. Named witnesses: the bailiff, the mayor, the coroners, the reeves, Walter Shirley, Walter Nalder, Thomas Mason, Robert Warmwell, Henry Man, John Swift, William Warwick, and the clerk

8 September 1423, at Salisbury

2516 By his indented charter William Warin, a citizen of Salisbury, granted to a younger John Pope, draper, of Salisbury, and his wife Alice a corner messuage, with conjoined shops and cottages, in Winchester Street and Culver Street between a tenement of an elder John Pope in Winchester Street on the west side and a yard of John Hampton, grocer, in Culver Street on the south side. The messuage, with the shops and cottages, was held jointly by William Walter, now dead, of late a citizen of Salisbury, and William Warin by a grant of Richard Spencer, formerly a citizen of Salisbury, and it is to be held for ever by John and Alice and that John's heirs and assigns. Clause of warranty. The grant was perfected on condition that, if John and Alice, either one of them, or anyone on their behalf were to pay to William Warin or his executors 20s. at the following Christmas, 20s. at the following Easter, 20s. on the following 24 June, and 100s. a year for the four following years, it would stand in its validity and effect. Clause to permit permanent repossession if John and Alice were to default for a month on a payment. Seals: those of the parties to the parts of the charter in turn and the common and mayoral seals of the city. Named witnesses: the bailiff, a coroner, the reeves, Walter Shirley, Walter Nalder, Thomas Mason, Robert Warmwell, Henry Man, John Swift, William Warwick, and the clerk

22 September 1423, at Salisbury

2517 By his indented charter John Noble, a citizen of Salisbury, an executor of Thomas Bower, of late a citizen of Salisbury, on the strength of Thomas's will granted to William Hamlin, of Guernsey, a tenement in Winchester Street, between a tenement of late Thomas Bonham's on the east side and Isabel Plummer's tenement on the west side, to be held for ever by him and his heirs and assigns. The grant was perfected on condition that, if William or his heirs or executors, or anyone else on behalf of him or them, were to pay to John or his executors 100s. a year for the four following years, beginning next Christmas, until £20 had been paid, it would keep its validity and effect. Clause to permit permanent repossession if William were to default for a year on a payment. Seals: those of the parties to the parts of the charter in turn and the common and mayoral seals of the city. Named witnesses: the bailiff, the mayor, the coroners, a reeve, Walter Shirley, Walter Nalder, Thomas Mason, Robert Warmwell, Henry Man, John Swift, William Warwick, and the clerk

2518 By their charter Thomas Hussey and Richard at the mill, [?both] of

Salisbury, granted to Thomas Frog, of Salisbury, a messuage, with a cellar, shops, gardens, and a corner cottage, in New Street and Carter Street [*margin*: Bull Corner] between cottages of late John Upton's in Carter Street on the north side and Robert Ashley's cottage in New Street on the west side. The messuage, with the cellar, shops, gardens, and corner cottage, was held by Thomas Hussey and his wife Joan, now dead, by a grant of Thomas Upton, a clerk, and it is to be held for ever by Thomas Frog and his heirs and assigns. Clause of warranty in respect of Thomas Hussey. Seals: those of Thomas Hussey and Richard at the mill and the common and mayoral seals of the city. Named witnesses: the bailiff, the mayor, the coroners, a reeve, Walter Shirley, Walter Nalder, Thomas Mason, Robert Warmwell, Henry Man, John Swift, William Warwick, and the clerk

20 October 1423, at Salisbury
2519 Approval of the will of Edward Gilbert, dubber, a citizen of Salisbury, made on 9 July 1423. <u>Interment</u>: in St. Edmund's church, in front of the altar of the Blessed Mary, beside the tomb of Richard Spencer. <u>Bequests</u>: 20*d.* to the fabric of the cathedral church; 6*s.* 8*d.* to the fabric of St. Edmund's church, 40*d.* to the provost for his forgotten and badly assessed tithes, and 20*d.* to Henry Clere, the parochial chaplain; 6*s.* 8*d.* to William Halstead; the rest of his goods to his wife Joan and, after her death, to his daughter Cecily; all the vessels pertaining to his craft, including a furnace and a beater, to John Shergold, his servant, Edward, his godson, and Thomas Sprackman, to be shared among them equally. <u>Devises</u>: to his wife Joan for life his land, tenements, rent, services and reversions in the city and in Andover, except a tenement, which he acquired from Robert Deverill and in which John Swift, dyer, dwells, beside the [upper: *cf. **2520**]] bridge of Fisherton Anger on the east side. The excepted tenement should be sold immediately by his executors for paying his debts and laying out on behalf of his soul and the souls of others. On Joan's death the rest of the land, tenements, rent, services, and reversions should remain for ever to his daughter Cecily and her issue, and if Cecily were to die without issue they should be sold by Edward's executors. The money received should be handed out among his kinsmen and among paupers. Edward devised to his brother John Gilbert a tenement, with 25 acres, in Shrewton parish to be held for ever by him and his heirs and assigns. <u>Executors</u>: his wife Joan and his brother John; overseer, William Halstead. <u>Proved</u> on 28 July 1423 in front of John Pedwell, the subdean; the administration was entrusted to the executors. <u>Approved</u> at a court held in front of the bailiff, the mayor, and other citizens; the seisin of the land, tenements, rent, services, and reversions [in the city] was released to the legatees.
2520 By their charter John Gilbert, a brother, and an executor, of Edward Gilbert, dubber, of late a citizen of Salisbury, and Joan, Edward's relict and John's co-executor, on the strength of Edward's will granted to Robert Warmwell, a citizen of Salisbury, a tenement, in which John Swift, dyer, dwells, beside the upper bridge of Fisherton, between cottage property of late John Butt's on the east side and the Avon on the west side. The tenement was appointed by Edward to be sold by his executors for his debts to be paid, and it is to be held for ever

by Robert and his heirs and assigns as that which Robert bought from them in good faith for a sum of money, reaching its true value, to be laid out according to Edward's will. Seals: those of John and Joan and the common and mayoral seals of the city. Named witnesses: the bailiff, the mayor, the coroners, a reeve, Walter Shirley, Walter Nalder, Thomas Mason, Henry Man, John Swift, William Warwick, John Bromley, and the clerk

2521 By his writing John Deverill, of Salisbury, quitclaimed to Robert Warmwell, a citizen of Salisbury, his right or claim to a tenement, in which John Swift, dyer, dwells, beside the upper bridge of Fisherton, [*as in* **2520**]. The tenement was formerly that of Robert Deverill, John's father. Seals: John Deverill's and the common and mayoral seals of the city. Named witnesses: the bailiff, the mayor, the coroners, a reeve, Walter Shirley, Walter Nalder, Thomas Mason, Henry Man, John Swift, Robert Warmwell, John Bromley, and the clerk

29 December 1423, at Salisbury

2522 By their charter William Warin, a citizen of Salisbury, William Lord, and John Marshall, of Salisbury, executors of William Walter, merchant, of late a citizen of Salisbury, on the strength of William's will granted to William Halstead, butcher, of Salisbury, six conjoined cottages, with gardens and a dovecot, in Culver Street between cottages of the hospital of the Holy Trinity on the north side and Robert Earl's cottage property on the south side. One of the six cottages, with a garden, was held for their life by Robert Chapman, dyer, and his wife Maud, both now dead, by William Walter's devise and, with the other five, remains after their death to be sold by the executors. The money received from the sale should be laid out among poor priests, Franciscan friars, and Dominican friars, on celebrating masses, among poor girls to be given in marriage, on visiting the decrepit and bedridden, and on linen and woollen clothing, and shoes, to be given to the indigent, to pray for William's soul and the souls of others. The six cottages, with the gardens and dovecot, are to be held for ever by William Halstead and his heirs and assigns as that which William bought in good faith from the executors for a sum of money, reaching their true value, to be wholly laid out according to the terms of William Walter's will. Seals: those of the grantors and the common and mayoral seals of the city. Named witnesses: the bailiff, the coroners, the reeves, Walter Shirley, Thomas Mason, Robert Warmwell, Henry Man, John Swift, William Warwick, and William Reynold

8 March 1424, at Salisbury

2523 By his charter William Bailiff, called Weston, granted to Thomas Brown, weaver, of Salisbury, a cottage, with a garden, in Gigant Street between William Alexander's tenement on the north side and a cottage of late Margaret Godmanstone's, which John Horn, weaver, holds, on the south side. The cottage, with the garden, was devised by Margaret to William and his heirs for ever, and it is to be held for ever by Thomas and his heirs and assigns. Clause of warranty. Seals: William's and the common and mayoral seals of the city. Named witnesses: the bailiff, the mayor, the coroners, the reeves, Walter Shirley, Thomas Mason,

Robert Warmwell, Henry Man, John Swift, John Bromley, and the clerk

2524 By his indented charter John Wishford granted to Robert Chinchin a corner tenement in Endless Street and Scots Lane between a tenement of late John Lymington's on the north side and a tenement of late Adam Morris's on the west side. The tenement is to be held for ever by Robert and his heirs and assigns, paying a yearly rent of 53s. 4d. to John Wishford and his assigns for John's life and meeting all other charges incumbent on the tenement for that period. Robert and his heirs and assigns should maintain and repair the tenement in all things necessary at their own expense in John's lifetime, without causing any waste or destruction, so that the rent would not be lost. Clause to permit re-entry if the rent were to be in arrear for 15 days, distraint, and the keeping of distresses until the unpaid rent and other losses were recovered; also, to permit permanent repossession if the rent were to be in arrear for a month or Robert or his heirs or assigns were not to maintain and repair the tenement in John's lifetime. Clause of warranty. Seals: those of the parties to the parts of the charter in turn and the common and mayoral seals of the city. Named witnesses: the bailiff, the mayor, the coroners, the reeves, Henry Man, Robert Warmwell, John Bromley, John Wylye, and John Shad

22 March 1424, at Salisbury

2525 Approval of the will of Alice, the wife of Thomas Field and the relict of John Baker, draper, made on 21 December 1423. Interment: in the graveyard of St. Thomas's church. Bequests: 12d. to the fabric of the cathedral church; a rosary of amber beads, with a silver and gilt crucifix, to St. Thomas's church; the rest of her goods to Thomas, her husband, to be laid out for the salvation of her soul and for praying. Devise: she appointed a tenement, in which she dwelt, in Carter Street, between William Warin's tenement on the north side and a tenement of late John Upton's on the south side, to be sold by Thomas, her husband and executor. The money received from the sale should be laid out, on pious uses, on behalf of Alice's soul and John Baker's soul. Alice appointed that in the purchase of the tenement Thomas should be preferred to all others, and he should have the tenement for £40 as a best price for the very great labour which he undertook in her weakness. From the sale of the tenement, when it happened, she bequeathed 5 marks each to Joan Cambo and Joan's son John, to be delivered to them by the hand of Thomas Field. Executor: Thomas Field, her husband. Proved on 7 February 1424 in front of an officer of the subdean; the administration was entrusted to the executor, who accounted with an officer and was dismissed. Approved at a court held in front of the bailiff, the mayor, and other citizens; the seisin of the tenement was released to the legatee.

5 April 1424, at Salisbury

2526 By his charter John Shad, a citizen of Salisbury, granted to Walter Hobbs, carpenter, of Salisbury, a tenement, with a cottage and a garden, in Drake Hall Street, between John's cottage property on the north side and Thomas Cook's cottage on the south side, extending from that street as far as Freren Street. The tenement, with the cottage, measures 57½ ft. in width at its frontage on the street; the part of the garden which lies on the north side of Thomas Cook's garden measures 63½ ft. in width from that garden towards the north, and the rest of the garden, which extends to Freren Street, measures 48 ft. in width at the end of 'that garden'. The tenement, with the cottage and garden, is to be held for ever by Walter and his heirs and assigns. Clause of warranty. Seals: John Shad's and the common and mayoral seals of the city. Named witnesses: the bailiff, the mayor, the coroners, the reeves, Walter Shirley, Thomas Mason, Robert Warmwell, Henry Man, John Swift, and the clerk

17 May 1424, at Salisbury
2527 Approval of the will of William Moore, a citizen of Salisbury, made on 12 April 1424. <u>Interment</u>: in St. Thomas's church, on the north side of the font, where his wife Agnes was buried. <u>Bequests</u>: 12*d.* to the fabric of the cathedral church; 12*d.* to the fabric of St. Edmund's church, 12*d.* to the provost for his forgotten tithes and oblations, 12*d.* to the lord Henry Clere, 4*d.* to each collegiate chaplain, and 2*d.* to each other chaplain celebrating mass there; 12*d.* to the fabric of St. Thomas's church, and 4*d.* to each chaplain; 2*s.* 6*d.* to the Dominicans of Fisherton Anger; 40*d.* to the paupers in the hospital of the Holy Trinity, [to be shared] among them equally; a coverlet, two linen sheets, two blankets, a basin with a laver, a mazer, and a new brass pot to William, his godson and his servant; 40*d.* to Agnes Taylor; a best gown to John Shapwick; the rest of his goods to his wife Susan to be disposed of on behalf of his soul and the souls of others. <u>Devises</u>: to Susan a tenement, in which he dwelt, with a shop, opposite the Guildhall, between a tenement of the dean and chapter of Salisbury on the north side and Thomas Harding's tenement on the south side. The tenement, with the shop, is to be held for her life by Susan and her assigns, and immediately after Susan's death should be sold by William Warwick, mercer, a citizen of Salisbury, and Philip Baron or by their executors or the executors of those executors. From the money received from the sale William appointed 20 marks to the fraternity and light of St. John the Baptist for the tailors' craft to hold his obit yearly in St. Thomas's church on 6 May for ever. The fraternity should give security to his executors and their overseer for holding the obit thus; otherwise it should not have the legacy, and the 20 marks should be laid out by the executors and their overseer. The rest of the money from the sale should be laid out by William Warwick and Philip Baron, by their executors, or by subsequent executors on behalf of William's soul, the souls of his wives, and the souls of others. <u>Executors</u>: his wife Susan, the principal executor, and Philip Baron; overseer, William Warwick. William Moore bequeathed 6*s.* 8*d.* to Philip and, to be paid to them from the sale of the tenement, 20*s.* each to him and William Warwick. <u>Proved</u> on 8 May 1424 in front of an officer of the subdean; the administration was entrusted to the executors, who at length appeared, accounted with an officer, and were dismissed. <u>Approved</u> at a court held in front of the bailiff, the mayor, and other citizens; the seisin of the tenement was released to the legatees.

31 May 1424, at Salisbury

2528 Approval of the will of Thomas Read, a citizen of Salisbury, made on 11 November 1423. Interment: in St. Edmund's church, opposite the window of St. John the Evangelist. Bequests: 20s. to the fabric of that church; 6s. 8d. each to the fabric of St. Martin's church and the fabric of St. Thomas's church; 40d. to the fabric of the cathedral church; 40d. both to the Franciscans of Salisbury and the Dominicans of Fisherton; 40d. to the hospital of the Holy Trinity; 20s. beyond his stipend to John, his servant, on condition that he serves his wife Agnes before others; 13s. 4d. to Marion, his servant, on the same condition; a striped gown, of the fashion of John Swift while he was mayor, with fur, to Nicholas Colling, of Coombe; 6d. to each of his godchildren; the rest of his goods to his wife Agnes. Devises: he appointed to the provost of St. Edmund's church and the chaplains of the college a rent of 5s. a year receivable by them on the feast of St. German the Bishop [?28 May] from Thomas's tenement, in which he dwelt, in Winchester Street between Robert Earl's corner tenement on the west side and John Pope's tenement on the east side, to be held from the day of the perfection of Thomas's will for the following 20 years. If the rent were to be in arrear at that feast the provost and chaplains might enter on the tenement, distrain, and keep distresses until the unpaid rent was recovered. Thomas devised to his wife Agnes that same tenement, with shops, to be held for ever by her and her heirs and assigns. He devised to Agnes for life a tenement, with a shop, in New Street between John Pope's tenement on the west side and a tenement of the hospital of the Holy Trinity on the east side. On Agnes's death the tenement, with the shop, should remain for ever to a younger Thomas Andrew and Alice, Thomas Read's daughter, and Alice's issue, and for lack of issue it would remain to Thomas Read's executors to be sold. The money received from the sale should be laid out on behalf of Thomas Read's soul and the souls of others. After the 20 years the rent of 5s. a year should be sold by his executors. The money received from the sale should be delivered to the provost and chaplains of St. Edmund's church for the time being to pray for ever for Thomas's soul and the souls of others. Executors: his wife Agnes and, to both of whom he bequeathed 20s., an elder William Lord and John Wantage, weaver. Witnesses: William Spicer, the parochial chaplain of St. Martin's church, John Pope, and Hugh Andrew. Proved on 15 December 1423 in front of Simon Sydenham, the dean of Salisbury, in that matter deputed a commissary of Henry [Chichele], the archbishop of Canterbury; the administration of the goods within the province of Canterbury was entrusted to Agnes, reserving the power to entrust it to William Lord and John Wantage when they might come to seek it. Approved at a court held in front of the bailiff, the mayor, and other citizens; the seisin of the tenements was released to the legatees.

12 July 1424, at Salisbury

2529 By their indented charter Thomas Williams, otherwise called Thomas Llandaff, of Longbridge Deverill, and his wife Agnes, a daughter and heir of Adlin Gaunt and his wife Catherine, appearing in court granted to John Morris, of Salisbury, and his wife Edith a chief tenement, with a lane, in New Street between Agnes Ettshall's tenement on the east side and a tenement, in which Henry Chubb dwells, on the west side. The lane extends from the tenement to the Avon on the west side, between Agnes's stone wall on the north side and Henry's tenement and fence on the south side. The tenement, with the lane, is to be held for ever by John and Edith and their heirs and assigns. Clause of warranty. The grant was made on condition that, if John and Edith, their heirs or executors, or anyone for them were to pay £8 to Thomas and Agnes or their executor or attorney at Salisbury on the following 25 December, it would stand in its validity and effect. Clause to permit permanent repossession if John and Edith defaulted on the payment. Seals: those of the parties to the parts of the charter in turn and the common and mayoral seals of the city. Named witnesses: the bailiff, the mayor, the coroners, the reeves, Walter Shirley, Thomas Mason, Robert Warmwell, Henry Man, John Swift, John Bromley, and the clerk

26 July 1424, at Salisbury
2530 By his indented charter Walter Shirley, a citizen of Salisbury, granted to Richard Cooper and his wife Alice a corner tenement, with shops and sollars, in Wineman Street between the chief entrance to Walter's messuage on the east side and a kitchen appurtenant to the messuage on the north side; also four conjoined shops in Wineman Street between the chief entrance to Walter's messuage on the west side and Walter's shops on the east side; also free ingress and egress to and from the corner tenement through that chief entrance for repairing and roofing as often as necessary, at due times, in all things necessary, and at the expense of Richard and Alice and their heirs. The corner tenement, shops, sollars, and free ingress are to be held for ever by Richard and Alice and their heirs and assigns, paying to Walter and his heirs and assigns a rent of 10s. a year, and at their own expense repairing and maintaining a dormer of a chief room of the messuage falling above the easternmost of the four shops for the whole width of the dormer. Clause to permit distraint in the tenement and shops, with the sollars, if the repair and maintenance were not carried out or if the rent were to be in arrear for 15 days, in respect of both a penalty sum of money and the rent in arrear, and the keeping of distresses until the unpaid rent, the penalty sum, and other losses incurred in the matter and in the case of non-repair of the dormer, were recovered; also, to permit permanent repossession if the rent were to be in arrear for six weeks. Clause of warranty. Seals: those of the parties to the parts of the charter in turn and the common and mayoral seals of the city. Named witnesses: the bailiff, the mayor, the coroners, the reeves, Thomas Mason, Robert Warmwell, Henry Man, John Swift, John Bromley, and the clerk

9 August 1424, at Salisbury
2531 By his charter John Shad, a citizen of Salisbury, granted to Walter Hobbs, carpenter, of Salisbury, a tenement, with a cottage and a garden, in Drake Hall Street, [*as in 2526*]. The tenement, with the cottage, measures [*as in 2526*]; the part of the garden which lies on the north side of Thomas Cook's garden measures

[*as in 2526*], and the rest of the garden, which extends to Freren Street, measures [*as in 2526*]. The tenement, with the cottage and garden, is to be held for ever by Walter and his heirs and assigns, to whom John quitclaimed all his right or claim to it. Clause of warranty. Seals: John's and the common and mayoral seals of the city. Named witnesses: the bailiff, the mayor, the coroners, the reeves, Walter Shirley, Thomas Mason, Robert Warmwell, Henry Man, John Swift, and the clerk

6 September 1424, at Salisbury
2532 By his charter Stephen Leonard, fuller, of Salisbury, granted to William Harding, a scholar of de Vaux college, a tenement in Winchester Street between William's tenement, in which Robert Hindon dwells, on the west side and a tenement of late Richard Spencer's on the east side. The tenement measures 104 ft. 10 in. in length from the street as far as William's garden and 20 ft. 5 in. in width from William's tenement as far as Richard's tenement. It is to be held for ever by William and his heirs and assigns. Clause of warranty. Seals: Stephen's and the common and mayoral seals of the city. Named witnesses: the bailiff, the mayor, the coroners, the reeves, Walter Shirley, Thomas Mason, Robert Warmwell, Henry Man, John Swift, and the clerk

20 September 1424, at Salisbury
2533 By his charter Nicholas Upton, a brother of Thomas Upton, a clerk, a son of John Upton, of late a citizen of Salisbury, and his wife Edith, granted to John Upton, a son of that John Upton and Margaret, his second wife, six conjoined shops in Carter Street between a chief tenement, formerly that of the elder John Upton, on the south side and a tenement, in which Thomas Field dwells, on the north side; also five shops, near the pillories, opposite the Cheese Corner; also the reversion of two conjoined shops in Carter Street when they fell due on the death of Thomas Hussey. One of the shops stands above a cellar of late that of the elder John, and the other stands between that shop on the south side and the chief tenement on the north side. All those shops, with the reversion of the two shops when they fell due, are to be held for ever by the younger John and his heirs and assigns. Clause of warranty. Seals: Nicholas's and the common and mayoral seals of the city. Named witnesses: the bailiff, the mayor, the coroners, the reeves, Walter Shirley, Thomas Mason, Robert Warmwell, Henry Man, John Swift, and the clerk

23 September 1424, at Salisbury
2534 By his writing Nicholas Upton, a son of John Upton, of late a citizen of Salisbury, quitclaimed to John, a son of that John Upton and Margaret, his second wife, and his heirs and assigns his right or claim to six conjoined shops in Carter Street [*as in 2533*]; also to five shops near the pillories [*as in 2533*]; also to two conjoined shops in Carter Street [*as in 2533*]. Seals: Nicholas's and the common and mayoral seals of the city. Named witnesses: the bailiff, the mayor, the coroners, the reeves, Walter Shirley, Thomas Mason, Robert Warmwell,

Henry Man, John Swift, and the clerk

4 October 1424, at Salisbury
2535 By their charter Walter Shirley, a citizen of Salisbury, an executor of John Camel, of late a citizen of Salisbury, and Alice Bonham, the relict of Thomas Hart and of John Camel, Walter's co-executor, granted to John Scot their estate in a tenement in Winchester Street between William Hamlin's tenement on the west side and a trench of running water on the east side. The tenement and that estate in it are to be held for ever by John and his heirs and assigns, so that neither Walter or Alice, nor their executors, could have any future claim to it. Seals: those of Walter and Alice and the common and mayoral seals of the city. Named witnesses: the bailiff, the mayor, Thomas Mason, Robert Warmwell, Henry Man, John Swift, William Warwick, John Bromley, and the clerk
2536 By her letters of attorney Alice Bonham, the relict of Thomas Hart and of John Camel, as a co-executor of Walter Shirley, a citizen of Salisbury, an executor of John, appointed John Gilbert, of Fovant, and John Hampton, grocer, of Salisbury, to deliver to John Scot and his heirs and assigns the seisin of a tenement in Winchester Street [*as in 2535*] according to the terms of a charter, dated 4 October 1424, perfected for them by Walter and her. Seals: Alice's and the mayoral seal of the city

27 December 1424, at Salisbury
2537 By her charter Joan, the relict of Edward Dubber, of late a citizen of Salisbury, in her widowhood and full power granted to a younger Thomas Fadder, weaver, of Salisbury, and her daughter Cecily her estate in a messuage in Castle Street between a tenement of late Thomas Farrant's on the north side and a tenement of late Edward's on the south side. The messuage, and Joan's estate in it, is to be held by Thomas Fadder and Cecily for Joan's life. Joan quitclaimed to that Thomas and Cecily and to Thomas's heirs and assigns her right or claim to the messuage on the strength of Edward's will. Seals: Joan's and the common and mayoral seals of the city. Named witnesses: the bailiff, the mayor, the coroners, the reeves, William Warin, Walter Shirley, Thomas Mason, Robert Warmwell, Henry Man, John Swift, and the clerk
2538 By his writing Walter Shirley, a citizen of Salisbury, quitclaimed to Thomas Mason, draper, and John Swift, ironmonger, citizens of Salisbury, and to Henry Warin, a chaplain, and their heirs and assigns his right or claim to a tenement, with a garden, which Ralph Lockyer holds, in Endless Street between a tenement of late John Mower's on the south side and the street called Scots Lane on the north side. The tenement, with the garden, together with other land, tenements, shops, cottages, rent, and reversions, was of late held by Walter Shirley, William Walter, now dead, Thomas Mason, John Swift, and Henry Warin by a grant of John Mower, of late a citizen of Salisbury. Seals: Walter's and the common and mayoral seals of the city. Named witnesses: the bailiff, the mayor, the coroners, the reeves, William Warin, Robert Warmwell, Henry Man, and the clerk

10 January 1425, at Salisbury

2539 Approval of the will of William West, a citizen of Salisbury, made on 28 September 1415. <u>Interment</u>: in St. Thomas's church. <u>Bequests</u>: 6s. 8d. to the fabric of that church on condition that his corpse should rest entombed there, and 6d. each to the light of St. Michael, the light of St. James, and the light of St. John the Baptist; 12d. to the fabric of the cathedral church; three sheep, a brass pot, a basin (*concium*), and 12d. to Thomas, his household servant; 20s. or goods of that value, to his sister; 20s. to Margaret, his goddaughter, his sister's daughter; 2s. 6d. both to the Dominicans of Fisherton and the Franciscans of Salisbury; 12d. to each of his godchildren; a gown and a blue hood of medley to John Tidpit; a gown and a hood of green and blue to Richard Ballfoot; a sheep to each of five children; the rest of his goods to his wife Agnes to be laid out on behalf of his soul. <u>Devise</u>: to Agnes for life a corner tenement, with shops, in New Street and Brown Street between a tenement of late William Warmwell's on the west side and a tenement of late John Upton's on the south side. After Agnes's death the tenement should be sold by William West's executors or their executors. The money received from the sale should be laid out, on celebrating masses and doing other charitable deeds, on behalf of William's soul, Agnes's soul, and the souls of others. <u>Executors</u>: his wife Agnes and Richard Ballfoot. <u>Proved</u> on 7 November 1415 in front of an officer of the subdean; the administration was entrusted to the executors. <u>Approved</u> at a court held in front of the bailiff, the mayor, and other citizens; the seisin of the tenement, with the shops, was released to the legatee.

2540 By their charter Thomas Mason, draper, and John Swift, ironmonger, citizens of Salisbury, and Henry Warin, a chaplain, granted to Joan, the wife of Walter Shirley, a tenement, with a garden, in Endless Street, between a tenement of late John Mower's on the south side and the street called Scots Lane on the north side, to be held for ever by her and her heirs and assigns. Seals: those of Thomas, John, and Henry and the common and mayoral seals of the city. Named witnesses: the bailiff, the mayor, the coroners, the reeves, William Warin, Robert Warmwell, Henry Man, and the clerk

2541 By his charter [*see* **2625**] Walter Shirley, a citizen of Salisbury, granted to Thomas Hain, of Winchester, John Swift, ironmonger, of Salisbury, Henry Warin, a chaplain, and William Lord all his land and tenements, with shops, cottages, gardens, meadows, rent, pasture, and feeding rights, in Salisbury or elsewhere in Wiltshire to be held for ever by them and their heirs and assigns. Clause of warranty. Seals: Walter's and the common and mayoral seals of the city. Named witnesses: the bailiff, the mayor, the coroners, the reeves, William Warin, Robert Warmwell, Henry Man, and John Bromley

2542 By his charter [*dated to the Wednesday after the feast of St. Hilary (17 January) probably in error for the Wednesday before that feast (10 January)*] John Sampson, of Salisbury, granted to John Hill, of Salisbury, three conjoined cottages in Brown Street between three cottages of John Sampson on the north side and Henry Southwick's cottage on the south side. The three cottages being granted, with other land and tenements in the city, were bought by John Sampson and Edith, of late his wife, now dead, from an elder John Chandler, and they are to be held for ever by John Hill and his heirs and assigns. Clause of warranty. Seals: John Sampson's and the common and mayoral seals of the city. Named witnesses: the bailiff, the mayor, the coroners, the reeves, William Warin, Walter Shirley, Thomas Mason, Robert Warmwell, Henry Man, John Swift, and the clerk

24 January 1425, at Salisbury
2543 By her charter Agnes, the relict of Roger Enterbush, of Salisbury, granted to Alice Sutton a tenement, with a garden, in Mealmonger Street between William Mead's tenement on the south side and a tenement of late Adam Dummer's on the north side. The tenement, with the garden, by the name of two cottages and gardens, was bought by Roger from Edmund Friday for himself and his heirs for ever, and it is to be held for ever by Alice and her heirs and assigns. Clause of warranty. Seals: Agnes's and the common and mayoral seals of the city. Named witnesses: the bailiff, the mayor, the coroners, the reeves, William Warin, Thomas Mason, Robert Warmwell, Henry Man, John Swift, and the clerk

21 February 1425, at Salisbury
2544 By their indenture Agnes, the relict of Thomas Read, of late a citizen of Salisbury, and William Lord granted to a younger Thomas Andrew and his wife Alice a tenement, with a shop and a garden, in New Street between a tenement of a younger John Pope on the west side and a tenement of the hospital of the Holy Trinity on the east side. The tenement, with the shop and garden, was formerly that of Nicholas Hayward, of Salisbury, and is to be held for ever by Thomas and Alice and their heirs and assigns, paying a rent of 8s. a year for Agnes's life to Agnes and her assigns. Clause to permit re-entry if the rent were to be in arrear for 15 days, distraint, and the keeping of distresses until the unpaid rent was recovered; also, to permit repossession for Agnes's life if the rent were to be in arrear for six weeks and sufficient distresses could not be found. Seals: those of the parties to the parts of the indenture in turn and the common and mayoral seals of the city. Named witnesses: the bailiff, the mayor, the coroners, the reeves, William Warin, Thomas Mason, Robert Warmwell, Henry Man, John Swift, and John Bromley
2545 By his writing William Lord, an executor of Thomas Read, of late a citizen of Salisbury, quitclaimed to a younger Thomas Andrew and his wife Alice and their heirs and assign his right or claim to a tenement, with a garden, in New Street [*as in* **2544**]. Seals: William's and the common and mayoral seals of the city. Named witnesses: the bailiff, the mayor, the coroners, the reeves, William Warin, Thomas Mason, Robert Warmwell, Henry Man, John Swift, and John Bromley

18 April 1425, at Salisbury
2546 By their charter Thomas Mason, draper, and Laurence Groom, a chaplain, granted to William Oving, chandler, of Salisbury, a garden, with racks, in Freren Street, between a garden, which William Doncaster, dyer, holds, on the south side and a garden of John Plowman, carpenter, on the north side, extending from that street as far as the garden of Thomas Cook's tenement in Drake Hall Street

(*Dragorounstrete*), to be held for ever by him and his heirs and assigns. Clause of warranty in Laurence's name. Seals: those of Thomas and Laurence and the common and mayoral seals of the city. Named witnesses: the bailiff, the mayor, the coroners, the reeves, William Warin, Robert Warmwell, Henry Man, John Swift, John Bromley, and the clerk

27 June 1425, at Salisbury
2547 By his charter Richard Coof, a citizen of Salisbury, granted to William Papillon, a clerk, and Simon Poy and his wife Alice a tenement in Endless Street between a tenement of late Roger Enterbush's on the south side and a corner tenement of William Dunning, weaver, on the north side. The tenement was held by Edward Frith, now dead, and Richard by a grant of Nicholas Baynton, a son and heir of Nicholas Baynton, of Faulston, and is to be held by William, Simon, and Alice and the joint issue of Simon and Alice. If Simon and Alice were to die without such issue it would remain for ever to the direct heirs of William, Simon, and Alice and to the last of their descendants. Clause of warranty. Seals: Richard's and the common and mayoral seals of the city. Named witnesses: the bailiff, the mayor, the coroners, the reeves, William Warin, Thomas Mason, Robert Warmwell, Henry Man, John Swift, John Bromley, and the clerk

11 July 1425, at Salisbury
2548 By his charter John Hobbs, brewer, of Salisbury, granted to Robert Warmwell, a citizen of Salisbury, and a younger John Pope, of Salisbury, a tenement in St. Martin's Street between a tenement of the provost of St. Edmund's church on the east side and a tenement of the vicars of the cathedral church on the west side. The tenement was held by John Hobbs and his wife Cecily, now dead, by a grant of William Bower, and is to be held for ever by Robert Warmwell and John Pope and their heirs and assigns. Clause of warranty. Seals: John Hobbs's and the common and mayoral seals of the city. Named witnesses: the bailiff, the mayor, the coroners, the reeves, William Warin, Thomas Mason, John Swift, Henry Man, John Bromley, and the clerk

22 August 1425, at Salisbury
2549 Approval of the will of Simon Bradley, a baker, a citizen of Salisbury, made on 17 April 1424. Interment: in the graveyard of St. Edmund's church. Bequests: 6s. 8d. to the fabric of that church, 2s. to the provost for his forgotten tithes and oblations, and 12d. to Henry Clere, [the parochial chaplain]; 2s. to the fabric of the cathedral church; 12d. to the fabric of St. Thomas's church; 12d. to the paupers in the hospital of the Holy Trinity, to be paid among them equally; 2s. 6d. both to the Dominicans of Fisherton Anger and the Franciscans of Salisbury; three brass pots, three brass pottles, two basins with two lavers, and half a dozen pewter vessels, *genisiat'* (or *gemsiat'*), to his son Edward; 6s. 8d. to Ralph Lockyer; 40d. to John Anketell; 12d. each to Gillian and Alice, his wife's daughters; a coverlet, a blanket, and a linen sheet to John Power, of late his apprentice; a blue coat and 6d. to William at the lake, his apprentice; 6d. to John May; 6d. to

Agnes, his maid; a hat each to John Batter, Philip Baron, and Thomas Hawkins; 40s. to be handed out to paupers on the day of his burial on behalf of his soul and the souls of others; the rest of his goods to his wife Alice to be disposed of on behalf of his soul and the souls mentioned below; 6d. to Joan, a daughter of Robert Stonard; his harnessed dagger to his son Edward. Devise: to his wife Alice a tenement, in which he lived, in Scots Lane, between William Dunning's cottages on the east side and Robert Linden's cottages on the west side, to be held for her life by her and her assigns. On Alice's death the tenement should remain for ever to Simon's son Edward and Edward's issue, and if Edward were to die without issue it should be sold by Simon's executors, their executors, or subsequent executors. The money received from the sale should be laid out by the executors on masses and other charitable deeds on behalf of Simon's soul, the souls of his wives, and the souls of others. Executors: his wife Alice as principal executor, and Ralph Lockyer and John Anketell as co-executors. Proved on 5 May 1425 in front of an officer of the subdean; the administration was entrusted to Alice, reserving the power to entrust it to Ralph and John when they might come to seek it. Afterwards Alice appeared, accounted with an officer, and was dismissed, and afterwards Ralph appeared in front of the officer of the subdean and the administration was entrusted to him. Approved at a court held in front of the bailiff, the mayor, and other citizens; the seisin of the tenement was released to the legatees.

19 September 1425, at Salisbury
2550 By his charter Walter Messenger granted to William Warin, a citizen of Salisbury, three conjoined shops, with a cellar, in Carter Street between the shop of a tenement of William, formerly Robert Beechfount's, on the south side and a messuage formerly that of John Preston, grocer, and sometime since Agnes Bodenham's, on the north side. The shops were formerly those of John Wallop, carder. Walter also granted to William that messuage, with shops and gardens, in Carter Street between those shops on the south side and a tenement of late William Tull's, formerly Robert Beechfount's, on the north side. The shops, with the cellar, and the messuage, with the shops and gardens, are to be held for ever by William Warin and his heirs and assigns. Seals: Walter's and the common and mayoral seals of the city. Named witnesses: the bailiff, the mayor, the coroners, the reeves, Thomas Mason, Robert Warmwell, Henry Man, John Swift, John Bromley, Richard Coof, and the clerk

3 October 1425, at Salisbury
2551 By his charter William Harding, a scholar of de Vaux college, granted to Thomas Harding, draper, his brother, a citizen of London, a tenement in Winchester Street between William's tenement, in which Robert Hindon of late dwelt, on the west side and a tenement of late Richard Spencer's on the east side. The tenement measures 104 ft. 10 in. in length from the street as far as a garden of William's and 20 ft. 5 in. in width from William's tenement as far as the tenement of late Richard Spencer's. William also granted to Thomas a cottage in Gigant

Street between the entrance of a garden of a tenement of Thomas's on the north side and a cottage, in which Robert Edmund, carpenter, dwells, on the south side; also the reversion of the cottage in which Robert dwells, in Gigant Street on the south side of that cottage, when it fell due on Robert's death. The tenement, the cottage, and the reversion are to be held for ever by Thomas and his heirs and assigns. Clause of warranty. Seals: William's and the common and mayoral seals of the city. Named witnesses: the bailiff, the mayor, the coroners, the reeves, William Warin, Thomas Mason, Robert Warmwell, Henry Man, John Swift, John Bromley, and the clerk

2552 By his letters of attorney William Harding, a scholar of de Vaux college, appointed Gilbert Marshall or Simon Westby to deliver to Thomas Harding, draper, his brother, a citizen of London, the seisin of a tenement in Winchester Street and of a cottage in Gigant Street according to the terms of a charter perfected by William for Thomas. Seals: William's and the mayoral seal of the city

2553 By his writing John Preston, a son of John Preston, grocer, of late of Salisbury, and his wife Clarice, quitclaimed to William Warin, a citizen of Salisbury, and his heirs and assigns his right or claim to three conjoined shops, with a cellar, in Carter Street [*as in* **2550**]; also his right or claim to a messuage, with shops and gardens, in Carter Street [*as in* **2550**]. Clause of warranty. Seals: John's and the common and mayoral seals of the city. Named witnesses: the bailiff, the mayor, the coroners, the reeves, Thomas Mason, Robert Warmwell, Henry Man, John Swift, John Bromley, Richard Coof, and the clerk

31 October 1425, at Salisbury

2554 By his charter John Franklin, of Salisbury, granted to Thomas Daniel, draper, of Salisbury, a toft, or empty plot of land, in Endless Street between John Line's tenement, which John Gay holds, on the north side and Peter Daw's tenement, of late Robert Arnold's, on the south side. The toft was formerly that of the master William Ferrer and his wife Isabel, was held by John Franklin and by John Warminster and John Dean, both now dead, by a grant of Isabel, then William's relict, and is to be held for ever by Thomas and his heirs and assigns. Seals: John Franklin's and the common and mayoral seals of the city. Named witnesses: the bailiff, the mayor, the coroners, the reeves, William Warin, Thomas Mason, Robert Warmwell, Henry Man, John Swift, John Bromley, and the clerk

14 November 1425, at Salisbury

2555 Approval of the will of Giles Litchborough, otherwise called Giles Avery, a citizen of Salisbury, made at Salisbury on 8 October 1424. <u>Interment</u>: in the graveyard of St. Martin's church. <u>Bequests</u>: 6*d.* each to the fabric of that church and the fabric of the cathedral church; the rest of his goods to his wife Joan. <u>Devise</u>: to Joan a tenement, with cottages, in St. Martin's Street, at Ivy bridge, between John Moore's tenement, of late Thomas Focket's, on the east side and cottages of late Thomas Bridgehampton's on the west side. The tenement, with the cottages, was acquired by Giles from Richard Coof and Walter Short, executors of William Sall, of late a citizen of Salisbury, and is to be held for ever by Joan and her heirs and assigns. Executors: his wife Joan and Richard Coof, a citizen of Salisbury. Proved on 21 October 1424 in front of an officer of the subdean; the administration was entrusted to Joan, Richard expressly refusing to undertake it. Approved at a court held in front of the bailiff, the mayor, and other citizens; the seisin of the tenement was released to the legatee.

6 February 1426, at Salisbury
2556 By his charter Walter Warwick, a chaplain, granted to Henry Friend a tenement, with yards, in New Street between Robert Ashley's cottage on the east side and John Ladd's cottage property on the west side. The tenement, with the yards, was held by Walter by a grant of William Friend, Henry's father, and is to be held for ever by Henry and his heirs and assigns. Seals: Walter's and the common and mayoral seals of the city. Named witnesses: the bailiff, the mayor, the coroners, the reeves, William Warin, Thomas Mason, Robert Warmwell, Henry Man, John Swift, John Bromley, and the clerk
2557 By his charter Robert Gilbert, tanner, of Salisbury, a kinsman and heir of John Amesbury, of late a citizen of Salisbury, granted to John Moore, baker, of Salisbury, an empty plot in the high street which is called Minster Street between Laurence Gowan's tenement on the south side and a tenement of de Vaux college on the north side. The plot measures 36 ft. in length towards the east end and 13 ft. 8 in. fronting on the street. It is to be held for ever by John and his heirs and assigns. Seals: Robert's and the common and mayoral seals of the city. Named witnesses: the bailiff, the mayor, the coroners, the reeves, William Warin, Thomas Mason, Robert Warmwell, Henry Man, John Swift, John Bromley, and the clerk
2558 By his charter William Oving, chandler, of Salisbury, granted to William Mohun, of Salisbury, a corner tenement, with shops and cottages, in Winchester Street between Richard Forster's tenement on the west side and Laurence Gowan's tenement on the south side [*the tenement is described slightly differently in* **2505**]. The tenement, with the shops and cottages, is to be held for ever by William Mohun and his heirs and assigns, paying a rent of £4 a year for the following 16 years to John Wishford and his assigns if John were to live so long. If John were to die within that term the payment of the rent would cease, and for the rest of the term a rent of 40s. a year should be paid to John's daughter Margaret, a nun of Wherwell abbey, if she were to live so long. If Margaret were to die within the 16 years the payment of the rent would cease. Clause of warranty. Seals: William Oving's and the common and mayoral seals of the city. Named witnesses: the bailiff, the mayor, the coroners, the reeves, William Warin, Thomas Mason, Robert Warmwell, Henry Man, John Swift, John Bromley, and the clerk
2559 By his charter John Herring, of Winterbourne, granted to John Shad, draper, of Salisbury, two conjoined tenements, with a cellar, in Culver Street between Richard Butler's tenement on the north side and John Deverill's garden on the south side. The tenements, by the name of two tenements, with a cellar and a dovecot, were held sometime since by John Herring and William Walter, now dead, by a grant of Thomas Read, a son and heir of Richard Read, formerly a citizen of Salisbury, and, with the cellar, are to be held for ever by John Shad

and his heirs and assigns. Seals: John Herring's and the common and mayoral seals of the city. Named witnesses: the bailiff, the mayor, the coroners, the reeves, William Warin, Thomas Mason, Robert Warmwell, Henry Man, John Swift, John Bromley, and the clerk

2560 By his writing Thomas Read, a son and heir of Richard Read, of late a citizen of Salisbury, quitclaimed to John Shad, draper, of Salisbury, and his heirs and assigns his right or claim to two conjoined tenements, with a cellar, in Culver Street [*as in 2559*]. Seals: Thomas's and the common and mayoral seals of the city. Named witnesses: the bailiff, the mayor, the coroners, the reeves, William Warin, Thomas Mason, Robert Warmwell, Henry Man, John Swift, John Bromley, and the clerk

6 March 1426, at Salisbury
2561 Approval of the will of John Hampton, brewer, a citizen of Salisbury, made on 12 May 1419. Interment: in St. Edmund's church, behind the high altar, in the south part of the place in which the corpse of William Wallop, a parochial chaplain of that church, lies buried; or at all events in the graveyard of that church. Bequests: 40*d.* to the fabric of that church; 20*d.* to the fabric of the cathedral church; 12 lb. of wax to be burned around his corpse on the day of his burial; the rest of his goods to his wife Margery and his daughters Pauline, Olive, and Alice. Devises: to his daughter Pauline a cottage in Gigant Street, between Joan Warmwell's cottages on the south side and John Teffont's cottages on the north side, and to his daughter Olive a cottage in Mealmonger Street, between a gate of [Ive's Corner], his chief tenement in that street, on the south side and cottages of late William Warmwell's on the north side. The cottages are to be held seperately by Pauline and Olive and their issue for ever. If Pauline were to die without issue in the lifetime of Olive, or if Olive were to die in the lifetime of Pauline, the two cottages should remain for ever to the one who lived longer and to her issue. If Pauline and Olive were to die without issue the two cottages should be sold by John's executors, their executors, or subsequent executors. The money issuing from the sale should be laid out by the executors on pious uses for the salvation of John's soul. John devised to his daughter Alice three shops or dwelling houses in Wineman Street, one between a gate of John's chief tenement in Wineman Street on the east side and William Chapman's tenement on the west side, the other two in the same street between a gate of the same chief tenement on the west side and Mealmonger Street on the east side. The three shops or dwelling houses are to be held for ever by Alice and her issue, if Alice were to die without issue they would remain for ever to Pauline and Olive and their issue, and if Pauline and Olive were to die without issue they should be sold by John's executors, their executors, or subsequent executors. The money received from the sale should be laid out by the executors on the salvation of John's soul. John devised to his wife Margery for life as dower [Ive's Corner], a chief tenement, in which he dwelt except the cottages and shops or dwelling houses devised above, in Wineman Street and Mealmonger Street between a shop devised to his daughter Alice on the west side, the two shops or dwelling houses devised

to Alice in Wineman Street on the east side, and the cottage devised to Olive in Mealmonger Street on the north side. The ovens and other vessels appurtenant to his craft as a brewer should remain in the chief tenement for Margery's use, and for the maintenance of Pauline, Olive, and Alice, for life. On Margery's death the chief tenement, with the ovens and the vessels, should remain for ever to Pauline and her issue, if Pauline were to die without issue they would remain for ever to Olive and her issue, and if Olive were to die without issue they would remain for ever to Alice and her issue. If Pauline, Olive, and Alice, or their issue, were to die without surviving issue the chief tenement, with the ovens and the vessels, should be sold by John's executors, their executors, or subsequent executors. The money issuing from the sale should be laid out on the salvation of his soul and the souls of others. Executors: his wife Margery, John Hain, loader, and John Collingbourne, tucker. Proved on 14 January 1422 in front of John Pedwell, the subdean; the administration was entrusted to the executors, who afterwards appeared, accounted with an officer, and were dismissed. Approved at a court held in front of the bailiff, the mayor, and other citizens; the seisin of the tenements was released to the legatee.

20 March 1426, at Salisbury
2562 By his charter Hildebrand Elwell, grocer, a citizen of London, granted to Stephen Cooper, mercer, of Salisbury, three conjoined shops in Pot Row between Robert Earl's shop on the west side and a shop of Thomas Freeman, mercer, on the east side. The three shops were held by Hildebrand by a grant of Thomas Freeman and are to be held for ever by Stephen and his heirs and assigns. Seals: Hildebrand's and the common and mayoral seals of the city. Named witnesses: the bailiff, the mayor, the coroners, the reeves, William Warin, Thomas Mason, Robert Warmwell, Henry Man, John Swift, John Bromley, John Noble, Thomas Freeman, mercer, and the clerk

3 April 1426, at Salisbury
2563 By their charter Richard Ballfoot and Agnes, the relict of William West, baker, of late a citizen of Salisbury, William's executors, on the strength of William's will granted to Henry Ham, of Salisbury, a corner tenement, with shops, in New Street and Brown Street between a tenement of William Huggin, carpenter, on the west side and John Upton's tenement on the south side. William West appointed the tenement, with the shops, to be sold by his executors or their executors. The money received from the sale should be laid out on behalf of his soul and the souls of others. The tenement, with the shops, is to be held for ever by Henry and his heirs and assigns. Seals: those of Richard and Agnes and the common and mayoral seals of the city. Named witnesses: the bailiff, the mayor, the coroners, the reeves, William Warin, Thomas Mason, Robert Warmwell, Henry Man, John Swift, John Noble, and the clerk
2564 By his deed John Weston, a merchant, a burgess of Bristol, quitclaimed to Richard Weston, of Salisbury, his father, and his heirs and assigns his right or claim to two conjoined cottages, which of late he held by Richard's grant, in

Gigant Street between William Cambridge's tenement on the north side and a garden of late Agnes Ball's on the south side. Seals: John's and the common and mayoral seals of the city. Named witnesses: the bailiff, the mayor, the coroners, the reeves, William Warin, Thomas Mason, Robert Warmwell, Henry Man, John Noble, and the clerk

2565 By his charter William Bailey, of Stratford, an executor of Margaret Godmanstone, on the strength of Margaret's will granted to John Hunt, a citizen of Salisbury, a cottage, with a garden, in Gigant Street between cottages of late William Warmwell's on the south side and a cottage devised by Margaret to William Bailey on the north side. Margaret appointed the cottage to be sold by her executors. The money received from the sale should be laid out on behalf of her soul. The cottage, with the garden, is to be held for ever by John and his heirs and assigns as that which John bought from William in good faith for a sum of money reaching its true value. Seals: William's and the common and mayoral seals of the city. Named witnesses: the bailiff, the mayor, the coroners, the reeves, William Warin, Thomas Mason, Robert Warmwell, Henry Man, John Swift, John Bromley, John Noble, and the clerk

17 April 1426, at Salisbury
2566 Approval [*dated, erroneously, to the Wednesday before the feast of St. Thomas the Martyr in the 4th year of the reign of Henry VI (26 December 1425); perhaps the most likely date for the approval is the Wednesday before the feast of St. George the Martyr in that year (17 April 1426)*] of the will of Thomas Yeovil, a tailor, a citizen of Salisbury, made on 24 December 1425. <u>Interment</u>: in the graveyard of St. Thomas's church. <u>Bequests</u>: 40*d.* to the fabric of that church, and 12*d.* to the high altar for his forgotten tithes and oblations; 6*d.* to the fabric of the cathedral church; 2*s.* 6*d.* both to the Dominicans of Fisherton Anger and the Franciscans of Salisbury; 20*s.* to the mayor and commonalty of Salisbury to pray for his soul when they might be together and to be of good friendship to his wife Joan if she were to have need of it in the future; a striped gown, coloured blue and lined with white fur, and 6*s.* 8*d.* to his brother Nicholas; cloth to the value of 6*s.* 8*d.* or 6*s.* 8*d.* in money, according to the will of his wife Joan, to Edith, the wife of Richard Ballard, of Britford; 6*s.* 8*d.* to William, a servant of John Pope; his appropriate scissors, and cloth to the value of 6*s.* 8*d.*, to Roger Hardy, tailor; 6*s.* 8*d.* to Thomas Coffin, of late his apprentice; a gown and 6*s.* 8*d.* to Richard Bristow, his servant; £10 to be handed out in alms by his executors immediately after his death; £10 for funeral expenses and rites; 6*s.* to each of his godchildren, *viz.* Agnes, a daughter of Gerard Goldsmith, Thomas, a son of John Avery, a daughter of Nicholas Mower, George, a son of a younger John Lake, Thomas, a son of William Lake, Thomas, a son of John Power, a daughter of Thomas Pillinger, and a daughter of John Still; the rest of his goods to his wife Joan to pray for his soul. <u>Devise</u>: to Joan for life a tenement, in which he dwelt, with shops attached on the west side, in the street called Old Poultry between a tenement of late Thomas Play's, now John Lippiatt's, on the west side and a tenement of late Thomas Knoyle's, now Robert Earl's, on the east side. The tenement, with the shops, is to be held by Joan for

holding Thomas's obit once a year for her lifetime in St. Thomas's church, and immediately after her death it should be sold by her executors, their executors, or subsequent executors. The money received from the sale should be laid out, on masses and doing other charitable deeds, on behalf of Thomas's soul, Joan's soul, and the souls of others. <u>Executor</u>: his wife Joan; overseer, Philip Baron. <u>Proved</u>: on 6 February 1426 in front of an officer of the subdean; the administration was entrusted to the executor. <u>Approved</u> at a court held in front of the bailiff, the mayor, and other citizens; the seisin of the tenement was released to the legatee.

14 October 1426, at Salisbury
2567 An indenture agreed on by Peter Daw, mercer, of Salisbury, and Thomas Daniel, draper, of Salisbury. On behalf of himself and his heirs and assigns Peter granted to Thomas a licence to lay a lead gutter 22 ft. long on a house of Peter's, built and ordained as a kitchen and workhouse, within a cottage, which John Franklin, weaver, holds of Peter, in Endless Street between a newly built tenement of Thomas's on the north side and Peter's cottage, which William Sims holds, on the south side. The house on which the gutter will be lain stands on the south side of a house of Thomas's. Thomas and his heirs should maintain and repair the gutter at their own expense so that, by the want of such maintenance and repair, no rot should occur to the timber or walls of Peter's house, and the gutter should incur no loss to Thomas and his heirs. Seals: those of the parties to the parts of the indenture in turn and the mayoral seal of the city

16 October 1426, at Salisbury
2568 A deed of John Manning and John Draper, clerks, executors of Thomas Manning, who appointed cottages in Brown Street, between [?a tenement of: *cf.* *2577*] the hospital of the Holy Trinity on the south side and a tenement of St. Nicholas's hospital on the north side, and a yard in Gigant Street, between Peter Upavon's tenement on the north side and John Lea's tenement on the south side, by the name of all the land and tenements which he acquired from Richard Mawardine and his wife Edith, to be sold by his executors. John Swift, a citizen of Salisbury, and Richard Gater, of Salisbury, have paid to John Manning and John Draper a sum of money, reaching the true value of the cottages and the yard, to be laid out wholly on behalf of Thomas's soul and the souls specified in his will, and on the strength of the will John Manning and John Draper granted the cottages and the yard to them, to be held for ever by them and their heirs and assigns as that which they bought from John and John in good faith for that sum. Seals: those of John Manning and John Draper and the common and mayoral seals of the city. Named witnesses: the mayor, the coroners, the reeves, William Warin, Robert Warmwell, Thomas Mason, Henry Man, John Swift, John Noble, and the clerk
2569 By their letters of attorney John Manning and John Draper, clerks, executors of Thomas Manning, appointed Richard Walker, mercer, of Salisbury, to deliver to John Swift, a citizen of Salisbury, and Richard Gater, of Salisbury, the seisin of cottages in Brown Street [*as in* *2568*] and of a yard in Gigant Street [*as in* *2568*].

Seals: those of John Manning and John Draper and the mayoral seal of the city

13 November 1426, at Salisbury
2570 Approval of the will of Thomas Andrew, a citizen of Salisbury, made on 7
July 1426. <u>Interment</u>: in St. Edmund's church. <u>Bequests</u>: 12*d.* to the fabric of the
mother church of Salisbury; 18*s.* 9*d.*, which John Kimmeridge owes to him, to
the fabric of St. Edmund's church, 20*d.* to the high altar for his forgotten tithes
and oblations and lesser benefactions, and 2*s.* 6*d.* to the members of the college
to celebrate mass on behalf of his soul; 2*s.* 6*d.* both to the Franciscans of Salisbury
and the Dominicans of Fisherton to pray on behalf of his soul and the souls of
others; his best horse, with a saddle, a bridle, and all the equipment, and four
sheep to his son John; his second-best horse and four sheep to his son Ralph;
three horses, a cart with all the equipment, and a plough with all the equipment
to his son Thomas; six sheep and 6*s.* 8*d.* to his daughter Cecily; 6*d.* to each of his
godchildren; 40*d.* to John Butler; the rest of his goods to his wife Joan. <u>Devise</u>:
to Joan for life a messuage, in which he dwelt, in Gigant Street between William
Alexander's tenement on the north side and a tenement which John Smith
holds on the south side. On Joan's death the messuage should remain for ever to
Thomas's son Ralph and his issue, for want of such issue it would remain for ever
to Thomas's son John and his issue, for want of such issue it would remain for ever
to Thomas's daughter Cecily and her issue, and for want of such issue it should
remain to Thomas's executors, if they were then living, to Joan's executors, or to
the executors of Thomas's children to be sold. The money received from the sale
should be laid out on pious uses, giving alms, repairing churches, and celebrating
masses. <u>Executors</u>: his wife Joan and John Butler. <u>Proved</u> on 20 July 1426 in front
of an officer of the subdean; the administration was entrusted to the executors,
who accounted with an officer and were dismissed. <u>Approved</u> at a court held,
while the bishopric was vacant, the temporalities of the bishop were in the king's
hand, and the mayor and other officers of the city were present as officers of the
king, in front of the mayor, and other citizens; the seisin of the messuage was
released to the legatee.

27 November 1426, at Salisbury
2571 By his charter Peter Daw, mercer, of Salisbury, granted to Stephen Cooper,
mercer, of Salisbury, two conjoined cottages in Endless Street between a tenement
of Thomas Daniel, draper, of Salisbury, on the north side and John Machin's
tenement on the south side. The cottages were of late held by Robert Warmwell,
a citizen of Salisbury, William Stout, weaver, of Salisbury, and Peter, with the
reversion of the tenement in which Peter dwelt, by a grant of Richard Weston,
weaver, and his wife Alice, now dead. By their deed Robert and William released
their right in them for ever to Peter and his heirs, and they are to be held for
ever by Stephen and his heirs and assigns. Clause of warranty. Seals: Peter's and
the common and mayoral seals of the city. Named witnesses: the mayor, the
coroners, the reeves, William Warin, William Warwick, Thomas Mason, John
Swift, Henry Man, John Bromley, and the clerk

2572 A deed of Thomas Randolph and his wife Alice. By his deed dated at Salisbury on 15 February 1419 [*2369*] William Packing enfeoffed Thomas and Alice in all the land, tenements, with shops and cottages, and reversions which he held in Endless Street and Chipper Lane [Chipper Street *in 2369*], to be held for ever by them and their heirs on condition that, if within the following eight years he would pay 160 marks to them, the feoffment would be counted for nothing and William and his heirs might enter on the premises, take back possession, and keep his former estate. William afterwards paid the 160 marks to Thomas and Alice, Thomas and Alice acknowledged it to have been paid to them, and William entered on the premises. By their deed Thomas and Alice quitclaimed to William and his heirs and assigns their right or claim to the premises. Seals: those of Thomas and Alice and the common and mayoral seals of the city. Named witnesses: the mayor, the coroners, the reeves, William Warin, Robert Warmwell, William Warwick, Thomas Mason, Henry Man, John Swift, and the clerk

11 December 1426, at Salisbury
2573 By his charter John Durnford, dyer, of Salisbury, granted to Robert Gilbert, a citizen of Salisbury, a tenement in Castle Street, between Thomas Daniel's tenement, formerly that of John Sexhampcote, the vicar of Whiteparish, on the north side and a tenement of John Marshall, dyer, sometime since Edward Breamore's, on the south side, to be held for ever by him and his heirs. Clause of warranty. Seals: John Durnford's and the common and mayoral seals of the city. Named witnesses: the bailiff, the mayor, the coroners, the reeves, William Warin, Robert Warmwell, Thomas Mason, William Warwick, Henry Man, John Bromley, John Swift, and the clerk

15 January 1427, at Salisbury
2574 A deed of Thomas Field, an executor of Alice, the relict, and an executor, of John Baker, draper, of Salisbury. John devised to Alice for life a place or tenement, with shops, and with a garden with a stone wall and houses inclosed [within it], in which he dwelt, in Carter Street between William Warin's tenement on the north side and a tenement of John Upton, a son of a late elder John Upton, on the south side. He appointed the tenement, with the shops and garden, to remain on Alice's death to his son Richard and on Richard's death to his daughter Gillian; after the death of Alice, Richard, and Gillian it should be sold by his executors or the executors of Alice, Richard, or Gillian. The money received from the sale should be laid out, on celebrating masses in St. Thomas's church and the churches of the Franciscans of Salisbury and the Dominicans [?of Fisherton] and handed out among paupers, on behalf of his soul and the souls of Alice and his children. Alice appointed Thomas her executor, Richard and Gillian are dead, and the place or tenement, with the shops and garden, pertains to Thomas as Alice's executor to be sold. Robert Ishmael, of Devizes, has paid to Thomas a sum of money reaching the true value of the place or tenement, with the shops and garden, and by his charter, and on the strength of John Baker's will, Thomas granted the premises to Robert to be held for ever by him and his heirs and

assigns as that which he bought from Thomas in good faith for the sum of money to be wholly laid out as described above. Seals: Thomas's and the common and mayoral seals of the city. Named witnesses: the bailiff, the mayor, the coroners, the reeves, William Warin, Thomas Mason, Robert Warmwell, Henry Man, John Swift, John Bromley, and the clerk

2575 By their charter Thomas Mason, draper, and John Swift, ironmonger, citizens of Salisbury, and Henry Warin, a chaplain, granted to William Shipton, a cordwainer, of Salisbury, and his wife Maud two conjoined tenements, with a garden, in Chipper Lane between a messuage of late Nicholas Baynton's on the east side and a tenement of late John Mower's, which Thomas Saddler holds, on the west side. The tenements, with all the land, tenements, shops, cottages, rent, and reversions which John Mower held in Salisbury, were held by William Walter and Walter Shirley, both now dead, and by Thomas, John, and Henry by a grant of John Mower, and, with the garden, they are to be held for ever by William and Maud and their heirs. Seals: those of the grantors and the common and mayoral seals of the city. Named witnesses: the bailiff, the mayor, the coroners, the reeves, William Warin, Robert Warmwell, Henry Man, John Bromley, and the clerk

5 February 1427, at Salisbury

2576 By their writing Thomas Randolph, a citizen of Salisbury, and John Moore, baker, of Salisbury, quitclaimed to Robert Ishmael, of Devizes, and his heirs and assigns their right or claim to a place or tenement, with shops and a garden, in Carter Street [*as in* **2574**], which Robert held by a grant of Thomas Field, an executor of Alice, the relict of John Baker, draper. Seals: those of Thomas Randolph and John Moore and the common and mayoral seals of the city. Named witnesses: the bailiff, the mayor, the coroners, the reeves, William Warin, Thomas Mason, Robert Warmwell, Henry Man, John Swift, John Bromley, and the clerk

5 March 1427, at Salisbury

2577 By their charter John Swift, ironmonger, and Richard Gater, citizens of Salisbury, granted to Richard Ballfoot, tailor, of Salisbury, a tenement, with a garden, and with two walls on the north side of the tenement and of the garden, in Brown Street between a tenement of the hospital of the Holy Trinity on the south side and two tenements, in which John Crickmore dwells, on the north side; also half a well for taking his profit from or for drawing water from for himself and his heirs for ever. The tenement, with the garden and walls, and the half of the well are to be held for ever by Richard Ballfoot and his heirs and assigns. Seals: those of John Swift and Richard Gater and the common and mayoral seals of the city. Named witnesses: the bailiff, the mayor, a coroner, the reeves, William Warin, Thomas Mason, Robert Warmwell, Henry Man, John Bromley, and the clerk

2578 By their charter John Swift, ironmonger, and Richard Gater, citizens of Salisbury, granted to John Crickmore, a parchmenter, of Salisbury, two tenements, with gardens, in Brown Street between Richard Ballfoot's tenement on the south side and a tenement of St. Nicholas's hospital on the north side; also half a well for taking his profit from or drawing water from for himself and his heirs for ever. The tenements, with the gardens, and the half of the well are to be held for ever by John Crickmore and his heirs and assigns. Seals: those of John Swift and Richard Gater and the common and mayoral seals of the city. Named witnesses: the bailiff, the mayor, a coroner, the reeves, William Warin, Thomas Mason, Robert Warmwell, Henry Man, John Bromley, and the clerk

19 March 1427, at Salisbury
2579 By his writing John Manning, a chaplain, quitclaimed to Richard Ballfoot, tailor, of Salisbury, and his heirs and assigns his right or claim to a tenement, with a garden, and with two walls on the north side of the tenement and of the garden, in Brown Street [*as in* **2577**]; also his right or claim to half a well [*as in* **2577**]. Clause of warranty, provided that the warrant would not extend against John and his heirs to pay for its value but only to exclude them for ever. Seals: John's and the common and mayoral seals of the city. Named witnesses: the bailiff, the mayor, the coroners, the reeves, William Warin, Thomas Mason, Robert Warmwell, Henry Man, John Swift, John Bromley, and the clerk
2580 By his writing John Manning, a chaplain, quitclaimed to John Crickmore, parchmenter, of Salisbury, and his heirs and assigns his right or claim to two tenements, with gardens, in Brown Street [*as in* **2578**]; also his right or claim to half a well [*as in* **2578**]. Clause of warranty, provided that the warranty would not extend against John and his heirs to pay for its value but only to exclude them for ever. Seals: John Manning's and the common and mayoral seals of the city. Named witnesses: the bailiff, the mayor, the coroners, the reeves, William Warin, Thomas Mason, Robert Warmwell, Henry Man, John Swift, John Bromley, and the clerk

The copy of the following charter is unfinished and its date is missing. It appears between a charter dated 11 December 1426 and a will approved on 17 September 1427
2581 By his charter Laurence Groom, a chaplain, an executor of William Buck, of late a vicar of the cathedral church, on the strength of William's will granted to Thomas Farrant, of Salisbury, and his wife Joan a rent of 8*s.* a year issuing from a corner tenement, formerly that of Eleanor, the wife of Edmund Bramshaw, in which Thomas and Joan dwell, in Endless Street [and Chipper Lane: *cf.* **2651**] between a tenement of late William Duke's on the south side and cottages formerly Thomas Burford's on the west side. The rent is to be held for ever by Thomas and Joan and their heirs and assigns as that which Thomas and Joan bought from Laurence in good faith for a sum of money reaching its true value, and Laurence quitclaimed to Thomas and Joan and their heirs and assigns his right or claim to the corner tenement or the rent.

17 September 1427, at Salisbury
2582 Approval of the will of Christine, the relict of William Dowding, of Salisbury, made on 12 September 1426. <u>Interment</u>: in St. Thomas's church, beside

William's grave. <u>Bequests</u>: 6*s*. 8*d*. to the fabric of the cathedral church; 20*s*. and a silver and gilded cross to the fabric of St. Thomas's church, and she wished that the cross might be of greater value than other things in the church to keep her soul and the souls of John King, a brewer, and her husband William in prayers there on Sundays; 6*s*. 8*d*. to the rector of that church for her forgotten tithes, 40*d*. to the parochial chaplains to pray for her soul, a mazer bound with silver and gilded, with an altar cloth, to the chantry, 6*s*. 8*d*. to John Kill, a chaplain there, 12*d*. to each other chaplain celebrating mass in the church to pray for her soul, 8*d*. to the deacon, 6*d*. to the sacristan, and 6*s*. 8*d*. to the light of the fraternity of St. Michael; 6*s*. 8*d*. to the fabric of St. Edmund's church to pray for her soul and the soul of her daughter Alice; 40*d*. to the fabric of St. Martin's church; 20*s*. to the Dominicans of Fisherton Anger to pray for her soul and the souls of John King and William Dowding, of late her husbands; 6*s*. 8*d*. to the Franciscans of Salisbury to pray likewise; 40*d*. to the master (*domini*) and paupers of the almshouse of Salisbury; 6*s*. 8*d*. to the fabric of Netheravon church to pray for her soul and the souls of her father and mother lying at rest there; a silver bowl with a cover all gilded, to Robert Warmwell, and a belt of green silk harnessed with silver *grapis* and *batis*, her best tablecloth with a best altar cloth, and two best towels of linen cloth to his wife Margaret; 12 best silver spoons with gilded pommels, a piece of silver with a second-best cover, a coverlet of red worsted, a pair of best linen sheets, a tablecloth with an altar cloth and two protective cloths, and a large pillow with tars to William Knolle, her kinsman, her best gown, with fur, a best hat with her best kirtle, her best silvered and gilded belt, a tablecloth with an altar cloth and two protective cloths, and a rosary of silver beads with a cross in it to his wife Agnes, and 40*s*. to his daughter Joan; a gown of motley sendal and six silver spoons marked with the letter D to the wife of John Woodhay; 6*s*. 8*d*. to the servant of John Wylye, mercer; her second-best gown and a blue silvered belt, with a rosary of amber beads with a cross hanging on it, to Laurence, the wife of Richard Butler; a second-best mazer to Joan, the wife of George Westby, 40*d*. to her daughter Alice, and 40*d*. to her daughter Margaret, a goddaughter of Christine; 6*s*. 8*d*. and a rosary of coral beads to Gillian, a daughter of William Warin, a goddaughter of Christine; 20*d*. to each of her other godchildren; a bowl called Nut with a foot harnessed with silver gilt and with a cover of the same style to Maud, a daughter of William Alexander; a pair of linen sheets to each of 20 paupers dwelling in in the city; a smock with a belt to each of 20 poor men of the city; a smock to each of 20 poor women of the city; a pair of shoes to each of the poor men and women of the city; her executors should ordain 100 masses to be celebrated on behalf of her soul before her burial, and should hand out £3 in bread to paupers of the city on that day; a flat piece of silver, with a cover, to Walter Short, serjeant, and a green silvered belt to his wife Margaret; 20*s*., a piece of silver *de quarta secte*, a tablecloth with an altar cloth, a basin with a laver, a posnet with barley feet ('berefet'), and a box to Henry Draper; a rosary of silver beads and a tongue with a cross to Christine Swift; a brass pot containing 2 gallons, and a basin with a laver, to Isabel, of late her servant; 40*d*. to Alice, the wife of Richard Walker, and 40*d*. to her sister Catherine; a cloak of medley to Isabel, the

wife of Stephen Saddler; a flat piece of silver to Walter Cook; 6s. 8d. to the friar
Thomas Glassingbury; 10s. each to Thomas Knolle and Richard Knolle; 6s. 8d. to
John Harleston; a brass pot marked with a fleshknife to Alice Bridmore; a cloak of
russet to Alice Smith; a black gown to Agnes, her servant; the rest of her goods to
her executors to be disposed of on behalf of her soul, the souls of her husbands,
and the souls of others. Devises: to her kinsman William Knolle a tenement,
in which she dwelt, [in Winchester Street: cf. *2399*] between John Woodhay's
tenement on the east side and William Alexander's tenement on the west side.
The tenement is to be held for ever by William and his heirs and assigns to pay
Christine's debts, legacies, and funeral expenses about her burial immediately
after her death, to lay out on chaplains celebrating mass in St. Thomas's church
to celebrate on behalf of her soul, the souls of John King and William Dowding,
of late her husbands, and the souls of others, and to hand out to paupers in
the city. Christine appointed a tenement in Gigant Street, between a tenement
formerly William Sall's on the north side and William Stout's tenement on the
south side, to be sold by Robert Warmwell and William Knolle, her executors,
immediately after her death. The money received from the sale should be laid
out, on celebrating masses in St. Thomas's church, for the salvation of the souls
of William Warmwell, William Dowding, and Robert Warmwell and his wife
Edith, and of her own soul. Christine appointed that William Alexander, Robert
Long, William Warin, John Judd, Henry Man, and Richard Gage, feoffees in two
tenements and an empty plot, should enfeoff her executors in those premises. The
tenements stand in Carter Street, one, called Abbey, between a tenement of late
Richard Spencer's on the south side and a tenement of John Moore, baker, on the
north side, the other between a tenement of late John Preston's on the south side
and a tenement of late that of John Newman, cardmaker, on the north side. The
empty plot, formerly William Tull's, lies in Wineman Street and Culver Street, on
a corner of them. The tenements and the empty plot are to be held for ever by
Robert Warmwell and William Knolle, the executors, and their heirs and assigns
to be sold immediately after Christine's death. The money received from the
sale should be laid out for the salvation of Christine's soul, the souls of William
Tull and his wife Alice, and the souls mentioned above. Christine appointed that
her executors should cause a chaplain to celebrate mass in St. Thomas's church
for the two years immediately following her death on behalf of her soul and
the souls mentioned above. Executors: Robert Warmwell and William Knolle;
overseer, Henry Draper. Witnesses: William Ogbourne and John Kill, chaplains,
Walter Short, serjeant, and others. Proved on 24 August 1427 in front of John
Pedwell, the subdean; the administration was entrusted to the executors, who
afterwards appeared, accounted with an officer, and were dismissed. Approved at
a court held in front of the bailiff, the mayor, and other citizens; the seisin of the
tenements was released to the legatees.

15 October 1427, at Salisbury
2583 A deed of William Knolle, a kinsman of Christine, the relict of William
Dowding, of late a citizen of Salisbury. Christine devised to William a tenement,

in which she dwelt, in Winchester Street, between John Woodhay's tenement on the east side and William Alexander's tenement on the west side, to be held for ever by him and his heirs and assigns to pay her debts and legacies, and to meet other charges, on behalf of her soul, the souls of John King, brewer, and William Dowding, her husbands, and the souls of others. William Charling, mercer, of Salisbury, has paid to William Knolle a sum of money, reaching the true value of the tenement, to be laid out wholly according to the terms of Christine's will, and by his charter William Knolle granted the tenement to him to be held for ever by him and his heirs and assigns. Seals: William Knolle's and the common and mayoral seals of the city. Named witnesses: the bailiff, the mayor, the coroners, the reeves, William Warin, Thomas Mason, Robert Warmwell, Henry Man, John Swift, John Bromley, and the clerk

16 October 1427, at Salisbury
2584 By their writing Robert Warmwell and William Knolle, executors of Christine, the relict of William Dowding, of Salisbury, quitclaimed to William Charling, mercer, a citizen of Salisbury, and his heirs and assigns their right or claim to a tenement in Winchester Street [*as in* **2583**]. Seals: those of Robert Warmwell and William Knolle and the common and mayoral seals of the city. Named witnesses: the bailiff, the mayor, the coroners, the reeves, William Warin, Thomas Mason, Henry Man, John Swift, John Bromley, and the clerk

10 December 1427, at Salisbury
2585 Approval of the will of John Clive, tanner, a citizen of Salisbury, made on 14 November 1427. <u>Interment</u>: in the graveyard of St. Edmund's church. <u>Bequests</u>: 6s. 8d. to the fabric of that church, and 12d. to the provost; 20d. to the fabric of the cathedral church; 20d. to the Dominicans of Fisherton Anger; 20d. to the Franciscans of Salisbury to pray for his soul and the souls of others; 12d. to the fabric of St. Thomas's church; 12 marks to his son John; 40s. to his daughter Edith; 60s. to his daughter Cecily; the rest of his goods to his wife Joan. <u>Devise</u>: to Joan for life a chief tenement, in which he dwelt, with two cottages attached to it and with gardens, in Endless Street between John Hogman's tenement on the north side and a tenement of the hospital of the Holy Trinity on the south side. On Joan's death the tenement, with a garden, should remain for ever to his son John and John's issue, and if John were to die without issue it should be sold by the elder John's executors, their executors, or subsequent executors. The money received from the sale should be laid out on pious uses on behalf of the soul of the elder John, Joan's soul, and the souls of others. John appointed a cottage, with a garden, in which Richard Dorset and John Mild dwell, in Endless Street beside John Hogman's tenement to remain on Joan's death to his own daughter Cecily for life, and on Cecily's death to remain to the younger John Clive and his issue for ever. He appointed a cottage, with a garden, in which John Holme and his own daughter Edith dwell, to remain on Joan's death to Edith for life, and on Edith's death to the younger John and his issue for ever. If that John were to die without issue the two cottages, with the gardens, should remain to the elder

John's executors to be sold. The money received from the sale should be laid out by the executors on behalf of that John's soul and the souls mentioned above. Executors: his wife Joan, his son John, and John Holme. Proved on 21 December 1427 in front of an officer of the subdean; the administration was entrusted to the executors, who accounted with an officer and were dismissed. Approved at a court held in front of the bailiff, the mayor, and other citizens; the seisin of the tenement was released to the legatee.

3 March 1428, at Salisbury
2586 A deed of Robert Warmwell, an executor of William Warmwell, of late a citizen of Salisbury. William devised to William Dowding a tenement, with a garden, in Gigant Street between William Stout's tenement on the south side and a tenement of late William Sall's on the north side. The tenement was to be held by William Dowding on condition that, if within the two years following William Warmwell's death he would pay to William's executors £10 in each of the two years, the tenement, with the garden, would be held for ever by him and his heirs and assigns; otherwise the executors should sell it. The money received from the sale should be laid out on behalf of William Warmwell's soul and the souls of others. William Dowding did not pay the £20 to the executors. By his present deed Robert, an executor of William Warmwell, granted the tenement, with the garden, to Thomas Randolph, a citizen of Salisbury, and his wife Alice to be held for ever by them and their heirs and assigns as that which Thomas and Alice bought from him in good faith for a sum of money, reaching its true value, to be laid out wholly according to the terms of William's will. Seals: Robert's and the common and mayoral seals of the city. Named witnesses: the bailiff, the mayor, the coroners, the reeves, William Warin, Thomas Mason, Henry Man, John Swift, John Marshall, Richard Ecton, and the clerk

24 March 1428, at Salisbury
2587 By his charter an elder William Lord, of Salisbury, granted to William Warin, a citizen of Salisbury, William Alexander, Thomas Mason, William Packing, Robert Ogbourne, Thomas Harding, draper, of London, Richard Oliver, a chaplain, John Pope, and Henry Blackmoor the land, tenements, gardens, shops, and cottages, with the meadows, pastures, feeding rights, rent, services, and reversions, which he held in Salisbury, Fisherton Anger or Old Sarum, and elsewhere in England to be held for ever by them and their heirs and assigns. Clause of warranty. Seals: William Lord's and the common and mayoral seals of the city. Named witnesses: the bailiff, the mayor, the coroners, the reeves, Robert Warmwell, Henry Man, John Swift, William Warwick, John Noble, and Thomas Randolph

14 April 1428, at Salisbury
2588 By her deed Joan, the relict of Thomas Yeovil, of Salisbury, in her widowhood and full power granted to John Noble, a citizen of Salisbury, her estate in three conjoined shops in Old Poultry between John Lippiatt's shop on

the west side and a shop formerly Thomas Knoyle's, beside a lane, on the east side. She held an estate in the three shops for her life by a demise of them, under the name of a messuage, by John Judd, a citizen of Salisbury, to her and Thomas, of late her husband, and to Thomas's heirs. The shops are to be held for Joan's life by John Noble. Seals: Joan's and the common and mayoral seals of the city. Named witnesses: the bailiff, the mayor, the coroners, the reeves, William Warin Thomas Mason, Robert Warmwell, Henry Man, John Swift, and the clerk

17 April 1428, at Salisbury
2589 A charter of Joan, the relict, and an executor, of Thomas Yeovil. In his will Thomas appointed the reversion of a tenement, with shops, [in the street called Old Poultry: *cf.* **2566**] to be sold by his executors or their executors after Joan's death or by Joan in her lifetime. The money received from the sale should be laid out by Joan or the executors on behalf of Thomas's soul, Joan's soul, and the souls of others. By her deed Joan granted her estate in the tenement, with the shops, for her life to John Noble and his heirs. Now, because it seemed to her better for the souls mentioned above for the reversion to be sold in her lifetime, and the money issuing from the sale to be laid out on behalf of the souls, than for the sale to be delayed, in as much as her husband's will might perhaps be impeded by such delay to the grave damage of her soul, by her charter Joan, in her widowhood and full power, for a sum of money reaching the true value of the reversion of the tenement, with the shops, on the strength of Thomas's will granted that reversion, when it fell due, to John Noble to be held for ever by him and his heirs and assigns as that which John bought from her in good faith for a sum of money, extending to its true value, to be laid out wholly on behalf of the souls mentioned above. Joan quitclaimed to John and his heirs and assigns her right or claim to the tenement, with the shops. Seals: Joan's and the common and mayoral seals of the city. Named witnesses: the bailiff, the mayor, the coroners, the reeves, William Warin, Thomas Mason, Robert Warmwell, Henry Man, John Swift, and the clerk

21 July 1428, at Salisbury
2590 Approval of the will of Agnes, the wife of Thomas Davy, a citizen of Salisbury, made on 20 November 1427. <u>Interment</u>: in the chancel of St. Martin's church. <u>Bequests</u>: 6s. 8d. to the fabric of the cathedral church; 6s. 8d. to the fabric of St. Martin's church, 6s. 8d. to William Spicer, a chaplain of that church, 12d. each to John Went and William Westage, chaplains of that church, 8d. to John, the deacon, and 6d. to Richard, the sacristan; 40d. each to the fabric of St. Edmund's church and the fabric of St. Thomas's church; 40d. to the paupers of the almshouse of the Holy Trinity; 6s. 8d. each to her brothers John and Thomas; a blue gown furred with squirrel to both her sister Denise and Alice Read; a good brass pot, a pan, a bowl with a laver, a bed with all its bedding, a green belt, a tunic lined with black fur, and a rosary of black beads to Edith Porter; a gold ring set with a stone (*or* stones) to Christine Pope; a gold ring each to Maud Halstead and Joan Cox; 20d. to the poor men of the leper's hospital of Harnham; 40s. to

paupers, to be handed out to them as bread on the day of her obit; a red hat to Agnes Davy; a 'frend' of sendal, a smock, and a rosary of amber beads to Alice Davy, a sister of Thomas Davy; 12*d.* to each of her godchidren; the rest of her goods to her husband Thomas. <u>Devise</u>: to Thomas for life a tenement, in which she dwelt, with shops, in Winchester Street between John Pope's tenement on the east side and Robert Earl's tenement, previously Thomas Knoyle's, on the west side. After Thomas's death the tenement, with the shops, should be sold immediately by her executors. The money received from the sale should be laid out, on celebrating masses, giving alms, and doing other charitable deeds, on behalf of Agnes's soul, the souls of Thomas Read, John Courtman, and Cecily Read, and the souls of others. <u>Executors</u>: her husband Thomas and William Cox. <u>Proved</u> on 10 January 1428 in front of an officer of the subdean; the administration was entrusted to Thomas, reserving the power to entrust it to William when he might come to seek it, and Thomas was dismissed by an officer. <u>Approved</u> at a court held in front of the bailiff, the mayor, and other citizens; the seisin of the tenement was released to the legatee.

2591 Approval of the will of John Beccles, the parson of the church of Stanton Harcourt, made on 31 October 1427. <u>Interment</u>: in the chancel of that church. <u>Bequests</u>: 3*s.* 4*d.* to the mother church of Lincoln; 2 qr. of barley to the fabric of the church of Stanton Harcourt, and 8*d.* to each light there; a hog to each of his godchildren; 40*s.* to Richard Talbot, his kinsman; 20*s.* to Thomas 'Rodberd', his servant, and 10*s.* to Agnes, his wife; 10*s.* to John Kers, his shepherd; 10*s.* to John, his servant; the rest of his goods to Walter Trusthorpe, the parson of the church of Farnborough, and Thomas Mauger, of Witney, for them to lay out on the celebration of masses on behalf of his soul and the souls of others, and on giving alms to paupers in his parish and elsewhere. <u>Devise</u>: to Walter Trusthorpe and Thomas Mauger all his burgages and tenements, rent, services, and reversions in Salisbury, in a place called Cheese Corner and elsewhere, to be held for ever by them and their heirs and assigns. <u>Executors</u>: Walter and Thomas, with the power of adding and deducting in all things mentioned above; overseer, the master Thomas Beckington, a clerk. <u>Proved</u> on 22 November 1427 in front of an officer of the archdeacon of Oxford; the administration was entrusted to the executors. <u>Approved</u> at a court held in front of the bailiff, the mayor, and other citizens; the seisin of the tenement was released to the legatees.

2592 By his charter John Noble, a citizen of Salisbury, granted to Thomas Davy, of Salisbury, and his wife Joan three conjoined shops in Old Poultry [*as in **2588**].* The shops were bought by John from Joan, while she was unmarried, as the executor of Thomas Yeovil, formerly a citizen of Salisbury, and they are to be held for ever by Thomas and Joan and their heirs and assigns. Seals: John's and the common and mayoral seals of the city. Named witnesses: the bailiff, the mayor, the coroners, the reeves, William Warin, Thomas Mason, Robert Warmwell, Henry Man, John Swift, Thomas Randolph, William Packing, and the clerk

2593 A deed [*dated to the Wednesday after the feast of St. Margaret the Virgin in the 7th year of the reign of Henry VI (27 July 1429), evidently in error for the Wednesday after that feast in the 6th year of that reign (21 July 1428)*] of Agnes, the relict, and an executor, of Thomas Frog, of late a citizen of Salisbury. In his will Thomas appointed a tenement, with a cellar, in which he dwelt, in Carter Street and New Street [*cf. description in 2518*] to be sold after his death by his executors. The money received from the sale should be laid out on the discharge of his debts. John Upton has paid to Agnes a sum of money reaching the true value of the tenement, with the cellar, and by her charter she, as Thomas's executor, granted to John and his wife Isabel the tenement, with the cellar, to be held for ever by them and their heirs and assigns. Seals: Agnes's and the common and mayoral seals of the city. Named witnesses: the bailiff, the mayor, the coroners, the reeves, William Warin, Thomas Mason, Robert Warmwell, Henry Man, John Swift, Thomas Randolph, William Packing, and the clerk

22 July 1428, at Salisbury
2594 By their deed Agnes, the relict, and an executor, of Thomas Frog, and Nicholas Shute and John Gower, her co-executors, quitclaimed to John Upton and his heirs and assigns their right or claim to a tenement, with a cellar, a shop (*or shops*), gardens, and cottages, in New Street and Carter Street between John Upton's cottages in Carter Street on the north side and Robert Ashley's shop in New Street on the west side [*cf. description in 2518*]. Thomas Hussey bought those premises from Thomas Upton, a clerk, and Nicholas Upton, and he granted his estate in them to Thomas Frog and his heirs. Seals: those of Agnes, Nicholas Shute, and John Gower and the common and mayoral seals of the city. Named witnesses: the bailiff, the mayor, the coroners, the reeves, William Warin, Thomas Mason, Robert Warmwell, Henry Man, John Swift, Thomas Randolph, William Packing, and the clerk

18 August 1428, at Salisbury
2595 By his charter William Oving, chandler, of Salisbury, granted to William Spine, of Britford, a tenement in New Street, between cottages of late those of Thomas Upton, a clerk, on the west side and an empty plot formerly that of Robert Netton, a chaplain, on the east side, which he held by a grant of Agnes, the relict of John Bedford, skinner, and a daughter and heir of Richard of Otterbourne, a public notary; also a toft, with a garden, which was of late Robert Netton's, in New Street between that tenement on the west side and a tenement sometime ago that of John Stone, of Wilton, on the east side. The tenement and the toft, with the garden, are to be held for ever by William Spine and his heirs and assigns. Clause of warranty. Seals: William Oving's and the common and mayoral seals of the city. Named witnesses: the bailiff, the mayor, the coroners, the reeves, William Warin, Thomas Mason, Robert Warmwell, Henry Man, John Swift, William Warwick, John Noble, William Packing, and the clerk

13 October 1428, at Salisbury
2596 A charter of Robert Warmwell, a citizen of Salisbury, an executor of William Warmwell, of late a citizen of Salisbury. William appointed rent of 10s. a year issuing from two cottages, of late those of Thomas Ferring, weaver, and

his wife Edith, in Mealmonger Street between cottages of late Thomas Bonham's on the north side and cottages of John Breamore, weaver, on the south side to his executors. He also appointed three conjoined cottages in the same street, between cottages of late those of John Hampton, brewer, on the south side and John Slegge's cottages on the north side, to be sold by his executors. The money received from the sale should be laid out on behalf of William's soul and the souls of others. Edward Goodyear, draper, of Salisbury, has paid to Robert a sum of money reaching the true value of the rent and the cottages, to be laid out according to the terms of William's will, and by his charter Robert, as William's executor, on the strength of the will granted the rent and the cottages to him to be held for ever by him and his heirs and assigns. Seals: Robert's and the common and mayoral seals of the city. Named witnesses: the bailiff, the mayor, the coroners, the reeves, William Warin, Thomas Mason, Henry Man, John Swift, John Noble, William Packing, and the clerk

2597 By his charter Robert Warmwell, a citizen of Salisbury, an executor of William Warmwell, of late a citizen of Salisbury, on the strength of William's will granted to Edward Goodyear, draper, of Salisbury, and his wife Denise two conjoined cottages, of late those of Thomas Ferring, weaver, and his wife Edith, in Mealmonger Street, [*as in* **2596**], to be held for ever by them and Edward's heirs and assigns. Seals: Robert's and the common and mayoral seals of the city. Named witnesses: the bailiff, the mayor, the coroners, the reeves, William Warin, Thomas Mason, Henry Man, John Swift, John Noble, William Packing, and the clerk

5 January 1429, at Salisbury
2598 By their writing Joan, the relict of Walter Shirley, of late a citizen of Salisbury, in her celibate widowhood and full power, and Richard Shirley, a son and heir of Walter and Joan, appearing at the court held on that day quitclaimed to Thomas Mason and John Swift, citizens of Salisbury, and to Henry Warin, a chaplain, and to their heirs and assigns their right or claim to conjoined cottages called Bedredin Row [Bedmin Row *in* **2631**], in the street on the way from Scots Lane towards St. Edmund's church, between a corner tenement of late Walter's, in which Richard Lockyer of late dwelt, on the west side and a tenement of John Marshall, dyer, on the east side. The cottages, with shops, cottages, rent, and reversions, were of late held by William Walter and Walter Shirley, both dead, and by Thomas Mason, John Swift, and Henry Warin by a grant of John Mower, some time since a citizen of Salisbury. Seals: Joan's and Richard's and the common and mayoral seals of the city. Named witnesses: the bailiff, the mayor, the coroners, the reeves, William Warin, Robert Warmwell, Henry Man, John Noble, John Bromley, Thomas Randolph, and the clerk

2599 By his charter John London, mason, of Gloucester, granted to John Hain, of Salisbury, and his wife Margaret three cottages, with gardens and racks, in Mealmonger Street between Alice Witney's cottages, of late Edmund Friday's, on the south side and a garden of John Cross, a son and heir of John Cross, saddler, on the north side. The cottages, with the gardens and racks, were held by John London by a devise of his wife Joan, a daughter of Edmund Cofford. William Penton, who, with Robert Cocklot, weaver, was seised in them by Joan while she was chaste, after Robert's death released his right in them to John London and his heirs. The cottages, with the gardens and racks, are to be held by John Hain and Margaret and John's heirs and assigns. Clause of warranty. Seals: John London's and the common and mayoral seals of the city. Named witnesses: the bailiff, the mayor, the coroners, the reeves, William Warin, Thomas Mason, Robert Warmwell, Henry Man, John Swift, John Noble, John Bromley, Thomas Randolph, and the clerk

2600 By his indented charter Stephen Hart, a citizen of Salisbury, granted to Thomas Randolph, a citizen of Salisbury, and John Park, draper, of Salisbury, seven conjoined shops in St. Martin's Street, between a tenement of late Henry Southwick's on the north side and John Bailey's tenement on the east side, to be held for ever by them and their heirs and assigns. The grant was made on condition that, if Stephen, his heirs, his executors, or anyone else on his or their behalf, were to pay to Thomas and John, to either of them, or to their executors or attorney 15s. on 25 March 1429, 15s. on 24 June 1429, 15s. on 29 September 1429, 15s. on 25 December 1429, and 60s. a year for the five following years, until £18 had been paid, the charter and the grant would be of no value and counted for nothing. In such case Stephen and his heirs might enter on the shops, take back possession, and keep them for themselves for ever. If Stephen were to default on any payment the charter and the grant would keep their force and effect, that is for Thomas and John and their heirs and assigns for ever. Clause of warranty. Seals: those of the parties to the parts of the charter in turn and the common and mayoral seals of the city. Named witnesses: the bailiff, the mayor, the coroners, the reeves, William Warin, Thomas Mason, Robert Warmwell, Henry Man, John Bromley, John Swift, and the clerk

16 March 1429, at Salisbury

2601 A charter of John Judd and John Purvis, a citizen of London, executors of William Mercer, of late a citizen of Salisbury. In his will William appointed two tenements at the east end of Pot Row to be sold after the death of his wife Edith by his executors, their executors, or subsequent executors. The money received should be laid out, on celebrating masses, giving alms to the poor, repairing ways and bridges, and doing other charitable deeds, on behalf of his soul and the souls of others. It seemed to the executors better for those souls that the reversion of the tenements should be sold in their lifetime, and the money issuing from the sale laid out on behalf of the souls, than that the sale of the tenements should be delayed, inasmuch as William's will might be culpably impeded by such delay to the grave damage of the souls. By their charter, for a sum of money reaching the true value of the tenements, the executors on the strength of William's will granted to John Hain, a citizen of Salisbury, and his wife Margaret the reversion when it fell due on Edith's death. The two tenements are to be held for ever, after Edith's death, by John and Margaret and John's heirs and assigns. Seals: those of John Judd and John Purvis and the common and mayoral seals of the city.

Named witnesses: the bailiff, the mayor, the coroners, the reeves, William Warin, Thomas Mason, Robert Warmwell, Henry Man, John Swift, John Noble, John Bromley, and the clerk

30 March 1429, at Salisbury
2602 By his charter John Bodenham, a citizen of Salisbury, granted to John Noble, a citizen of Salisbury, Richard Wise, draper, and John Partridge, a clerk, a tenement in Castle Street, between Richard Ecton's tenement on the north side and a tenement of late Nicholas Longstock's, now Richard Gage's, on the south side, to be held for ever by them and their heirs and assigns. Clause of warranty. Seals: John Bodenham's and the common and mayoral seals of the city. Named witnesses: the bailiff, the mayor, the coroners, the reeves, William Warin, Henry Man, Robert Warmwell, Thomas Mason, John Wylye, and the clerk

25 May 1429, at Salisbury
2603 By his charter Thomas Pinchbeck, cook, of Salisbury, granted to John Eastbury, of Salisbury, a cottage, with a garden, in Drake Hall Street between William Phebis's tenement on the south side and a tenement of Walter Plowman, carpenter, on the north side. The cottage, with the garden, extends from Drake Hall Street as far as a garden, with a rack, of William Oving, chandler, in Freren Street on the east side. The cottage, with the garden, by the name of a yard, was held by Thomas by a grant of John [?Waltham *or* Chandler], now dead, formerly the bishop of Salisbury, and is to be held for ever by John Eastbury and his heirs and assigns. Clause of warranty. Seals: Thomas's and the common and mayoral seals of the city. Named witnesses: the bailiff, the mayor, the coroners, the reeves, William Warin, Robert Warmwell, Henry Man, John Noble, John Bromley, and the clerk
2604 By his charter Thomas Mason, a citizen of Salisbury, granted to William Stamford, of Ashbosom, Dorset, two conjoined tenements, with gardens, in Minster Street, which is called Castle Street, between a tenement of late Walter Chippenham's, called the Cage, on the south side and a tenement of late Philip of Bristol's, now Ralph Packer's, on the north side. The tenements were formerly those of the master Richard Leach, a citizen of Salisbury, now dead, and are to be held for ever by William and his heirs and assigns. Clause of warranty. Seals: Thomas's and the common and mayoral seals of the city. Named witnesses: the bailiff, the mayor, the coroners, the reeves, William Warin, Robert Warmwell, Henry Man, John Swift, John Noble, John Bromley, Thomas Randolph, and the clerk

15 June 1429, at Salisbury
2605 By their writing William Lord and Richard Weston quitclaimed to William Stamford and his heirs and assigns their right or claim to two conjoined tenements, with gardens, in Minster Street, which is called Castle Street, [*as in* **2604**], formerly those of the master Richard Leach, a citizen of Salisbury, now dead. Seals: those of William and Richard and the common and mayoral seals

of the city. Named witnesses: the bailiff, the mayor, the coroners, the reeves, William Warin, Robert Warmwell, Henry Man, John Swift, John Noble, John Bromley, Thomas Randolph, and the clerk

29 June 1429, at Salisbury
2606 By their charter Walter Trusthorpe, the parson of the church of Farnborough, and Thomas Mauger, of Witney, granted to Stephen Cooper, mercer, of Salisbury, a corner tenement called Cheese Corner, with a cellar, shops, and sollars, in Carter Street [and Winchester Street], opposite a corner tenement called Dyne's Corner, between Thomas Biston's tenement [in Winchester Street: *cf. 2644*] on the east side and his shop, which Henry Hellier holds, on the north side. The tenement was of late that of John Beccles, the parson of the church of Stanton Harcourt, and, with the cellar, shops, and sollars, is to be held for ever by Stephen and his heirs and assigns. Clause of warranty. Seals: those of Walter and Thomas and the common and mayoral seals of the city. Named witnesses: the bailiff, the mayor, the coroners, the reeves, William Warin, Robert Warmwell, Henry Man, John Swift, John Bromley, William Warwick, John Noble, Richard Ecton, and the clerk

29 June 1429
2607 By his letters of attorney Walter Trusthorpe, the parson of the church of Farnborough, appointed Richard Needler and John Saunders, of Salisbury, to deliver to Stephen Cooper, mercer, of Salisbury, the seisin of a corner tenement called Cheese Corner, with a cellar, shops, and sollars, in Carter Street [and Winchester Street]; also the seisin of a shop in Carter Street between William Cambridge's shop on the south side and John Camel's shop on the north side. Seals: Walter's, that of the office of the sheriff of Oxfordshire, of his castle there, and the mayoral seal of the city of Oxford

20 July 1429, at Salisbury
2608 By his charter John Judd, of Salterton, granted to Richard Pain, of Salisbury, a garden, with yards and racks built in them, in Martin's Croft opposite the graveyard of St. Edmund's church, which he held by a grant of John Sexhampcote, a chaplain, to be held for ever by Richard and his heirs and assigns. Clause of warranty. Seals: John Judd's and the common and mayoral seals of the city. Named witnesses: the bailiff, the mayor, the coroners, the reeves, William Warin, Robert Warmwell, Henry Man, John Swift, John Noble, John Bromley, Thomas Randolph, and the clerk

27 July 1429, at Salisbury
2609 Approval of the will of John Wantage, a citizen of Salisbury, made on 5 March 1429. Interment: in the graveyard of St. Edmund's church. Bequests: 6*d.* each to the fabric of the cathedral church, the fabric of St. Edmund's church, the paupers of the hospital of the Holy Trinity, the Franciscans of Salisbury to pray for his soul, the paupers of St. Nicholas's hospital to pray for his soul, the Dominicans

[?of Fisherton] to pray for his soul, and the fabric of St. Thomas's church; two bows, with all the arrows and bolts, a small harnessed dagger, and a leather belt harnessed with silver to his son William; a blue and lined gown, a plain red gown, a leather doublet, and a long coat to Robert, his servant, to whom he remitted 10*s*. of the 20*s*. which he owed to him; a green and lined gown to Robert Rous, of late his apprentice; 10*s*. to William Goddard, his servant; a silk belt, harnessed, and a cloak of rabbit fur to his sister Alice, and a bow to Edward Goodyear, her husband; a pair of knives with maple-wood handles to Henry Lowing, a cordwainer, and 12*d*. to Joan Carpenter, his daughter. <u>Devise</u>: he appointed his two cottages in Freren Street, between a small portion of ground beside the stone wall of the Franciscans on the north side and a yard of St. Nicholas's hospital on the south side, to be sold by his executors immediately after his death, when it could be done advantageously. The money issuing from the sale, and the rest of his goods not bequeathed above, his debts, legacies, and funeral expenses having been paid and fulfilled, should be divided into three equal portions. He assigned one portion to his wife Christine, one to his executors to be laid out on pious uses for the salvation of his soul, and one to his son William to pray for his soul. William's portion should be assigned to him at the discretion of John's executors at his majority. If William were to die before he reached his majority that portion, or a part if anything were then to be in goods of any kind, should revert to John's executors to be laid out on behalf of John's soul and William's soul. <u>Executors</u>: Nicholas Shute, to whom John bequeathed 6*s*. 8*d*., and Richard Cooper, to whom he bequeathed a bow and 6*s*. 8*d*. <u>Proved</u> on 26 July 1429 in front of John Pedwell, the subdean; the administration was entrusted to the executors, who afterwards accounted with an officer and were dismissed. <u>Approved</u> at a court held in front of the bailiff, the mayor, and other citizens; the seisin of the cottages was released to the legatees.

3 August 1429, at Salisbury
2610 By their charter Nicholas Shute, weaver, of Salisbury, and Richard Cooper, of Salisbury, executors of John Wantage, of late a citizen of Salisbury, on the strength of John's will granted to Christine, John's relict, cottages, with yards and racks, in Freren Street between a small portion of ground beside a stone wall of the Franciscans of Salisbury on the north side and a yard of St. Nicholas's hospital on the south side [*margin*: Mr. Griffith's garden]. The cottages, with the yards and racks, were appointed by John in his will to be sold by his executors immediately after his death, and they are to be held for ever by Christine and her heirs and assigns as that which she bought from Nicholas and Richard in good faith for a sum of money reaching their true value. Seals: those of Richard and Nicholas and the common and mayoral seals of the city. Named witnesses: the bailiff, the mayor, the coroners, the reeves, William Warin, Robert Warmwell, Henry Man, John Swift, John Noble, John Bromley, Thomas Randolph, and the clerk
2611 By his charter Stephen Hart, weaver, of Salisbury, granted to Thomas Randolph, a citizen of Salisbury, two corner tenements, with gardens, of which one stands, opposite a croft, between a street called Nuggeston on the south

side and Mealmonger Street on the east side, and the other stands, opposite the graveyard of St. Edmund's church, between Mealmonger Street on the east side and a garden of Thomas Freeman, mercer, on the west side [cf. *2382*]. The tenement, with the garden, in Nuggeston [*margin*: the corner garden and the corner house opposite Green Croft] extends from there as far as the garden of the corner tenement opposite the graveyard. The two tenements, with the gardens, were held by Stephen by a grant of John Wishford, a citizen of Salisbury, and are to be held by Thomas and his heirs and assigns. Clause of warranty. Seals: Stephen's and the common and mayoral seals of the city. Named witnesses: the bailiff, the mayor, the coroners, the reeves, William Warin, Robert Warmwell, Henry Man, John Swift, John Noble, John Bromley, and the clerk

28 September 1429, at Salisbury
2612 By their charter William Vivian, mercer, of Salisbury, and his wife Alice, appearing at the court held on that day, granted to John Wylye, a citizen of Salisbury, and his wife Joan two conjoined shops in Carter Street, between a tenement, in which Nicholas Bell of late dwelt, on the south side and John Wylye's shop on the north side, to be held for ever by John and Joan and their heirs and assigns. Seals: those of William and Alice and the common and mayoral seals of the city. Named witnesses: the bailiff, the mayor, the coroners, the reeves, William Warin, Robert Warmwell, Henry Man, John Swift, John Noble, John Bromley, Thomas Randolph, and the clerk

12 October 1429, at Salisbury
2613 By his writing William Warin, a citizen of Salisbury, an executor of Alice, who was the wife of John Heath, on the strength of Alice's will quitclaimed to John Wylye, a citizen of Salisbury, and his wife Joan, William's daughter, and their heirs and assigns, his right or claim to a shop in Carter Street [*as in **2612***]. The shop, by the name of two shops, was granted by William Vivian and his wife Alice to John and Joan and their heirs. Seals: William Warin's and the common and mayoral seals of the city. Named witnesses: the bailiff, the mayor, the coroners, the reeves, Robert Warmwell, Henry Man, John Swift, John Noble, John Bromley, and the clerk
2614 By his charter John Shad, draper, of Salisbury, granted to Stephen Cooper, mercer, of Salisbury, two conjoined tenements, with a cellar, in Culver Street between Richard Butler's tenement on the north side and John Deverill's garden on the south side. The tenements were held by John Shad by a grant of John Herring, of Winterbourne, and are to be held for ever by Stephen and his heirs and assigns. Clause of warranty. Seals: John Shad's and the common and mayoral seals of the city. Named witnesses: the bailiff, the mayor, the coroners, the reeves, William Warin, Robert Warmwell, Henry Man, John Noble, John Bromley, Thomas Randolph, and the clerk
2615 By their charter John Swift and Richard Gater, citizens of Salisbury, granted to William Packing and Thomas Randolph, citizens of Salisbury, a messuage, with a garden, in Gigant Street between Peter Upavon's tenement on the north

side and a tenement of John Lea, a son of the late Nicholas Lea on the south side. The messuage, with the garden, by the name of a cottage, with a garden, was held by John and Richard by a feoffment of John Manning, a chaplain, and John Draper, a clerk, executors of Thomas Manning, and is to be held for ever by William and Thomas and their heirs and assigns. Clause of warranty. Seals: those of John Swift and Richard Gater and the common and mayoral seals of the city. Named witnesses: the bailiff, the coroners, the reeves, William Warin, Robert Warmwell, Henry Man, John Swift, John Noble, John Bromley, and the clerk

26 October 1429, at Salisbury
2616 By their charter William Packing and Thomas Randolph, citizens of Salisbury, granted to Richard Gater and his wife Alice a messuage, with a garden, in Gigant Street [*as in* **2615**]. The messuage, with the garden, was held by William and Thomas by a grant of John Swift and Richard Gater, citizens of Salisbury, and is to be held for ever by Richard and Alice and their heirs and assigns. Seals: those of William and Thomas and the common and mayoral seals of the city. Named witnesses: the bailiff, a coroner, the reeves, William Warin, Robert Warmwell, Henry Man, John Swift, John Noble, John Bromley, and the clerk

23 November 1429, at Salisbury
2617 By their charter John Noble, a citizen of Salisbury, and Richard Wise, draper, granted to John Bodenham, a citizen of Salisbury, and his wife Eleanor a tenement in Castle Street [*as in* **2602**], to be held for ever by them and John's heirs and assigns. John and Richard also quitclaimed to John and Eleanor and John's heirs and assigns their right or claim to the tenement. Seals: those of John Noble and Richard Wise and the common and mayoral seals of the city. Named witnesses: the bailiff, the mayor, the coroners, the reeves, William Warin, Henry Man, John Swift, John Bromley, William Packing, Thomas Randolph, and the clerk

7 December 1429, at Salisbury
2618 By their charter John Noble, Richard Shail, Henry Man, and John Woodhurst granted to John Bodenham, of Salisbury, a messuage, which Stephen Cooper, mercer, holds, opposite the market place, between Robert Chamberlain's tenement on the east side and Thomas Hall's tenement on the west side; also 60 acres of arable land and 4 acres of meadow land in Charlton. The messuage and the land were held by the grantors by a grant of John Bodenham and his wife Joan, as is evident through a fine levied between them in Michaelmas term 1429, and are to be held for ever by John and his heirs and assigns. Seals: those of the grantors and the common and mayoral seals of the city. Named witnesses: the bailiff, the mayor, the coroners, the reeves, William Warin, John Bromley, Thomas Ringwood, David Cervington, Thomas Gerberd, Thomas Merriott, Thomas Martin, and the clerk

21 December 1429, at Salisbury
2619 By his charter John Heathwolf, a son and heir of Richard Heathwolf, of

Coate, in Bishop's Cannings hundred, granted to John Corscombe, tucker, of Salisbury, and his wife Margaret two tenements, with a garden, in Gigant Street between John Butler's tenement on the north side and William Alexander's tenement on the south side. The tenements, with the garden, descended to John by right of inheritance on Richard's death, were bought by Richard under the name of a tenement, with a garden, from William Shilling, and are to be held for ever by John and Margaret and their heirs and assigns. Clause of warranty. Seals: John Heathwolf's and the common and mayoral seals of the city. Named witnesses: the bailiff, the mayor, the coroners, the reeves, William Warin, Henry Man, John Swift, John Bromley, John Noble, William Packing, and the clerk

1 March 1430, at Salisbury

2620 A charter of John Judd, of Salisbury, and John Purvis, executors of William Mercer, of late a citizen of Salisbury. William devised to his wife Edith for life a tenement, in which he dwelt, in Wineman Street between a tenement then Robert Bowyer's on the east side and a tenement then John Lewisham's on the west side, and on Edith's death the tenement would remain for ever to Christine, a kinswoman of William, and her issue. William appointed the tenement to be sold by his executors or their executors if Christine were to die without issue. The money received from the sale should be laid out, on celebrating masses, giving alms to paupers, repairing ways and bridges, and doing other charitable deeds for the salvation of his soul and the souls of others. Christine has died without surviving issue, Edith survives, and the reversion of the tenement pertains to the executors to be sold. John Corscombe has paid to the executors a sum of money reaching the true value of the reversion, and by their charter John Judd and John Purvis have granted it to him and his wife Margaret. The tenement is to be held for ever by John Corscombe and Margaret and their heirs and assigns from when it fell due on Edith's death. Seals: those of John Judd and John Purvis and the common and mayoral seals of the city. Named witnesses: the bailiff, the mayor, the coroners, the reeves, William Warin, Henry Man, John Swift, John Noble, John Bromley, William Packing, and the clerk

15 March 1430, at Salisbury

2621 By their writing Robert Warmwell, John Bromley, and Thomas Randolph, citizens of Salisbury, quitclaimed to Henry Man, a citizen of Salisbury, and his heirs and assigns their right or claim to the shops, cottages, and gardens which Henry and they held, with other land and tenements in Salisbury, by a feoffment of John Moore. The shops, cottages, and gardens are situated in Shit Lane between Richard Gage's tenement on the north side and a tenement of Robert Gilbert, tanner, on the east side [*margin*: Jacob's lands]. Seals: those of Robert, John, and Thomas and the common and mayoral seals of the city. Named witnesses: the bailiff, the mayor, the coroners, the reeves, William Warin, John Swift, John Noble, William Packing, and the clerk

29 March 1430, at Salisbury

2622 By their charter Robert Warmwell, Henry Man, John Bromley, and Thomas Randolph, citizens of Salisbury, granted to Robert Gilbert, tanner, of Salisbury, a messuage, with a garden, in St. Martin's Street between cottages of the provost of St. Edmund's church on the west side and a tenement of the choristers of the cathedral church on the east side. The messuage, with the gardens, contains in it two dwelling houses, was of late that of John Moore, baker, and is to be held for ever by Robert Gilbert and his heirs and assigns. Seals: those of the grantors and the common and mayoral seals of the city. Named witnesses: the bailiff, the coroners, the reeves, William Warin, John Swift, John Noble, William Packing, and the clerk

2623 By his charter Henry Ham, of Salisbury, granted to William Clitour, a miller of the bishop of Salisbury, a corner tenement, with shops, in New Street and Brown Street between a tenement of late that of William Huggin, carpenter, on the west side and John Upton's tenement on the south side. The tenement, with the shops, was held by Henry by a feoffment of Richard Ballfoot and Agnes, the relict of William West, baker, of late a citizen of Salisbury, and is to be held for ever by William Clitour and his heirs and assigns. Clause of warranty. Seals: Henry's and the common and mayoral seals of the city. Named witnesses: the bailiff, the mayor, the coroners, the reeves, William Warin, Henry Man, John Swift, John Noble, John Bromley, William Packing, and the clerk

12 April 1430, at Salisbury

2624 By his charter John Upton, of Martock, granted to Peter Devereux a tenement, with shops and a cellar, in New Street and Carter Street [*cf.* Bull Corner: *2518*] between Robert Ashley's cottage in New Street on the west side and cottages of late John Upton's in Carter Street on the north side. The tenement, with the shops and cellar, was held by John by a feoffment of Agnes, the relict, and an executor, of Thomas Frog, of late a citizen of Salisbury, and is to be held for ever by Peter and his heirs and assigns. Clause of warranty. Seals: John's and the common and mayoral seals of the city. Named witnesses: the bailiff, the mayor, the coroners, the reeves, William Warin, Henry Man, John Swift, John Noble, John Bromley, William Packing, and the clerk

19 April 1430, at Salisbury

2625 Tripartite letters of William Spaldington, the provost of the college of St. Edmund's, and the fellows of the college, and of Thomas Hain, of Winchester, and John Swift, ironmonger, Henry Warin, a chaplain, and William Lord, all of Salisbury. By his charter given at Salisbury on 10 January 1425 [*see* **2541**] Walter Shirley, of late a citizen of Salisbury, granted to Thomas Hain, John Swift, Henry Warin, and William Lord all his land and tenements, with shops, cottages, gardens, meadows, rent, pastures, and feeding rights in Salisbury and elsewhere in Wiltshire. To that grant he added the following conditions and terms. An indenture testified that by his charter Walter granted to Thomas, John, Henry, and William all his land and tenements [*as above*] to be held for ever by them and their heirs and assigns on the following conditions. As soon after his death as it could be reasonably done the grantees should sell two tenements in Castle Street which were of late Alice Body's. The money received from the sale should be handed over to the provost and collegians of St. Edmund's church. The grantees should grant to John Park, hosier, a tenement, with two shops, in which Thomas Roper dwells, in Wineman Street, for the term of years through which John could receive the rest of what was owed to him of the £32 12s. beyond what he received from the tenement, at the discretion of those feoffees. After the debt was levied the tenement should remain or revert to Walter's executors and the feoffees to be sold. The money received from the sale should be handed to the provost and collegians of St. Edmund's church to build over as great an empty plot in the city as, by a licence of the progenitors of the present king, they bought for themselves and their successors, just as the money suffices; also to hold a yearly obit of Walter and his wife Joan in St. Edmund's church for ever in the manner described below; also to pray for the souls of John Camel, of late Walter's master, and his wife Edith, the souls of the master Richard Prentice and John Mower, and the souls of others. The feoffees should grant to Walter's wife Joan for life a tenement, in which Richard Marshall, tucker, dwells, in Castle Street on the south side of a tenement of William Lord, and on Joan's death the tenement should remain to the executors and the feoffees, and their executors, to be sold. The money issuing from the sale should be handed to the provost and collegians of St. Edmund's church on the terms mentioned above. The feoffees should grant to John Wilmot, a servant of Walter, and to Catherine, a servant of Walter, a cottage, with a gate built there, and with three houses, which John Stop of late held, within that gate on the north side of it, between Roger Fadder's cottage on the west side and a palisade appurtenant to [Ball's Place: *cf. below*], a chief messuage which John Hobbs holds, on the east side, saving free ingress and egress through the gate for carts and other things going in as far as the chief messuage [*margin*: to be noted for the tenement called Ball's Place]. The cottage is to be held by John and Catherine for life and the life of the one of them living longer on condition that they would be lawfully married. On the death of John and Catherine the cottage should remain or revert to the executors and the feoffees, or their executors, to be sold. The money received from the sale should be handed to the provost and collegians of St. Edmund's church on the terms mentioned above. The feoffees should grant to Isabel, a servant and kinswoman of Walter, for life two cottages, one in Wineman Street, between a tenement, with shops, which Thomas Roper holds, on the east side and Richard Cooper's cottages on the west side, and the other, which John Purbeck holds, in Scots Lane. On Isabel's death the cottages should remain or revert to the executors and the feoffees, or their executors, to be sold. The money received from the sale should be handed to the provost and collegians of St. Edmund's church on the terms mentioned above. The feoffees should grant to Walter's wife Joan for life a chief messuage, with a garden, called Ball's Place, in which John Hobbs dwells, in Wineman Street [*heading*: the will of Walter Shirley concerning Ball's Place in Wineman Street and

Brown Street]. On Joan's death the messuage should remain to John Eastbury and his wife Amice for life and the life of the one of them living longer, and on their death it should remain to the executors and the feoffees, or their executors, to be sold. The money received from the sale should be handed to the provost and collegians of St. Edmund's church on the terms mentioned above. The feoffees should grant to Walter's wife Joan for life all the other land, tenements, and meadows which, on the day mentioned above, Walter held in the city, except those in which she stood jointly enfeoffed in fee simple with him. On Joan's death the premises thus granted should remain for ever to Walter's and Joan's son Richard and his issue, and for want of such issue should remain to the executors and the feoffees to be sold. The money received from the sale should be paid to the provost and collegians of St. Edmund's church on the terms mentioned above. Otherwise the feoffees, within a reasonable time, a licence of the king and of all those it concerned having been obtained previously, should grant such land and tenements, with shops, cottages, meadows, rent, pasture, and feeding rights, except the estates and terms of the parties named above, to the provost and fellows of the college of St. Edmund's church, to be held for ever by them and their successors. Every year at the feast of St. Vincent, that is on the day of Walter's obit, the provost for the time being of St. Edmund's church, should for ever hold an obit for Walter and his wife Joan in that church, and on the same day should hand out 30s. 4d. among paupers of the city, *viz.* 1d. to each pauper, 12d. to each collegiate chaplain being in the college at the time, 4d. to each other chaplain celebrating mass in St. Edmund's church, 4d. to the deacon, 4d. to the sacristan, and 2d. to each of the two beadsmen of the city to pray for the souls of Walter and Joan. Seals: those of the parties to the parts of the indenture in turn and the mayoral seal of the city. The indenture was given at Salisbury on 10 January 1425. Thomas Hain, John Swift, Henry Warin, and William Lord carefully considered the poverty of the college, the difficulty in these days of an appropriation of that land and those tenements being obtained by the college, that beforehand the reversions would have fallen due, that with the passage of time the memory of men would have been fading, and that there is a threat to those houses from lawsuits, pleas, and ruin. They noted in addition that the college has many sites in the city, appropriated long ago, which for lack of repair are now vacant and laid waste, by reason of which the college's rent is very much reduced. Whereupon they, bearing in mind those and other matters and wishing to give effect to Walter's will and pious disposition as quickly and as best they could, with the express consent of the provost and fellows of the college, by these tripartite letters, given at Salisbury on 19 April 1430, granted all the reversions, when they fell due, of such land and tenements, with the shops, cottages, meadows, pasture, and feeding rights, except what was excepted above, to Joan Shirley, a widow, Walter's relict, for £80, to be held for ever by her and her heirs and assigns. All that, and the money mentioned above, should be spent on the building and repair of houses of the college to increase its rent and on maintaining all the buildings yearly. William, the provost, and his fellows promise for themselves and their successors to observe inviolably [their obligations under the terms of the indenture] for ever.

Seals: those of Thomas Hain, John Swift, Henry Warin, and William Lord, the mayoral seal of the city, the common seal of the college, and the common seal of the city to the part of the indenture in Joan Shirley's possession, those of Thomas, John, Henry, and William and the common and mayoral seals of the city to the part in the possession of the provost and members of the college, and the common seal of the college and the mayoral and common seals of the city to the third part of the indenture in the possession of Thomas, John, Henry, and William. Robert [Nevill], the bishop of Salisbury, ratified the agreements, grants, and confirmations of charters contained in the indenture, saving to him and his successor bishops escheats, rent, services, suits, and customs from the messuages, land, shops, cottages, yards, gardens, meadows, pasture, and feeding rights owed or customary, and, so far as it concerned him and for himself and his successors, confirmed the tenor of the indenture. Seal: the oblong seal of the bishop. Given on the bishop's manor of Ramsbury on 16 July 1429.

26 April 1430, at Salisbury
2626 By his charter Stephen Mercer, otherwise called Stephen Cooper, of Salisbury, granted to Reynold Kentwood, the dean of St. Paul's church, London, Walter Fettiplace, William Goodyear, John Judd, Henry Guildford, and Thomas Cutler all his land and tenements, with shops, cottages, cellars, and gardens, which he held in fee simple in Salisbury and elsewhere, to be held for ever by them and their heirs and assigns. Clause of warranty. Seals: Stephen's and the common and mayoral seals of the city. Named witnesses: the bailiff, the mayor, the coroners, the reeves, William Warin, Henry Man, John Swift, John Noble, John Bromley, William Packing, and the clerk
The above entry has been crosed through
2627 Approval of the will of John Bodenham, a citizen of Salisbury, made on 13 March 1430. <u>Interment</u>: in the graveyard of the church of St. Nicholas in Atrio, Wilton, in the tomb of John Bodenham, his late father. <u>Bequests</u>; 40*d*. to the fabric of the cathedral church; 40*d*. to the fabric of St. Thomas's church, and 6*s*. 8*d*. to the parson for his forgotten tithes; 2*s*. 6*d*. both to the Dominicans of Fisherton Anger and the Franciscans of Salisbury; 2*s*. to the fabric of St. Giles's church, near Wilton; the rest of his goods to his executors to be laid out on behalf of his soul. <u>Devises</u>: he appointed that his feoffees should enfeoff William Bodenham, his brother, in all his land, tenements, meadows, pasture, feeding rights, rent, and services in the vill and fields of Charlton, near Downton, to be held for ever by William and his heirs and assigns. John devised to William Pelt, hosier, of Salisbury, his estate for a term of years in land, tenements, meadows, pasture, feeding rights, rent, reversions, and services which he held by a grant of Roger Cordray in the vill and fields of Chute. He devised to his wife Eleanor for life as dower two conjoined tenements in Castle Street between Richard Ecton's tenement on the north side and Richard Gage's tenement on the south side, and he appointed the tenements to be sold by his executors, their executors, or subsequent executors after Eleanor's death. The money received from the sale should be laid out on celebrating masses on behalf of his soul and the souls of

others. John appointed a tenement, opposite the market place where grains are
sold, between Robert Watercombe's tenement on the east side and a tenement of
late Thomas Stalbridge's on the west side, to be sold by his executors immediately
after his death, reserving to Stephen Cooper the term which he held in it. He
assigned the money received from the sale for discharging his debts. He appointed
his land, tenements, meadow, pasture, feeding rights, rent, and reversions in
the borough of Wilton to be sold by his executors immediately after his death.
He assigned the money received from the sale for them to pay his debts and
legacies, and the cost of his funeral, for the relief of his soul. Executors: the lord
William Bodenham, his brother, William Pelt, and Edmund Penstone; overseers,
John Everard, John Davy, and John Fonthill. Proved on 7 April 1430 in front of
the subdean; the administration was entrusted to the executors. Approved at a
court held in front of the bailiff, the mayor, and other citizens; the seisin of the
tenements was released to the legatees.

7 June 1430, at Salisbury
2628 By his charter Adam Body, of Canterbury, a son and heir of Robert Body,
of late a citizen of Salisbury, granted to Robert White of Farnham, Surrey, a
corner tenement, with shops and cottages, in Wineman Street and Brown Street
between Henry Ham's tenement on the west side and a stable of John Popham,
esq., on the north side. The tenement, with the shops and cottages attached to
it, is to be held for ever by Robert White and his heirs and assigns. Clause of
warranty. Seals: Adam's, the common and mayoral seals of the city, and the seal of
the office of the bailiffs of Canterbury. Named witnesses: the bailiff, the mayor,
the coroners, the reeves, William Warin, Henry Man, John Noble, John Bromley,
William Packing, and the clerk
2629 By his letters of attorney Adam Body, of Canterbury, a son and heir of
Robert Body, of late a citizen of Salisbury, now dead, appointed the master John
Wareham and Robert Needler, citizens of Salisbury, to deliver to Robert White,
of Farnham, Surrey, the seisin of a corner tenement, with shops and cottages
attached to it, in Wineman Street and Brown Street [*as in 2628*]. Seals: Adam's
and, because his seal is unknown to many, at his request the seal of the office of
the bailiffs of Canterbury

1 July 1430, 6 October 1430, at Westminster
2630 A final agreement reached in the king's court on the octave of the nativity
of St. John the Baptist in front of William Babington, John Martin, John Juyn,
James Strangewish, John Cottesmore, and William Paston, justices, and afterwards
on the octave of Michaelmas, between Elizabeth, the relict of John Lisle, kt.,
and Henry Lisle, plaintiffs, and John Becket, defendant, concerning a messuage
in Salisbury which Alice Becket holds of John's inheritance for her life. John
acknowledged the messuage to be the right of Henry and granted that on Alice's
death it would not revert to himself and his heirs but would remain for ever to
Elizabeth and Henry and Henry's heirs. Clause of warranty. Consideration, 100
marks cash

5 July 1430, at Salisbury
2631 By their charter Thomas Mason, draper, and John Swift, ironmonger, granted to Henry Man, John Bromley, William Packing, and Richard Gater, citizens of Salisbury, a messuage, with shops, cottages, a latrine, and sollars, at the upper bridge of Fisherton Anger; also conjoined cottages, called Bedmin Row [Bedredin Row *in* **2598**], in the street on the way from a bridge in Endless Street towards St. Edmund's church, between a lane of running water on the east side and Joan Shirley's corner tenement, which Ralph Lockyer of late held, on the west side. The messuage and the cottages, with the shops, latrine, and sollars, are to be held for ever by the grantees and their heirs and assigns. Seals: those of Thomas Mason and John Swift and the common and mayoral seals of the city. Named witnesses: the bailiff, the mayor, the coroners, the reves, William Warin, John Noble, Thomas Randolph, and the clerk

19 July 1430, at Salisbury
2632 Approval of the will of Thomas Biston, a citizen of Salisbury, made on 12 June 1430. Interment: in the graveyard of St. Thomas's church. Bequests: 12*d.* to the fabric of that church, and 4*d.* to each chaplain of it present at his funeral rites and masses on the day of his burial; 12*d.* to the fabric of the cathedral church; 10 marks to his daughter Edith in the name of her share of all his goods on condition that she would remit, and by her deed release, to Thomas's executors all actions, real and personal, against them on account of her share of his goods to be demanded from them or on account of any other cause concerning his will; if Edith were to refuse to observe that condition, and would not be content with that money, the 10 marks should be laid out by Thomas's executors on behalf of his soul and the souls of others; the rest of his goods to his wife Margery. Devise: to Margery and her heirs and assigns for ever a tenement, in which he dwelt and which he held by a feoffment of William Warmwell and William River, citizens of Salisbury, in New Street, between a tenement of late John Kingbridge's on the east side and a tenement of John Hunt, tucker, on the west side, extending from New Street in the front as far as the ditch of the close of the cathedral church at the back. Executors: his wife Margaret and Robert Cave, a clerk. Proved on 12 July 1430 in front of the subdean, having the archidiaconal jurisdiction of Salisbury and its suburbs; the administration was entrusted to Margaret, Robert expressly declining to undertake it. Approved at a court held in front of the bailiff, the mayor, and other citizens; the seisin of the tenement was released to the legatee.

27 September 1430, at Salisbury
2633 By his indented charter Robert Potter, a cordwainer, of Salisbury, granted to Robert Gilbert, tanner, of Salisbury, four conjoined shops, with a skilling of the length of the shops on their north side, with a stable below the skilling at their east end, with the principal post of the door of the west shop of the four, 13 in. wide, and with another post set above that post, saving to Robert Potter and

his heirs and assigns the foundation, with the wall set above it, as it extends from the principal post towards the north, in length and breadth from the foundation to the top of the wall. The shops stand in Chipper Street between the hall of a corner shop, which John Eustace, tapster, holds, on the west side and John Parch's cottages on the east side. Robert Potter also granted to Robert Gilbert free ingress and egress through the chief entrance of the chief tenement, in which he dwells, in Castle Street for the repair and improvemant of the four cottages [?*rectius* shops], with the skilling, as often as necessary at due and most suitable times. Robert Gilbert granted to Robert Potter and his heirs and assigns that all the water coming from the washing of any kind of things on Robert Potter's side, and the rainwater falling above Robert Potter's ground, should for ever go out through Robert Gilbert's gutter running down on the east side of the four shops, above the ground, all the way into Chipper Street. If in the future the gutter were to become blocked on Robert Potter's side by anything filthy or rotten, by means of Robert Gilbert, inmates of his house, or his heirs, Robert Gilbert should put an end to the blockage by cleaning the gutter at his own expense and taking it away. The four cottages [?*rectius* shops], with the skilling, stable, posts, and free ingress and egress, are to be held for ever by Robert Gilbert and his heirs and assigns. Clause of warranty. Seals: those of the parties to the parts of the charter in turn and the common and mayoral seals of the city. Named witnesses: the bailiff, the mayor, the coroners, the reeves, William Warin, Henry Man, John Swift, John Noble, John Bromley, William Packing, Thomas Randolph, and the clerk

2634 Approval of the will of Joan Andrew, the relict of Thomas Andrew, of Salisbury, made on 20 August 1430. <u>Interment</u>: in the graveyard of St. Edmund's church, beside the gate of the college, near her sons. <u>Bequests</u>: 6s. 8d. to the fabric of Broad Hinton church, with her best kerchief for the image of the Blessed Mary; a brass pot worth 5s., or 5s., with a kerchief, to the fabric of Garston church; 12d. to the fabric of the cathedral church; 6s. 8d. to the fabric of St. Edmund's church, 6d. to the high altar, and 2s. 6d. to the serving priests of that church for a trental mass; 5s. to the Franciscans of Salisbury and the Dominicans of Fisherton for two trental masses; all her brewing vessels except two ovens and two pans, six pewter dishes, a half-gallon pot, a pewter half-pottle, a silver bowl, a tablecloth with a towel and two protective cloths, an aumbry, a box, and a green bed of his own making with a pair of linen sheets, two blankets, and two pillows to her son Thomas; her best gown with her best scarlet hat, a best cloak, a best smock for a woman, two cotton kerchiefs, two kerchiefs of Paris, three dishes (*scutellas*), two dishes (*discos*), three salt-cellars, a half-gallon pot, a quart pot of pewter, a coverlet or tester, a pair of linen sheets, a pair of blankets, three pillows, a red coat, a tablecloth, a towel, two protective cloths, a belt harnessed with silver, a rosary of silver beads, a box, a press, a small mazer, and a basin with a laver to her daughter Cecily; a green bed, a pair of linen sheets, a belt studded with silver, a pair of harnessed knives, a mazer, and six silver spoons to her son William; a kerchief of Paris to Edith, the wife of William Andrew, a black hat and a silk kerchief to his daughter Maud, and a silk kerchief to his daughter Joan; a blood-red gown, a coat, and a smock for a woman to her daughter Joan, of Chaddington; a gown of 'Blakofbre', a blue coat, and a smock for a woman to Alice Simond; a green gown, a green coat, and a smock for a woman to Gillian Witts; her best basin, with a laver, to the lord William Pentridge; a small basin, a small posnet with a handle (*manucipio*), and a small pan with a handle (*manucipio*) to Thomas, a son of John Simond; a 3-gallon pan, a mattress, a linen sheet, and a blanket to Robert, a son of John Simond; a brass pot, a coverlet stained red, a linen sheet, and a pair of candlesticks of latten to Isabel, her servant; a kerchief lined with yarn (*de filo*), a rosary of jet beads above with an image of the crucifixion to Edith Limeburner; a 1½-gallon pan, a candlestick, and a 'folet' of yarn (*de filo*) to Cecily, a daughter of John Simond; a kerchief of Paris to Edith, a daughter of William Cox; a kerchief lined with yarn (*de filo*) to Joan Rentis; a 'folet' lined with yarn (*de filo*) to Edith, a daughter of Edith Witts; a long box to the children of John Simond; a rosary of jet beads, with a silver paternoster, to Alice, a daughter of Hugh Limeburner; 6*d*. to each of her godsons and goddaughters; the rest of her goods should be disposed of, at the discretion of her son Thomas and her daughter Cecily, on behalf of her soul. Devise: as an executor of Thomas, of late her husband, she granted to her son Thomas, for his good and praiseworthy service frequently devoted to her, laid low in various ailments in her old age, and especially at the point of her death, a tenement, in which she dwelt, in Gigant Street between William Alexander's tenement on the north side and John Griffith's tenement on the south side, to be held for ever by him and his heirs. If Joan's daughter Cecily were to die without issue Joan's obit and that of her husband Thomas, Cecily's father, should be held yearly in St. Edmund's church on the Thursday before the Thursday in Easter week as long as Joan's son Thomas might live, and until 10 marks for the fee of the tenement to be held by that Thomas shall have been paid out on it. If Cecily's estate could be acquired by Thomas in augmentation of his estate in the tenement, as was agreed in Joan's presence, another 10 marks to pay for the obit should be held by him as promised. Executors: her son Thomas; overseer, William Lord, to whom Joan bequeathed 3*s*. 4*d*. for his work. Proved on 31 August 1430 in front of the subdean; the administration was entrusted to the executor, who afterwards appeared, accounted with an officer, and was dismissed. Approved at a court held in front of the bailiff, the mayor, and other citizens; the seisin of the tenement was released to the legatee.

2635 Approval of the will of John Paul furbisher, of Salisbury, made on 20 June 1430. Interment: in St. Thomas's church. Bequests: 6*s*. 8*d*. to the fabric of that church, 40*d*. to the rector for his forgotten tithes and lesser benefactions, 6*d*. to Henry, the parochial chaplain, and 4*d*. to each chaplain celebrating mass there; 6*d*. to the fabric of the cathedral church; immediately after the death of his wife a standing mazer to his son William, if William were to outlive her, or otherwise it should remain to William's surviving brothers and sisters; after the death of his wife a small mazer to his daughter Joan, if Joan were to outlive her, or otherwise it should remain to Joan's surviving brothers and sisters; 6*s*. 8*d*. to Margery, his servant; if his apprentice were to fulfil his apprenticeship agreement well and in good faith according to the terms of the indenture perfected between them he should have 40*s*. after the completion of his term; 6*s*. 8*d*. to Maud, his servant; 10*s*.

to Robert Warmwell; 10s. to Robert Leving; 10s. to the master John Pedwell, the subdean of Salisbury; the rest of his goods to his wife Christine for keeping [their] male children at school and educating [their] female [children] in other arts, and so that she might bestow food and clothing until the majority of those children. Devises to Christine for life two conjoined tenements in the high street [called Minster Street: cf. *2496–7*] between Laurence Groom's tenement on the south side and Thomas Randolph's tenement on the north side. John appointed those tenements on Christine's death to his son William and William's issue for ever, if William were to die without issue he appointed them for ever to his daughter Isabel and her issue, if Isabel were to die without issue he appointed them for ever to his daughter Joan and her issue, and if Joan were to die without issue he appointed them to be sold by his executors, their executors, or subsequent executors. The money received from the sale should be laid out by the executors on pious uses such as the celebration of masses, the repair of ways, and other charitable deeds. John devised to Christine for life a tenement in the high street [called Minster Street: cf. *2496–7*] between a tenement called the Rose on the south side and Laurence Groom's tenement on the north side. He appointed that tenement on Christine's death to Joan and Joan's issue for ever, if Joan were to die without issue he appointed it for ever to Isabel and her issue, if Isabel were to die without issue he appointed it for ever to William and William's issue, and if William were to die without issue he appointed it to be sold by the executors. The money received from the sale should be laid out by the executors in the way described above. Executors: Robert Warmwell and Robert Leving; overseer, John Pedwell. Proved on 18 August 1430 in front of the subdean; the administration was entrusted to Robert Lewin, reserving the power to entrust it to Robert Warmwell when he might come to seek it. Approved at a court held in front of the bailiff, the mayor, and other citizens; the seisin of the tenements was released to the legatee.

25 October 1430, at Salisbury
2636 By his charter John Noble, a citizen of Salisbury, granted to Simon Horsehill, and his wife Christine, of Ramsbury parish, a tenement, with shops, in Winchester Street between John Pope's tenement on the east side and a corner tenement formerly Thomas Knoyle's on the west side. The tenement was held by John Noble by a grant of Thomas Davy, butcher, and, with the shops, is to be held for ever by Simon and Christine and their heirs and assigns. Clause of warranty. John also granted to Simon and Christine a lead 'sistlie' [?sester], two ovens, and a cauldron remaining within the tenement. Seals: John's and the common and mayoral seals of the city. Named witnesses: the bailiff, the mayor, the coroners, the reeves, William Warin, Henry Man, John Swift, John Bromley, William Packing, Thomas Randolph, and the clerk

8 November 1430, at Salisbury
2637 Approval of the will of John Bonham made on 27 September 1430. Interment: in the graveyard of the church of St. Peter and St. Paul, Longbridge

Deverill. Bequests: 6 sheep to the fabric of that church, and 2 sheep to Thomas [Wilcock], the vicar; 6*d.* to the fabric of the cathedral church; a gown to William Bishop; a doublet to John Baker; 80 sheep to his daughter Elizabeth; the rest of his goods to his wife Alice so that she might dispose of them on behalf of his soul. Devises: to Alice and the joint issue of him and her all his tenements in Salisbury which John Bonham, his father, devised to him and his heirs and assigns. If such issue were to die without issue the tenements would remain for ever to Alice's heirs and assigns. John also devised to Alice and their joint issue all his tenements, land, pasture, and feeding rights in Woodminton and Bower Chalke, and if such issue were to die without issue those premises would remain for ever to Alice's heirs and assigns. John also devised to Alice and their joint issue all his land, tenements, rent, and services in Compton Chamberlayne which his father devised to him and his heirs and assigns. Executor: his wife Alice. Witnesses: Thomas, the vicar of Longbridge Deverill, John Pain, Thomas Sherlock, Richard Cottel, William Belcher, an elder John Cottel, Thomas Clark, John Whitbread, John Prior, and others. Proved on 16 November 1430 [?*rectius* October] in front of an officer of the archdeacon of Salisbury; the administration was entrusted to the executor, who afterwards appeared, accounted with an office, and was dismissed. Approved at a court held in front of the bailiff, the mayor, and other citizens; the seisin of the tenements was released to the legatee.

22 November 1430, at Salisbury
2638 Approval of the will of Richard Needler made on 30 August 1430. Interment: in St. Edmund's church. Bequests: 20*d.* to the fabric of that church, 12*d.* to the provost for his forgotten tithes and lesser benefactions, 6*d.* to each collegiate chaplain present at his funeral rites and mass, and 4*d.* to each annual chaplain; 6*d.* each to the fabric of the cathedral church and the fabric of St. Martin's church; a silver cup with a cover, a nut with a cover, and two dozen best spoons to his wife Agnes; a silver bowl with a cover, a mazer, and 12 third-best silver spoons to his son John; a quart mazer, a piece of silver standing on three lions, and 12 silver spoons to his daughter Isabel; a mazer, a swaging piece, and a … [*MS. blank*] to his daughter Agnes; the rest of his goods to his wife Agnes. Devises: to his wife Agnes for life a tenement in Wineman Street between William Cambridge's tenement on the west side and John Collingbourne's tenement on the east side. Richard appointed the tenement on Agnes's death to his son John and John's issue for ever, if John were to die without issue he appointed it for ever to his daughter Isabel and her issue, if Isabel were to die without issue he appointed it for ever to his daughter Agnes and her issue, and if Agnes were to die without issue he appointed it to be sold by his executors. The money received from the sale should be laid out on pious uses, on celebrating masses, giving alms, and doing other charitable deeds, for the salvation of the soul of John Needler, his father, his own soul, the soul of his wife Agnes, and the souls of others. Richard appointed two shops in New Street, beside a tenement of late John Lippiatt's, to be sold by his executors. The money received from the sale should be laid out by the executors on pious uses. Richard devised to John Needler, his kinsman,

a tenement in Mealmonger Street, which he held by that John's grant, to be held for ever by John and his heirs and assigns on condition that, within the year after he received notice of Richard's death, he were to pay 20 marks to Richard's executors; otherwise the tenement should be sold by Richard's executors, who should release to John all the money from the sale beyond the 20 marks. Richard appointed a messuage, with gardens, a croft, a piece of meadow, and 20 acres of arable land in the vill and fields of Stratford-sub-Castle and Old Sarum, to his wife Agnes to be sold immediately after his death to discharge his debts; he wished that William Lord should be preferred in the purchase. Executors: his wife Agnes and William Lord. Proved on 7 October 1430 in front of the subdean; the administration was entrusted to Agnes, reserving the power to entrust it to William Lord when he might come to seek it. Approved at a court held in front of the bailiff, the mayor, and other citizens; the seisin of the tenements was released to the legatees.

9 May 1431, at Salisbury
2639 By his charter Robert Ogbourne, of Salisbury, granted to William Alexander and John Newbury, a chaplain, the land, tenements, messuages, and cottages which he held by a demise of Gunnore, his mother, in Salisbury, as they were delimited in indentures perfected between him and her on 14 April 1429. The premises, the reversions of which should have passed to Robert on Gunnore's death, are to be held for ever by William and John and their heirs and assigns. Clause of warranty. Seals: Robert's and the common and mayoral seals of the city. Named witnesses: the bailiff, the mayor, the coroners, the reeves, William Warin, Robert Warmwell, Henry Man, John Swift, John Noble, John Bromley, William Packing, and the clerk

17 May 1431
2640 A deed of John Becket, a son and heir of John Becket, of late a citizen of Salisbury. The elder John devised to his wife Alice, still living, for life a tenement in New Street, in which William Debden of late dwelt, between John Wishford's tenement on the east side and John Hathaway's tenement on the west side. On Alice's death the tenement was to remain to the younger John Becket and his heirs, and Alice stands seised of it in her demesne as freehold with reversion to him. By his charter that John granted to Elizabeth, the relict of John de Lisle, kt., and her son Henry de Lisle and his heirs that the tenement would remain for ever to them on Alice's death. Clause of warranty. Seals: John Becket's. Named witnesses: Oliver Digley, a canon of Salisbury, Robert Digley, esq., Henry Man, William Thursby, and Thomas Lyon

23 May 1431, at Salisbury
2641 By their charter William Alexander and John Newbury, a chaplain, granted to Robert Ogbourne, of Salisbury, and his wife Idony the land, tenements, messuages, and cottages in Salisbury, which they held by Robert's grant, to be held for ever by them and their joint issue. If Robert and Idony were to die

without such issue the premises would remain for ever to Robert's direct heirs. Seals: those of William and John and the common and mayoral seals of the city. Named witnesses: the bailiff, the mayor, the coroners, the reeves, William Warin, Robert Warmwell, Henry Man, John Swift, John Noble, John Bromley, William Packing, Thomas Randolph, and the clerk

18 July 1431, at Salisbury

2642 By his writing Richard Fitton quitclaimed to Robert White, of Farnham, and his heirs and assigns his right or claim to a corner tenement, with shops and cottages, in Wineman Street and Brown Street [*as in 2628*]. Seals: Richard's and the common and mayoral seals of the city. Named witnesses: the bailiff, the mayor, the coroners, the reeves, William Warin, Robert Warmwell, Henry Man, John Swift, John Noble, John Bromley, William Packing, Thomas Randolph, and the clerk

1 August 1431, at Salisbury

2643 By their charter Thomas Randolph and John Hain, citizens of Salisbury, granted to Richard Plowman and his wife Catherine a messuage in New Street, between a tenement of Reynold Kingsbridge, a chaplain, on the west side and a tenement of late that of Walter Warwick, a vicar of the cathedral church, on the east side, to be held for ever by them and their heirs and assigns. Seals: those of Thomas and John and the common and mayoral seals of the city. Named witnesses: the bailiff, the mayor, the coroners, the reeves, William Warin, Robert Warmwell, Henry Man, John Swift, John Bromley, John Noble, William Packing, Thomas Freeman, mercer, and the clerk

15 August 1431, at Salisbury

2644 By her charter [*dated to the Wednesday before the feast of St. Laurence the Martyr (8 August), possibly in error for the Wednesday after that feast (15 August)*] Margery, the relict of Thomas Biston, of late a citizen of Salisbury, a daughter and heir of William Hoare, in her chaste widowhood granted to John Morris, a chaplain, a messuage, with two cottages next to it, in Winchester Street between William Warin's tenement on the east side and Stephen Cooper's tenement on the west side; also a tenement opposite the Cole Corner, in Carter Street, of late called High Street, in which Henry Hellier dwells, between Stephen Cooper's tenement on the south side and John Purvis's tenement on the north side; also a toft, with racks and gardens next to it, in Gigant Street and Brown Street; also a toft, with an adjacent garden in New Street, near Barnwell's cross, between a tenement of John Bromley on either side; and all her land and tenements, with the rent and reversions, in the city. All those premises, with the rent and reversions, are to be held for ever by John Morris and his heirs and assigns. Seals: Margery's and the common and mayoral seals of the city. Named witnesses: the bailiff, the mayor, the coroners, the reeves, Henry Man, Robert Warmwell, William Warwick, Richard Ecton, and the clerk

29 August 1431, at Salisbury

2645 By his charter John Eastbury, of Salisbury, granted to John Tutsay, of Salisbury, a cottage, with a garden, between William Phebis's tenement on the south side and a tenement of Walter Plowman, carpenter, on the north side. The cottage, with the garden, extends from Drake Hall Street as far as a garden, with a rack, of William Oving, chandler, in Freren Street on the east side. It was held by John Eastbury by a grant of Thomas Pinchbeck, cook, of Salisbury, and is to be held for ever by John Tutsay and his heirs and assigns. Clause of warranty. Seals: John Eastbury's and the common and mayoral seals of the city. Named witnesses: the bailiff, the mayor, the coroners, the reeves, William Warin, Robert Warmwell, Henry Man, John Swift, John Noble, John Bromley, William Packing, Thomas Randolph, and the clerk

26 September 1431, at Salisbury

2646 Approval of the will of William Harnhill, barber, of Salisbury, made on 30 March 1430. Interment: in the graveyard of St. Edmund's church, in the processional way in front of the west gate. Bequests: 40d. and an altar cloth measuring 3 yd. to the fabric of that church, 6d. to the provost for his forgotten tithes, 6d. to the lord William Spicer and 4d. to each other collegiate chaplain present at his funeral rites and mass on the day of his burial, and 4d. to each annual chaplain present likewise; 6d. to the fabric of the cathedral church, and 2s. to the light of the fraternity of barbers; 12d. to the fabric of St. Martin's church, and 4d. to each chaplain except William Spicer; 6d. to the lord John Crosier; William appointed that his executors should cause 100 masses to be celebrated on behalf of his soul on the day of his obit if, his debts having been paid, his goods were of sufficient value, and he appointed that they should cause two trentals of St. Gregory to be celebrated as soon as possible on behalf of his soul and of the condition of his wife Alice, his father John, his mother Margery, his brother John and his wife Alice, and others; 2s. 6d. both to the Franciscans of Salisbury and the Dominicans of Fisherton Anger to pray for his soul; 40d., at 6d. a week while the 40d. lasted, to the paupers of the hospital of the Holy Trinity; 4d. to each of his godchildren; his best gown, with a hood, to John Young, chandler; 6s. 8d. to Thomas Rayner; 13s. 4d. to John Park; the rest of his goods to his executors to be disposed on behalf of his soul. Devise: to his wife Alice for life two cottages [with gardens] in the street on the way to St. Martin's church between Henry Man's cottages on the north side and John Hampton's cottages on the south side. If it seemed best for his soul and for hers Alice might sell the reversion of the cottages in her lifetime, or his executors, their executors, or subsequent executors should sell the cottages after Alice's death. From the money from the sale William assigned 40d. to the paupers of the hospital of the Holy Trinity, to be laid out by Alice or the executors on eating and drinking worth 6d. as long as the 40d. might last; what remained should be laid out by Alice or the executors on pious uses for the salvation of his soul and the souls of those mentioned above. Executors: his wife Alice, John Young, chandler, and John Park, hosier. Proved on 20 April 1430 in front of John Pedwell, the subdean; the administration was entrusted to John

Young and John Park, reserving the power to entrust it to Alice when she might come to seek it. Approved at a court held in front of the bailiff, the mayor, and other citizens; the seisin of the cottages and gardens was released to the legatees. **2647** By their indented charter Alice, the relict, and an executor, of William Harnhill, barber, of Salisbury, and John Young, chandler, of Salisbury, Alice's co-executor, for a sum of money reaching their true value, and on the strength of William's will, granted to Robert Leving, saddler, of Salisbury, two cottages, with gardens, in the street on the way to St. Martin's church, [*as in* **2646**]. In his will William appointed the reversion of the cottages, and the gardens, to be sold in Alice's lifetime if it seemed to her most advantageous for his soul and hers, and Alice fulfilled that appointment for the greatest profit of those souls on the following terms. The cottages, with the gardens, were to be held for ever by Robert Leving and his heirs and assigns. After the grant to him Robert granted the cottages, with the gardens, to Alice, to be held by her for life for a rent of a red rose a year to be paid to him and his heirs and assigns. On Alice's death the cottages, with the gardens, would remain for ever to Thomas Rayner and his wife Alice and their heirs and assigns. Seals: those of the parties to the parts of the charter in turn and the common and mayoral seals of the city. Named witnesses: the bailiff, the mayor, the coroners, the reeves, William Warin, Robert Warmwell, Henry Man, John Swift, William Packing, and the clerk

10 October 1431, at Salisbury
2648 By their charter Simon Horsehill and his wife Christine, appearing in court in front of the bailiff, the mayor, and others, citizens of Salisbury, Christine being examined according to the custom of the city, granted to John Hain, of Salisbury, a tenement, with shops, in Winchester Street between John Pope's tenement on the east side and a corner tenement formerly Thomas Knoyle's on the west side. The tenement, with the shops, was held by Simon and Christine by a grant of John Noble, a citizen of Salisbury, and is to be held for ever by John Hain and his heirs and assigns. Clause of warranty. Seals: those of Simon and Christine and the common and mayoral seals of the city. Named witnesses: the bailiff, the mayor, the coroners, a reeve, William Warin, Robert Warmwell, Henry Man, John Bromley, William Packing, Thomas Randolph, and the clerk

14 November 1431, at Salisbury
2649 By his charter John Morris, a chaplain, granted to Robert Cove and his wife Margery, the relict of Thomas Biston, a messuage, with two cottages next to it, in Winchester Street [*as in* **2644**]; also a tenement opposite the Cole Corner, in Carter Street, of late called High Street, in which Henry Hellier dwells, [*as in* **2644**]; also a toft, with racks and gardens, in Gigant Street and Brown Street; also a toft, with an adjacent garden, in New Street, near Barnwell's cross, [*as in* **2644**]; also all the land and tenements, with the rent and reversions, [*as in* **2644**]. All those premises, with the rent and reversions, are to be held for ever by Robert and Margery and their heirs and assigns. Clause of warranty. Seals: John's and the common and mayoral seals of the city. Named witnesses: the bailiff, the

mayor, the coroners, the reeves, William Warin, Robert Warmwell, Henry Man, William Warwick, Richard Ecton, John Marshall, and the clerk

21 November 1431, at Salisbury
2650 By his charter Robert White, of Farnham, Surrey, granted to John Jarvis, merchant, of Salisbury, a corner tenement, with shops and cottages, in Wineman Street and Brown Street [*as in 2628*]. The tenement, with the shops and cottages, was held by Robert by a grant of Adam Body, a son and heir of Robert Body, of late a citizen of Salisbury, and is to be held for ever by John and his heirs and assigns. Clause of warranty. Seals: Robert's and the common and mayoral seals of the city. Named witnesses: the bailiff, the mayor, the coroners, the reeves, William Warin, Robert Warmwell, John Swift, John Noble, John Bromley, William Packing, Richard Gater, Thomas Randolph, and the clerk
2651 By his charter Thomas Farrant, of Salisbury, granted to Richard Pain, a citizen of Salisbury, a corner tenement, with shops, cottages, and yards, [*margin: the corner house overright the weavers' corner house*] in Endless Street and Chipper Lane, between a tenement of late William Duke's, formerly Stephen Shearer's, on the south side and cottages of late William Tull's on the west side. The tenement, with the shops, cottages, and yards, was held by Thomas by a grant of Eleanor Bramshaw, a confirmation of Robert and William, sons of Edmund Bradshaw, and of Emme, a daughter of Edmund, and a release of Edmund Friday, all perfected for him and his heirs for ever. It would have remained to Edmund Friday and his heirs for ever for want of issue of Robert, William, and Emme, and it is to be held for ever by Richard Pain and his heirs and assigns. Thomas Farrant quitclaimed to Richard and his heirs and assigns his right or claim to it or to any rent issuing from it. Clause of warranty. Seals: Thomas's and the common and mayoral seals of the city. Named witnesses: the bailiff, the mayor, the coroners, the reeves, William Warin, Robert Warmwell, John Swift, John Noble, John Bromley, William Packing, Richard Gater, Thomas Randolph, and the clerk

2 January 1432, at Salisbury
2652 A charter of William Warwick, a citizen of Salisbury, and of Edward Say and his wife Margaret, the relict, and an executor of Philip Baron, an executor of William Moore, tailor, of late a citizen of Salisbury. William Moore devised to his wife Susan for life a tenement, with a shop, opposite the Guidhall, between Thomas Harding's tenement on the south side and a tenement of the dean and chapter of Salisbury on the north side. On Susan's death the tenement should be sold. The money received from the sale should be laid out by William Warwick and Philip Baron or their executors on pious uses on behalf of the soul of William Moore and the souls of his wives and others. Edward Goodyear, tailor, and his wife Denise have paid to William, Edward, and Margaret a sum of money, reaching the true value of the reversion of the tenement and the shop, to be laid out wholly according to the terms of William Moore's will. By their charter William, Edward, and Margaret on the strength of that will granted the reversion

to Edward Goodyear and Denise, and the tenement, with the shop, when it fell due on Susan's death, is to be held for ever by Edward and Denise and Edward's heirs and assigns. Seals: those of the grantors and the common and mayoral seals of the city. Named witnesses: the bailiff, the mayor, the coroners, the reeves, William Warin, Robert Warmwell, John Swift, John Noble, John Bromley, William Packing, Richard Gater, Henry Baron, and the clerk

9 January 1432, at Salisbury
2653 Approval of the will of George Goss, tucker, a citizen of Salisbury, made on 13 December 1431. Interment: in St. Edmund's church. Bequests: his best brass pot to the fabric of that church, and 12*d*. to Edward, the parochial chaplain; 6*d*. to the fabric of the cathedral church; 4*d*. to each priest present at his funeral rites; a silver bowl, a mazer, and his best gown, furred, to the lord John, his son; six silver spoons to his daughter Joan; his best basin to John Glazier [?John Ox, glazier: *cf. below*], and a book containing a psalter with offices of the dead to John's son George; a basin with a laver to Joan, his household servant; a brass pot to Alice, his household servant; a pan containing 2 gallons to Agnes, his household servant; the rest of his goods to his wife Alice. Devises: to his wife Alice a shop, with rooms and sollars built above it, which John Curtis, a cordwainer holds, on the south side of the entrance of a chief messuage, in which George himself dwells, in Castle Street, to be held by her for life as completely as John Curtis holds it. On Alice's death the shop, with the rooms and sollars, should remain for ever to Richard Pain and his heirs and assigns. George devised to Richard the chief messuage, with a garden next to it, to be held for ever by him and his heirs and assigns. He appointed a shop, with a house called Workhouse, and a hall in a sollar of the shop, with a room there, which he granted to John Ox, glazier, and his wife Joan, George's daughter, and their joint issue, which for want of such issue would revert to George himself, to remain for ever to Richard Pain and his heirs and assigns. Witnesses: Henry Man, the mayor, William Lord, and others. Executors: his wife Alice and his son John. Proved on 5 January 1432 in front of the subdean; the administration was entrusted to the executors. Approved at a court held in front of the bailiff, the mayor, and other citizens; the seisin of the tenements was released to the legatees.

12 March 1432, at Salisbury
2654 By his charter John Rew, of Wells, granted to John Bromley, a citizen of Salisbury, a messuage, with three shops next to it, in New Street between a tenement of the abbot of Stanley on the east side and Richard Needler's tenement on the west side. The messuage, with the shops, was held by John Rew by a grant of John Lippiatt and his wife Alice, and is to be held for ever by John Bromley and his heirs and assigns. Seals: John Rew's and the common and mayoral seals of the city. Named witnesses: the bailiff, the mayor, the coroners, the reeves, William Warin, Robert Warmwell, John Swift, John Noble, William Packing, Richard Gater, Henry Baron, and the clerk

7 May 1432, at Salisbury

2655 By his charter William Oving, chandler, of Salisbury, granted to William Warin, a citizen of Salisbury, and Thomas Kittle, of Salisbury, a tenement, with a garden, in New Street, between Richard Ecton's tenement on the west side and Alice Becket's messuage on the east side, to be held for ever by them and Thomas's heirs and assigns. Clause of warranty. Seals: William Oving's and the common and mayoral seals of the city. Named witnesses: the bailiff, the mayor, the coroners, the reeves, Robert Warmwell, John Swift, John Noble, John Bromley, William Packing, Richard Gater, Henry Baron, and the clerk

21 May 1432, at Salisbury

2656 A deed of Walter Bugien, dubber, of Salisbury, and his wife Christine, the relict of Edmund Purdy, of late a citizen of Salisbury. Edmund devised to Christine for life a tenement, in which he dwelt, in Castle Street, beyond the lower bars, on the west side of the street, between a tenement of Robert Long, a cordwainer, on the north side and Edith Starr's cottages on the south side, and he appointed it on Christine's death to his son John and John's heirs for ever. Walter and Christine, appearing in court on that day, surrendered the tenement for ever to John and his heirs and assigns. Seals: those of Walter and Christine and the common and mayoral seals of the city. Named witnesses: the mayor, the coroners, the reeves, William Warin, Robert Warmwell, John Noble, John Bromley, William Packing, Richard Gater, Henry Baron, and the clerk

4 June 1432, at Salisbury

2657 Approval of the will of John Shute made on 16 April 1432. Interment: in the graveyard of St. Edmund's church, in front of the cross on the way into the graveyard on its west side. Bequests: 12*d.* to the fabric of the cathedral church; 6*s.* 8*d.* each to the fabric of St. Edmund's church and the fabric of King's Somborne church; 20*s.* and a furred gown of sendal to Simon Shute, a chaplain, to pray for his soul; a gown of green motley to Thomas Lavend, his servant; a dozen cloths, the best of all his cloths, and a red box to his son Nicholas; 6*s.* 8*d.* to Parnel Daw; 6*s.* 8*d.* to Richard Gage for his work in helping to bury his corpse; all his goods should be divided into two equal parts with Richard's oversight, and he appointed one half to his son Nicholas to be laid out on pious uses for the salvation of his soul and the souls of others. Devises: to his wife Alice for life a lower room in his tenement in Endless Street between John Everard's tenement on the south side and Margery Witney's tenement on the north side, with free ingress and egress. John devised that tenement, except that room, for ever to his son Nicholas and his heirs and assigns for finding food and drink for his mother, John's wife Alice, for her life. He appointed that, for her life, Alice should pay 6*s.* 8*d.* a year to Nicholas for repairing the room becomingly. On Alice's death the room should remain for ever to Nicholas and his heirs and assigns. Executors: his son Nicholas and his wife Alice; overseer, Richard Gage. Proved on 25 April 1432 in front of John Pedwell, the subdean; the administration was entrusted to the executors. Approved at a court held in front of the bailiff, the mayor, and other citizens; the seisin of the tenement and the room was released to the legatees.

30 July 1432, at Salisbury
2658 By her charter Christine, the relict of John Wantage, of late a citizen of Salisbury, in her chaste widowhood and full power granted to William Warwick, a citizen of Salisbury, cottages, with yards and racks, in Freren Street between a small portion of ground beside a stone wall of the Franciscans on the north side and a yard of St. Nicholas's hospital on the south side. The cottages, with the yards and racks, were bought by Christine from Nicholas Shute, weaver, of Salisbury, and Richard Cooper, executors of John Wantage, and they are to be held for ever by William Warwick and his heirs and assigns. Clause of warranty. Seals: Christine's and the common and mayoral seals of the city. Named witnesses: the bailiff, the mayor, the coroners, the reeves, William Warin, Robert Warmwell, John Swift, John Noble, John Bromley, Henry Baron, and the clerk

10 September 1432, at Salisbury
2659 By his charter Richard Gater, a citizen of Salisbury, granted to John Shad, of Salisbury, cottages, with a yard (*or* yards), a vacant site, and a portion of meadow land. The cottages, with the yard(s), stand in Drake Hall Street between John Popham's yard on the north side and a new ditch of the city on the south side. The portion of meadow lies, in the same street, between that ditch on the north side and John Upton's meadow on the south side. All those premises are to be held for ever by John Shad and his heirs and assigns. Seals: Richard's and the common and mayoral seals of the city. Named witnesses: the bailiff, the mayor, the coroners, the reeves, William Warin, Robert Warmwell, John Swift, John Noble, John Bromley, William Packing, Henry Baron, and the clerk
2660 By his charter John Shad, draper, of Salisbury, granted to John Sigley and his wife Parnel a cottage, with a garden, and a small house next to the cottage in Drake Hall Street between a trench of running water on the north side and the door of a lane of John Shad's to his garden on the south side. The cottage measures 28½ ft. 3 in. in width at its frontage on the street, 26½ ft. in length from the street as far as the extreme east end of the small house, 33½ ft. in width from the south gutter of the small house as far as the trench of running water, and 35 ft. 8 in. in width to the east end of the garden. The cottage, with the garden, measures 135 ft. in length from the street as far as the east end of the garden. The cottage, with the garden and small house, is to be held for ever by John Sigley and Parnel and Parnel's heirs and assigns. Clause of warranty. Seals: John Shad's and the common and mayoral seals of the city. Named witnesses: the bailiff, the mayor, the coroners, the reeves, William Warin, Robert Warmwell, John Swift, John Noble, John Bromley, William Packing, Richard Gater, Henry Baron, and the clerk

5 November 1432, at Salisbury
2661 By their writing Henry Man and Robert Warmwell, citizens of Salisbury, quitclaimed to John Park, draper, of Salisbury, and his heirs and assigns their right

or claim to conjoined cottages, or shops, in St. Martin's Street and Brown Street, on a corner between William Sever's tenement in Brown Street on the north side and a tenement of John Wheeler, weaver, in St. Martin's Street on the east side. Seals: those of Henry and Robert and the common and mayoral seals of the city. Named witnesses: the bailiff, the coroners, the reeves, William Warin, John Swift, John Noble, John Bromley, William Packing, Richard Gater, Henry Baron, and the clerk

14 January 1433, at Salisbury
2662 By his charter John Hogman, weaver, of Salisbury, granted to William Warwick, a citizen of Salisbury, a tenement in Endless Street between William's cottages on the north side and Joan Clive's cottage on the south side. The tenement, with gardens, was bought by John from John Twyford and, with the gardens, is to be held for ever by William and his heirs and assigns. Clause of warranty. Seals: John Hogman's and the common and mayoral seals of the city. Named witnesses: the bailiff, the mayor, the coroners, the reeves, William Warin, Robert Warmwell, Henry Man, John Swift, John Noble, John Bromley, William Packing, Richard Gater, and the clerk
2663 By his letters of attorney John Hogman, weaver, of Salisbury, appointed Walter Short to deliver to William Warwick, a citizen of Salisbury, the seisin of a tenement, with gardens, in Endless Street [*as in* **2662**]. Seals: John's and the mayoral seal of the city
2664 Approval of the will of Henry Harborough, a canon of the cathedral church, made on 13 September 1432. <u>Interment</u>: in the cathedral church. <u>Bequests</u>: all his vestments ordained for the preparation of divine service, except a vestment of red velvet, and all his gold and silver plate should be sold by his executors; the excepted vestment, a dalmatic, [and] two blue tunicles, for a deacon and a subdeacon, of one style, and worked with vernicles and gold stars with orphreys with various images, to God and the cathedral church to pray for his soul; from the money issuing from the sale of the rest his debts, if there were to be any, should be paid, and his servants and other persons by whom he is held [dear] should be rewarded, as will be made clear below; various sums of money owed to him from his benefice and elsewhere should be levied by his executors and laid out on those same payments and rewards. The debts which are owed to him, as mentioned above, for the most part are these: £200 from the various reeves of the lordship of Charminster and Bere, beyond that £220 from Thomas Freeman, of late a bailiff there, by means of a statute merchant, 180 marks from Hugh at the haw, the farmer of 'Routebury', and £313 in the hands of his friend Henry Ridgely, for which he has to answer; other, lesser, sums owed to him, which he cannot fully record now without other evidences, should be levied and laid out on behalf of his soul at the discretion of his executors. The master Nicholas Bilston owes 200 ducats to him from the chamber without the exchange (*camera sine cambio*). Henry bequeathed £60 of the £100 for which the tenements of 'Horew' were sold, with the £20 received from the lord John Frank for two letters sent for him by Henry after Henry's arrival from the court of Rome, to his

kinsman William Hartshorn; a silver bowl, gilded, standing, swaged, with a cover, worked with various branches, and £40 in money for his marriage, with a bed of red and green worsted with all the bedding, to Richard Lambard; a silver bowl, gilded, which he received from George [?Lowthorpe], a former treasurer of the cathedral church, and £40 for his marriage, with a bed of red and white worsted with all the bedding, to John Guy; a silver bowl, standing, gilded, plain, of which the feet are lions, a bed with falcons with all the bedding, and 40 marks to Henry Burnage; a bed of red worsted, with all the bedding, hanging in a room below … [word illegible], £10 cash, and a pot and a pan each containing 3 gallons to Janis [male], his long-time servant; 10 marks and a pot and a pan each containing 3 gallons to Walter Brown; 40s. to Robert Cann; 50 ducats from the chamber with the exchange (camera cum cambio) to the friar Peter of Rome, and another 50 ducats to celebrate mass and pray on behalf of his soul and to go on a pilgrimage for him to the Holy Sepulchre; 100[?s.] to the master John Symondsbury; 100s. to the master Robert Brown; a porteous, with two volumes bound with red leather, to the lord Hugh ApEvan; a silver bowl, standing, with a cover to Thomas Chapman, of Rome; 10 marks to Thomas Chapman, of Charminster, his bailiff, and a silver bowl with a plain cover to Thomas's wife Maud; 100s. to Thomas Freeman, of Haddenham, on condition that he would satisfy him concerning the sum contained in the statute merchant; 2 marks each to John Cook (Coco), Thomas of 'Butria', and William Compton; his bed of red worsted, which Thomas Hatfield has in his keeping, with all the bedding, viz. a mattress, blankets, linen sheets, tablecloths, and towels, to that Thomas and his wife; 20s. to Thomas Massy. The rest of his goods should be sold by his executors and disposed of for the salvation of his soul. Devises: to Richard Lambard the reversion of a house in London which he bought from Marion Blyth of London. He devised all his tenements in Salisbury to John Guy. Executors: John Symondsbury and Robert Brown, canons of Salisbury, Hugh ApEvan, Richard Lambard, John Guy, and Henry Burnage, a clerk; overseer, John Frank, the Master of the Rolls. Proved on 5 October 1432 in the cathedral church in front of Edward Prentice, the precentor, deputed a commissary of Henry [Chichele], the archbishop of Canterbury; the administration was entrusted to Richard Lambard, John Guy, and Henry Burnage, the other executors rejecting the burden of it. Approved at a court held in front of the bailiff, the mayor, and other citizens; the seisin of the tenements was released to the legatees.

2665 By their charter John Lippiatt and his wife Alice, the relict of Thomas Play, of late a citizen of Salisbury, granted to Edward Prentice, Nicholas Upton, William Ingram, William Swift, and Thomas Cirencester, canons of the cathedral church, and John Golding, Laurence Groom, Robert Driffield, and Walter Dash, vicars of that church, a tenement, opposite the cross where poultry are sold, between a tenement of the dean and chapter on the west side and a corner shop of late John Becket's on the east side, to be held for ever by them and their heirs and assigns. Clause of warranty. Seals: those of John and Alice and the common and mayoral seals of the city. Named witnesses: the bailiff, the mayor, the coroners, the reeves, William Warin, Robert Warmwell,

Henry Man, John Swift, John Noble, John Bromley, William Packing, Richard Gater, and the clerk

25 January 1433, at Wells
2666 By their letters of attorney John Lippiatt and his wife Alice, the relict of Thomas Play, of late a citizen of Salisbury, appointed George Westby, Gilbert Marshall, and William Lord to deliver to Edward Prentice and others [*as in 2665*] the seisin of a tenement opposite the cross where poultry are sold [*as in 2665*]. Seals: those of John and Alice and, because their seals are unknown to many, at their request the seal of the office of John Wheatley, the master of the city of Wells

2667 By his letters John Play, a son and heir of Thomas Play, of late a citizen of Salisbury, acknowledged that he had examined a charter of John Lippiatt and his wife Alice, his mother, sealed with their seals, and, on behalf of himself and his heirs and assigns, approved of and confirmed all it contained. Seals: John's and, because his seal is unknown to many, at his request the seal of the office of John Wheatley, the master of the city of Wells. Named witnesses: John Rook, John Godwin, Richard Hall, John Pedwell, Richard Goodrich, John Collis, cutler, and Richard Dyer

28 January 1433, at Salisbury
2668 By their writing Ralph Hogman, of London, a son of John Hogman, and John Linley and his wife Agnes quitclaimed to William Warwick, a citizen of Salisbury, and his heirs and assigns their right or claim to a tenement, with gardens, in Endless Street [*as in 2662*]. Seals: those of Ralph, John Linley, and Agnes and the common and mayoral seals of the city. Named witnesses: the bailiff, the mayor, the coroners, the reeves, William Warin, Robert Warmwell, Henry Man, John Swift, John Noble, John Bromley, William Packing, Richard Gater, and the clerk

3 June 1433, at Salisbury
2669 By his charter John Gage, of Salisbury, granted to William Warwick, a citizen of Salisbury, a messuage, called the Cage, in Castle Street, between William Stamford's tenement on the north side and Thomas Freeman's tenement on the south side, to be held for ever by him and his heirs and assigns. Clause of warranty. Seals: John's and the common and mayoral seals of the city. Named witnesses: the bailiff, the mayor, the coroners, the reeves, William Warin, Robert Warmwell, Henry Man, John Swift, John Bromley, William Packing, Richard Gater, Stephen Cooper, mercer, and the clerk

1 July 1433, at Salisbury
2670 By their charter John Glazier, chandler, of late of Salisbury, and his wife Agnes, appearing in court on that day, granted to Henry Man, a citizen of Salisbury, the estate or term which they held in a tenement, opposite the poultry cross, between a corner tenement of late Thomas Bower's, now that of John and

Agnes, on the east side and a tenement of late Gunnore Bowyer's, now Robert Ogbourne's, on the west side. The tenement, by the name of a toft or vacant ground, was held by John and Agnes by a grant of John at the burgh, esq., for a term of 77 years, of which 5½ years have passed, and their estate or term in it is to be held by Henry and his assigns from the day on which this charter was perfected for the following 71½ years for the rent and other charges specified in the charter perfected between John and Agnes and John at the burgh. John and Agnes also granted to Henry the corner tenement, between a tenement of St. Edmund's church on the north side and the tenement which is held of John at the burgh on the west side, to be held for ever by him and his heirs and assigns. Clause of warranty in respect of the corner tenement. Seals: those of John and Agnes and the common and mayoral seals of the city. Named witnesses: the bailiff, the mayor, the coroners, the reeves, William Warin, Robert Warmwell, John Bromley, William Packing, Richard Gater, Stephen Mercer, and the clerk

22 July 1433, at Salisbury
2671 By their charter Thomas Mason, draper, and Richard Gater granted to William Warwick, a citizen of Salisbury, a tenement in Minster Street, otherwise called Castle Street, between a tenement of Richard Milbourne, esq., on the north side and a tenement of Robert Potter, a cordwainer, on the south side. The tenement was acquired by Thomas and Richard, together with Walter Shirley, Walter Nalder, Stephen Edington, and Richard Weston, all now dead, and with William Lord, who released all his right in it for ever to them and their heirs, by a grant of Nicholas Harding, of late a citizen of Salisbury. Thomas and Richard also granted to William Warwick a messuage in Chipper Street between a tenement of late William Purchase's on the west side and John Noble's tenement on the east side. The tenement and the messuage are to be held for ever by William Warwick and his heirs and assigns. Clause of warranty, given by Thomas Mason. Seals: those of Thomas Mason and Richard Gater and the common and mayoral seals of the city. Named witnesses: the bailiff, the mayor, the coroners, the reeves, William Warin, Robert Warmwell, Henry Man, John Swift, William Packing, Stephen Mercer, and the clerk

12 August 1433, at Salisbury
2672 A charter of John Noble, a citizen of Salisbury, an executor of Thomas Bower, of late a citizen of Salisbury. Thomas devised to his wife Ellen for life [Grandon's Corner, opposite the market place: *cf.* ***1219, 2015, 2017***], a chief tenement in which he dwelt, on a corner of Wineman Street, between John Hampton's tenement on the east side and a tenement of late William Bowyer's on the south side. Thomas appointed the tenement to be sold by John Noble after Eleanor's death or, if it could be done advantageously, the reversion to be sold by him as executor in Eleanor's lifetime. Eleanor, with Richard Gage, her husband, granted her estate in the tenement to William Knolle, otherwise called William Cormell, and John Mundy, of Wilton, who together granted it to John Noble. William has paid to John Noble a sum of money reaching the true value of the

reversion of the tenement, and by his charter John granted the corner tenement to William and his wife Agnes to be held for ever by them and William's heirs and assigns. John quitclaimed to William and Agnes and William's heirs and assigns all his right or claim to the tenement. Seals: John Noble's and the common and mayoral seals of the city. Named witnesses: the bailiff, the mayor, the coroners, the reeves, William Warin, Robert Warmwell, John Swift, Henry Man, John Bromley, William Packing, Richard Gater, Stephen Mercer, and the clerk

26 August 1433, at Salisbury
2673 Approval [*the approval is dated to the Wednesday after the feast of St. Barnabas in the 11th year of the reign of Henry VI (17 June 1433), evidently in error for the Wednesday after the feast of St. Bartholomew in that year (26 August 1433)*] of the will of John Park, a citizen of Salisbury, made on 23 June 1433. <u>Interment</u>: in the chapel of St. John the Baptist in St. Edmund's church. <u>Bequests</u>: 20s. to the fabric of that church, 6s. 8d. to the light of St. James, and 2s. 6d. to Edward, the parochial chaplain [?of that church: *cf.* ***2653***]; 12d. to the fabric of the cathedral church; 40d. each to the fabric of St. Thomas's church and the fabric of St. Martin's church; 12d. to the fabric of St. Clement's church, Fisherton; 40d. both to the friars of Fisherton and to the convent of the Franciscans of Salisbury; a furred gown of blood-red and a green gown furred with rabbit skins to Thomas Peasenhall; his best silver belt and dagger, with a silver chape, and a blue gown with a red hood to John Cooper; 40d. to the paupers of the hospital called Almshouse; 6s. 8d. for the repair of the way from Brend mill; his best sword, a poleaxe, and two hauberks, with a satchel, to John Andrew; two boxes, his best brass pot, and £3 6s. 8d. to his daughter Emme; a basin with a hanging laver to Edith, a daughter of John Andrew; 40s. to John, 20s. to William, and 10s. to Richard, each a son of John Andrew; six silver spoons to William Conning, his brother; 3s. 4d., a gown of motley, two best smocks, and an English book to William Draper; a hat of ray sendal to Adam of Cranborne; two bows, with all the arrows, and three coats to John Risby; 20s. and a russett gown to John Andrew, one of his executors, for his work; 20s. to John Wyatt, his other executor; 8s. 4d. to be handed out before the day of his burial among priests celebrating masses; the rest of his goods to his wife Margaret. <u>Devises</u>: to Margaret his estate in two tenements in Wineman Street, one of which is held by John Preece, fewster, and the other by John Rowe, loader. The tenements, under the name of a tenement with two shops next to it, were held by John Park by a grant of Thomas Hain, of Winchester, John Swift, ironmonger, of Salisbury, Henry Warin, a chaplain, and William Lord to be held by him and his heirs and assigns for a term of 24 years according to an indented charter dated 21 February 1425. John devised to Margaret for life six conjoined shops [*or* cottages] in St. Martin's Street and Brown Street, on a corner, between William Sever's tenement in Brown Street on the north side and a tenement of John Wheeler, weaver, in St. Martin's Street on the east side [*margin*: Hooper's land in the ...]. Those shops were held jointly by Thomas Randolph, now dead, and John Park by a grant of Stephen Hart, to be held for ever by them and their heirs and assigns. John appointed the cottages to Stephen and his heirs and assigns

for ever if Stephen would pay £18 6s. 8d. to John's wife Margaret or her assigns in her lifetime, and the keeping and expenses which John, Margaret, or their assigns incurred about the cottages. If Stephen were to fail to pay the £18 6s. 8d. or the keeping and expenses, on Margaret's death the cottages would remain for ever to John's daughter Emme and her issue, and if Emme were to die without issue they should be sold by John's executors or their executors. The money received from the sale should be laid out on behalf of John's soul and the souls of others. <u>Executors</u>: his wife Margaret, John Andrew, and John Wyatt, to dispose of his goods for the salvation of his soul. <u>Proved</u> on 4 August 1433 in front of the subdean; the administration was entrusted to Margaret; John Wyatt and John Andrew, appearing in person, expressly declined it; afterwards Margaret appeared, accounted with an officer, and was dismissed. <u>Approved</u> at a court held in front of the bailiff, the mayor, and other citizens; the seisin of the tenements and cottages was released to the legatees.

21 April 1434, at Salisbury
2674 By his indented charter William Warwick, a citizen of Salisbury, granted to John Collingbourne, tucker, of Salisbury, and his wife Alice a tenement in Castle Street, on the east side of the street, between a tenement of Richard Milbourne, esq., on the north side and Robert Potter's tenement on the south side; also a messuage on the north side of Chipper Street between a tenement of John Chitteris on the west side and John Noble's tenement on the east side. The tenement and the messuage were held by William by a feoffment of Thomas Mason and Richard Gater, and they are to be held for ever by John and Alice and their heirs and assigns, paying a rent of £10 a year on 25 March to William and his heirs and assigns for the following eight years until £80 had been paid. Clause to permit permanent repossession if nothing were to be paid on the first 25 March; also, if John and Alice were to fail to make a payment of £10 on any 25 March after the first one, to permit William and his heirs and assigns to enter on the tenement and the messuage, distrain, and keep distresses, or to take back possession if they preferred, until that unpaid £10 was recovered. Seals: those of the parties to the parts of the charter in turn and the common and mayoral seals of the city. Named witnesses: the bailiff, the mayor, the coroners, the reeves, Robert Warmwell, Henry Man, John Bromley, John Swift, Richard Ecton, and the clerk

12 May 1434, at Salisbury
2675 By their charter William Alexander and Henry Man, executors of John Becket, of late a citizen of Salisbury, and Alice, the relict, and an executor, of John, on the strength of John's will, and for a suitable sum of money paid to them in advance, granted to Richard Holt, William Chamberlain, and John Shapwick shops, opposite a corner shop, in which John Swift, ironmonger, of late dwelt, on the way to the New Inn, between a tenement in which Edward Potticary of late dwelt, now that of the dean and chapter of Salisbury, on the west side opposite the cross where poultry are sold, a lane leading from the north end of the shops

towards the New Inn on the east side, and a shop formerly Gunnore Bowyer's on the south side. The shops are to be held for ever by the grantees and their heirs and assigns. Seals: those of the grantors and, because their seals are unknown to many, the common and mayoral seals of the city. Named witnesses: the bailiff, the mayor, the coroners, the reeves, Robert Warmwell, William Warwick, John Bromley, William Packing, Richard Gater, Stephen Cooper, mercer, and the clerk

4 June 1434, at Salisbury
2676 By their writing William Alexander, Robert Warmwell, Henry Man, and Alice, the relict of John Becket, of late a citizen of Salisbury, quitclaimed to Richard Holt, William Chamberlain, and John Shapwick and their heirs and assigns their right or claim to shops [*as in* **2675**]. The shops are to be held for ever by Richard, William, and John and their heirs and assigns. Seals: those of William, Robert, Henry, and Alice and the common and mayoral seals of the city. Named witnesses: the bailiff, the mayor, the coroners, the reeves, William Warwick, John Bromley, William Packing, Richard Gater, Stephen Cooper, mercer, and the clerk

21 July 1434, at Salisbury
2677 By their writing Thomas Scot, clothier, a citizen of London, and William Priddy, weaver, of Salisbury, quitclaimed to Henry Man and John Bromley, citizens of Salisbury, and their heirs and assigns their right or claim to a corner tenement, with shops and cottages, in Winchester Street and Brown Street between Richard Forster's tenement in Winchester Street on the west side and Laurence Goodwin's tenement in Brown Street on the south side. Seals: those of Thomas and William and the common and mayoral seals of the city. Named witnesses: the bailiff, the mayor, the coroners, the reeves, Robert Warmwell, William Warwick, Richard Ecton, John Swift, and the clerk

25 August 1434, at Salisbury
2678 Approval of the will of Thomas Farrant, a citizen of Salisbury, made on 23 March 1433. Interment: in the graveyard of St. Edmund's church. Bequests: 12*d.* to the provost of that church; 12*d.* to the fabric of the cathedral church; 2*s. 6d.* to John Oakington, a chaplain; 20*d.* to William Goodacre, his kinsman; the rest of his goods to his wife Joan. Devise: to Joan a tenement, in which he dwelt, in Castle Street, between William Lord's tenement on the north side and a tenement of late Thomas Beeton's on the south side, to be held for ever by her and her heirs and assigns. Executor: his wife Joan, to dispose of his goods for the salvation of his soul. Proved on 13 August 1434 in front of John Pedwell, the subdean; the administration was entrusted to the executor, who afterwards accounted with an officer and was dismissed. Approved at a court held in front of the bailiff, the mayor, and other citizens; the seisin of the tenement was released to the legatee.
2679 By their indented charter Henry Man and John Bromley, citizens of Salisbury, granted to John Adkin, dyer, of Salisbury, and his wife Edith a corner

tenement, with shops and cottages, in Winchester Street [and Brown Street: *cf.* **2677**] between Laurence Goodwin's tenement on the south side and a tenement of Richard Forster, of Bristol, on the west side. The tenement is to be held for ever by John and Edith and their heirs and assigns on condition that, if they would pay £10 to Henry and John, or to their attorney, on the following 24 June, the charter would stand in its validity and effect. If, on 24 June, John and Edith were to fail to pay the £10 Henry and John and their heirs and assigns might enter on the tenement, take back possession, and keep their former estate. Clause of warranty. Seals: those of the parties to the parts of the charter in turn and the common and mayoral seals of the city. Named witnesses: the bailiff, the mayor, the coroners, the reeves, John Fadder, then the alderman of St. Martin, Robert Warmwell, John Swift, William Warwick, William Packing, Richard Gater, Henry Baron, Stephen Mercer, and the clerk

BOOK 7

(WSA 23/1/215)

31 October 1408, at Heytesbury

2680 By her charter Sibyl Baynton, a daughter and heir of William Bowtest and his wife Clarice, a sister and heir of the master William Heytesbury, in her chaste and perpetual widowhood granted to John Malet and Robert Leverage her land and tenements, houses, gardens, messuages, cottages, yards, tofts, arable land, meadows, pastures, feeding rights, commons, closes, hedges, ditches, waters, ways, footpaths, rent, services, and reversions which must fall to her by right of inheritance in the vills and fields of Heytesbury, Sutton Veny, and Newnham, or elsewhere in Wiltshire, to be held for ever by them and their heirs and assigns. Clause of warranty. Seal: Sibyl's. Named witnesses: Walter Hungerford, kt., Ralph Green, the lord of Warminster, Peter Stantor, John Rous, of Imber, John Osborne, Walter Park, Robert Backham, John Andrew, and Amaury Thurston

3 March 1409, at Heytesbury

2681 By their charter John Malet and Robert Leverage granted to Sibyl Baynton and to her son Thomas and his wife Edith land and tenements, which they held by Sibyl's grant, in the vills and fields of Heytesbury, Sutton Veny, and Newnham, or elsewhere in Wiltshire, to be held for ever by them and the heirs and assigns of Thomas and Edith. Seals: those of John and Robert. Named witnesses: William Cheyne, kt., Ralph Green, the lord of Warminster, John Rous, of Imber, Peter Stantor, John Osborne, Walter Park, Robert Backham, John Andrew, and Richard Kember

15 October 1427, at Salisbury

2682 By his charter Robert Netton, a chaplain, granted to John Ford, William Lord, and William Penton a cottage, with a garden, in Gigant Street between William Stout's cottage property on the north side and John Teffont's cottages on

the south side. The cottage, with another cottage of William Stout, by the name
of a tenement, was held by Richard Stout, of Bulford, now dead, and Robert by
William's grant and, with the garden, is to be held for ever by John Ford, William
Lord, and William Penton and by John's heirs and assigns. Seals: Robert's and the
common and mayoral seals of the city. Named witnesses: the bailiff, the mayor,
the coroners, the reeves, William Warin, Henry Man, John Swift, John Bromley,
William Warwick, and John Marshall

16 October 1427, at Salisbury
2683 By his writing William Stout, of Salisbury, quitclaimed to John Ford,
William Lord, and William Penton and John's heirs and assigns his right or claim
to a cottage, with a garden, in Gigant Street [*as in 2682*]. Clause of warranty. Seals:
William Stout's and the common and mayoral seals of the city. Named witnesses:
the bailiff, the mayor, the coroners, the reeves, William Warin, Thomas Mason,
Robert Warmwell, Henry Man, John Swift, John Bromley, and John Marshall
A second copy of that witing, without the clause of warranty, immediately
follows the first

8 October 1432, at Salisbury
2684 By his writing an elder William Lord, of Salisbury, quitclaimed to John
Fowey, of Up Sydling, and his wife Alice, a sister, as it is said, and heir of John
Ford, of late an attorney in the king's court of Common Bench, and to Alice's
heirs and assigns his right or claim to a tenement in Gigant Street between
William Stout's tenement on the north side and John Teffont's cottages on the
south side. Seals: William Lord's and the common and mayoral seals of the city.
Named witnesses: the bailiff, the mayor, the coroners, the reeves, William Warin,
Robert Warmwell, John Swift, John Noble, John Bromley, William Packing,
Richard Gater, Henry Baron, and the clerk
2685 By their charter John Fowey, of Up Sydling, and his wife Alice, appearing
in court on that day, granted to an elder William Lord, of Salisbury, and Henry
Brice, of Britford, a tenement in Gigant Street, [*as in 2684*], to be held for ever
by William and Henry and their heirs and assigns. Clause of warranty perfected
by John and Alice in respect of themselves and Alice's heirs and assigns. Seals:
those of John and Alice and the common and mayoral seals of the city. Named
witnesses: the bailiff, the mayor, the coroners, the reeves, William Warin, Robert
Warmwell, John Swift, John Noble, John Bromley, William Packing, Richard
Gater, Henry Baron, and William Warwick

22 October 1432, at Salisbury
2686 By their charter an elder William Lord, of Salisbury, and Henry Brice,
of Britford, granted to John Fowey, of Up Sydling, and his wife Alice and to
Christine, the relict of William Penton, a tenement in Gigant Street, [*as in 2684*],
to be held for ever by them and Alice's heirs and assigns. Seals: those of William
and Henry and the common and mayoral seals of the city. Named witnesses: the
bailiff, the mayor, the coroners, the reeves, William Warin, Robert Warmwell,

John Swift, William Warwick, John Noble, John Bromley, William Packing, Richard Gater, and Henry Baron

24 October 1439, at Salisbury
2687 By his charter Warter of London, skinner, granted to John Edmund, otherwise called Young, husbandman, of West Harnham, and his wife Tamsin a garden in Drake Hall Street between a tenement of late John Hemby's on the north side and a garden of late John Popham's on the south side. The garden, with other land and tenements, was held by Warter by a feoffment of John Bromley and William Swayne, of Salisbury, and is to be held for ever by John and Tamsin and their heirs and assigns. Seals: that of Warter and the common and mayoral seals of the city. Named witnesses: the bailiff, the mayor, the coroners, the reeves, William Warin, Robert Warmwell, Thomas Freeman, and Stephen Cooper, mercer

after 2 August 1441
2688 The will of Henry Chubb, a baker, of Salisbury, made on 28 June 1441. Interment: in the graveyard of the cathedral church, in front of the west door. Bequests: a silver-plated crescent to the fabric of that church; 20*d.* to the fabric of St. Thomas's church, 20*d.* to the high altar for his forgotten tithes, 6*d.* to each chaplain celebrating mass in that church, 4*d.* to the deacon, and 2*s.* 6*d.* to John Green, the parochial chaplain; 2*s.* 6*d.* to the lord Thomas Still; 20*s.* and a lined gown, coloured blue, with a hood to John Hill, baker, his apprentice, having completed his years; 6*s.* 8*d.* to the friar Henry Wake, of Ilchester; 6*s.* 8*d.* to Joan Bloxwich, a nun of Wilton; the rest of his goods to his wife Agnes to pray for his soul. Devise: Agnes and her assigns should hold for her life three conjoined tenements, beside the lower bridge of the city which leads towards Fisherton, between John Gower's tenement on the east side and John Upton's tenement on the west side, according to the terms of a charter perfected by Margaret Godmanstone for him and Agnes and his assigns. On Agnes's death the tenements should remain to Richard Still, cook, and his wife Agnes, Henry's daughter, and their joint issue, and if Richard and Agnes were to die without such issue, which God forbid, the tenements would revert to the nearest direct heirs of Henry's blood to be sold. The money received from the sale should be laid out by such heirs, on charitable deeds, for the salvation of Henry's soul, the soul of his wife Agnes, the souls of Richard Still and his wife Agnes, and the souls of others. Executor: his wife Agnes; overseer, Richard Still. Proved on 2 August 1441 in front of John Pedwell, the subdean; the administration was entrusted to Agnes, who accounted with an officer and was dismissed.

29 September 1447, at Salisbury
2689 By his charter William Fowey, of Up Sydling, Dorset, granted to Richard Cocklet, weaver, of Salisbury, a tenement in Gigant Street, between a tenement of late William Stout's on the north side and a cottage of late John Teffont's on the south side, to be held for ever by him and his heirs and assigns. Clause of warranty.

Seals: William's and the common and mayoral seals of the city. Named witnesses: the bailiff, the mayor, the coroners, the reeves, William Swayne, William Hoare, Richard Pain, John Wyatt, and Simon Poy

2 October 1447, at Salisbury
2690 By his writing John Fowey, of Up Sydling, Dorset, quitclaimed to Richard Cocklet, weaver, of Salisbury, and his heirs and assigns his right or claim to a tenement in Gigant Street, [*as in* **2689**]. The tenement is to be held for ever by Richard and his heirs and assigns. Clause of warranty. Seals: John's and the common and mayoral seals of the city. Named witnesses: the bailiff, the mayor, the coroners, the reeves, William Swayne, William Hoare, Richard Pain, John Wyatt, and Simon Poy

5 October 1447, at Salisbury
2691 By his writing William Hill, a chaplain, a kinsman and heir of Alice, the relict of an elder John Fowey, quitclaimed to Richard Cocklet, weaver, of Salisbury, and his heirs and assigns his right or claim to a tenement in Gigant Street, [*as in* **2689**]. The tenement is to be held for ever by Richard and his heirs and assigns. Clause of warranty. Seals: William's and the common and mayoral seals of the city. Named witnesses: the bailiff, the mayor, the coroners, the reeves, William Swayne, William Hoare, Richard Pain, John Wyatt, and Simon Poy

5 December 1449, at Salisbury
2692 By their indented charter Thomas Hussey, esq., of Dorset, and his wife Isabel granted to Robert Metgyff, baker, of Salisbury, and his wife Margaret conjoined tenements in Castle Street, which is called Minster Street, between a tenement of late William Lord's, now John Man's on the south side and a tenement formerly that of John Marshall, dyer, now that of John Wise, vintner, on the north side. The tenements are to be held for ever by Robert and Margaret and their heirs and assigns on condition that they would pay 55 marks to Thomas and Isabel, that is £12 4s. 5d. on 13 January in each of the years 1451–3. Clause to permit permanent repossession if Robert and Margaret and their heirs were to fail to make a payment. Clause of warranty. Seals: those of Thomas and Isabel to the part of the charter remaining in the possession of Robert and Margaret, those of Robert and Margaret to the part remaining in the possession of Thomas and Isabel, and the common and mayoral seals of the city. Named witnesses: the bailiff, the mayor, the coroners, the reeves, William Swayne, William Hoare, John Port, John Wyatt, and Simon Poy

25 March 1450, at Salisbury
2693 By his charter John Hobbs, a clerk, a son and heir of John Hobbs, brewer, of late of Salisbury, and his wife Cecily, granted to Thomas Leaker, tanner, of Salisbury, the reversion of a tenement in St. Martin's Street between a tenement of the provost of St. Edmund's church on the east side and a tenement of the vicars of the cathedral church on the west side. The tenement was held by the elder

John and Cecily by a grant and devise of William Bower, was held by John in his demesne as of fee at his death, descended to the younger John on the elder John's death, and is held for life as dower by the elder John's relict Isabel. The reversion, when it fell due on Isabel's death, is to be held for ever by Thomas and his heirs and assigns. Clause of warranty. Seals: John Hobbs's and the common and mayoral seals of the city. Named witnesses: the bailiff, the mayor, the coroners, the reeves, William Swayne, William Hoare, Richard Pain, John Wyatt, and Simon Poy

5 December 1451, at Salisbury
2694 By his deed William Parchment quitclaimed to William Wreath and his wife Alice and William's heirs and assigns his right or claim to a corner tenement in Castle Street and Scots Lane between a tenement of late Walter Hind's on the south side and Robert Linden's tenement on the east side. Seals: William Parchment's and the mayoral seal of the city. Named witnesses: the bailiff, the mayor, a coroner, William Swayne, John Port, and William Cormell

after 16 August 1453
2695 The will of William Wreath, of Salisbury, made on 15 April 1453. Interment: in the chapel of St. John the Baptist in St. Edmund's church, on the way from the vestry to the high altar. Bequests: 20*d.* to the fabric of the cathedral church; 6*s.* 8*d.* to the fabric of St. Edmund's church; 3*s.* 4*d.* both to the Dominicans of Fisherton and the Franciscans of Salisbury; the rest of his goods to his wife Alice. Devise: his land and tenement(s) in Castle Street [*cf.* **2694**] to Alice for life. William appointed those premises to remain on Alice's death to an elder John Page and his wife Joan for their life and the life of the one of them living longer, on the death of John and Joan to their daughter Alice and her issue, if that Alice were to die without issue, which God forbid, on her death to John, a son of John and Joan, and his issue, and if that John were to die without issue, which God forbid, on his death to be sold by his own executors or their executors. The money received from the sale should be laid out on pious uses. Executors: his wife Alice and John Pyville, the provost of the collegiate church of St. Edmund; overseer, Nicholas Shute. Proved: on 12 June 1453 in front of the subdean; the administration was entrusted to Alice, who appeared, accounted with an office, and was dismissed on 16 August 1453.

6 October 1455, at Salisbury
2696 By his charter Richard Still, cook, of Salisbury, granted to William Hunt and his wife Idony three conjoined tenements, beside the lower bridge of the city which leads to Fisherton, between a tenement of Edith, the relict of John Gower, on the east side and John Upton's tenement on the west side, to be held by them and their heirs and assigns. Clause of warranty. Seal: Richard's. Named witnesses: the mayor, William Lightfoot, Robert Newman, John Thursby, and John Wright

21 July 1456, at Salisbury
2697 By his charter William Swayne, a citizen of Salisbury, granted to William

Bedwell and his wife Agnes two tenements in Castle Street, beyond the bars, between a tenement of John Shipton, dubber, on the south side and a tenement of John Mowe, a clerk of the bishop, of late William Warin's, on the north side. The tenements, among others, were bought by William Swayne from Idony, the relict of Robert Ogbourne, and John Newbury, Robert's executors, and they are to be held for ever by William Bedwell and Agnes and that William's heirs and assigns. Clause of warranty. Seals: William Swayne's and, because his seal is unknown to many, the common and mayoral seals of the city. Named witnesses: the mayor, the bailiff, a coroner, the reeves, John Wyatt, William Hoare, William Cormell, and the clerk

20 September 1458, at Salisbury
2698 By his indented deed John Ashford, a tailor, a citizen of Salisbury, granted to the keepers of the commonalty of the guild of St. John the Baptist in the city, and their successors, two tenements in Minster Street, otherwise called Castle Street, beside the new gate, between William Lord's tenement on the south side and a ditch of running water on the north side, which he bought from Nicholas Shute, an executor of Edith Fewster. John also granted to those keepers the reversion of a corner tenement, called Lockyer's Corner, with shops, when it fell due on the death of Cecily, the wife of Henry Friend; the tenement stands in Endless Street, between a tenement of late Edward Frith's on the south side and the street which leads to St. Edmund's church on the north side, and was bought from John Eastbury, of late an executor of Richard Shirley, a son and heir of Walter Shirley, of late a citizen of Salisbury. The two tenements and the reversion are to be held for ever by the keepers and their successors on the following terms and conditions. From immediately after John's death the keepers and their successors should hold an anniversary mass yearly and for ever on 12 April in St. Edmund's church for 10s. cash issuing from the profits of the tenements. The 10s. should be laid out as follows: 2s. 2d. to the priests of that church celebrating mass in the night of the day of his funeral to say and chant placebo, dirge, and mass, and being present to celebrate mass on the morrow, if all the priests should happen to be present in the church at the high mass on the day of the anniversary mass, 2s. on bread, 2s. on ale, 16d. on wine, 12d. on cheese, 4d. on ringing the great bell, 2d. to beadsmen on behalf of the souls mentioned above [?*rectius* below], 6d. to the keepers of the guild for their work, and 6d. to the paupers of the charity of the fraternity of the tailors present in that church on that day in that month to pray for the soul of John Conge, of late the provost of that church, the souls of John Ashford and his wives Joan and Christine, Thomas Whiting and his wife Edith, the souls of the brothers and sisters of the guild of St. John the Baptist, and the souls of others. If the keepers and their successors were to fail to do those things the provost of St. Edmund's church and his successors might distrain in the tenements and keep distresses until the keepers held the anniversary mass yearly to pray for the souls mentioned above in the way described above. Clause of warranty. Seals: John's to the part of the deed remaining in the possession of the keepers and, because his seal is unknown to many, the common and mayoral

seals of the city, and the common seal of the guild to the part remaining in the possession of the provost. Named witnesses: the bailiff, the mayor, a coroner, the reeves, William Swayne, John Hall, John Port, William Hoare, and the clerk

22 November 1458

2699 By her writing Joan Pain, a daughter and heir of Richard Pain, and an executor of Alice Pain, her mother, who was an executor of Richard, quitclaimed to Hugh FitzRichard every kind of personal action which she could have against him. Seals: Joan's and, because her seal is unknown to many, the mayoral seal of the city

11 June 1459, at Plaitford

2700 By his charter John Uphill, otherwise called Carlidon, granted to John Stourton, the lord of Stourton, and Thomas Bagot all his land, tenements, meadows, pastures, feding rights, and woodland in the vill and fields of Plaitford, called Ruddock, to be held for ever by them and Thomas's heirs and assigns. Clause of warranty. Seals: John's and, because his seal is unknown to many, the mayoral seal of Salisbury. Named witnesses: Maurice Berkeley, kt., Thomas Ringwood, Walter at the barrow, Simon Milbourne, esq., and John Estcourt

12 June 1459, at Salisbury

2701 By their charter John Bodington, salmonmonger, of Salisbury, and his wife Evelyn granted to William Jones, otherwise called Taverner, of Salisbury, a tenement, in the street called Chipper Lane, between a tenement of Robert Gilbert, gent., on the west side and a tenement of late John Chitterne's, now that of John Wylye, draper, on the east side, to be held for ever by him and his heirs and assigns. Clause of warranty. Seals: those of John and Evelyn and, because their seals are unknown to many, the common and mayoral seals of the city. Named witnesses: the mayor, the bailiff, a coroner, the reeves, an elder William Hoare, John Wise, draper, John Wylye, draper, and the clerk

24 July 1459, at Salisbury

2702 By his indented deed William Swayne, a merchant, a citizen of Salisbury, granted to Henry Swayne and his wife Catherine three conjoined tenements, with shops, in Minster Street, which is called Castle Street, between a tenement of late William Warwick's, now that of his chantry, called the Cage, on the north side, a tenement of late that of John Justice, of Calne, now John Chaffin's, on the south side, and the river Avon on the west side. The tenements, with the shops, are to be held for ever by Henry and Catherine and their joint issue paying a rent of £10 a year to William for his life. All the utensils in Robert Pett's house, called Dyeing House, in which Robert dwells, part of the tenements, the ovens, cisterns, 'odefats', troughs, 'shetis', and all the other things there appurtenant to Robert's house, are reserved to William for his life; also the utensils in the bakehouse, in which William Hawkin, a baker, dwells at the will of William, are reserved to William for his life. If Henry and Catherine were to die without joint issue William appointed that the tenements, with the shops, would revert for ever to him and his heirs and assigns. Clause to permit William, in his lifetime, if the rent were to be in arrear for a month, to enter on the tenements, with the shops, distrain, and keep distresses until the unpaid rent and other losses were recovered; also, to permit permanent repossession if the rent were to be in arrear for six weeks and sufficient distresses could not be found. Clause of warranty. On Catherine's death the tenements, with the shops, should be charged, with other land and tenements appointed by William for the purpose, with a rent, as he wished, for the maintenance of a perpetual chaplain to pray every day for ever in the chapel of the Blessed Mary in St. Thomas's church for the good condition of William and his wife Christine while they lived, for their souls when they were dead, and for the souls of others. Seals: William's to the part of the deed remaining in the possession of Henry and Catherine, those of Henry and Catherine to the part remaining in William's possession, and the common and mayoral seals of the city. Named witnesses: the mayor, the bailiff, a coroner, the reeves, William Hoare, John Hall, William Lightfoot, John Wheeler, and the clerk

14 September 1459, at Winchester
2703 Letters patent of Henry VI. *The king has been informed that some of his subjects in various parts of his realm have stirred up unlawful assemblies and associations by way of rebellion and, in contempt of him and in breach of his peace, daily continue to do so. Contrary to the terms of proclamations and prohibitions often made those men will disturb the whole realm, and all the people of it, unless they are quickly stopped. The king, unwilling to endure such riots, assemblies, and associations, and wishing both to restrain those rashly attempting such things and to punish them according to their faults, appointed his kinsman James [Butler], earl of Wiltshire, as his liegeman of that county, trusting in the earl's fealty and wisdom. The earl is required to muster, arm, and equip as many men as he might think fit, of whatever estate, degree, and status they might be, and, whenever it might be necessary, to proceed with them to repress the rebels and unlawful assemblies. The king gave him full power to lead and command such liegemen. The king, moreover, ordered the sheriff of Wiltshire and all the mayors, bailiffs, constables, and other officers and liegemen of the county to obey the orders given to them by the earl in those matters, on pain of their allegiance.* [*Heading:* this commission was received on 19 September 1459]

5 November 1459
2704 By her letters of attorney Alice Freeman, a widow, the relict of Walter Freeman, merchant, of late of Salisbury, and a daughter and heir of Robert Oliver, esq., of Middlesex, appointed Thomas Freeman, merchant, of Salisbury, and Richard Freeman, merchant, of Salisbury, to manage her place called Oliver's Place, and all the land and tenements appurtenant to it, in Sandon, Hertfordshire, together with all the land and tenements in Middlesex, Berkshire, and Hertfordshire which fell to her by right of inheritance on Robert's death; with full power and a special mandate to let the premises at farm, to collect the rent and money owed to her from them, to distrain on them if it were necessary, to expel the farmers and tenants if it were necessary, to put in new ones, to reach,

seal, and determine acquittances in her place and name, and to do everything else necessary in those premises. Seals: Alice's and, because her seal was unknown to many, the mayoral seal of Salisbury

20 April 1460
2705 A deed of Henry Wigmore, a clerk. By his charter William Alexander, of late the lord of Thornton, Dorset, granted to Henry and to Walter Messenger, now dead, land, tenements, meadows, pastures, feeding rights, rent, services, and reversions in Shipton Bellinger (*Benger*), in Hampshire, and in Farley, Winterslow, Porton, Winterbourne Gunner, Winterbourne Ford, and Winterbourne Cherburgh, with the advowson of Winterbourne Cherburgh church. By his deed Henry confirmed to Thomas Hussey, esq., and his wife Isabel, the relict of William Alexander, the estate which they hold in that land and those tenements *etc.* and in the advowson, and he quitclaimed his right or claim to them to Thomas and Isabel and Isabel's heirs and assigns. Seals: Henry's and the mayoral seal of Salisbury. Named witnesses: William Stourton, kt., John Baynton, kt., Simon Milbourne, Edmund Ashley, and Walter [at the] barrow

14 June 1460, at Salisbury
2706 By his charter John Salman granted to William Jones, otherwise Taverner, merchant, of Salisbury, and his wife Joan a messuage, near the graveyard of St. Thomas's church, between a tenement of late William Lord's, now William Swayne's, on the south side and a tenement of late Edward Potticary's, now that of Richard Wise, mercer, on the north side. The messuage was held by John by a devise of Richard Gater, of late a citizen of Winchester, and is to be held for ever by William and Joan and their heirs and assigns. Clause of warranty. Seals: John's and, because his seal is unknown to many, the common and mayoral seals of the city. Named witnesses: the mayor, the bailiff, a coroner, William Swayne, John Wise, draper, John Chippenham, and Roger Buckbridge

19 October 1461, at Salisbury
2707 By his charter John Greening, a chaplain, a son and heir of William Greening, weaver, of late of Salisbury, granted to William Bedwell and his wife Agnes four tenements, with gardens, in Castle Street, outside the new gate. Two of the tenements stand conjoined, on the east side of the street, between Denise Dix's tenement on the south side and William Ludlow's tenement on the north side. The other two stand conjoined, on the west side of the street, between a tenement of late William Knolle's on the south side and John Hood's tenement on the north side. The four, with the gardens, are to be held for ever by William and Agnes and their heirs and assigns. Clause of warranty. Seals: John Greening's and, because his seal is unknown to many, the mayoral and common seals of the city. Named witnesses: the mayor, the bailiff, a coroner, the reeves, William Swayne, John Port, Simon Poy, Thomas Whiting, and Edmund Penstone
2708 By their deed John Winterbourne and his wife Agnes, a daughter of William Greening, weaver, of late of Salisbury, John Winterbourne and Agnes

Winterbourne, a son and a daughter of John and Agnes, and William Wilkin and his wife Alice, another daughter of John and Agnes, quitclaimed to William Bedwell and his wife Agnes and their heirs and assigns their right or claim to four tenements, with gardens, in Castle Street, outside the new gate. Two of the tenements stand conjoined on the east side of the street [*as in 2707*]. The other two stand conjoined on the west side of the street [*as in 2707*]. Seals: those of the men and women who quitclaimed and, because their seals are unknown to many, the mayoral and common seals of the city. Named witnesses: the mayor, the bailiff, a coroner, the reeves, William Swayne, John Port, Simon Poy, Thomas Whiting, and Edmund Penstone

24 February 1462

2709 A deed of William Swayne, a citizen of Salisbury, and Robert Saucer, gent. By his deed dated at Salisbury on 3 December 1455 John Wylye, draper, a citizen of Salisbury, granted to William and Robert, with other land and tenements, a tenement, with sollars, near the graveyard of St. Thomas's church, between a tenement of late that of Richard Milbourne, esq., on the north side and a tenement of late Robert Warmwell's, formerly William Godmanstone's, on the south side. John held the tenement, among other land and tenements, by a feoffment of Robert Warmwell, and it was to be held for ever by William and Robert and their heirs and assigns. By their deed William and Robert, on the strength of that deed granted the tenement to John Cranborne, William Mitchell, John Wallop, John Martin, John Cook, John Hughson, and Thomas Stephenson, clerks, to be held for ever by them and their heirs and assigns. Seals: those of William and Robert and the common and mayoral seals of the city and, for greater proof, John Wylye's. Named witnesses: the mayor, the bailiff, a coroner, the reeves, Philip Morgan, John Hall, William Hoare, Simon Poy, and the clerk

27 February 1462

2710 By his writing John Wylye, draper, a citizen of Salisbury, quitclaimed to John Cranborne, William Mitchell, John Wallop, John Martin, John Cook, John Hughson, and Thomas Stephenson, clerks, his right or claim to a tenement, with sollars, near the graveyard of St. Thomas's church, [*as in 2709*]. John Wylye of late held the tenement, with other land and tenements, by a feoffment of Robert Warmwell. Seals: John Wylye's and the common and mayoral seals of the city

13 April 1462, at Salisbury

2711 By their charter John Christmas and his wife Christine granted to William Jones, otherwise called William Taverner, a tenement in Endless Street, in which Robert Russell, weaver, dwells, between a tenement of late Gilbert Marshall's on the north side and a tenement of late Robert Chinchin's, now William's, on the south side, to be held for ever by him and his heirs and assigns. Clause of warranty. Seals: those of John and Christine and, because their seals are unknown to many, the mayoral and common seals of the city. Named witnesses: the mayor, the bailiff, a coroner, the reeves, Thomas Freeman, Simon Poy, Thomas Whiting, and the clerk

18 December 1462, at Salisbury

2712 A charter of John Bodington, salmonmonger, of Salisbury, and his wife Evelyn, executors of Thomas Pain, of late of Salisbury, a son and heir of Thomas Pain, weaver, of late of Salisbury, and his wife Edith. The younger Thomas devised to John and Evelyn a tenement, in which the elder Thomas and Edith of late dwelt, in Chipper Street, between a tenement formerly John Collingbourne's on the west side and a tenement of late Edward Doll's on the east side, to be held for ever by them and their heirs and assigns. By their charter John and Evelyn, on the strength of the younger Thomas's will, granted the tenement to William Jones, otherwise called William Taverner, a citizen of Salisbury, to be held for ever by him and his heirs and assigns. Clause of warranty. Seals: those of John and Evelyn and, because their seals are unknown to many, the common and mayoral seals of the city. Named witnesses: the mayor, the bailiff, a coroner, the reeves, an elder William Hoare, William Swayne, Simon Poy, and the clerk

9 June 1463, at Salisbury

2713 By their deed Richard Spershore, saddler, of Salisbury, and his wife Agnes quitclaimed to Agnes Walsh, a widow, the relict of John Walsh, and her heirs and assigns a tenement, with an adjacent garden, in Mealmonger Street between Edward Alexander's tenement on the north side and a tenement of John Mowe, gent., on the south side. Clause of warranty. Seals: those of Richard and his wife Agnes and, because their seals are unknown to many, the common and mayoral seals of the city. Named witnesses: the mayor, the bailiff, a coroner, the reeves, an elder William Hoare, Simon Poy, John Wheeler, William Wootton, and the clerk

28 June 1464, at Salisbury

2714 By his charter Richard Pile, a son and heir of Robert Pile, a weaver, of late of Salisbury, granted to John Ludlow, Edmund Penstone, John Chaffin, and John Hampton a messuage, with an adjacent garden, in Endless Street between a tenement of late Richard Gage's, now that of the guild of the weavers of Salisbury, on the north side and a tenement of Thomas Gowan, esq., on the south side. The messuage, with the garden, descended to Richard Pile on the death of his father and is to be held for ever by the grantees and their heirs and assigns. Clause of warranty. Seals: Richard's and, because his seal is unknown to many, the mayoral seal of the city. Named witnesses: the mayor, Thomas Freeman, an elder William Hoare, John Port, and John Wylye

10 August 1464

2715 A deed of William Wootton, the mayor of Salisbury, and the commonalty of the city. Richard [?Mitford], of late the bishop of Salisbury, with the assent of the dean and chapter, granted to two chaplains a toft which, a parcel of the bishop's mills, extends from the graveyard of St. Thomas's church as far as the pond of the mills. The chaplains were to celebrate mass every day in St. Thomas's church on behalf of the soul of Robert Godmanstone, of late of Salisbury, and the souls of others, on the terms of the ordination of the chantry, and they have no land or tenement in the city for their own use because the toft is not part of the city. By their deed the mayor and the commonalty therefore exonerate for ever Richard White and William Oak, the chaplains of the chantry, and their successors, celebrating mass in that church, from all offices appurtenant to the city by virtue of that grant of the toft. Seals: the common and mayoral seals of the city

1 July 1465, at Salisbury

2716 By their deed William Keynell, William Palmer, Robert Honeycode, and Thomas Watts quitclaimed to John Watts, a son and heir of Robert Watts, now dead, of late of Chapmanslade, their right or claim to the land and tenements in Salisbury which they held, with other land and tenements in Devon, Somerset, and Wiltshire, by John's grant. Seals: those of the four who quitclaimed and the common and mayoral seals of the city. Named witnesses: the mayor, the bailiff, the coroners, John Wylye, draper, John Chaffin, William Buckett, William Easton, and John Chippenham

after 28 September 1465

2717 A copy, under the mayoral seal of the city, of the will of John Canford made on 25 July 1465. <u>Interment</u>: in the church of the Franciscans of Salisbury, in the holy tomb. <u>Bequests</u>: 6*d.* to the fabric of the cathedral church; 6*d.* to the fabric of St. Thomas's church, 12*d.* to the high altar for his forgotten tithes, and 6*d.* to the fraternity of Jesus; 3*s.* 4*d.* to the Franciscans of Salisbury; the rest of his goods to his wife Joan. <u>Devises</u>: he appointed his messuage in Brown Street, with a garden, to be sold by the hand of John Mowe. Of the money issuing from the sale 100*s.* should be handed to the Franciscan friars of Salisbury to pray for the souls of William Oving, chandler, and his wife Alice, John's soul, and the souls of others; the rest should be given to his wife Joan. <u>Executor</u> Joan; overseers, Richard Gilbert and Richard Charity. <u>Witnesses</u>: Richard Bruin, the parochial chaplain of St. Thomas's church, William Wastell, Hugh Bennett, and many others. <u>Proved</u> on 28 September 1465 in front of William Nessingwick, the subdean; the administration was entrusted to the executor, who at length [accounted] with an office and was dismised.

20 July 1466

2718 A deed of John Farley, gent., of Stockton. By his deed dated 22 July 1440 John Alexander, a son and heir of William Alexander and his wife Edith, a daughter and heir of John Beer, esq., confirmed to William the estate which William held in the manors of Thornton and Little Kington, Dorset, and in the advowson of the church of Studland on Purbeck and of the chapel of Thornton, Dorset. The manors and advowsons were to be held for ever by William and his heirs. By his deed John Farley, a kinsman and heir of William Alexander, being the son of William's sister Margaret, confirmed to an elder Thomas Hussey, esq., and his wife Isabel the estate which they hold in the advowson of Studland church, and he quitclaimed his right or claim to it to them and their heirs and assigns. Clause of warranty. Seals: John Farley's and the mayoral seal of the city of Salisbury

2 November 1466, at Salisbury
2719 By his charter Richard Haynes, esq., granted to William Jones, otherwise Taverner, and his wife Joan two conjoined tenements, with gardens, in Scots Lane, on the north side of the street, between William's tenement on the east side and a tenement of William Watts and his wife Christine on the west side; also five conjoined cottages, with gardens, in Mealmonger Street, on the east side of the street, between cottages of John Wise, vintner, on the north side and Edward Bowyer's cottage property on the south side. The tenements and the cottages, with the gardens, are to be held for ever by William and Joan and their heirs and assigns. Clause of warranty. Seals: Richard's and, because his seal is unknown to many, the common and mayoral seals of the city. Named witnesses: the mayor, the bailiff, a coroner, an elder William Hoare, John Wise, draper, Edmund Penstone, and Andrew Brant

5 November 1466, at Salisbury
2720 By his deed Richard Haynes, esq., quitclaimed to William Jones, otherwise Taverner, and his wife Joan and their heirs and assigns his right or claim to two conjoined tenements, with gardens, in Scots Lane, [*as in* **2719**]; also his right or claim to five conjoined cottages, with gardens, in Mealmonger Street, [*as in* **2719**]. Clause of warranty. Seals: Richard's and, because his seal is unknown to many, the common and mayoral seals of the city. Named witnesses: the mayor, the bailiff, a coroner, an elder William Hoare, John Wise, draper, Edmund Penstone, and John Wise, vintner

4 March 1467, at Salisbury
2721 By his indented charter Henry Friend, a citizen of Salisbury, granted to John Pettifer, a merchant, of Sherborne, Dorset, a tenement, with a yard (*or* yards), in New Street between a cottage of late Robert Ashley's, now that of Edmund Ashley, esq., on the east side and cottage property of late John Ladd's, now that of John Coof, weaver, on the west side. The tenement, with the yard(s), is to be held for ever by John and his heirs and assigns on condition that, if he or they were to pay to Henry or his executors or assigns 33s. 4d. on 29 September 1467 and thereafter 33s. 4d. quarterly until £43 6s. 8d. had been paid, the charter would keep its validity and effect. Clause to permit permanent repossession if within 30 days after any term John or his heirs or assigns were to fail to make a payment. Clause of warranty. Seals: Henry's to the part of the charter remaining in John's possession, John's to the part remaining in Henry's possession, and, because their seals are unknown to many, the common and mayoral seals of the city. Named witnesses: the mayor, the bailiff, a coroner, an elder William Hoare, William Swayne, and Edmund Penstone

3 June 1467, at Salisbury

2722 By their charter John Sheriff, mercer, of Salisbury, and his wife Margaret, the relict of Robert Metgyff, baker, of late of Salisbury, granted to William Jones, otherwise Taverner, merchant, and John Gardener, clothmaker, citizens of Salisbury, their land and conjoined tenements in Castle Street, which is called Minster Street, between a tenement of late William Lord's, afterwards John Man's, now William Lord's, on the south side and a tenement formerly that of John Marshall, dyer, now that of John Wise, vintner, on the north side. The land and tenements were held by Margaret, together with Robert, by a grant of Thomas Hussey, esq., of Dorset, and his wife Isabel, and they are to be held for ever by William Jones and John Gardener and their heirs and assigns. Clause of warranty. Seals: those of John Sheriff and Margaret and, because their seals are unknown to many, the common and mayoral seals of the city. Named witnesses: the mayor, the bailiff, a coroner, John Hall, John Wise, draper, and John Wise, vintner

5 June 1467, at Salisbury

2723 By their charter William Jones, otherwise Taverner, merchant, and John Gardener, clothmaker, citizens of Salisbury, granted to John Sheriff, mercer, of Salisbury, and his wife Margaret their land and conjoined tenements in Castle Street, which is called Minster Street, [*as in* **2722**]. The land and tenements were held jointly by William and John by a grant of John and Margaret and are to be held for ever by John and Margaret and their heirs and assigns. Seals: those of the grantors and, because their seals are unknown to many, the common and mayoral seals of the city. Named witnesses: the mayor, the bailiff, a coroner, John Wise, draper, Edmund Penstone, John Wise, vintner, and Andrew Brant

8 June 1467, at Salisbury

2724 By his charter a younger William Hoare, grocer, of Salisbury, granted to William March, tailor, of Salisbury, a tenement, with gardens and racks built in it, in St. Edmund's Street between a garden of the provost of St. Edmund's church on the south side and a garden of late Alice Pain's on the north side; also two conjoined tenements, with a garden, in the street called Rolleston between a tenement of late Henry Man's, now John Frank's, on the north side and a tenement of the provost of that church on the south side. The tenements, with the gardens and racks, are to be held for ever by William and his heirs and assigns. Clause of warranty. Seals: William Hoare's and the common and mayoral seals of the city. Named witnesses: the bailiff, the mayor, Thomas Freeman, John Wise, draper, John Wylye, Edmund Penstone, and John Mowe

22 June 1467, at Salisbury

2725 By their charter an elder Thomas Hussey, esq., of Dorset, and his wife Isabel granted to William Carent, esq., John Newborough, esq., Nicholas Kimmer, John Hussey, the master Ellis Hussey, Henry Wigmore, a clerk, John Messenger, a clerk, and Edmund Penstone all their land, and tenements, shops, gardens, rent, services, and reversions, in Salisbury; also their land, and tenements, meadows, pastures, feeding rights, woods, rent, services, and reversions, in Winterbourne Cherburgh, Winterbourne Gunner, Porton, Winterslow, and Farley near Clarendon, with the advowson of Winterbourne Cherburgh church. The land, and tenements *etc.*, and the advowson, are to be held for ever by the grantees and their heirs and assigns. Clause of warranty. Seals: those of Thomas and Isabel and the mayoral seal of the city. Named witnesses: the mayor, the bailiff, Henry Long, Edmund Ashley, and John Hall, esq.

3 August 1467, at Salisbury
2726 A charter of a younger John Pinnock, an executor of Alice Hendy, a widow, the relict, and an executor, of Stephen Hendy, tailor, of late of Salisbury. Alice appointed a chief tenement, in which she dwelt, in Winchester Street, between a tenement of late William Alexander's, now Thomas Hussey's, on the east side and a tenement of Walter [at the] barrow, esq., on the west side, to be sold by John. The money received from the sale should be laid out, on repairing ways and bridges and on other things charitable, for the salvation of Alice's soul, Stephen's soul, and the souls of others. By his charter John, on the strength of Alice's will and for a sum of money paid to him in advance, granted the tenement to John Gardener, otherwise called Pease, clothmaker, of Salisbury, and his wife Joan to be held for ever by them and John's heirs and assigns. Clause of warranty. Seals: John Pinnock's and, because his seal is unknown to many, the common and mayoral seals of the city. Named witnesses: the mayor, the bailiff, a coroner, John Hall, esq., and John Wise, draper

20 October 1467, in the hospital of the Holy Trinity, Salisbury
2727 An indenture perfected between John Port, the mayor of Salisbury and the master of the hospital of the Holy Trinity and St. Thomas the Martyr founded in Salisbury, and the brothers and sisters of the hospital, on the one side and John Jenkins, butcher, of Salisbury, on the other side. The mayor as master, and the brothers and sisters, granted to John a tenement in the street called Butcher Row, between a tenement of Thomas Hampton, esq., on the east side and a tenement of Henry Upton, esq., on the west side. The tenement was of late held by John Hayter, butcher, and is to be held by John Jenkins for 30 years from Michaelmas 1467 for a rent of 36s. 8d. a year. The mayor as master, and the brothers and sisters, will repair and maintain the tenement, and will make a canopy capable of protecting against wind and rain, at their own expense during that term. Clause to permit re-entry if the rent were to be in arrear for 15 days, distraint, and the keeping of distresses until the unpaid rent was recovered; also, to permit permanent repossession if the rent were to be in arrear for six months. Clause of warranty. Seals: the common seal of the hospital and the mayoral seal of the city to the part of the indenture in the possession of John Jenkins, that of John to the part in the possession of the mayor as master and of the brothers and sisters

27 January 1468, at Salisbury
2728 By his charter an elder William Hoare, merchant, a citizen of Salisbury,

granted to John Hall, merchant, of Salisbury, and his wife Joan a messuage, with
shops attached to it, opposite the market place where fleeces are sold, between a
tenement of late William Bowyer's on the north side and a tenement of the dean
and chapter of Salisbury on the south side. The messuage, and the shops, were
held by William by a grant of William Warwick, mercer, of late of Salisbury,
and is to be held for ever by John and Joan and their heirs and assigns. Clause of
warranty. Seals: William Hoare's and, because his seal is unknown to many, the
common and mayoral seals of the city. Named witnesses: the mayor, the bailiff, a
coroner, John Wise, draper, Edmund Penstone, and Andrew Brant

28 January 1468, at Salisbury
2729 By their deed a younger William Hoare, grocer, of Salisbury, Richard
Gilbert, gent., and William Marchy, tailor, quitclaimed to John Hall, merchant,
of Salisbury, and his wife Joan and their heirs and assigns their right or claim to
a messuage, with shops attached to it, opposite the market place where fleeces
are sold, [*as in 2728*], which an elder William Hoare, merchant, of Salisbury, of
late held by a grant of William Warwick, mercer, of late of Salisbury. Clause of
warranty perfected by the younger William Hoare. Seals: those of the younger
William Hoare, Richard Gilbert, and William Marchy and, because their seals are
unknown to many, the common and mayoral seals of the city. Named witnesses:
the mayor, the bailiff, a coroner, John Wise, draper, Edmund Penstone, and John
Wise, vintner

16 March 1468, at Salisbury
2730 By his charter Richard Cocklet, weaver, of Salisbury, granted to William
Buckett, merchant, of Salisbury, a tenement in Gigant Street, between a tenement
of late that of a younger William Stout on the north side and cottage property of
late John Teffont's, now that of Agnes Knolle, a widow, on the south side, to be
held for ever by him and his heirs and assigns. Clause of warranty. Seals: Richard's
and the common and mayoral seals of the city. Named witnesses: the mayor, the
bailiff, a coroner, an elder William Hoare, John Wise, draper, William Jones,
[?otherwise] Taverner, Thomas Copter, and William Harris

18 March 1468, at Salisbury
2731 By his deed Richard Cocklet, weaver, of Salisbury, quitclaimed to William
Buckett, a merchant, of Salisbury, and his heirs and assigns his right or claim
to a tenement in Gigant Street between a tenement formerly that of an elder
William Stout, and of late that of his son, a younger William Stout, on the north
side and cottage property formerly John Teffont's, now that of Agnes Knolle, a
widow, on the south side. The tenement was of late held by Richard by a grant of
William Fowey, of Up Sydling, Dorset. Clause of warranty. Seals: Richard's and
the common and mayoral seals of the city. Named witnesses: the mayor, Roger
Newton, a clerk, Edmund Penstone, Henry Swayne, esq., John Chaffin, William
Lord, and Richard Wise

20 March 1468, in the hospital of the Holy Trinity, Salisbury
2732 An indenture perfected between John Port, the mayor of Salisbury and the master of the hospital of the Holy Trinity and St. Thomas the Martyr founded in Salisbury, and the brothers and sisters of the hospital, on the one side and Peter White, joiner, of Salisbury, on the other side. The mayor as master, and the brothers and sisters, granted to Peter two tenements in Carter Street, between a tenement of the hospital, in which Alice Allen dwells, on the north side and a tenement of late John Prettyjohn's, now John Ranger's, on the south side, to be held by Peter and his assigns from 25 March 1468 for the following 70 years for a rent of 20s. a year, provided that the mayor as master, and the brothers and sisters, remitted to Peter and his assigns the rent issuing from the tenements from that date to 25 December 1468. Peter has met the cost incurred on the very great repair of the tenements, henceforward is anxious to do more of the same to those tenements which, on his entry, were totally dilapidated, and he and his assigns will repair and maintain the tenements, and build anew when necessary, at their own expense for the duration of the term. Clause to permit re-entry if the rent were to be in arrear for 15 days, distraint, and the keeping of distresses until the unpaid rent was recovered; also, to permit permanent repossession if the rent were to be in arrear for six months. Clause of warranty. Seals: the common seal of the hospital and the mayoral seal of the city to the part of the indenture in the possession of Peter White, that of Peter to the part in the possession of the mayor as master and of the brothers and sisters

25 March 1468
2733 By her writing Elizabeth, the relict of William Stout, yeoman, of late of Salisbury, otherwise called Elizabeth Stout, widow, quitclaimed to John Lilley, otherwise called Elbold Arnold, otherwise called Arnold Elbold, cordwainer, of Salisbury, all actions, real and personal, against him on any grounds whatsoever. Seals: Elizabeth's and, because her seal is unknown to many, the mayoral seal of the city

28 March 1468, at Salisbury
2734 By her deed Joan, the relict of Richard Cocklet, weaver, of late of Salisbury, sometime since dead, quitclaimed to William Buckett, a merchant, of Salisbury, and his heirs and assigns her right or claim to a tenement, of late Richard's, in Gigant Street [*as in 2730*]. Seals: Joan's and the common and mayoral seals of the city. Named witnesses: the mayor, Roger Newton, a clerk, Edmund Penstone, Henry Swayne, esq., John Chaffin, William Lord, and Richard Wise

3 June 1468
2735 *By his letters of attorney John Frank, of late a citizen of Salisbury, appointed William Palmer, merchant, of London, and Richard Blackmoor to receive from Johannes 'Vannegyn', Cornelius 'Buke', Segrus 'Permatire', and Mateys 'Bonetmakere', of Bruges, in Flanders, £60 which they owe to him by means of his paper bill sealed with their seals. Of a sum of £80 John received £20 from those debtors by the hand of William Barlow,*

of Salisbury, so that they owe the £60 to him. Because of a failure to pay the debt John gave a power to his attorneys, according to the laws and customs of Flanders, to arrest the debtors, imprison them and keep them imprisoned, recover the debt from them, release them from prison according to the exigency of the law, and do anything else suitable and necessary in his name. Seals: John Frank's and, because his seal is unknown to many, the mayoral seal of Salisbury

19 August 1468, at Salisbury

2736 By his letters of attorney John Palmer, yeoman, of late of Salisbury, appointed Laurence Vivian, mercer, of Debenham, Suffolk, to seek, levy, and receive from Geoffrey Palmer, otherwise Diss, husbandman, of late of Buxhall, Suffolk, 40s. which Geoffrey owes to him and unjustly withholds. John gave Laurence the power to do whatever was necessary and appropriate in the matter. Seals: John's and, because his seal is unknown to many, the mayoral seal of Salisbury

12 September 1468, at Salisbury

2737 By their deed John Stephens, of late of Leigh, in Westbury parish, and John Chaffin granted to Edward Alexander, otherwise called Bowyer, seven conjoined cottages, with gardens, in Gigant Street and Nuggeston between a tenement of late that of John Battin, smith, on the south side and a tenement of late William Knolle's on the east side; also a tenement newly built there between the tenement of late William Knolle's on the east side and a corner cottage, in which Robert Walshman dwells, on the west side; also two conjoined cottages, with gardens, in Nuggeston between Peter Grant's tenement on the east side and the tenement of late William Knolle's on the west side. The cottages, with the gardens, were held by John Stephens and John Chaffin by a grant of Edward and of John Dyer, deceased, of late of Leigh, and, with the tenement and the gardens, are to be held for ever by Edward and his heirs and assigns. Seals: those of John Stephens and John Chaffin and, because their seals are unknown to many, the mayoral seal of the city. Named witnesses: the mayor, the bailiff, William Swayne, an elder William Hoare, and William Taverner

11 October 1468

2738 By their writing William Beckley and Nicholas Beckley, husbandmen, of Hurstbourne Tarrant (*Husbourne Regis*), Hampshire, acknowledged that, on the day that the writing was perfected, they had received from Robert Anker, by the hand of John Cranborne, a clerk and a residentiary of the cathedral church of Salisbury, 60s., in full payment of £12 on account of arbitration, now owed to them. They acknowledge Robert and his heirs and his executors to be quit. Seals: those of William and Nicholas and, because their seals are unknown to many, the mayoral seal of the city

20 November 1468

2739 By his letters of attorney Gabriel Corbet, a son and heir of Thomas Corbet, of late a burgess of Southampton, appointed John Gamlin, a merchant, of Salisbury, to levy and receive from John Herdman and Roger Olding, husbandmen, of Eling parish, Hampshire, the money which they owed to him for arrears of the rent from his messuages, cottages, tofts, yards, land, tenements and woods in Eling parish. Also he appointed John to bring a suit against John and Roger in whatever court he pleased in respect of the waste perpetrated by them to his premises and to recover his losses and costs in the matter; also to remove John and Roger from the premises, to lease the premises for a term of years, and for the following eight years to cut down, sell, and carry away timber and underwood growing and being on the land and tenements. Seals: Gabriel's and, because his seal is unknown to many, the mayoral seal of Salisbury

1 February 1469
2740 By their deed Roger Sheeter and his wife Margaret, a daughter and heir of William Ryborough, of late of Wilton, and his wife Joan, a daughter and heir of John Vallis, of late of Wilton, quitclaimed to Thomas Pirie, hardwareman, of Salisbury, all actions, real and personal; they also quitclaimed to Thomas and his heirs and assigns their right or claim to all the land, tenements, yards, rent, and services in Wilton which were formerly those of John Vallis, Margaret's grandfather. Clause of warranty. Seals: those of Roger and Margaret and, because their seals are unknown to many, the mayoral seal of Salisbury. Named witnesses: the mayor of Salisbury, John Wise, draper, John Hampton, John Hood, Richard Plowman, Nicholas Millbridge, and John Gamlin

8 March 1469
2741 By his deed John Stone quitclaimed to Thomas Pirie, hardwareman, of Salisbury, his right or claim to all the land, tenements, yards, rent, and services in the borough of Wilton which, with Thomas, he of late held by a grant of William Ryborough by means of William's charter perfected for them and dated at Wilton on 15 October 1463. Seals: John's and, because his seal is unknown to many, the mayoral seal of Salisbury. Named witnesses: the mayor of Salisbury, John Wise, vintner, John Hill, William Marchy, John Grey, and James Lint

25 July 1469
2742 By her charter Joan Botreaux, a daughter and heir of William Botreaux, a son and heir of Ralph Botreaux, in her chaste maidenhood granted to Richard Trevelyan a tenement, with land, meadows, pastures, and feeding rights in 'Trerubio' which descended to her on William's death and which Ralph bought from Stephen Smallhill and died seised of. The tenement, with the land, meadows, pastures, and feeding rights, is to be held for ever by Richard and his heirs and assigns. Clause of warranty. Seal: Joan's. Named witnesses: John Courteney, John Porquin, John Hayden, Stephen Craddock, and John Hoare. Given on 8 July 1469 at 'Trerubio'. The charter was examined by John Port, the mayor of Salisbury, who, in testimony of it and at the request of Richard Trevelyan, affixed the mayoral seal of the city to it.

23 August 1469, at Salisbury
2743 By his deed John Stone, merchant, of Salisbury, quitclaimed to his son William and William's heirs his right or claim to a messuage, with shops and cellars, in Castle Street, opposite the market, between a tenement of late Robert Ogbourne's, now John Chaffin's, on the south side and John Port's tenement on the north side. Seals: John Stone's and, because his seal is unknown to many, the common and mayoral seals of the city. Named witnesses: the mayor, the bailiff, a coroner, John Wise, draper, John Chaffin, John Wise, draper [?*rectius* vintner], and Roger Buckbridge

26 August 1469, at Salisbury
2744 By his indented deed William Stone, a citizen of Salisbury, granted to his father John Stone, merchant, of Salisbury, a messuage, with shops and cellars, in Castle Street, opposite the market, [*as in 2743*], to be held for his life by him and his assigns, rendering a red rose a year on 24 June to William if requested. John and his assigns should repair and maintain the messuage, with the shops and cellars, at their own expense for the life of John. Clause of warranty. Seals: William's to the part of the deed remaining in John's possession, John's to the part remaining in William's possession, and, because William's seal is unknown to many, the mayoral seal of the city. Named witnesses: the mayor, the bailiff, a coroner, John Chaffin, and Roger Buckbridge

10 January 1470, at Salisbury
2745 By his indented charter William Jones, otherwise Taverner, merchant, of Salisbury, granted to John Rycroft, smith, of Salisbury, and his wife Edith a tenement in Chipper Street, otherwise called Chipper Lane, between a tenement of late John Chitterne's, afterwards John Wylye's, and now that of Margaret Wylye, a widow, on the east side and Richard Gilbert's tenement on the west side. The tenement was of late that of Thomas Pain, brewer, afterwards John Beddington's, and was held by William by that John's grant. It is to be held for ever by John and Edith on condition that, if John or his heirs or assigns were to pay to William or his assigns 20s. a year for the following 11 years, the charter would keep its full force. Clause to permit permanent repossession if John or his heirs or executors failed to make a payment within 15 days after any term. Clause of warranty. Seals: William's to the part of the charter remaining in the possession of John and his heirs, and John's to the part remaining in William's possession; because William's seal is unknown to many he procured the common and mayoral seals of the city to be affixed. Named witnesses: the mayor, the bailiff, a coroner, John Wise, draper, and John Chaffin

2 April 1470, at Salisbury
2746 By his charter Thomas Ballfoot, tailor, a citizen of Salisbury, a son of the late Richard Ballfoot, granted to Peter Mowtier, merchant, a citizen of Salisbury, a tenement, with a garden next to it and two walls on the north side of the tenement and of the garden, in Brown Street between a tenement of the hospital

of the Holy Trinity on the south side and a tenement of late John Crickmore's, now that of John Warin, weaver, on the north side; together with half a well there for making a profit for Peter or for drawing water from. The tenement, with the garden and its other appurtenances, are to be held for ever by Peter and his heirs and assigns. Clause of warranty. Seals: Thomas's and, because his seal is unknown to many, the common and mayoral seals of the city. Named witnesses: the mayor, the bailiff, a coroner, William Wootton, and Thomas Hussey

4 April 1470, at Salisbury
2747 By their deed Thomas Ballfoot, tailor, a citizen of Salisbury, and his son John quitclaimed to Peter Mowtier, merchant, a citizen of Salisbury, and his heirs and assigns their right or claim to a tenement, with a garden next to it and two walls on the north side of the tenement and of the garden, in Brown Street [*as in 2746*]; together with half a well there [*as in 2746*]. Clause of warranty. Seals: those of Thomas and John and, because their seals are unknown to many, the common and mayoral seals of the city. Named witnesses: the mayor, the bailiff, a coroner, William Wootton, Edmund Penstone, William Easton, and William Pingbridge

25 May 1470, at Salisbury
2748 An indenture perfected between Joan Chamber, widow, on the one side and John Alwin, esq., on the other side. Joan granted to John two conjoined tenements in Culver Street between a tenement of the provost of St. Edmund's church on the north side and John's tenement on the south side. The tenements are to be held for ever by John and his assigns from 25 March 1470 for the following 40 years, rendering to the chief lord of the city such payments and services as are due and paying to Joan and her heirs and assigns a rent of a red rose a year on 24 June for the 40 years if requested. John and his assigns should repair and maintain the tenements at their own expense. Clause of warranty. Seals: those of the parties to the parts of the indenture in turn and, because their seals are unknown to many, the mayoral seal of the city

20 October 1470, at Salisbury
2749 By his charter John Watts, a son and heir of Robert Watts, deceased, of Chapmanslade, granted to John Port, a citizen of Salisbury, and William Woodward, mercer, of Salisbury, four conjoined tenements in Brown Street and St. Martin's Street between William Sever's tenement, formerly Henry Southwick's, on the north side and John Wheeler's tenement, formerly William Sall's, on the east side. The tenements were held by Robert by a grant of Philip Morgan, by the name of all the land and tenements which Philip, with John Twinho, deceased, held by a grant of Stephen Hart, of late of Salisbury, and they are to be held for ever by John Port and William Woodward and John's heirs and assigns. Clause of warranty. Seals: John Watts's and the common and mayoral seals of the city. Named witnesses: the mayor, the bailiff, the coroners, John Wheeler, William Wootton, William Easton, Richard Freeman, Andrew Corn, and Robert South

7 March 1471, at Salisbury

2750 By his charter John Sheriff, a citizen of Salisbury, granted to John Hampton, gent., Andrew Corn, and William Harris, citizens of Salisbury, his land and conjoined tenements in Castle Street, which is called Minster Street, between a tenement of late William Lord's on the south side and a tenement formerly that of John Marshall, dyer, now that of John Wise, vintner, on the north side. The land and tenements were held by John Sheriff and his late wife Margaret by a grant of William Jones, otherwise Taverner, merchant, and John Gardener, clothmaker, citizens of Salisbury, to them and their heirs and assigns for ever, and they are to be held for ever by John Hampton, Andrew Corn, and William Harris and their heirs and assigns. Clause of warranty. Seals: John Sheriff's and, because his seal is unknown to many, the common and mayoral seals of the city. Named witnesses: the mayor, the bailiff, a coroner, Edmund Penstone, and John Mowe

8 May 1471, at Salisbury

2751 By his charter Thomas Bower, a son and heir of Edward Bower, of late a citizen of Salisbury, granted to William Naggington and John Horman, tailor, all his land and tenements in Salisbury, to be held for ever by them and their heirs and assigns. Clause of warranty. Seals: Thomas's and, because his seal is unknown to many, the mayoral seal of the city. Named witnesses: the mayor, the bailiff, a coroner, John Port, John Chaffin, Robert South, Henry Vincent, and John Malpass

15 May 1471, at Salisbury

2752 By their charter William Naggington and John Horman, tailor, granted to Thomas Bower and Emmotte, William's daughter, all the land and tenements in Salisbury which they held by Thomas's grant, to be held for ever by them and their joint issue. Clause of warranty. Seals: William's and John's and, because their seals are unknown to many, the mayoral and common seals of the city. Named witnesses: the mayor, the bailiff, a coroner, John Port, John Chaffin, Robert South, Henry Vincent, and John Malpass

1 August 1471, at Salisbury

2753 By their charter John Hampton, gent., Andrew Corn, and William Harris, citizens of Salisbury, granted to William Jones, otherwise Taverner, a citizen of Salisbury, their land and conjoined tenements in Castle Street, which is called Minster Street, [*as in* **2750**]. The land and tenements were held jointly by the grantors by a grant of John Sheriff, a citizen of Salisbury, to them and their assigns for ever, and they are to be held for ever by William Jones, otherwise Taverner, and his heirs and assigns. Seals: those of the grantors and the common and mayoral seals of the city. Named witnesses: the mayor, the bailiff, a coroner, John Port, John Wheeler, John Wise, vintner, and William Easton

23 August 1471, at Salisbury

2754 By his deed John Sheriff, a citizen of Salisbury, quitclaimed to William

Jones, otherwise Taverner, a citizen of Salisbury, and his heirs and assigns his right or claim to land and conjoined tenements in Castle Street, which is called Minster Street, [*as in* **2750**]. Clause of warranty. Seals: John's and, because his seal is unknown to many, the common and mayoral seals of the city. Named witnesses: the mayor, the bailiff, a coroner, John Port, and John Hampton

13 November 1471, at Salisbury

2755 By his charter John Hood, glover, of Salisbury, granted to Guy Rutter, patten maker, a citizen of Salisbury, a tenement in Castle Street, beyond the bars, on the west side of the street, between a tenement of late that of John Shipton, dubber, on the north side and a tenement of John Greening, a clerk, on the south side. The tenement was held by John Hood by a grant of John Purdy, hosier, of late of Salisbury, and is to be held for ever by Guy and his heirs and assigns. Clause of warranty. John Hood appointed Anselm Withier and William Wynne his attorneys to deliver the seisin of the tenement to Guy and his heirs and assigns. Seals: John Hood's and, because his seal is unknown to many, the common and mayoral seals of the city. Named witnesses: the mayor, the bailiff, a coroner, William Swayne, Edmund Penstone, John Mowe, and William Bedwyn

2 January 1472, at Salisbury

2756 By her charter Alice, a widow, the relict of Thomas Durnford, of Salisbury, granted to Robert South and his wife Alice a corner tenement, with gardens, shops, and cottages next to it, on the east side of a street called Castle Street and Minster Street, between a tenement of late John Camel's on the north side and a tenement, of late John Hain's, in Scots Lane on the east side. The tenement, with the gardens, shops, and cottages, was held by Alice Durnford by a grant of Thomas, who held it by a grant of Margaret, formerly his wife, and it is to be held for ever by Robert South and his wife Alice and Robert's heirs and assigns. Seals: Alice Durnford's and, because her seal is unknown to many, the common and mayoral seals of the city. Named witnesses: the mayor, the bailiff, a coroner, John Port, John Chaffin, Richard Freeman, John Bushel, and William Bedwell

2757 By her charter Margaret Wylye, a widow, the relict of John Wylye, draper, of late a citizen of Salisbury, granted to Nicholas Martin, merchant, of Salisbury, a tenement or messuage in Bridge Street, beside the upper bridge of Fisherton Anger, between a tenement of late that of John Butt, a cordwainer, now William Poole's, on the east side, the Avon on the west side, and a tenement of late that of John Parrant, goldsmith, on the north side. The tenement or messuage was held by Margaret by a devise of John Wylye who, while her husband, held it by a grant of William Savernake, a clerk, and Henry Eliot, of late a citizen of Salisbury, and it was held by William and Henry by a grant of Robert Himmerford, esq., as is shown in Robert's charter perfected for them. It is to be held for ever by Nicholas and his heirs and assigns. Clause of warranty. Margaret appointed John Hampton and William Wynne her attorneys to deliver the seisin of the tenement or messuage to Nicholas and his heirs and assigns. Seals: Margaret's and, because her seal is unknown to many, the common and mayoral seals of the city. Named witnesses: the mayor, the bailiff, William Swayne, John Hall, John Port, Edmund Penstone, and John Chippenham

19 February 1472, at Salisbury
2758 By his charter Guy Rutter, patten maker, a citizen of Salisbury, granted to Anselm Withier, Edward Champflour, a chaplain, and Thomas Pirie a tenement in Castle Street, beyond the bars, [*as in 2755*]. The tenement was held by Guy by a grant of John Hood, glover, of Salisbury, and is to be held for ever by Anselm, Edward, and Thomas and their heirs and assigns. Seals: Guy's and, because his seal is unknown to many, the mayoral seal of the city. Named witnesses: the mayor, the bailiff, John Wise, draper, John Port, John Chaffin, John Bushell, and William Bedwyn

29 February 1472, at Salisbury
2759 By his deed Edward Champflour, a chaplain, quitclaimed to Anselm Withier and Thomas Pirie his right or claim to a tenement in Minster Street, or Castle Street, beyond the bars, between a tenement of late that of John Shipton, dubber, on the north side and a tenement of late that of John Greening, a clerk, on the south side. The tenement extends from the street on the east side as far as the Avon on the west side. Edward, with Anselm and Thomas, held it by a grant of Guy Rutter, patten maker, a citizen of Salisbury. Seals: Edward's and the mayoral seal of the city. Named witnesses: the mayor, the bailiff, John Wise, draper, John Wise, vintner, Nicholas Edmond, Robert South, Andrew Corn, James Lint, and the clerk

10 March 1472, at Salisbury
2760 By his charter Richard Haynes, esq., granted to Robert South, a citizen of Salisbury, a messuage or tenement, with a yard (*or* yards) adjacent, in Scots Lane between a tenement of William Taverner, merchant, on the east side and Robert's cottage property on the west side. The messuage or tenement, with the yard(s), was held, among other land and tenements, by Richard by a grant and devise of John Haynes, his father, of late a citizen of Salisbury, and it is to be held for ever by Robert and his heirs and assigns. Clause of warranty. Richard appointed Richard Gilbert and John Hampton his attorneys to deliver the seisin of the messuage or tenement, with the yard(s), to Robert and his heirs and assigns. Seals: Richard Haynes's and, because his seal is unknown to many, the common and mayoral seals of the city. Named witnesses: the mayor, the bailiff, John Wise, draper, Andrew Brant, Nicholas Mason, and William Bedwyn

8 March 1473, at Salisbury
2761 By their charter Anselm Withier and Thomas Pirie granted to John Hood, glover, of Salisbury, a tenement in Minster Street, or Castle Street, beyond the bars, on the west side of the street [*as in 2759*]. The tenement extends to the Avon on the west side. It was held by Anselm and Thomas by a grant of Guy Rutter, patten maker, a citizen of Salisbury, and is to be held for ever by John and

his heirs and assigns. Seals: those of Anselm and Thomas and the mayoral seal of the city. Named witnesses: the mayor, the bailiff, John Port, John Wise, draper, Robert South, William Bedwell, Andrew Corn, James Lint, and the clerk

15 March 1473, at Salisbury
2762 By his charter John Hood, glover, of Salisbury, granted to Anselm Withier, glover, of Salisbury, a tenement in Minster Street, or Castle Street, beyond the bars, on the west side of the street, between a tenement of late that of John Shipton, dubber, on the north side and a tenement of late that of John Greening, a clerk, now William Bedwell's, on the south side. The tenement extends to the Avon. It was held by John Hood by a grant of John Purdy, hosier, of late of Salisbury, and is to be held for ever by Anselm and his heirs and assigns. Clause of warranty. Seals: John Hood's and the common and mayoral seals of the city. Named witnesses: the mayor, the bailiff, John Port, John Hampton, William Easton, Robert South, Richard Gilbert, Andrew Corn, William Bedwell, John Selwood, and the clerk

1 May 1473, at Salisbury
2763 By their charter Bartholomew Johnson and his wife Joan, the relict of an elder John Page, of Salisbury, and a daughter of William Wreath, of late a citizen of Salisbury, granted to William Bedwell, dubber, of Salisbury, and his wife Agnes a messuage, with a cottage (*or* cottages), shops, and a yard (*or* yards), in Castle Street and Scots Lane, on a corner, on the east side of Castle Street and the south side of Scots Lane, between a messuage formerly George Goss's, of late Walter Hind's, in Castle Street on the south side and cottages formerly Thomas Sexhampcote's, of late Robert Linden's, in Scots Lane on the east side. The messuage, with the cottage(s), shops, and yard(s), was held by William Wreath by a grant of William Ludlow and John Wylye, executors of Robert Warmwell, formerly a citizen of Salisbury, to whom it descended on the death of William Bower, his kinsman, and William Bower held it by grant of Thomas Chaplin and his wife Joan. It is to be held for ever by William Bedwell and his wife Agnes and William's heirs and assigns. Clause of warranty. Seals: those of Bartholomew and Joan and the common and mayoral seals of the city. Named witnesses: the mayor, the bailiff, John Port, John Wise, draper, William Easton, Robert South, and the clerk

3 May 1473
2764 By her charter Cecily Friend, a widow, a daughter and heir of Thomas Andrew, of late a citizen of Salisbury, granted to John Pettifer, a citizen of Salisbury, a messuage in Gigant Street, between a tenement of late William Alexander's, now Thomas Hussey's, on the north side and a tenement of late that of Thomas Ham, tailor, afterwards Henry Friend's, on the south side, to be held for ever by him and his heirs and assigns. Clause of warranty. Seals: Cecily's and, because her seal is unknown to many, the common and mayoral seals of the city. Named witnesses: the mayor, the bailiff, John Hall, William Taverner, Edmund Penstone,

John Mowe, and William Merriott

5 May 1473, at Salisbury
2765 By her deed Cecily Friend, a widow, the relict, and an executor, of Henry
Friend, formerly a citizen of Salisbury, quitclaimed to John Pettifer, a merchant,
of late of Sherborne, Dorset, otherwise called John Pettifer, a citizen of Salisbury,
and to his heirs and assigns her right or claim to a tenement, with a yard (*or* yards),
in New Street between a cottage of late Robert Ashley's, now that of Edmund
Ashley, esq., on the east side and cottage property of late John Ladd's, now John
Coof's, on the west side. The tenement, with the yard(s), was of late Henry's.
Seals: Cecily's and the common and mayoral seals of the city. Named witnesses:
the mayor, the bailiff, William Swayne, John Hall, John Mowe, and Nicholas
Noble

20 May 1473, at Salisbury
2766 By their deed Bartholomew Johnson and his wife Joan, a daughter and heir
of William Wreath, a citizen of Salisbury, and the sole executor of Alice Wreath,
her mother, the relict, and sole executor, of William, quitclaimed to William
Bedwell, dubber, of Salisbury, and his wife Agnes and that William's heirs and
assigns their right or claim to a messuage, with a cottage (*or* cottages), shops,
and a yard (*or* yards), in Castle Street and Scots Lane, [*as in* **2763**]. By the will
of William Wreath the messuage, with the cottage(s), shops, and yard(s), should
have reverted to Joan and her executors on the death of her daughter Alice and
Alice's heirs to be sold. Clause of warranty. Seals: those of Bartholomew and Joan
and the common and mayoral seals of the city. Named witnesses: the mayor, the
bailiff, Nicholas Edmond, Henry Swayne, Edmund Penstone, John Pettifer, and
the clerk

1 June 1473, at Salisbury
2767 By their deed John Gronow, and his wife Alice, the only daughter of
John Page and his wife Joan, a daughter and heir of William Wreath, of late a
citizen of Salisbury, quitclaimed to William Bedwell, dubber, of Salisbury, and his
wife Agnes and that William's heirs and assigns their right or claim to a corner
tenement or messuage, with a cottage (*or* cottages), shops, and a yard (*or* yards),
in Castle Street, or Minster Street, and Scots Lane, [*as in* **2763**]. The tenement
or messuage, with the cottage(s), shops, and yard(s), should have descended to
Alice and her heirs on the death of Joan, her mother. Clause of warranty. Seals:
those of John Gronow and Alice and the common and mayoral seals of the city.
Named witnesses: the mayor, the bailiff, John Wise, vintner, John Chaffin, John
Hampton, Andrew Corn, and the clerk

31 August 1473
2768 By his deed John Lea, gent., of Flamston, quitclaimed to Richard Chuck,
kt., Hugh Pavey, a clerk, John Port, John Chaffin, and John Bushell and their
heirs and assigns his right or claim to the manor of Upper Eldon near King's

Somborne, Hampshire, and the advowson of the church appurtenant to the manor when it fell due, with all the land, tenements, rent, reversions, services, woods, moors, meadows, pastures, and feeding rights, which he of late held by a grant of Robert Piston and his wife Margaret. Seals: John Lea's and the mayoral seal of the city of Salisbury. Named witnesses: the mayor, John Wise, draper, John Hampton, William Easton, and Hugh FitzRichard

26 September 1477, at Salisbury
2769 By his indented charter John Mowe, a citizen of Salisbury, granted to his son Thomas and Thomas's wife Joan, a daughter of John Hatchford, two conjoined tenements, with attached cottages and gardens, called Mowe's Abbey, in Carter Street between a tenement of Edmund Ashley, esq., on the south side and a tenement of late Roger Mayne's on the north side; also two other conjoined tenements in Carter Street between a tenement of William Stourton, kt., the lord of Stourton, on the north side and a tenement, or gardens, of late John Preston's on the south side; also two other tenements in Carter Street between Robert Inkpen's tenement on the north side and William Easton's tenement on the south side; also a toft, or garden, with racks built in it, and a small house at the end of the garden, in the street called Rolleston between John White's gardens on the south side and a tenement of late Thomas Warbleton's on the north side. The tenements, cottages, and gardens are to be held for ever by Thomas and Joan and Thomas's issue, if Thomas were to die without issue they would remain for ever to William Wynne and his wife Catherine, John's daughter, and to Catherine's issue, and for lack of such issue they would revert, and remain for ever, to John and his heirs and assigns. John appointed William Cropper his attorney to deliver the seisin of the tenements, cottages, and gardens, to Thomas and Joan and Thomas's issue. Seals: John's and, because his seal is unknown to many, the common and mayoral seals of the city. Named witnesses: the mayor, the bailiff, a coroner, William Easton, Henry Swayne, John Chippenham, and Robert South

4 August 1478, at Salisbury
2770 By his charter an elder Thomas Knoyle, of East Lulworth (*Lulworth St. Andrew's*), Dorset, granted to John Newborough, a son and heir of William Newborough, kt., Richard Hampden, John FitzJames, Edward Belknap, a son and heir of Henry Belknap, John Newborough, a son of an elder John Newborough, John Knoyle, a clerk, John Lea, of Flamston, Thomas Copcutt, Thomas Stoner, of Rotherfield Peppard, Thomas Gate, John Doyle, William Marmion, of Adwell, William Temmes, of Rood Ashton, Alexander Knoyle, Laurence Normerton, and Richard Cary, of Wycombe, a chief tenement in Winchester Street, above the ditch, between John Mowe's tenement on the east side and a tenement of the elder John Newborough on the west side; also a tenement in Pot Row between a tenement of late Edmund Penstone's on the east side and John Lea's tenement on the west side; also a tenement in Butcher Row, in which John Chippenham dwells, between that John's tenement on the west side and John Mowe's tenement on the east side; also two tenements in Carter Street between a garden, which

William Buckett holds, on the south side and a tenement of the poor almsmen of the house of the Holy Trinity, called Almshouse, on the north side. Those premises are to be held for ever by the grantees and their heirs and assigns. Clause of warranty. Seals: Thomas Knoyle's and, because his seal is unknown to many, the common and mayoral seals of the city. Named witnesses: the mayor, the bailiff, the coroners, John Hall, esq., William Easton, and the clerk

5 August 1478
2771 By his letters of attorney an elder Thomas Knoyle, of East Lulworth (*Lulworth St. Andrew's*), Dorset, appointed John Knolle, William Wynne, and Richard Crimp his executors to deliver to John Newborough and others [*as listed in 2770*] the seisin of a chief tenement in Winchester Street, above the ditch, a tenement in Pot Row, a tenement in Butcher Row, in which John Chippenham dwells, and two tenements in Carter Street according to the terms of his charter given on 4 August 1478. Seal: Thomas's

WITNESSES TO DOCUMENTS

As the bailiff of Salisbury (the bishop's bailiff)
John Cheyne, an Esquire of the Body, 2769–70
John FitzJames, 2756–67
John of Hillsley, 2170
Thomas Hungerford, kt., 2174
Nicholas Lea, 2326–8, 2330, 2333–9
Robert Long, 2573–80, 2582–2606, 2608–24, 2626–8, 2631–9, 2641–55, 2657–
    62, 2664–5, 2668–79, 2682–7
William Westbury, 2178–9, 2182–2202, 2204–9, 2211–61, 2263, 2265–7, 2269,
    2271–5, 2277, 2280–1, 2283–96, 2298–2302, 2304, 2306–11, 2314, 2316, 2319–
    25, 2341–2, 2344, 2346–52, 2354–61, 2363–5, 2367–72, 2374–92, 2394–2404,
    2406–23, 2425–9, 2431–47, 2449–51, 2453–8, 2460–6, 2468–74, 2476–87,
    2489–2512, 2514–35, 2537–51, 2553–66
John Whittocksmead, 2689–94, 2697–8, 2701–2, 2706–9, 2711–13, 2716, 2719–
    26, 2728–30, 2737, 2743–47, 2749–55

As the mayor of the city
Henry Baron, 2662, 2664–5, 2668–73
John Becket, 2179, 2182–92
John Bromley, 2585–97
William Buckett, merchant, 2761–8
John Camel, 2692–3
Thomas Chadworth, 2712–13
Richard Gater, fuller, tucker, 2638–9, 2641–9
John Hall, esq., merchant, 2719–20
William Jones, otherwise William Taverner, merchant, 2756–60
John Judd, 2330–1, 2333–5, ?2336, 2338–9, 2341–2, 2344, 2346–52, 2354
John Lewisham, 2224–52
William Lightfoot, 2694
Henry Man, 2431–51, 2453–4, 2456, 2650–60, 2684–7
Thomas Mason, draper, 2193–2202, 2204–9, 2211–23
Walter Nalder, draper, merchant, 2178
John Noble, 2570–80, 2582–4, 2682–3
Nicholas Noble, 2769
William Packing, 2598–2606, 2608–14
John Port, 2689–91, 2701–2, 2706, 2716, 2721–6, 2728–31, 2734, 2737, 2740–1,
    2743–7, 2749
Robert Poynant, 2355–61, 2363–5, 2367–72, 2374–92, 2394–7
John Salisbury, grocer, 2174
Walter Shirley, merchant, 2292–2301, 2304, 2307–11, 2314, 2316, 2319–26, 2328–9

William Swayne, merchant, 2696, 2770
John Swift, ironmonger, 2455, 2457, 2460–6, 2468–74, 2476–87, 2489, 2491–3
William Taverner, *see* William Jones
Reynold of Tidworth, 2170
William Warin, grocer, 2253–61, 2263, 2265–7, 2269, 2271–5, 2277–81, 2283–91,
    2494–2515, 2517–21, 2523–35, 2674–9
Robert Warmwell, 2398–2404, 2406–17, 2419, 2421, 2423, 2425, 2427–9, 2617–
    21, 2623–4, 2626–8, 2631–7
William Warwick, mercer, 2537–51, 2553–66, 2568
John Wheeler, weaver, 2698
John Wise, draper, 2707–9, 2711, 2750–5
William Wootton, 2714
John Wylye, draper, 2697

A a coroner of the city
John Bromley, 2472–4, 2476–7, 2479–81, 2484–7, 2489, 2491
Robert Cove, 2689–94, 2697–8, 2701–2, 2706–9, 2711–13, 2716, 2719–23, 2726,
    2728–30, 2743–7, 2749–56
William Cox, grocer, 2517–18, 2520–4, 2526, 2529–34, 2537–8, 2540–8, 2550–1,
    2553–4, 2556–60, 2562–3, 2565, 2568–ex.2571–80, 2583–4, 2586–9, 2592–2606,
    2608, 2610–24, 2626–7, 2631, 2633, 2636, 2639, 2641–5, 2647, 52, 2654–6,
    2658–62, 2665, 2668–72, 2674–7, 2679, 2682–7
Robert Deverill, 2178
Richard Gater, fuller, tucker, 2515–18, 2520–2, 2524, 2526, 2530–4, 2537–8,
    2540–8, 2550–1, 2553–4, 2556–60, 2562–5, 2568, 2571–6, 2579–80, 2583–4,
    2586–9, 2592–2606, 2608, 2610–15, 2617–24, 2626, 2631, 2633, 2636, 2682–3
Edward Gilbert, 2515
Robert Gilbert, tanner, 2639, 2641–5, 2647–52, 2654–6, 2658–62, 2665, 2668–
    72, 2674–7, 2679, 2684–7
William Halstead, butcher, 2689–93
Roger Holes, 2769–70
John Judd, 2189–92, 2195–7, 2199–2202, 2204–5, 2207–9, 2211–17, 2222, 2224,
    2226, 2228–34, 2239–44, 2246–9, 2251–2, 2254, 2257–61, 2263, 2265–7, 2269,
    2271–4, 2277–8, 2280–1, 2283–94, 2296–7, 2299–2302, 2304, 2306–11, 2314,
    2316, 2319–27, 2329, ?2334–6, ?2351, 2356–61, 2363–5, 2367–72, 2374–7,
    2380–3, 2386–92, 2394, 2396–8, 2402–4, 2406–12, 2414–15, 2417–20, 2422–3,
    2426–8, 2431–9, 2442–4, 2446–51, 2453–8, 2461–6, 2468–9, 2472–4, 2476–7,
    2479–81, 2484–7, 2489, 2491
John of Knoyle, 2170
John Mowe, gent., 2770
Edmund Penstone, 2716, 2749
John Swift, ironmonger, 2189–92, 2195–7, 2199–2202, 2204–5, 2207–9, 2211–
    17, 2222–4, 2226, 2228–34, 2239–44, 2246–9, 2257–61, 2266, 2269, 2271–5,
    2277–80, 2283–94, 2296–7, 2299–2302, 2304, 2306–11, 2314, 2316, 2319–24,
    2326–7, 2329, 2331, ?2334–6, 2337–9, 2341–2, 2344, 2347–50, ?2351, 2352,

2356–61, 2364–5, 2367–72, 2374–8, 2380–3, 2385–92, 2394, 2396–8, 2402–4, 2406–12, 2414–15, 2417–19, 2422–3, 2426–8, 2431–9, 2442–4, 2446–51, 2453–4, 2456, 2564, 2628
John Wylye, mercer, 2523, 2529

As a reeve of the city
Edward Alexander, 2707–8
Thomas Allaker, 2687
John Bodenham, 2224, 2226, 2229–34, 2239–44, 2247, 2249, 2251–2
Thomas Bower, draper, 2195–7, 2199, 2201–2, 2204, 2207–9, 2211–17, 2222–3
William Bowyer, 2178
John Bromley, 2331, 2334–9, 2341–2, 2344, 2346–52
John Butler, 2598–2606, 2608, 2610–16
John Camel, 2537–8, 2540–8, 2550–1, 2553–4
William Chapman, 2662, 2665, 2668–72
William Child, 2674–7, 2679
Stephen Cooper, mercer, 2586–9, 2592–7
John Corscombe, tucker, 2650–2, 2654–6, 2658–61, 2684–6
William Cox, grocer, 2494, 2496–2501, 2503–6, 2508, 2510–16
Edward Dubber, 2356–61, 2363–5, 2367–72, 2374–8, 2380–3, 2385–92, 2394, 2396–7
Richard Ecton, 2537–8, 2540–8, 2550–1, 2553–4
William Fewster, 2178
Hugh Fox, 2170
Thomas Freeman, mercer, 2522–4, 2526, 2529–34
Edward Frith, 2254, 2257–61, 2263, 2265–7, 2269, 2271–5, 2277–81, 2283–91
Richard Gage, 2182–7, 2189–92
Richard Gater, fuller, tucker, 2455, 2457, 2461–6, 2468–74, 2476–7, 2479–81, 2484–7, 2489–93
Robert Gilbert, tanner, 2356–61, 2363–5, 2367–72, 2374–8, 2381–3, 2385–6, 2388–92, 2394, 2396–7
Geoffrey Goldsmith *see* Geoffrey Mansel
Edward Goodyear, ?draper, tailor, 2674–7, 2679
William of Hagbourne, 2170
John Hain, 2586–9, 2592–7
William Halstead, butcher, 2650–2, 2654–6, 2658–61, 2684–6
John Hampton, grocer, 2617–24, 2626, 2628, 2631, 2633, 2636
John Hart, 2697
Anselm Hebbing, 2689–91
John Hunt, merchant, 2522–4, 2526, 2529–34
elder Thomas Hussey, esq., 2709, 2711
Thomas Knoyle, 2698
William at the lea, fishmonger, merchant, 2224, 2226, 2228–34, 2239–41, 2243–4, 2246–9, 2251–2
John Loud, 2698

William Lord, 2414–15, 2417–18, 2421–3, 2426–7, 2433–9, 2442–4, 2446–51, 2453–8, 2461, 2465–6, 2469, 2471–4, 2476–7, 2479–81, 2485–7, 2489, 2491–2, 2494, 2497–2501, 2503–6, 2508, 2510–12, 2514–18, 2520–1, 2523, 2526, 2529–35, 2537–8, 2542–3, 2546–8, 2550–1, 2553–4, 2556–60, 2562–5, 2568, 2571–80, 2583–4, 2586, 2588–9, 2592–2606, 2608, 2610–24, 2626, 2628, 2631, 2633, 2636, 2639, 2641–5, 2647–52, 2654–6, 2658–62, 2665, 2668–72, 2674–7, 2679, 2684

Thomas Pirie, 2759, 2761–3, 2766–7

As a citizen

Edmund Ashley, 2725

Henry Baldry, 2170

Henry Baron, 2652, 2654–6, 2658–61, 2679, 2684–6

John Becket, 2204–5, 2213–15, 2217, 2224, 2241, 2246, 2248, 2257–8, 2260, 2265–6, 2272–3, 2278, 2280, 2283–6, 2288

William Bedwell, dubber, 2756, 2761–2

William Bedwyn, 2755, 2758, 2760

Nicholas Bell, 2201, 2211, 2223

John Bishop, 2170

William Bishop, merchant, 2195, 2200, 2212, 2223–4, 2226, 2234, 2246, 2251, 2254, 2259, 2261, 2265, 2272, 2274, 2277–8, 2284–6, 2288–9, 2293, 2296, 2308–9, 2314, 2316, 2319, 2323, 2325–7, 2329, 2338, 2342, 2344, 2347, 2356–8, 2360, 2363, 2369, 2371–2, 2374, 2378, 2380, 2382, 2385, 2387–9, 2397, 2407, 2410–12, 2414–15, 2417–18, 2428, 2431–2

Thomas Bleacher, 2244

John Bodenham, 2301, 2310

Thomas Bower, draper, 2247, 2249, 2271, 2273, 2277, 2280, 2300, 2341, 2388, 2396–8, 2402, 2404, 2406, 2409, 2480, 2484

Andrew Brant, 2719, 2723, 2728, 2760

John Bromley, 2375, 2387, 2398, 2418, 2420, 2427–8, 2431–9, 2442–4, 2446–51, 2453–4, 2455–8, 2461–5, 2468, 2470, 2490, 2498, 2501, 2503, 2506, 2508, 2510–14, 2520–1, 2523–4, 2529–30, 2535, 2541, 2544–8, 2550–1, 2553–4, 2556–60, 2562, 2565, 2571, 2573–80, 2583–4, 2598–2601, 2603–6, 2608, 2610–20, 2623–4, 2626, 2628, 2633, 2636, 2639, 2641–3, 2645, 2648, 2650–2, 2655–6, 2658–62, 2665, 2668–70, 2672, 2674–6, 2682–6

Roger Buckbridge, 2706, 2743–4

John Bushell, 2756, 2758

John Chaffin, 2716, 2731, 2734, 2743–5, 2751–2, 2756, 2758, 2767

Robert Cheese, 2170

John Chippenham, 2706, 2716, 2757, 2769

Richard Coof, draper, 2337, 2380, 2392, 2397–8, 2411–12, 2550, 2553

Stephen Cooper, *otherwise* Stephen Mercer, mercer, 2669–72, 2675–6, 2679, 2687

Thomas Copter, 2730

William Cormell, *see* William Knolle

Andrew Corn, 2749, 2759, 2761–2, 2767

William Cox, grocer, 2291, 2301

William Dowding, draper, merchant, 2182, 2184, 2187, 2191, 2200, 2202, 2209, 2213, 2215, 2224, 2226, 2228, 2230–2, 2234, 2242, 2248, 2252, 2258–61, 2263, 2266, 2271, 2276, 2278–80, 2283, 2290, 2292, 2296–7, 2304, 2308–9, 2314, 2316, 2319–23, 2325–7, 2329, 2331, 2334–9, 2341–2, 2344, 2349, 2352, 2357, 2361, 2363–4, 2369–72

William Easton, 2716, 2747, 2749, 2753, 2762–3, 2768–70

Richard Ecton, 2586, 2606, 2644, 2649, 2674, 2677

Nicholas Edmond, 2759, 2766

John Fadder, alderman of St. Martin (Martin's ward), 2679

William Fewster, 2309, 2350–1, 2367–8

Hugh FitzRichard, 2768

Richard Freeman, 2749, 2756

Thomas Freeman, mercer, merchant, 2562, 2643, 2687, 2711, 2714, 2724

Edward Frith, 2311, 2346

Richard Gage, 2273, 2346, 2351, 2368, 2382, 2402–3, 2410, 2417

John Gamlin, merchant, 2740

Richard Gater, fuller, tucker, 2650–2, 2654–5, 2660–2, 2665, 2668–70, 2672, 2675–6, 2679, 2684–6

Richard Gilbert, 2762

Robert Gilbert, tanner, 2428

John Grey, 2741

John Hall, esq., merchant, 2698, 2702, 2709, 2722, 2725–6, 2757, 2764–5, 2770

Henry Ham, draper, ?2461

John Hampton, gent., 2740, 2754, 2762, 2767–8

Nicholas Harding, 2186, 2191, 2197, 2243, 2247, 2265, 2299, 2302, 2306, 2310, 2324, 2335, 2349, 2356–7, 2376, 2386, 2397

William Harris, 2730

John Hill, 2741

an elder William Hoare, merchant, 2689–93, 2697–8, 2701–2, 2709, 2712–14, 2719–21, 2730, 2737

John Hood, glover, 2740

an elder Thomas Hussey, esq., 2746

Adam Ironmonger, 2170

Thomas Ironmonger, 2170

William Jones, otherwise William Taverner, merchant, 2730, 2737, 2764

John Judd, 2421

William Knolle, otherwise William Cormell, 2694, 2697

Robert of Knoyle, 2170

John Lewisham, 2186, 2189, 2197, 2215, 2254, 2267, 2269, 2272, 2279, 2287, 2291–2, 2299–2302, 2306, 2323–4, 2327, 2334–6, 2339, 2342

William Lightfoot, 2696, 2702

James Lint, 2741, 2759, 2761

Henry Long, 2725

William Lord, 2731, 2734

2361

Henry Vincent, 2751–2

William Walter, merchant, 2178, 2185, 2191, 2195, 2197, 2201, 2204, 2207, 2219, 2222–4, 2226, 2229, 2243, 2246–7, 2249, 2254, 2257, 2259, 2263, 2267, 2269, 2274, 2276–7, 2279–81, 2287–9, 2291–2, 2294, 2297, 2299–2302, 2304, 2306–8, 2310–11, 2324

William Warin, grocer, 2184, 2189–90, 2195–6, 2199, 2205, 2208–9, 2211, 2216–17, 2219, 2223, 2228–33, 2239–40, 2242–4, 2246, 2248–9, 2251–2, 2292–4, 2296–7, 2299, 2302, 2304, 2306–8, 2310–11, 2314, 2316, 2319–27, 2329, 2331, 2334, 2336–9, 2342, 2344, 2346–52, 2356–61, 2364–5, 2367–70, 2372, 2374–5, 2377–8, 2380–1, 2383, 2385, 2387–92, 2394, 2396, 2402, 2404, 2406–12, 2414–15, 2417–23, 2426, 2431–9, 2442–4, 2446–51, 2453–8, 2461–6, 2468–74, 2476–7, 2479–81, 2484–7, 2489–92, 2537–8, 2540–8, 2551, 2554, 2556–60, 2562–5, 2568, 2571–80, 2583–4, 2586, 2588–9, 2592–2606, 2608, 2610–12, 2614–24, 2626, 2628, 2631, 2633, 2636, 2639, 2641–3, 2645, 2647–52, 2654, 2656, 2658–62, 2665, 2668–72, 2682–7

Robert Warmwell, 2200, 2239, 2267, 2281, 2290, 2297, 2309, 2314, 2316, 2325, 2327, 2329, 2337, 2348, 2357–8, 2360, 2363, 2365, 2367, 2374, 2376–7, 2381–2, 2385–6, 2390, 2394, 2433–9, 2442–4, 2446–9, 2451, 2453–8, 2461–5, 2468–74, 2476–7, 2479–81, 2484–7, 2489, 2491–4, 2496–2501, 2503–6, 2508, 2511–18, 2521–4, 2526, 2529–35, 2537–8, 2540–7, 2550–1, 2553–4, 2556–60, 2562–5, 2568, 2572–80, 2583, 2587–9, 2592–5, 2598–2606, 2608, 2610–16, 2639, 2641–5, 2647–52, 2654–6, 2658–60, 2662, 2665, 2668–72, 2674–5, 2677, 2679, 2683–7

William Warwick, mercer, 2455–6, 2480, 2484–7, 2489–90, 2494, 2496–7, 2500, 2504–5, 2515–18, 2520, 2522, 2535, 2571–3, 2587, 2595, 2606, 2644, 2649, 2675–7, 2679, 2682, 2685–6

John Wheeler, weaver, 2702, 2713, 2749, 2753

Thomas Whiting, 2707–8, 2711

William at the lea, fishmonger, merchant, 2321, 2344

John Wise, draper, 2701, 2706, 2719–20, 2722–4, 2726, 2728–30, 2740, 2743, 2745, 2758–61, 2763, 2768

John Wise, vintner, 2720, 2722–3, 2729, 2741, ?2743, 2753, 2759, 2767

Richard Wise, mercer, 2731, 2734

John Wishford, 2294, 2442

William Wootton, 2713, 2746–7, 2749

John Wright, 2696

John Wyatt, 2689–93, 2697

John Wylye, draper, 2701, 2714, 2716, 2724

John Wylye, mercer, 2524, 2602

INDEX ONE

General index: persons, places, and subjects

1430), 2635
Joan, dau. of John (d.
1430), 2635
John (fl. 1416), esq.,
2294, 2296
John (d. 1430), furbisher,
2496–7; will, 2635
Wm., s. of John (d.
1430), 2635
paupers, relief of, 2174,
2179, 2188, 2194–5,
2198, 2206, 2220–1,
2225, 2227, 2235–7,
2245, 2256, 2295,
2298, 2328, 2333,
2354–5, 2379, 2395,
2399, 2401, 2416,
2429, 2445, 2482–3,
2495, 2502, 2507,
2519, 2522, 2549,
2574, 2582, 2590–1,
2601, 2609, 2620,
2625, 2638, 2698; *and
see (for cross-references)*
hospitals
Pavey, Hugh, clerk, 2768
Pease, John, *see* Gardener
Peasenhall, Thos., chaplain,
2273–4, 2673
Pedwell, John, subdean of
Salisbury, 2355, 2384,
2395, 2401, 2429,
2483, 2495, 2502,
2519, 2561, 2582,
2609, 2635, 2646,
2657, 2667, 2678, 2688
Pelt, Wm., hosier, 2627
Penstone, Edm., 2627,
2714, 2725, 2770; *and
see* witnesses: coroner,
citizen
Penton
Christine, 2507
Christine (?same), relict
of Wm., 2686
Wm., dyer, 2225, 2249,
2360–2, 2397, 2479,
2507–8, 2599, 2682–3,
2686
Pentridge, the lord Wm.,
2634
Perch, John, clerk,

commissary, registrar
of [prerogative] court
of Canterbury, 2188,
2198, 2225
'Permatire', *Segrus*, 2735
Peter, apprentice, 2495
Pett, Rob., 2702
Pettifer, John, merchant,
2721, 2764–5; *and see*
witnesses: citizen
Pewsey, Wm., 2416
Phebis, Wm., weaver,
2195, 2224, 2226,
2231, 2240–1,
2292, 2325, 2384,
2387, 2428, 2437,
2603, 2645; *and see*
witnesses: reeve
Phelps, Wm., 2395
Pickard
John, 2253
Wm., 2293
Pierce, Agnes, 2509
Pile
Ric., s. of Rob., weaver,
2714
Rob., servant, 2496
Rob., weaver, 2714
Pilk, elder John, 2198,
2228, 2374, 2381, 2415
Pillinger, Thos., 2566
Pinch, John, tucker, 2191
Pinchbeck, Thos., cook,
2603, 2645
Pingbridge, Wm., *see*
witnesses: citizen
Pink, Thos., 2280
Pinnock
John, 2260
ygr. John (another), 2726
Pirie
Thos., hardwareman,
2740–1
Thos. (?another),
2758, 2761; *and see*
witnesses: clerk
Piston, Rob., and his w.
Marg., 2768
pit, at the, *see* Nicholas
Pitt, Wm., 2170
Place, John, 2198
placebo, 2245, 2698

Plaitford (estate called
Ruddock in), 2700
Play
Alice, relict of Thos., *see*
Lippiatt
John, s. of Thos., 2667
Marg., relict of Rob., *see*
Brown
Rob., ironmonger,
2173–4, 2176, 2216–
17, 2231, 2269–70,
2311
Thos., 2566, 2665–7
Plowman
Cath., w. of Ric., 2643
John, carpenter, 2546
Ric., 2643; *and see*
witnesses: citizen
Wal., carpenter, 2603,
2645
Plummer
Isabel, 2495, 2517
Thos., 2328, 2335
Polmond, John, burgess of
Southampton, 2184
Poole, Wm., 2757
Poole (Dors.), 2427
Pope
Alice, w. of ygr. John,
2516
Christine, w. of elder
John, 2463, 2508, 2590
Edith, relict of Hen.,
2244
Hen., 2243–4
John, chaplain, 2174,
2243–4
John, weaver, 2207–8
elder John, 2136, 2463,
2507–8, 2516
ygr. John, draper,
merchant, 2315, 2317,
2330, 2340, 2463,
2502, 2508, 2516,
2544–5, 2548; *and see*
witnesses: reeve
John (elder *or* ygr.),
2528, 2566, 2587,
2590, 2636, 2648
Sarah, 2207–8, 2243–4
Popes, Alice, 2225
Popham

2246, 2295, 2314–15,
2320–2, 2374, 2377,
2380, 2382, 2390,
2402, 2444–5, 2491,
2503, 2505, 2524,
2558, 2611, 2640; *and
see* witnesses: reeve,
citizen
Marg., dau. of John, nun
of Wherwell abbey,
2505, 2558
Reynold, 2307–8
Wm., 2179, 2201
Withier, Anselm, glover,
2755, 2758–9, 2761–2
Witney
Alice, 2599
Edm., 2441
Margery, 2657
Witney (Oxon.), 2591,
2606
Witts
Edith, 2634
her dau. Edith, 2634
Gillian, 2634
Wolf, Rob., 2343, 2393
wood, at the, *see* John
Woodborough
Alice, relict of Rob.,
2189, 2197
Cecily, dau. of Rob., ?w.
of John Forest, 2189,
2197
John, s. of Rob., 2189
Rob., 2189, 2197
Woodford, St. Margaret's
church, 2194
Woodham, Wm., 2384
Woodhay, John, 2399,

2582–4; *and see*
witnesses: reeve
Woodhurst, John, 2618
Woodlands (in Mere),
2223, 2249
Woodminton (in Bower
Chalke), 2637
Woodward, Wm., mercer,
2749
Wootton
Joan, relict of Wm. (d.
by 1419), 2382
John, 2225, 2316, 2382
Wm. (d. by 1419), 2382
Wm. (fl. 1470): as mayor,
2715; *and see* witnesses:
mayor, citizen
Worcester, Rob. of, rector
of Collingbourne
Kingston, 2170
Worcester, (cathedral)
church of, 2507
Wotton under Edge
(Glos.), 2507
Wreath
Alice, w. of Wm.,
2694–5, 2766
Joan, dau. of Wm., *see*
Johnson
Wm., 2694, 2763,
2766–7; will, 2695
Wyatt, John, 2673; *and see*
witnesses: citizen
Wycombe (*unspecified*,
?Bucks), 2770–1
Wylye
Joan, w. of John,
?mercer, dau. of Wm.
Warin, 2612–13

John (fl. 1419–29),
mercer, 2383, 2388–9,
2582, 2612–13; *and see*
witnesses: coroner,
reeve, citizen
John (fl. 1456–67,
?another), draper,
2701, 2709–10, 2745,
2757, 2763; *and see*
witnesses: mayor,
citizen
Marg., w. of John,
mercer, dau. of
William at the lea,
2379, 2383, 2388–9
Marg., relict of John,
draper, 2745, 2757
Wynne
Cath., w. of Wm., dau.
of John Mowe, 2769
Wm., 2755, 2757, 2769,
2771

yeomen, *see* Palmer; Stout
Yeovil
Joan, w. of Thos., *see*
Davy
Nic., bro. of Thos., 2566
Thos., tailor, 2588–9,
2592; will, 2566
York, 2179
Yorkshire, *see* Ripon; *and
see (for cross-reference)*
Bridlington
Young
John, chandler, 2646–7
John, husbandman, *see*
Edmund
Thos., tucker, 2354

INDEX TWO

Salisbury: buildings, locations, and institutions

(Cottages, gardens, shops, and yards are indexed when they constitute the principal subject of a conveyance or devise. They are not indexed when they are specified only as appurtenances of a messuage or tenement separately indexed. Cross-references to forenames and surnames are to those listed in index 1; cross-references to witnesses are to the lists entered above index 1)

Abbey (tenement in Carter Street), 2582; *cf.* Mowe's Abbey
Abbey, the (tenement in Chipper Street), 2209
Almshouse, *see* Holy Trinity hospital
archdeacon, 2637; *and see* Sydenham
Avon, river (as a boundary), 2283, 2309, 2351, 2395, 2468, 2520–1, 2529, 2702, 2757, 2759, 2761–2

bailiff, bishop's presiding over the bishop's court, 2186, 2648
and see witnesses
bakehouse, 2702
Ball's Place (in Brown Street and Wineman Street), 2176, 2223, 2249, 2625
Barnwell's cross, *see* New Street
bars, *see* Castle Street, beyond the bar; Wineman Street
?Batt's corner house (in St. Martin's Street), 2297
Bedmin (*otherwise* Bedredin) Row (cottages, in the street on the way from Scots

Lane to St. Edmund's church), 2598, 2631
Bert's Corner (Culver Street and Wineman Street), 2187
bishop, 2395
bailiff, *q.v.*
clerk, *see* Mowse
court, *q.v.* (for cross-references)
licence, 2179
mill, 2715
seal (oblong), 2625
sede vacante, 2570
seisin delivered by, 2315, 2318
surrenders into the hand of, 2203, 2262, 2264, 2270, 2303, 2312, 2317, 2332, 2340, 2343, 2345, 2353, 2362, 2366, 2393, 2405, 2424, 2452, 2467, 2475, 2488
and see Bubwith; Chandler; Erghum; Mitford; Nevill; Waltham
breweries, 2383, 2388–9; *and see (for cross-references)* index 1: brewers
Bridge Street
tenement or messuage, tenements, beside the upper bridge of Fisherton, 2757

cf. Fisherton, upper bridge
bridges, *see* Castle Street; Castle Street, beyond the bar; Endless Street; New Street; St. Martin's Street; *and see* Fisherton, lower bridge; Fisherton, upper bridge; index 1: bridges; *see also (for cross-references)* Friars bridge; Ivy bridge
Brown Street
cottages, corner, 2261–2, 2371, 2661, 2673
cottages (other), 2221, 2316, 2365–6, 2371, 2378, 2542, 2568–9
garden, extending to a trench, 2310, 2492
gate, of a tenement in Endless Street, 2385
messuage, chief, 2416
messuage, chief, corner, *see* Ball's Place
messuage, corner, 2275–6, 2278–9, 2372–3
messuage (other), 2717
shops, corner, 2225, 2261–2, 2661, 2673
shops (other), 2176, 2223, 2416
stable, 2628–9, 2642, 2650
tenements, corner, 2176, 2223, 2225, 2249,

2234, 2266, 2291,
2295, 2316, 2328,
2331–2, 2335–6, 2338,
2349, 2376, 2379,
2383, 2386, 2388–9,
2399, 2427, 2447,
2463, 2474–5, 2487–8,
2494–5, 2505, 2507–8,
2516–17, 2528, 2532,
2535–6, 2551–2, 2558,
2582–4, 2590, 2606,
2636, 2644, 2648–9,
2677, 2679, 2726,
2770; above the ditch,
2198, 2228, 2295,
2374, 2377, 2386,
2399, 2427; above the
ditch, extending to
Carter Street, 2383,
2388–9; beside the
ditch, 2323; beside a
trench, 2349, 2535–6;
opposite the trench
(above the ditch),
2338; *and see* Bull
Hall; 'Johnes'; New
Inn; 'Riole', the;

Warr's House
toft, corner, 2494
yard, 2323
and see New Inn (as a
landmark); ways
Wineman Street
cottages, 2360–2, 2397,
2479, 2561, 2625;
beside the ditch and
the bars, 2502
gate, 2561, 2625
houses, dwelling, 2561;
abutting Mealmonger
Street, 2561
kitchen, 2530
messuage, chief, corner,
see Ball's Place
messuage, corner, 2191;
and see Ive's Corner
messuage (other), 2530
plot, corner, 2582
shop, corner, 2225
shops (other), 2227,
2530, 2561, 2673;
abutting Mealmonger
Street, 2561
tenement, chief, 2511

tenements, chief,
corner, 2561; *and see*
Grandon's Corner
tenements, corner, 2173,
2176, 2223, 2225,
2249, 2280, 2316,
2326, 2334, 2352–3,
2379, 2502, 2511, 2530,
2628–9, 2642, 2650;
and see Ball's Place;
Bert's Corner
tenements (other),
2173, 2187, 2191,
2202–3, 2205, 2223,
2225, 2227, 2238,
2249, 2280, 2316,
2326, 2334, 2339–41,
2352–3, 2360–2, 2379,
2397, 2402, 2457,
2469, 2479, 2495,
2502, 2511, 2561, 2620,
2625, 2628–9, 2638,
2641, 2650, 2672–3
toft, 2457
Workhouse (?in Castle
Street), 2653

WILTSHIRE RECORD SOCIETY
(AS AT NOVEMBER 2024)

President: DR NEGLEY HARTE
Honorary Treasurer: IAN HICKS
Honorary Secretary: MISS HELEN TAYLOR
General Editor: DR TOM PLANT

Committee:
DR J. CHANDLER
DR J. HARE
S.D. HOBBS
MISS A. MCCONNELL
S. RAYMOND
I. SLOCOMBE
MRS S. THOMSON

Honorary Independent Examiner: C.C. DALE

PRIVATE MEMBERS

Honorary Members
OGBURN, SENR JUDGE R W
SHARMAN-CRAWFORD, MR T

ADAMS, MS S
BAINBRIDGE, DR V
BATHE, MR G,
BAYLIFFE, MR B G
BENNETT, DR N
BERRETT, MR A M
BERRY, MR C
BLAKE, MR P A
BOX, MR S D
BRAND, DR P A
BROCK, MRS C
BROWN, MR D A
BROWN, MR G R
BROWNING, MR E
BRYSON, DR A
CARTER, MR D
CAWTHORNE, MRS N
CHALMERS, MR D
CHANDLER, DR J H
CLARK, MR G A
COLCOMB, MR D M
COLLINS, MR A T
COUZENS, MR T

CRAVEN, DR A
CROOK, MR P H
CROUCH, MR J W
CROWLEY, DR D A
CUNNINGTON, MS J
DAKERS, PROF C
D'ARCY, MR J N
DODD, MR D
DYSON, MRS L
EDE, DR M E
ELLIOTT, DR J
ENGLISH, MS K
FORREST, DR M
GAISFORD, MR J
GALE, MRS J
GHEY, MR J G
GILES, MR D
GINGER, MR A
GODDARD, MR R G H
GRIFFIN, DR C
GRIST, MR M
HARE, DR J N
HARTE, DR N
HAWKINS, MR D
HEATON, MR R J
HELMHOLZ, PROF R W
HENLY, MR C

HERRON, MRS Pamela M
HICKMAN, MR M R
HICKS, MR I
HICKS, PROF M A
HILLMAN, MR R B
HOBBS, MR S
HOWELLS, DR Jane
INGRAM, DR M J
JOHNSTON, MRS J M
JONES, MS J
KITE, MR P J
KNEEBONE, MR W J R
KNOWLES, MRS V A
LANSDOWNE, MARQUIS OF
LAWES, MRS G
MARSH, REV R
MARSHMAN, MR M J
MARTIN, MS J
MOLES, MRS M I
NAPPER, MR L R
NEWBURY, MR C COLES
NEWMAN, MRS R
NICOLSON, MR A
NOKES, MR P M A
NOYCE, MISS S
OGBOURNE, MR J M V
OGBURN, MR D A

PARKER, Dr P F,
PATIENCE, Mr D C
PERRY, Mr W A
PLANT, Dr T
POWELL, Mrs N
PRICE, Mr A J R
RAILTON, Ms A
RAYMOND, Mr S
ROBERTS, Ms M
ROGERS, Mr K H
ROLFE, Mr R C
ROSE, Mr A

SAUNT, Mrs B A
SHELDRAKE, Mr B
SHEWRING, Mr P
SKINNER, Ms C
SLOCOMBE, Mr I
SMITH, Ms M
SMITH, Mr P J
SPAETH, Dr D A
STONE, Mr M J
SUTER, Mrs C
SUTTON, Mr A E
TATTON-BROWN, Mr T

TAYLOR, Miss H
THOMSON, Mrs S M
WADSWORTH, Mrs S
WILLIAMSON, Mr B
WILTSHIRE, Mr J
WILTSHIRE, Mrs P E
WOODFORD, Mr A
WOODWARD, Mr A S,
WRIGHT, Mr D P
YOUNGER, Mr C

UNITED KINGDOM INSTITUTIONS

Aberystwyth
    National Library of
    Wales
    University College of
    Wales
Birmingham. University
    Library
Bristol
    University of Bristol
    Library
Cambridge. University
    Library
Cheltenham. Bristol
    and Gloucestershire
    Archaeological
    Society
Chippenham
    Museum & Heritage
    Centre
    Wiltshire and Swindon
    History Centre
Coventry. University of
    Warwick Library
Devizes
    Wiltshire Archaeological
    & Natural History
    Society
    Wiltshire Family History
    Society

Durham. University
    Library
Edinburgh
    University Library
Exeter. University Library
Glasgow. University
    Library

Liverpool. University
    Library
London
    British Library
    College of Arms
    Guildhall Library
    Inner Temple Library
    Institute of Historical
    Research
    London Library
    The National Archives
    Royal Historical Society
    Society of Antiquaries
    Society of Genealogists
Manchester. John Rylands
    Library
Marlborough
    Memorial Library,
    Marlborough College
    Savernake Estate Office
Norwich. University of

East Anglia Library
Nottingham. University
    Library
Oxford
    Bodleian Library
    Exeter College Library
St Andrews. University
    Library
Salisbury
    Bourne Valley Historical
    Society
    Cathedral Library
    Salisbury and South
    Wilts Museum
Swansea. University
    College Library
Swindon
    Historic England
    Swindon Borough
    Council
Taunton. Somerset
    Archaeological and
    Natural History
    Society
Wetherby. British Library
    Document Supply
    Centre
York. University Library

INSTITUTIONS OVERSEAS

AUSTRALIA
Adelaide. University
Library
Crawley. Reid Library,
University of Western
Australia

CANADA
Halifax. Killam Library,
Dalhousie University
Toronto, Ont
Pontifical Inst of
Medieval Studies
University of Toronto
Library
Victoria, B.C. McPherson
Library, University of
Victoria

NEW ZEALAND
Wellington. National
Library of New
Zealand

UNITED STATES OF AMERICA
Ann Arbor, Mich. Hatcher
Library, University of
Michigan
Athens, Ga. University of
Georgia Libraries
Atlanta, Ga. The Robert

W Woodruff Library,
Emory University
Bloomington, Ind. Indiana
University Library
Boston, Mass. New
England Historic and
Genealogical Society
Boulder, Colo. University
of Colorado Library
Cambridge, Mass.
Harvard College Library
Harvard Law School
Library
Charlottesville, Va.
Alderman Library,
University of Virginia
Chicago
Newberry Library
University of Chicago
Library
Dallas, Texas. Public
Library
Davis, Calif. University
Library
East Lansing, Mich.
Michigan State
University Library
Evanston, Ill. United
Libraries, Garrett/
Evangelical, Seabury
Fort Wayne, Ind. Allen
County Public Library

Houston, Texas. M.D.
Anderson Library,
University of Houston
Iowa City, Iowa.
University of Iowa
Libraries
Ithaca, NY. Cornell
University Library
Los Angeles
Public Library
Young Research
Library, University of
California
Minneapolis, Minn.
Wilson Library,
University of
Minnesota
New York
Columbia University of
the City of New York
Salt Lake City, Utah.
Family History Library
San Marino, Calif. Henry
E. Huntington Library
Urbana, Ill. University of
Illinois Library
Washington. The Folger
Shakespeare Library
Winston-Salem, N.C.
Z.Smith Reynolds
Library, Wake Forest
University

LIST OF PUBLICATIONS

The Wiltshire Record Society was founded in 1937, as the Records Branch of the Wiltshire Archaeological and Natural History Society, to promote the publication of the documentary sources for the history of Wiltshire. The annual subscription is £15 for private and institutional members. In return, a member receives a volume each year. Prospective members should apply to the Hon. Secretary, c/o Wiltshire and Swindon History Centre, Cocklebury Road, Chippenham SN15 3QN. Many more members are needed.

The following volumes have been published. Price to members £15, and to non-members £20, postage extra. Most volumes up to 72 are still available from the Wiltshire and Swindon History Centre, Cocklebury Road, Chippenham SN15 3QN. Volumes 73 onwards are available from Hobnob Press, 8 Lock Warehouse, Severn Road, Gloucester GL1 2GA. Volumes 1-69 are available online, at www.wiltshirerecordsociety.org.uk.

1. *Abstracts of feet of fines relating to Wiltshire for the reigns of Edward I and Edward II*, ed. R.B. Pugh, 1939
2. *Accounts of the parliamentary garrisons of Great Chalfield and Malmesbury, 1645–1646*, ed. J.H.P. Pafford, 1940
3. *Calendar of Antrobus deeds before 1625*, ed. R.B. Pugh, 1947
4. *Wiltshire county records: minutes of proceedings in sessions, 1563 and 1574 to 1592*, ed. H.C. Johnson, 1949
5. *List of Wiltshire boroughs records earlier in date than 1836*, ed. M.G. Rathbone, 1951
6. *The Trowbridge woollen industry as illustrated by the stock books of John and Thomas Clark, 1804–1824*, ed. R.P. Beckinsale, 1951
7. *Guild stewards' book of the borough of Calne, 1561–1688*, ed. A.W. Mabbs, 1953
8. *Andrews' and Dury's map of Wiltshire, 1773: a reduced facsimile*, ed. Elizabeth Crittall, 1952
9. *Surveys of the manors of Philip, earl of Pembroke and Montgomery, 1631–2*, ed. E. Kerridge, 1953
10. *Two sixteenth century taxations lists, 1545 and 1576*, ed. G.D. Ramsay, 1954
11. *Wiltshire quarter sessions and assizes, 1736*, ed. J.P.M. Fowle, 1955
12. *Collectanea*, ed. N.J. Williams, 1956
13. *Progress notes of Warden Woodward for the Wiltshire estates of New College, Oxford, 1659–1675*, ed. R.L. Rickard, 1957
14. *Accounts and surveys of the Wiltshire lands of Adam de Stratton*, ed. M.W. Farr, 1959
15. *Tradesmen in early-Stuart Wiltshire: a miscellany*, ed. N.J. Williams, 1960
16. *Crown pleas of the Wiltshire eyre, 1249*, ed. C.A.F. Meekings, 1961
17. *Wiltshire apprentices and their masters, 1710–1760*, ed. Christabel Dale, 1961
18. *Hemingby's register*, ed. Helena M. Chew, 1963
19. *Documents illustrating the Wiltshire textile trades in the eighteenth century*, ed. Julia de L. Mann, 1964
20. *The diary of Thomas Naish*, ed. Doreen Slatter, 1965
21–2. *The rolls of Highworth hundred, 1275–1287*, 2 parts, ed. Brenda Farr, 1966, 1968
23. *The earl of Hertford's lieutenancy papers, 1603–1612*, ed. W.P.D. Murphy, 1969
24. *Court rolls of the Wiltshire manors of Adam de Stratton*, ed. R.B. Pugh, 1970
25. *Abstracts of Wiltshire inclosure awards and agreements*, ed. R.E. Sandell, 1971
26. *Civil pleas of the Wiltshire eyre, 1249*, ed. M.T. Clanchy, 1971
27. *Wiltshire returns to the bishop's visitation queries, 1783*, ed. Mary Ransome, 1972
28. *Wiltshire extents for debts, Edward I – Elizabeth I*, ed. Angela Conyers, 1973
29. *Abstracts of feet of fines relating to Wiltshire for the reign of Edward III*, ed. C.R. Elrington, 1974

30. *Abstracts of Wiltshire tithe apportionments*, ed. R.E. Sandell, 1975
31. *Poverty in early-Stuart Salisbury*, ed. Paul Slack, 1975
32. *The subscription book of Bishops Tounson and Davenant, 1620–40*, ed. B. Williams, 1977
33. *Wiltshire gaol delivery and trailbaston trials, 1275–1306*, ed. R.B. Pugh, 1978
34. *Lacock abbey charters*, ed. K.H. Rogers, 1979
35. *The cartulary of Bradenstoke priory*, ed. Vera C.M. London, 1979
36. *Wiltshire coroners' bills, 1752–1796*, ed. R.F. Hunnisett, 1981
37. *The justicing notebook of William Hunt, 1744–1749*, ed. Elizabeth Crittall, 1982
38. *Two Elizabethan women: correspondence of Joan and Maria Thynne, 1575–1611*, ed. Alison D. Wall, 1983
39. *The register of John Chandler, dean of Salisbury, 1404–17*, ed. T.C.B. Timmins, 1984
40. *Wiltshire dissenters' meeting house certificates and registrations, 1689–1852*, ed. J.H. Chandler, 1985
41. *Abstracts of feet of fines relating to Wiltshire, 1377–1509*, ed. J.L. Kirby, 1986
42. *The Edington cartulary*, ed. Janet H. Stevenson, 1987
43. *The commonplace book of Sir Edward Bayntun of Bromham*, ed. Jane Freeman, 1988
44. *The diaries of Jeffery Whitaker, schoolmaster of Bratton, 1739–1741*, ed. Marjorie Reeves and Jean Morrison, 1989
45. *The Wiltshire tax list of 1332*, ed. D.A. Crowley, 1989
46. *Calendar of Bradford-on-Avon settlement examinations and removal orders, 1725–98*, ed. Phyllis Hembry, 1990
47. *Early trade directories of Wiltshire*, ed. K.H. Rogers and indexed by J.H. Chandler, 1992
48. *Star chamber suits of John and Thomas Warneford*, ed. F.E. Warneford, 1993
49. *The Hungerford Cartulary: a calendar of the earl of Radnor's cartulary of the Hungerford family*, ed. J.L. Kirby, 1994
50. *The Letters of John Peniston, Salisbury architect, Catholic, and Yeomanry Officer, 1823–1830*, ed. M. Cowan, 1996
51. *The Apprentice Registers of the Wiltshire Society, 1817–1922*, ed. H. R. Henly, 1997
52. *Printed Maps of Wiltshire 1787–1844: a selection of topographical, road and canal maps in facsimile*, ed. John Chandler, 1998
53. *Monumental Inscriptions of Wiltshire: an edition, in facsimile, of Monumental Inscriptions in the County of Wilton, by Sir Thomas Phillipps*, ed. Peter Sherlock, 2000
54. *The First General Entry Book of the City of Salisbury, 1387–1452*, ed. David R. Carr, 2001
55. *Devizes Division income tax assessments, 1842–1860*, ed. Robert Colley, 2002
56. *Wiltshire Glebe Terriers, 1588–1827*, ed. Steven Hobbs, 2003
57. *Wiltshire Farming in the Seventeenth Century*, ed. Joseph Bettey, 2005
58. *Early Motor Vehicle Registration in Wiltshire, 1903–1914*, ed. Ian Hicks, 2006
59. *Marlborough Probate Inventories, 1591–1775*, ed. Lorelei Williams and Sally Thomson, 2007
60. *The Hungerford Cartulary, part 2: a calendar of the Hobhouse cartulary of the Hungerford family*, ed. J.L. Kirby, 2007
61. *The Court Records of Brinkworth and Charlton*, ed. Douglas Crowley, 2009
62. *The Diary of William Henry Tucker, 1825–1850*, ed. Helen Rogers, 2009
63. *Gleanings from Wiltshire Parish Registers*, ed. Steven Hobbs, 2010
64. *William Small's Cherished Memories and Associations*, ed. Jane Howells and Ruth Newman, 2011
65. *Crown Pleas of the Wiltshire Eyre, 1268*, ed. Brenda Farr and Christopher Elrington, rev. Henry Summerson, 2012
66. *The Minute Books of Froxfield Almshouse, 1714–1866*, ed. Douglas Crowley, 2013

Further details about the Society, its activities and publications, will be found on its website, www.wiltshirerecordsociety.org.uk.